Jane Austen and Co.

Jane Austen and Co.

Remaking the Past in Contemporary Culture

Suzanne R. Pucci
and
James Thompson, Editors

STATE UNIVERSITY OF NEW YORK PRESS

Published by
State University of New York Press, Albany

Printed in the United States of America

For information, address State University of New York Press,
90 State Street, Suite 700, Albany, NY 12207

Production by Marilyn P. Semerad
Marketing by Michael Campochiaro

Library of Congress Cataloging-in-Publication Data

Jane Austen and Co. : remaking the past in contemporary culture /
Suzanne R. Pucci and James Thompson, editors.
    p. cm.
  Includes bibliographical references and index.
  ISBN 0-7914-5615-3—ISBN 0-7914-5616-1 (pbk.)
    1. Austen, Jane, 1773–1817—Film and video adaptations.
  2. English fiction—Film and video adaptations.   3. Austen, Jane,
  1775–1817—Appreciation.   4. Historical films—History and criticism.
  5. England—In motion pictures.   6. Women in motion pictures.
  I. Pucci, Suzanne R. (Rodin), 1941–   II. Thompson, James, 1951–

PR4038.F55 J33   2003
791.43'6—dc21   2002029235

10 9 8 7 6 5 4 3 2 1

Contents

Introduction

The Jane Austen Phenomenon: Remaking the Past at the Millennium

Suzanne R. Pucci and James Thompson

Jane Austen's novels have never been out of print, so it seems strange to speak of an Austen revival. Nevertheless, a revival that some have termed "Austenmania" has produced a virtual industry flourishing widely in the United States and England, spawning in recent years nineteen film and television adaptations of this author's work, and over one hundred continuations, rewritings, and sequels of Austen's now almost two-hundred-year-old novels. This is a phenomenon not limited to the filming and screening of Austen's work because it spreads from Hollywood to movie theaters, television, bookstores, boutiques, and onto the Internet—from *Clueless* (Amy Heckerling's updated twentieth-century version of *Emma*); to the television serial based on this film; to the cross-marketing of such tie-ins as *Clueless* and *Pride and Prejudice* dolls, music to read Austen by, and organized tours of Jane Austen's England. Reaching an even larger population are the Web-based Austen discussion groups such as the "Republic of Pemberley" that extend effortlessly and limitlessly out into cyberspace.

Even though the world that Austen's novels represent is ostensibly located in the time, space, and conventions of early-nineteenth-century England, the story of Austen's recently exploding popularity across a proliferating variety of media and technologies (film, Internet, tourism, television) is an event, or rather a constellation of events—in other words, a phenomenon that has crystallized at a particular moment in our own contemporary culture.[1] Furthermore, Austen's novels, by far the most consistently (even obsessively) remade, provide a model and an incentive for the vogue of updating other classical texts into contemporary media, such as those of Henry James or of the eighteenth-century French writer Pierre Choderlos de Laclos.

Each of the following chapters explores diverse media representations of the past, particularly, but not exclusively, through the classical novels of Austen and, specifically, in relation to contemporary culture. We examine filmic, touristic, cyber, and literary strategies that these Austen adaptations have deployed in order to return to a past and to a sense of history. But, we are consistently attentive to the fact that this "past" is always in the process of being reinvented; for the past is remade from the perspectives of current cultural and social ambitions, politics, desires, market strategies, and historiography. This concept of "remake" thus denotes two different and complementary meanings that correspond to the major foci of our study. The past is made again—re-made as in a repetition, a re-presentation—and yet the past is always made anew. In the nature of all "heritage" productions is an attempt to promote a sense of unbroken tradition that confirms national identity and ostensibly works to repeat, to remake the past in film or through other objects or activities that represent a particular moment in the costume, speech, behavior, setting, or plot—in other words, a moment that has already gone by, already disappeared. Yet, either explicitly (such as in the film *Clueless* or as in the case of the revisionist *Mansfield Park* or *Metropolitan*) or implicitly, all these films—along with their accompanying products and activities—remake the past in the sense of making over, of shaping the past in the new fashions, styles, and desires of the present. The "Austen Phenomenon," in short, is about makeovers.

The striking surge in Austen's cultural capital has been most commonly explained away as "nostalgia," but such an explanation is at best a circular response, begging the question of what we are nostalgic for and why now. When academic and journalistic commentators designate the interest in Austen as an escape from modernity into some idealized past, such a response offers little explanation of what it is specifically that readers and viewers are seeking, and, moreover, what it is that they find. From somewhat diverse disciplinary (literature, film studies, history, geography) and cultural (English, French, American) perspectives, the present volume answers the principal question: What speaks so effectively and eloquently in these remakes to present-day needs and fantasies? What plots, what texts, what scripts are these films, rewrites, and objects (re)making? The answer to these questions involves identifying the tendencies of our own contemporary moment that keep returning to but also that keep making over texts of Jane Austen as well as other earlier texts in the likeness of late-twentieth- and early-twenty-first-century culture.

The studies in this volume, then, are ultimately concerned less with the notion of adaptation, less with the eventual similarity or difference between an Austen or other classical novel and the subsequent film, object, or event. Instead, they are more involved in an inquiry into those cultural, social, and pedagogical conditions that have motivated and shaped these remakes. While the films are the most visible manifestation of the present eruption of Austen appreciation, we understand the Austen phenomenon to encompass a whole range of interrelated forms, practices, and objects that include readers, reading groups, and reprints of the novels: Jane Austen guidebooks and guides to her England; screenplays; and the mass-market descriptions of the making of films. Unlike filmic adaptation, such as the two versions of *Cape Fear* or the sequence of Alfred Hitchcock's and Gus Van Sant's *Psychos*, the Austen films are not disposed in a chronological sequence, a definite series, with each successive iteration citing and playing upon its predecessors. Many of these films were produced simultaneously, as were the two *Emmas*, deriving from the same source, though in this case a novel, not another film. Yet these essays do not focus on the Austen films principally as translations in which the written text remains the primary and privileged original; as a consequence, they are not preoccupied with the accuracy or authenticity of adaptation. Throughout this collection, we explore the range of modern technologies and media that in a sense overwrite the verbal world of print culture. Just as much as the growing number of contemporary "sequels" to Austen's novels, these objects and activities—such as the CDs of music to read Jane Austen by, Elizabeth Bennet and *Clueless* dolls, or tourism around the sites of Austen's England—all attempt to continue and to update her fiction and so draw their past into the technologies, desires, and markets of the present.

In this respect, the Austen phenomenon is but the most obvious instance of remaking—of making over—the past at the millennium. The sheer number and variety of activities and objects related to Austen's novels—"tie-ins"—that have flooded the market make a special case that is nonetheless visibly discernible in remakes of other past novels and stories told in the seemingly flawless technologies of modern media. Both the remake and the makeover apply as well to a broad range of other films, television programs, and cultural objects. Thus, several of the chapters in this volume include heritage films that do not specifically derive from Austen. Virginia L. Blum (chapter 8) shows that remakes of Victorian novels, such as Henry James's *Wings of the Dove*, convey many of the same attractions that so captivate the late-twentieth- and early-twenty-first-century viewer in the Austen remakes. These chapters track the Austen phenomenon beyond Austen, into what Madeleine Dobie (chapter 12) calls, following Claire Monk, the "post-heritage" film, a kind of historical costume drama that uses the past in a deliberate or explicit way to explore current issues in cultural politics. And yet, the post-heritage film is not necessarily the antithesis of the Austen film because this intermingling of past and present interests can be found within the Austen remakes as well, and in a continuum that also emerges, for Dobie, in such recent films as *Metropolitan* (1990) and *Ruby in Paradise* (1993). In effect, to see the Austen and the historical film remake in general from perspectives that coincide with present cultural concerns is necessarily to position them with respect to the issues and viewpoints adopted in various other contemporary films. Martine Voiret (chapter 11) observes in the film *Bridget Jones' Diary* (2001) and in the popular television series *Ally McBeal* a continuation of the postfeminist backlash that she perceives as well within the Austen makeovers; while Sarah Maza (chapter 5) explores the film versions of the French eighteenth-century novel *Dangerous Liaisons,* which, placed within the British–American context, coincides both in its thematics and in its symbolics with the politics of this feminist backlash.

The Austen phenomenon, then, is not confined to Austen but in its extended sense serves as a model for examining and understanding how contemporary culture inevitably enters into those texts—visual, literary, and touristic—that remake and makeover the past. Kristina Straub devotes her chapter (3) to a contemporary American television series deriving from the feature-length film *Buffy the Vampire Slayer* in which the past itself becomes the principal antagonist that threatens and challenges the lives of present-day students, and there is violence that continues so long as they attempt to keep the past distant and separate from the present. The vampire in *Buffy* is used to dramatize the dangerous eruption of the past into the present, while the figure of the teacher, Straub shows, serves as mediator between students who occupy an eternal present and a threatening past that refuses to lie down and die.

How then does our fascination with Austen and Regency England, this shuttling back and forth between present and a desired/sometimes discarded, even feared past, affect that locale where it has always gone on—with students who have been asked, or directed, to read Austen for generation after generation? As teachers, this is the question that occupies us, indeed haunts us—as mediators how do we, how can we, bring the past into the present? In acknowledging those differences between the viewer and reader, between the film, TV program, and written text, the question can be broached—that often unspoken and yet tangible undercurrent felt (if not always articulated) by contemporary students that the literature of the past, of the last few centuries, has been replaced by more attractive, fast-paced media that correspond better and more directly to the pace and the interests of these students' own lives. But the past does not necessarily have to be construed as antagonistic because the classroom can become a site for comparing what a contemporary audience expects from and sees in the film and other remakes with what the texts of Jane Austen and others seem to ask of readers. By encouraging a familiarity with the skills of interpreting diverse media—reading novels and also viewing their filmic counterparts—students and readers in general can become engaged in the past in a new, perhaps more visual and intense way—one that necessarily and palpably links the present of their own cultural perception and experience with a distant historical and cultural location of the written text. This is not the usual procedure of contextualization that we normally understand as constituting literary study, but rather a simultaneous situating of present and past, and their mutual attractions and concomitant repulsions. Traditional literary study has always tried to bring the past to life, but here we insist on the contemporaneity of this conjuring trick, in our own interpretations and in our pedagogical efforts to reach and to engage students.

A major issue in these chapters brings to light the modes in which contemporary students and, now indeed, all of us consume culture. The Austen phenomenon is located within the interstices of the oral, visual, and spatial delivery systems, systems that reinforce each other and in turn reinforce the interaction among these media. Increasingly, this is the way cultural experiences are disseminated and consumed: see the film, read the book, buy the soundtrack, check out the Web site, visit the "actual" Austen sites in English country houses and countryside that Mike Crang (chapter 6) shows are to a large extent merely creations of the tourist industry. And, thus, our volume is not, strictly speaking, a volume of film criticism, though several of the chapters treat some specific aspect of film criticism (Virginia L. Blum's [chapter 8] demonstration of the close-up in film as a privileged late-twentieth-century technique introduced to exhibit an individual's supposedly "inner" feelings and truths; Maureen Turim's [chapter 2] tracking of the voice-over as well as the screwball comedy within the conventions of the history of film; Suzanne R. Pucci's [chapter 7] analysis of the camera shots that open most of the Austen remakes: the broad pan of the camera that each time narrows to define the enclosed spaces of domestic intimacy; and so forth). With the figure of Austen at the center of this proliferation of media, it becomes increasingly difficult and misleading to make sharp or convincing distinctions between high and low, elite and mass culture; between literature and popular entertainment. Rather, it is increasingly necessary to move back and forth between these realms so often kept separate within, or kept out of altogether, our college classrooms. Instead of denigrating or complaining about what popular film and media have "done to the novel," we take such activities as our point of departure in an attempt to help students compare their response to these films through their lived experience that both conditions and can also enhance and enrich their understanding of the novels embodied in past time and space.

In constructing this volume on remaking the past, all of the chapters circulate around the process of mediation between past and present, our moment of postmodernity and the nostalgic appeal of another more distant moment, most often Regency or Victorian England. The chapters also mediate between elite and popular culture—between the experiences of mass culture and the solitary pleasures of reading. Between a postfeminist moment acutely anxious about gender roles and classic novels of courtship that celebrate male and female harmony; between an age of sexual publicity and a period of reticence, privacy, intimacy, and repression; between the promise and threats of globalization and the circumscribed lure of domesticity and home; between an aristocratic, hierarchical, and patriarchal society and one that habitually imagines itself as level, democratic, even disaggregate. Our point here is not to insist on the categorical nature of these oppositions because the Austen phenomenon is all about the interaction among these differences. This is what we ask of our students when we ask them, through reading, viewing, and analysis, to imagine and try to understand themselves in relation to a past and to a changing present, not a transparent, static, eternal, or unreflexive present. Austen here is a sign through which desires as well as fantasies are channeled, about what we were, what we are, and what we want to be.

Thus, we propose the Austen Phenomenon as a blueprint for pedagogical practice that welcomes, indeed embraces, this promiscuous intermingling of reading, seeing, touring, and surfing. And in so doing, we underscore the importance of allowing the canon and its past to be complemented by and even in some sense to be supplanted by the tools and technologies of our contemporary culture and popular media. We retain much that earlier criticism and histories of literature and film taught us about the specificity of context and the historical transformations of form, and we add to that the layered questions posed by an intertextuality conceived as operating transhistorically and across diverse media. The broad aim of this collection is to open out onto the wider practices of reading as well as teaching texts: those of the novel and film, of tourism and cyberspace. We thus recurrently broach the subject of the teacher's role, the teacher who can function successfully as an intermediary between the past and present, student and text, and, in the case of film, television, and the Internet, between elite and popular culture.

Accordingly, we have organized the chapters into four interlocking and closely interrelated sections that move across, but nevertheless highlight, the major categories that we take to be formative of this contemporary phenomenon. *Jane Austen and Co.* takes place at several sites of contemporary culture that we will explore: In the Classroom (Part I); In the Nation (Part II); At Home (Part III); and In the Bedroom (Part IV). Accordingly, each of the above sites designates issues that these chapters discuss respectively: (1) pedagogy; (2) history and politics; (3) intimacy; and (4) gender and sexuality. We begin with James Thompson's (chapter 1) piece that offers an account of the record of Austen's ongoing appeal, from Sir Walter Scott's review of *Emma* in 1815 up through the present revival. What is the relation between the "professional" Austen—her place in the canon, in the curriculum, and in literary criticism—and the "amateur" Austen of the Janeites and mass culture? Maureen Turim (chapter 2) in turn explores the function of the Austen films in the classroom, particularly through *Clueless*, as she describes what she asks of her students: Which of these films reflects your life best, and what does it not account for? What does representation have to do with how we think about ourselves? *Clueless* occupies a prominent position in this volume, with three of our contributors writing on quite different aspects of this film precisely because here the makeover in its clearly contemporary scenario, decor, manners, language, and costumes says explicitly what the other films only imply. Austen's nineteenth-century England is transposed into modern-day Beverly Hills in a self-consciously explicit makeover of the past, of a past genre, as well as in the literal cosmetic makeovers of young people in constant search of the latest fad and identity. Within the tradition of screwball comedies, Maureen Turim (chapter 2) sees in the narrative and thematic formations of *Clueless*, in the interactivity of social, filmic, and computer technologies, a continuation of Austen's own sophisticated play with precedents. Thus, *Clueless* emerges here not as the modern, faddish, frivolous, and ephemeral version of a timeless classic but as an updated elaboration of Austen's own inventive experimentation with narrative technique and social analysis. Kristina Straub (chapter 3) addresses similar questions about makeovers, remaking, and the recycling of the past into the present through *Buffy the Vampire Slayer* (a television series and a feature-length film) that allegorizes history and our relation to it for a youth culture that is supposed to be resistant to history and the past. Here, the teacher–librarian and his books function in *Buffy* as the agent who mediates between past and present, between high and mass culture, between adult and youth culture.

Throughout, these chapters explore representations of the past—in terms of their conceptualization of history and in terms of their potential as pedagogical tools. Deidre Lynch (chapter 4) asks whether and how costume drama is history: "Do these remakes of classic texts from the past present us with opportunities to think historically—to perceive an organic and necessary relation between the bygone worlds they depict and our lived experience?" Lynch situates Austen's novels in a period of the modernization and professionalization of historiography, showing that these novels were already questioning the gendered assumptions of the new history. In turn, under the guise of fashion, *Clueless* remakes in the sense of making over the traditionalist's unproblematic and unitary time-line notion of history. Lynch thus situates Austen with respect to certain postmodern perspectives as she seeks to "de-idealize the time of genuine historicity that some contemporary cultural critics [insist on] locate[ing] only in the past." Sarah Maza (chapter 5) turns more explicitly to political history in exploring how the past is recycled into the present. In her analysis of the versions of *Dangerous Liaisons*, an eighteenth-century French novel, then British play, then British–U.S. film, Laclos's text becomes a vehicle for a heritage film in which political aspirations particularly of national destiny map the broad ambitions of Margaret Thatcher onto the demonized character of the infamous Marquise de Merteuil. Most specifically, the film "evoked some of the central obsessions of the 1980s: wealth, moral corruption, and female ambition." Laclos's novel, as made over into the Warner Brothers 1988 film, coincides with the feminist backlash that Maza identifies as operating in other films of the same period such as *Fatal Attraction*. Mike Crang (chapter 6) dwells in his chapter on the political significance of remaking through attention to the spatial thematics of heritage. In the tourism industry, houses and landscapes are singled out to commemorate a past and a now absent grandeur of former empire. With an analysis of specific tours that often offer only empty sites and spaces of nostalgia, where former homes and grounds once stood, Crang shows us the role of touring as an attempt to bring the past—in this case of Austen—into a material spatial and object reality that remains vestigial and ephemeral.

Suzanne R. Pucci (chapter 7) examines this spatialization of nostalgia through the visual lure of a "return home," a turning inward to the material places of domestic intimacy that open nearly every Austen film remake. A repeated filmic demarcation of familial enclosures appears to contrast sharply with, and yet here also dwells alongside, the unmarked borders of global cyberspace. Of course, any such transparency represented between a contemporary and a past moment as an intimate memory is never fully possible through actual objects or sites of the past. And yet, it is the fabrication of those objects for popular consumption that we are tracing in several of these chapters. The touristic object, the political, the historical object of the past, of memory itself, the intimate objects of the home, are accompanied by an attempt to recuperate lost sexual as well as love objects. Virginia L. Blum (chapter 8) shows how late-twentieth-century assumptions about sexuality pervade film adaptations of nineteenth-century novels as well as those of Austen, the period that was supposed to have repressed its sexual urges and hidden its desires, and yet which functions for us as the time when sexuality could have flourished precisely because it was hidden away from the glare of broadcasting and publicity. If, as Blum argues, sexual intimacy has become in our culture the place of supposed authenticity, it can only be found by resuscitating in certain of these contemporary films the structure of repression found in the Austen and James novels. In other words, we try to return in this age of supposed liberated sexuality to some semblance of repression. And we simulate this structure of repression as though structure alone were enough to revive what we imagine to be its content. Ruth Perry (chapter 10) is similarly interested in the ways in which film underwrites Austen novels with contemporary conceptualizations and representations of sexuality, romanticizing, and physicalizing her protagonists, and, most particularly, investing them with an anachronistic sense of physical disgust at the odious characters such as Mr. Collins. For Denise Fulbrook (chapter 9), *Clueless* offers an overtly presentist and revisionist cultural and sexual history because *Clueless* thoroughly rejects the Freudian Oedipal narrative of development and its presumed end of normative "adult" heterosexuality: Examining the sophistication with which the film treats youth cultures, Fulbrook reads *Clueless* as offering an array of resistances and alternatives to the expected comic closure of Cher's marriage—"As if: I'm only 17!" Martine Voiret (chapter 11) outlines a cultural history of sexuality by looking at the ways fashion is used in the costume drama to image and imagine altered gender roles in a series of films from *Pride and Prejudice* to *Ruby in Paradise* that offer the male body as spectacle of physical beauty for female viewers. And finally, for Madeleine Dobie (chapter 12), the heritage film as such becomes a vehicle to explore our conventional assumptions about gender: by its very marking of difference between past and present, the contemporary heritage film offers us a glimpse of what is in effect neither then nor now, but often tends toward the utopian.

Since all these chapters speak of this remaking in terms of making over, to what extent are we still able to think, as well as understand and imagine, historically? *Jane Austen and Co.* poses this question of our relation to the past. Is our ability to think historically significantly impaired, as some have argued (see Lynch on Fredric Jameson in chapter 4, this volume)? Is our cultural moment characterized by the absence of a sense of the past, the past as anathema, even in those places and landscapes that are supposed to appeal to our memory? Is our special attraction to Austen, heritage films, and Regency-England compensation for a postmodern failure or rejection of memory? Pierre Nora writes provocatively on these issues:

> Societies based on memory are no more: the institutions that once transmitted values from generation to generation—churches, schools, families, governments—have ceased to function as they once did. And ideologies based on memory have ceased to function as well, ideologies that once smoothed the transition from the past to future or indicated what the future should retain from the past, whether in the name of reaction, progress, or even revolution. More than that, our very perception of history has, with much help from the media, expanded enormously, so that memory, once the legacy of what people knew intimately, has been supplanted by the thin film of current events.[2]

Nora's statement both diminishes and expands the notions of memory and of history for our age. According to him, we experience an increasing lack of attachment through churches, schools, and families to shared ideologies that once provided us with narratives of our past. If this collective memory—once experienced as personal, as "intimate" knowledge and identity—has almost disappeared, history has nevertheless, also according to Nora, become present in the media that have expanded into all realms of our lives. The intimate memory of our past and its projection onto the future has been supplanted by the "thin film of current events." But we want to see this thin film also as the transparent celluloid of film itself that seems to make our past accessible by embodying memory in a seamless material and sensuous, albeit virtual, immediacy. Yet, this volume makes the point that the Austen Phenomenon is not sheerly compensatory, making up for a loss of communal memory, but that the individuation of media technologies parallels a privatization of the experience of the past: digital film, video, DVDs, and mpeg compression algorithms enable individuals to record, replay, rewatch the once-epic costume dramas as one would read a novel: all alone. In the place of a collective ideology of the past, the individual emerges as the seemingly sole or lonely consumer of histories that various markets compete to make current.

We are not condemned to a virtual amnesia, nor are we doomed to "pastiche," to remaking or recycling the bits and pieces, flotsam and jetsam of the past. Rather, the forms and media by which we are able to imagine and visualize the past have changed, and as a consequence we are seeing in our students a different form of memory/history/archive, as in *Buffy* and *Clueless*, which, in sophisticated ways, highlight the persistence of the past into the present, and live alongside the notion of an inheritance of the past. It is our generational as well as pedagogical challenge not to flatten out these new forms of memory into a nostalgia for the traditional notions of a linear history and thus of an absent past.

Notes

1. This sense of phenomenon as an extraordinary and public contemporary event—a happening—is appropriately of late-eighteenth-century vintage. As the *Oxford English Dictionary* defines it: "Something very notable or extraordinary; a highly exceptional or unaccountable fact or occurrence; colloq. a thing, person, or animal remarkable for some unusual quality; a prodigy." The public sense of phenomenon is best illustrated in their 1877 example: "1877 E. R. CONDER Bas. Faith (1884) App. I. iii. §8 note, The perversion of this word 'phenomenon' into the sense of 'prodigy'. Even educated people may be found speaking of a remarkable occurrence as 'Quite a phenomenon'."

2. Pierre Nora, *Realms of Memory* (New York: Columbia University Press, 1996), 2.

Part I
In the Classroom

1

How to Do Things
with Austen

James Thompson

If the ongoing revival of Jane Austen has a distinct extravagance to it, so does professional literary criticism on Austen: further, the discourse surrounding Austen has always been characterized by a certain extravagance, a certain excess, an almost erotic charge that for convenience sake I call "hysteria." I will try to describe that charge by working back and forth between classic nineteenth-century appreciations of Austen, and twentieth-century literary history and criticism, and exploring, lastly, the films and the commentary that the films have elicited in the popular press. The recent revival has a heady, almost carnivalesque, quality to it: Columbia Pictures, for instance, wanted to hire a ghostwriter to novelize Emma Thompson's script for *Sense and Sensibility*.[1] The last time Hollywood had drawn on Austen was 1940 with Robert Z. Leonard's *Pride and Prejudice*, but there are now sixteen films of Austen's six novels, including the most recent version of *Mansfield Park* released in November 1999. Austen made *People* magazine's "50 Most Fascinating People of 1995" list.[2] On February 4, 1996, *Sense and Sensibility* hit tenth place on the *New York Times* list of best-selling paperbacks. The most recent Signet edition of *Emma* comes with a sticker that announces "Now a Major Motion Picture," while the cover illustration for a recent Tor Press edition of *Sense and Sensibility* cites the conventions of the regency romance (if not quite the bodice ripper), when describing the contents as "Two sisters. Two romances. A tragic tale of love and deceit. . ." (ellipsis in the original).[3]

The fascination with Austen spreads well beyond books and film. For example, the July 1966 *House Beautiful* cover story (64–69) is an article with the eye-catching title, "Jane Austen Could Have Slept Here: A Self-Taught Decorator Brought up on English Novels Transforms a Bland Los Angeles Duplex into a Very Small Stately Home." Now, Austen never spent much time in Los Angeles, but the convergence of a decorative style coupled with Austen's name begs for investigation. The text concludes, "No doubt Jane Austen herself would feel at home." What interests me most here (aside from the intriguingly contradictory concept of "a very small stately home," a down-sized stately home for the 1990s) is the confidence that Austen easily fits into contemporaneity, that she would be comfortable in the culture of *Clueless*.[4] A story in circulation after *Clueless* appeared (perhaps an urban folktale) speaks to this play on Austen and contemporaneity. Supposedly after reviews indicated that *Emma* was the ultimate source for *Clueless*, talk show personnel were unable to turn up this Jane Austen person to appear on their shows. *People* magazine opens its review of *Emma* with "Call it a hat trick for Jane Austen," as if an author dead for 178 years is staging a personal comeback. Between 9 and 10 million British viewers watched the last episode of *Pride and Prejudice* (out of 47 million, which is an implausible 21 percent) and "the three part series earned A&E its highest rating ever when it aired here in January."[5] During the broadcast of this adaptation, sales of *Pride and Prejudice* hit 35,000 copies a week according to the *New York Times* (December 10, 1995, 14).[6] Jane Austen, in short, "has gone platinum." These divergent phenomena seem of their own accord to define the nature of this inquiry: the extravagant and irrational nature of Austen discourse. Why has her name such currency now? Further, how is Austen being stitched into contemporary culture?[7]

Austen's novels have never gone out of print, and they are among the few canonical works that are read inside and outside the academy. Alongside only the Brontës and Charles Dickens, Austen serves as both a canonical and a popular writer, the interest of a global Jane Austen Society and the subject of a widely displayed bumper sticker: "I'd Rather Be Reading Jane Austen."[8] Over the last three centuries, John Milton has never lost canonical status, but I have never seen an "I'd Rather Be Reading John Milton" bumper sticker. Thus, Austen has a peculiar status for literary professionals, in that our clientele apparently does not have to come to us for expertise or guidance (Roger Gard's relative study, *Jane Austen: The Art of Clarity*, is a three-hundred-page explanation of this single point: Austen's work is plain, clear, and self-evident, wanting no esoteric exegesis. If this is so, what role does it leave the teacher, whose accustomed role is as guide to the great but distant and difficult works of the past?) Austen, the Brontës, and Dickens alone are read inside and outside the academy.[9] Indeed, I have seen the "I'd Rather Be Reading Jane Austen" bumper sticker pasted on a colleague's door (though never one for the Brontës, Dickens, or—and this perhaps goes without saying—Milton).

Austen is, then, one of very few figures whose name and work muddies distinctions between high and low culture, between inside and outside the academy. I do not mean to construe Austen here as a utopian cyborg figure who deconstructs leaky distinctions, but rather I am interested in tracing enthusiasm for her in various domains to explore its cause, and to ask if there are any similarities in these various kinds of appeal. This leads ultimately to Bourdieuian questions concerning the rules of conversion among various types of cultural capital: How is it that a set of texts that have professional or academic value spread outside the university? Is the shift accidental or historical? Above all, is it replicable? That Austen appeals to both elite and popular, both academic and mass audiences, defies ordinary pedagogical practice, which is predicated on the need to build appeal. Such matters stimulate a distinct academic longing; in more than twenty-five years of teaching, this seems to be the first connection between a book I teach and contemporary taste, and so it tempts us to test the thickness of the firewall that seems to separate the academic from the ordinary world. There is, not surprisingly, some bemusement, if not superiority, in the academic reaction to the popularization of Austen. For example, in the collection *Jane Austen in Hollywood*, Carol M. Dole writes of the "prettification" expected of costume dramas after the Merchant/Ivory success.[10]

Austen may perform a different function in literary criticism and history compared with *Clueless*, but there are, I think, some significant congruities to the enthusiasm because the role Austen is asked to play in literary history is equally irrational. An adaptable figure, who can close eighteenth-century survey courses and go on to open nineteenth-century ones, she plays the missing link, as her novels exemplify if not perform the transition between neoclassicism and romanticism, between the eighteenth and the nineteenth centuries, between the old regime and the present. Jane Austen's novels are regularly connected with—asked to represent if not credited with—the advent of modernity, making her a curious agent of history. The various kinds of discourse on Austen I wish to examine, then, are four: literary history, literary criticism, film, and ultimately (the point at which these first three converge) pedagogy, to examine the curricular function of Austen.[11] If one of the objects of contemporary cultural studies is, as Gayatri Spivak puts it, "the techniques of knowledge production,"[12] we need to ask what kinds of knowledge has the canonization of Austen come to serve; what features are students asked to admire; what values does Austen come to embody? In other words, what is at stake when we direct students to admire Austen? In Slavoj Žižek's formulation of Jacques Lacan, "'*Che vuoi?*'—You're telling me that, but what do you want with it, what are you aiming at?"[13] In attempting to theorize the discourse surrounding Jane Austen, connecting the incessant claims of perfection and idealization with contemporary desires for closure, suture, and totality, we can use her work as a test case for canonical fiction, to specify what it is that we want when we ask others to read it. That is, can we isolate a set or constellation of desires that accrue to canonical authors? Such desires surely alter over time, but the history of

Austen readings shows considerable continuity, preserving something of the history of these desires. At the very least, with Austen specific questions and certain terms have persisted for almost three hundred years. I am not offering a description, a Jaussian trace of reception history, but rather an attempt to get at the question of what do we want from her and why these needs now?

The first thesis of this argument then is that the Austen Phenomenon is not confined to the popular. If the mark of professionalization is objectivity, even levelheaded professionals get emotional and extravagant when writing about Austen. Marvin Mudrick, for example, bemoans the fact that Austen "betrays" Marianne; Mudrick also asks plaintively, "Why must the Crawfords be sacrificed?"[14] In a not untypical example, A. C. Bradley (of *Shakespearean Tragedy* fame) writes of Elizabeth Bennet, "I was meant to fall in love with her and I do."[15] Nina Auerbach, who would seem far removed from Bradley, writes oddly similarly in *Romantic Imprisonment: Women and Other Glorified Outcasts*: "Alone among masters of fiction, Jane Austen commands the woman's art of making herself loved. She knows how to enchant us with conversational sparkle, to charm our assent with a glow of description, to entice our smiles with the coquette's practiced glee."[16] And it is not just literary critics who make extravagant claims in Austen's name. In *After Virtue: A Study of Moral Theory*, a story of the enlightenment as a fall into modernity, as a disintegration of a system or moral coherence, the philosopher Alisdair MacIntyre claims that Austen presents the last "synthesis": "Jane Austen is in a crucial way the last representative of the classical tradition." Austen in short provides the perfect model of community, distantly echoing Gilbert Ryle's claims:

> It is in her uniting of Christian and Aristotelian themes in a determinant social context that makes Jane Austen the last great effective imaginative voice of the tradition of thought about, and the practice of, the virtues which I have tried to identify. She thus turns away from the competing catalogues of virtues of the eighteenth century and restores a teleological perspective. Her heroines seek the good through their own good in marriage. The restricted households of Highbury and Mansfield Park have to serve as surrogates of the Greek city–state and the medieval kingdom.[17]

In a neat but prototypical little reversal, MacIntyre switches from the good in Austen to Austen as the embodiment, the representative, of these goods: virtue and the perfect communities before the fall, the Greek city–state and the medieval kingdom.

If MacIntyre seems to go a bit overboard in claiming for Austen the last understanding in Western culture of the unity of life, his praise is relatively judicious and temperate compared to Wayne Booth's in *The Rhetoric of Fic-*

tion. In a passage of profound admiration of *Emma*, Booth concludes that Austen's combination of transparency and authority produces human truth and perfection:

> When we read this novel, we accept her ["Jane Austen" or the narrator] as representing everything we admire most. She is as generous and wise as Knightley; in fact, she is a shade more penetrating in her judgment. She is as subtle and witty as Emma would like to think herself. Without being sentimental she is in favor of tenderness. She is able to put an adequate but not excessive value on wealth and rank. She recognizes a fool when she sees one, but unlike Emma she knows that it is both immoral and foolish to be rude to fools. She is, in short, a perfect human being, within the concept of perfection established by the book she writes; she even recognizes that human perfection of the kind she exemplifies is not quite attainable in real life. The process of her domination is of course circular; her character establishes the values for us according to which her character is then found to be perfect. But this circularity does not affect the success of her endeavor; in fact it insures it.
>
> The "omniscience" is thus a much more remarkable thing than is ordinarily implied by the term. All good novelists know all about their characters—all that they need to know. And the question of how their narrators are to find out all that *they* need to know, the question of "authority," is a relatively simple one. The real choice is much more profound than this would imply. It is a choice of the moral, not merely the technical, the angle of vision from which the story is to be told. [18]

To draw one last example from traditional literary criticism, I have argued elsewhere that Ian Watt's *Rise of the Novel* is based on *Pride and Prejudice*.[19] The function that Austen's work serves for Watt, or the problem it is asked to solve, is not merely technical or narratological, because almost inevitably in discussions such as this technical or narratological issues modulate into moral or ideological issues, issues that turn on the truth of her vision. Watt writes: "She was able to combine into a harmonious unity the advantages both of realism of presentation and realism of assessment, of the internal and of the external approaches to character; her novels have authenticity without diffuseness or trickery, wisdom of social comment without a garrulous essayist, and a sense of the social order which is not achieved at the expense of the individuality and autonomy of the characters."[20] What is at stake here is no longer technical prowess, but harmonious authenticity, not the way she conveys life stories, but what she conveys, another matter entirely. The slippage between formal and moral is absolutely central to

Austen criticism. For example, in Lionel Trilling's influential formulation, "The great charm, the charming greatness, of *Pride and Prejudice* is that it permits us to conceive of morality as style."[21] This is not quite the same thing as a stylization of life; rather, it is an aesthetization of morality, a slippage from goodness to grace, to style, to elegance: morality as elegance— almost a Platonic identification of the true, the good, and the beautiful. As Rebecca West writes in 1932, the protagonists of *Northanger Abbey* "are rich with the special charm that attends the conjunction of good souls and good breeding" (*JACH* 2:297).

Jane Austen's work is accorded a special place in the history of the novel because her work functions as a marker of transition;[22] her novels provide a convenient transition from the eighteenth-century to the nineteenth-century novel, in conventional terms from its rise to its triumph, or, as Julia Prewitt Brown puts it, "from tradition-directed to inner-directed society."[23] Her position in literary history as great innovator and her position in the canon as great novelist are related because discussions of the former inevitably seem to end up as discussions of the latter. In Watt, because Austen has a foot in the psychological world of Samuel Richardson and a foot in the sociological world of Henry Fielding, she is uniquely capable of negotiating that most fundamental contradiction of novelistic discourse: between subjectivity and objectivity, between individual subject position and collectivity. Despite the increasing transparency of her narrative, and its increasingly subjective form, Austen retains an authoritative narrative voice that checks the subjectivity of her protagonists. Duckworth, for example, argues that Austen's protagonists always overcome subjectivity, as they inevitably arrive at "a belief in the prior existence of certain imperatives for individual action."[24] Austen, in short, can suture personal and social together into a whole—she can explain the relation between the individual and the social whole—the intractable problem of modernity even if in this case, the social whole is imagined as three or four families in a village. Literary history—histories of the novel—have at this point internalized the plot of *Pride and Prejudice*, in which the marriage of Elizabeth and Darcy has come to represent the harmonious union of male and female, inner directed and outer directed, the (male) social responsibility of the eighteenth-century (aristocratic) tradition and the (feminine) subjectivity and emotionalism of nineteenth-century romanticism. Despite her small scale, Austen found the means of displaying the inside and the outside of human life, how her characters think and feel, along with how they interact with others. In this conventional view, then, Austen occupies a crucial spot in the development of the novel; not just showing more of life, but a leap to showing all of life. As F. R. Leavis puts it, Jane Austen makes possible George Elliot: "Jane Austen, in fact, is the inaugurator of the great tradition of the English novel."[25]

This was so from the start.[26] Essentially, the terms of Austen criticism are set in 1815 and do not really change, even with the advent of feminism in the 1980s. From Sir Walter Scott's review of *Emma* onward, Austen is small but perfect; her subject is common—ordinary, middling life—but exactly rendered (in an often-repeated phrase) in "minute detail" or with "minute fidelity to nature." Such a valuation reflects the aesthetic of realism, one that is connected invariably with her moral vision. That is to say, she sees things as they are and as they ought to be. The issue of limitation (often conveyed in the terms *condensation* or *concentration* and, later, *economy*) is by no means casual or extraneous, but is an essential half of an intricate aesthetic dialectic that reads Austen as formally limited and morally capacious.[27] So, too, the term *common* became the foundation of praise, as she is said to find greatness in the ordinary. Scott writes: "We, therefore, bestow no mean compliment upon the author of *Emma*, when we say that, keeping close to common incidents, and to such characters as occupy the ordinary walks of life, she has produced sketches of such spirit and originality, that we never miss the excitation which depends upon a narrative of uncommon events, arising from the consideration of minds, manners, and sentiments, greatly above our own. In this class she stands almost alone" (*JACH* 1:63–64). As Scott later writes in a letter of 1826, "That young lady had a talent for describing the involvement and feelings and characters of ordinary life which is to me the most wonderful I ever met with" (*JACH* 1:106; this judgment of small but true is also, implicitly, though often explicitly, gendered). Scott's praise of the exquisite, of the small but perfect, is expanded in Bishop Whately's 1821 review of *Northanger Abbey* and *Persuasion*: "Her fables appear to us to be, in their own way, nearly faultless"; "the minute fidelity of detail" gives "her fiction the perfect appearance of reality" (*JACH* 1:95, 96). By 1823, an anonymous reviewer describes Anne Elliot as "one of the most beautiful female characters ever drawn" (*JACH* 1:111) and by 1852, George Henry Lewes names Austen "the greatest artist who has every written, using the term to signify the most perfect mastery over the means to her end" (*JACH* 1:140). She becomes, via Thomas Babington Macaulay, George Henry Lewes, and Richard Simpson, the "prose Shakespeare" (*JACH* 1:122, 125, 243). Perfect within limitations, or more often perfect because of her limitations, has become commonplace; in 1866, "She sees and paints faithfully what she sees, and never tries beyond. She sees and paints as much of nature as we all see without reflecting upon it every day. Within this limitation she is absolute" (*JACH* 1:213). Richard Hutton writes in 1869, "And thus the limited work she had to do, she achieved with greater perfection and fineness and delicacy of touch than almost any other English author with whom we are acquainted. Never was a definite literary field so clearly marked out and so perfectly mastered as by Miss Austen" (*JACH* 2:164). To Margaret Oliphant in 1870, "Nothing could be more lifelike, more utterly real" (*JACH* 1:218); of Mr. Collins, she writes, "It is amazing in its unity and completeness—a picture perhaps unrivaled, certainly unsurpassed, in its way. It is, we repeat, cruel in its perfection"; "this pitiless perfection of art" is "so lifelike, so perfect and complete" (*JACH* 1:219, 220). Qualified perfection in 1913 becomes with Agnes Repplier "the fine, thin perfection of Miss Austen's work," as she connects "the flawlessness of Miss Austen's art and the narrowness of its boundaries" (*JACH* 2:206, 211).

The language of perfection often turns hyperbolic, habitually exorbitant, with its enthusiasm and passionate attachment producing an excess or surplus beyond rational claim. Reginald Farrer writes of Jane Austen in 1917 "as our greatest artist in English fiction," having "perfect mastery": "she is, in English fiction, as Milton in English poetry, the one completely conscious and almost unerring artist"; *Pride and Prejudice* is "the greatest miracle of English Literature," which Farrer characterizes as "this first fine careless rapture"; *Emma* is (anticipating Northrop Frye on *Paradise Lost*), "the Book of Books" (*JACH* 2:250, 259, 260, 265). As with Farrer, the language turns religious (though perhaps always tongue in cheek here, as when Arnold Bennet complains in 1927 that "[t]he reputation of Jane Austen is surrounded by cohorts of defenders who are ready to do murder for their sacred cause" (*JACH* 2:287); Leslie Stephen in 1876, writes, "I never, for example, knew a person so thoroughly deaf to humour who did not worship Miss Austen" (*JACH* 2:164); in his affection for Austen, A. C. Bradley (1911) numbers himself among "the faithful" (*JACH* 2:234); and to Reginald Farrer, "Jane Austen herself has long since taken rank as the center of a cult as ardent as a religion" (*JACH* 2:246). To William Dean Howells, "the refined perfection of Miss Austen" shortly becomes "the divine Jane" (*JACH* 2:203). In such passages, we should note that her work is plainly subject to being reread, as they all indicate: her text occasions extraordinary familiarity and affection (as with the therapeutic effects with Kipling's "Janeites" 1924). Jane Austen is E. M. Forster's "favorite Author" (*JACH* 2:279), and to Virginia Woolf, "the balance of her gifts was singularly perfect" (*JACH* 2:281). To Edith Wharton, "Jane Austen has given the norm, the ideal, of this type" (the novel of character [*JACH* 2:284]).

What connections are there among Victorian appreciation of Austen, later academic criticism, and the current investment? Is there a common appeal to this infinitely desirable, this small but perfect world? First, it must be said that such appeal is at least in part generically determined, again from Scott onward: Austen's value is quintessentially novelistic—a manageable, apprehensible slice of the real. Second and just as obvious, the appeal is even more broadly determined by comic form: as critics, readers, and viewers never tire of saying, the novels obtain satisfying closure; the perfect final completion of the process of secularizing (and sexualizing) providence, rewarding of the virtuous and punishing of the vicious. Slightly less obvious, but always present in commentary, is the Austen-specific mix of the comic and the ironic.[28] Romance of the courtship plot and domestic fiction in general is tempered by worldly-wise tartness. And as is clear I hope from the snippets of academic criticism mentioned previously, Austen presents a small but complete world, and the pleasures lie in that unusual relation between totality and diminutive size.

Much of this appeal can be collected under the rubric of Nostalgia. A continuing education seminar at the University of North Carolina entitled "Jane Austen: The Pleasures of a Good Novel" (July 15–17, 1996) attracted 150 people, who paid $125 for a few lectures on Austen. One surprisingly common response to the question of why people were so attracted to Austen now was that it is better than drugs. This turned out to mean not so much hallucinogens, nor opium dreams, but rather antidepressants. That is, for reducing stress, Austen is better than Prozac, because she represents a therapeutic return to something pleasurable, and an often-remembered pleasure. In both reviews and in conversation among amateur readers, the pleasure of reading Austen often refers backward, either or both to youth or to college experience. In her interview with *Rolling Stone* (August 22, 1996), Amy Heckerling, director of *Clueless*, said, "I needed a story a girl could go through. I wanted a comedy of manners—so I thought about Jane Austen and how much I loved *Emma* in college. The plot is perfect for any time." To appropriate a phrase from Oliver Sacks, "Austen mania" indicates a kind of "incontinent nostalgia."[29] Such nostalgia began early; an anonymous reviewer writes in 1866, "One of the greatest charms to us of Miss Austen's novels is the complete change of scene they afford: we are transferred at once to an old world which we can scarcely believe was England only half-a-century ago" (*JACH* 1:202).[30]

Austen then represents the lure of a small and perfect world: three or four families in a country village, a world often described, as in MacIntyre, as a community. What the language of closure, unity, wholeness, totality, what we would call suture, adds up to is an imaginable community. This is both idealized—transparently—utopian, but also peculiarly historical. Austen's novels are situated in a significantly reified moment, one so familiar it has a whole subgenre devoted to it, the regency romance. This moment is not accidental because it is historical but not distant, on the edge, as it were, of history. "Jane Austen's World" (as any number of the handbooks put it) constitutes a vague, abstracted, nonspecific past, before the railroad, before urbanization and industrialization, for example, the green world before the fall.[31] There is a close congruity between the academic and the popular Austen on this point. As René Balibar points out, the normative function of literary studies is explanatory and naturalizing, by "making a literary text appear in its context."[32] But with few exceptions (such as the studies of Marylin Butler and Alistair Duckworth), Austen has traditionally been contextless, a never-never land on the fold between history and modernity, touching but not part of either.

This idealized world finds its logic in miniaturization. Austen described her purview in a letter as "pictures of domestic life in country villages" (452), a scale that is condensed even further in another self-deprecating remark about her work, "the little bit (two Inches wide) of Ivory on which I work with so fine a Brush" (469).[33] Susan Stewart connects the miniature with childhood and innocence. Like the novel as such, miniaturization thematizes representation, accuracy to scale, the perfection of the techniques of replication—"a delirium of description" (46). "The miniature offers a world clearly limited in space but frozen and thereby both particularized and generalized in time—particularized in that the miniature concentrates upon the single instance and not upon the abstract rule, but generalized in that that instance comes to transcend, to stand for, a spectrum of other instances" (48). Ultimately, the miniature represents a controllable, manageable (downsized?) world. From this view, then, Austen represents a dollhouse, of which, Stewart notes, the two dominant motifs are "wealth and nostalgia" (61).[34]

But to describe the nostalgic appeal of Austen in terms of miniaturization does not explain why it has grown so acute now. Clearly there has been an appetite for costume dramas for some time, going back to Merchant/Ivory's *Room with a View* on up through *Howard's End* and Martin Scorsese's *Age of Innocence* and *Jefferson in Paris*. In his review of *Emma*, Roger Ebert (*Chicago Sun-Times*) writes, "In an impolite age, we escape to the movies to see good manners"; so too, Edward Rothstein's article on the Austen films is entitled "Manner's Envy" (*New York Times*, December 10, 1995). That may be so, but manners have been bad since anyone can remember, and there have always been costume dramas.[35] *Age of Innocence* did not provoke any Wharton mania, nor has any *Jane Eyre* film ever sent *Villette* or *Shirley* (or even *Jane Eyre* for that matter) onto the best-seller list. The opposition between good and bad mannered shows up in the pleasure reviewers take in odd coupling: *Clueless* and *Kids* (John Leland, *Newsweek* [July 24, 1995]); *Emma* and *Trainspotting* (Stanley Kauffmann, *The New Republic* [August 1996]).[36] In these oppositions, Austen is often set against Quentin Tarantino, or she is set up as "an antidote to the fungus infection of Joe Eszterhas" (Jack Kroll, *Newsweek* [December 18, 1995]). Such comparisons always seem to produce a derogation of the present because we need Austen more than ever in these degenerate times.[37] In his *The New Yorker* review of *Persuasion*, Anthony Lane sighs: "You look at Amanda Root and you see how patience has shifted into neurosis, how niceties have condensed into suffocation; the battle of wits is now a fight to the death."[38]

This antiseptic Austen presents a logical progression from the Merchant/Ivory–Forster films; Forster idolized Austen, and they share an oddly congruent (turn-of-the-century) historical and ideological appeal, as evidenced in Forster's *Two Cheers for Democracy* and his advocacy of an aristocracy of the plucky. As costume dramas, Forster and Austen can be figured as moments in which class as a brutal exclusionary force is being revisioned as elegance, style—as classiness. Both novelists can be read in terms of an aestheticization of morality or ethics. If the taste for costume drama is motored for a desire for pastoral, a past that is simple, attractive, manageable, better, nicer, kinder, and gentler, then who better to turn to than Austen? Some of the nostalgia may come from an older audience, long out of college, living into an age of canon reform, when "their" classics come under attack. Here the Austen costume dramas can be said to represent a purely white Englishness, before the fall into Empire and the politics of race.[39] Austen is the very embodiment of a white Englishness, especially for an Anglophile American audience. In Francis Mulhern's insightful reading of F. R. Leavis, his sense of tradition represents "precisely the continuity of Englishness": "Processes of change are described and interpreted, but only as the corrosive, demoralizing environment of something that is held to be essentially changeless, and whose value is the decisive theme of the retrospect. This is the past not as history but as 'tradition.'"[40] This view of the tradition as the persistence of Englishness in effect produces a negation of history, a preservation of a purely white England. Austen is an old comforting friend who celebrates the lasting values of morality, kindness, elegance via (and this phrase comes often in both conversation and reviews) "strong women."[41] So Austen is not simply made to look conservative and nostalgic but also slightly progressive at the same time. Judith Lowder Newton argued long ago that the appeal of *Pride and Prejudice* is that an entire class system can be overturned for one clever, witty, and lucky girl—and their marriage then represents "an aristocracy of the plucky." If Austen and the present appeal of Austen lies in her moment, which seems to transcode class into aesthetics and morality, then you could argue that what is happening in these films is the aesthetization of power—class, patriarchal, financial, political—powers that are given an elegant feminine gloss.

The new representations of Austen, then, present an aristocracy as attractive to nominal or residual democrats, an aristocracy at the point of its moralization and aesthetization into an abstract hierarchy, an aristocracy of the plucky, of the good, and the elegant, in which we can perceive morality as style. This operation turns on the transcoding of class from brute exclusionary practice to class as elegance and grace, to class in a commodity culture. This is an Austen superimposed with the look and feel of Ralph Lauren nostalgia for an available aristocracy, old money and *class* in the consumer sense of the term. The language of class is most evident in the marketing of Gwyneth Paltrow. In the *New York Times* review of *Emma* (August 2, 1996), Janet Maslin makes it clear that *Emma* thematizes stardom: like *Clueless*, this film "turns the role of Austen's best-loved busybody into a showcase for a show-stopping young star." Or, as Mike Clark writes in *USA Today* (August 12, 1995, p. 1), "Emma is Paltrow, Paltrow is Emma." But Paltrow is not just Emma: she is also Audrey Hepburn and Grace Kelly: "what used to be called class" (quoted in Richard Corliss, "A Touch of Class," *Times*, July 29, 1996, p. 2). As director McGrath puts it, "It's like, 'Shannen Doherty is Emma?' I don't think so" (Richard Corliss, "A Touch of Class," *Time* July 29, 1966. http://www.pemberley.com/kip/emma/

em2time.html). McGrath says in a *Vogue* article (August 1996), "the minute Gwyneth started speaking, I felt like I was looking at the perfect Emma" (214). It is in this context that Paltrow's election to the "50 Best Dressed People" in *People* magazine makes sense, her positioning as classic, understated elegance, as sheer class. In the text that accompanies her *Vogue* fashion layout, we are told, "'There's a Grace Kelly–Audrey Hepburn quality about her says Gucci's Tom Ford'. . . . 'She has a slightly removed elegance, a chic quality that we haven't seen in a long time'" (209). This is fashion before the fall into its globalization and corporatization, before supermodels, back when it could be envisioned as (relatively) innocent, something more about style and connected, with transparent, unproblematic cultural capital with the great houses, with individually named designers, and with the very rich and exclusive (this is the Hepburn of *Breakfast at Tiffany's*). The *Vogue* article closes as follows:

> And how does Pitt feel? "God, that's such an embarrassing question," says Paltrow. And then she takes the final sip of her second vodka tonic, and says, "He thinks I'm pretty good, you know? He always says, 'You're an *amazing* woman.' Another thing he says—oh gosh, this is *so* incredibly embarrassing, but another thing he always says is 'My girl's got class.'" And then, perhaps to prove that she has, Paltrow turns crimson. (209)

Within the films, the thematization of class as style and elegance is best exemplified in Ang Lee's *Sense and Sensibility*, in which the real actors are the great houses and the spectacular landscapes. Far grander than those Austen invokes, these houses and estates are the seats of grandees, of the great lords, dukes, and earls, with elaborate formal gardens. The scenery is so voluptuous that it regularly upstages the actors, so emphatically stitched together from some twenty different counties. Little attempt is made to connect the inside with the outside, either in landscape or weather. For example, Fanny mentions the avenue of trees that she plans to cut down, but the camera does not pan out of the window to display it. We see characters enter and exit, but where to is always obscured (often behind a screen). (In contrast, at least half of the locations used in the A&E *Pride and Prejudice* employ the same interior and exterior.) But it is the countryside, with its vast patchwork of lovely fields, meadows, hills, pastures, gardens, and unconnected coves that emphasize the beauty and riches of England and Englishness. Lee has produced a mélange of disconnected picture postcard-gift-calendar-perfect scenes, and in so doing offered fantasy space for place, the named places, the homes, the birthplaces that tie people and family to the land and to the farm: Norland, Cleveland, Combe Magna, Delaford. As Richard A. Blake, a reviewer for a magazine named *America* puts it, "*Sense and Sensibility* is beautifully photographed by Michael Coulter, whose camera caresses the glorious and ever moody English landscapes and the warm candlelit interiors of country homes" (March 9, 1996, 21). This is a post-Gainsborough, post-Constable landscape where the land is aesthetisized, removed from farming and production (though we do get the occasional sheep or some miscellaneous cattle milling about in a couple of scenes). The choice is thematized in the dispute concerning the room for Edward at Norland: the lovely set piece of the lake (never shown) versus the stables in back. This is a souvenir England, in which the hills and dales are movable, and interchangeable, an England without locality and connection between individual subjects and the land that supports them.

The connection between *Sense and Sensibility*'s anesthetized landscapes and its great houses, on the one hand, and the "small stately home" *House Beautiful* is so confident Jane Austen would admire, on the other, is a tenuous one, threaded along the historical transformation from class to classiness. The phrase *small stately home*, contains a double contradiction, between small and stately and between stately and home. The word *stately*, according to the *Oxford English Dictionary*, goes back to Chaucer, indicating elevated, dignified, befitting or indicating high estate, princely, noble, majestic. It is first applied to people (as in Jürgen Habermas's sense of aristocratic display and publicity), and only later to buildings, as in large and imposing: for example, Longleat, Wilton House, Blenheim Palace. The history of the word *stately* describes a gradual process of objectification, the end point of which is neatly specified by Walter Benjamin in "Paris: Capital of the Nineteenth Century," where he describes the world carefully contracted into decor: "the phantasmagorias of the interior."

> For the private person, living space becomes, for the first time, antithetical to the place of work. The former is constituted by the interior; the office is its complement. The private person who squares his accounts with reality in his office demands that the interior be maintained by his illusions. This need is all the more pressing since he has no intention of extending his commercial considerations into social ones. In shaping his private environment he represses both. From this spring the phantasmagorias of the interior. For the private individual the private environment represents the universal. In it he gathers remote places and the past: His drawing room is a box in the world theatre.[42]

Like the small stately home, Austen has come to figure for us the set of consumer objects that represent class and elegance, class miniaturized, something small we can own and hold, the last charm against an apparently brute world of violence. I want to close with a couple of moments from *Sense and Sensibility* and *Mansfield Park*. In a scene of fine comic buildup, when Lucy reveals her engagement to Edward, Fanny Dashwood physically expels Lucy, shoving her out a set of French doors. There has been no frame reverse frame to orient the viewer within that in the scene, but at its close, the glass clearly opens onto a modern block of apartments, a momentary portal into the present. This may be less of a suture of the present into the past than a sly expulsion of Lucy Steele into the present, into a more selfish and scheming age, a scapegoat of modern self-interest. So, too, at the end of the film, in the reciprocal image to Lucy's expulsion, we watch the wedding from a distance, from the subject position of the envious Willoughby. This Willoughby, with his contemporary male beauty and his unBritish, unantiqued accent, is also like Lucy—expedient and selfish—and so he, too, functions in a sense as a representative of our age, gazing longingly, but far removed, in the happy past.

This look of longing at the past appears reversed in the most aggressively presentist of recent Austen films—Patricia Rozema's 1999 gothic adaptation of *Mansfield Park*—in which Fanny Price, Austen's most physically delicate and repressive heroine, has been recast along the lines of a modernized Elizabeth Bennet: Frances O'Connor's portrayal of Fanny is a composite character of the novel's character, the novel's narrator, and a fantasy figuration of Austen as writer, with dialogue drawn from both the letters and the juvenilia—when Fanny addresses the camera/audience directly, as she frequently does, it is always as an authorial presence—most often reading from her own composition, but commonly delivering the narrator's judgments. This is not Trilling's fragile Christian heroine, but a sexualized, passionate, and athletic heroine who rides out in the night like Cathy in search of Heathcliff. The presentist composite of dates and periods is insistent here, as when the forward-looking Mary Crawford exclaims, "This is 1806, for heaven's sake." But in the penultimate scene, the Crawfords and their partners have a final moment of formally staring into the camera, as the voice-over intones, "Mary Crawford went to live in Westminster, and eventually she and Henry found partners who shared their more modern sensibility," fusing their incestuous "ménage a quarter" with a decadent modernity. *Mansfield Park*, then, closes with a brief return to the relative innocence of Fanny and Edmund, so despite Rozema's attempt to connect the Regency with a corrupt slavocracy, modernization still ends up as a slide into further disgrace and depravity.

These looks of longing on the past that the Austen films stage have their analogue in psychoanalysis: as Lacan summarizes Sigmund Freud's essay on love and hypnosis, "It is clear that, like all love, it can be mapped, as Freud shows, only in the field of narcissism. To love is, essentially, to wish to be loved."[43] Our moment's longing gaze on Austen ought to be validating; after all, we are the few who have the taste/elegance/class to recognize her worth, but of course there is no response from her: we are not loved in return. To draw on Lacan one more time, "When, in love, I solicit a look, what is profoundly unsatisfying and always missing is that—*You never look at me from the place from which I see you*" (103).

Notes

1. Emma Thompson, *The Sense and Sensibility Screenplay and Diaries* (New York: Newmarket Press, 1996), 215.

2. In a publication of the Ohio Wesleyan libraries, *At the Library* (Spring 1996, 4), Ruth Davies's article "The Year of Jane Austen" quotes Roger Rosenblatt on the *Lehrer News Hour* in January 1966, who said that the most important thing about 1995 was that "it brought Jane Austen back to life."

3. *Time* describes the movies *Persuasion* and *Sense and Sensibility* as revealing "the hidden hungers of the cautious soul" (December 25, 1995). For a critique of this kind of marketing, see Deborah Kaplan's "Mass Marketing Jane Austen: Men, Women, and Courtship in Two of the Recent Films," *Persuasions* 18 (1996): 171–181. Kaplan describes Ang Lee's and Douglas McGrath's films in terms of the harlequinization of Austen: "By harlequinization I mean that, like the mass-market romance, the focus is on a hero and heroine's courtship at the expense of other characters and other experiences" (172). In part, this is achieved by "amplifying and glamorizing Austen's heroes" (174), but she also means streamlining, simplification, stereotyping, and cliché. These procedures all serve the same end—mass-market appeal, e.g. profit."

4. Although there has been a steady stream of guidebooks to Austen for many years—almost a cottage industry in Britain—the pace accelerated from 1995 onward with several books on the making of Austen movies (including the scripts). Two examples of Austeniana suggest the confidence of timelessness in her work: Maggie Black and Deirdre le Faye suggest in their *The Jane Austen Cookbook* (Chicago: Chicago Review Press, 1995) that her recipes (or Martha Lloyd's) are just as good as they ever were. Similarly, in *Jane Austen's Little Instruction Book* (White Plains, NY: Peter Pauper Press, 1995), Sophia Bedford-Pierce assumes that Austen's advice is as good now as it was two hundred years ago; the advice consists largely of abstractable aphorisms, such as Mary's remark from *Pride and Prejudice*: "Vanity and pride are different things, though the words are often used synonymously" (26). I have myself compiled Jane Austen quotations for *The Columbia World of Quotations* (New York: Columbia University Press, 1996), and it is by no means easy to abstract from the rhetoric of specificity that the novels underwrite the aphoristic in Austen—as in the opening sentence of *Pride and Prejudice* "It is a truth universally acknowledged that a young man in possession of a good fortune must be in want of a wife"—is more often than not undercut by the plot.

The registration material for the 1996 Jane Austen Society of North America annual meeting includes two travel advertisements from two different companies offering Jane Austen tours of England. It also includes two advertisements for two different companies offering Jane Austen music CDs: the "Jane Austen Companion," from Nimbus Direct, which claims "Works by Mendelssohn, Fasch, J. Haydn, Boyce, J. C. Bach, M. Haydn and Schubert have been selected and sequenced to provide over an hour of inviting and relaxing listening. Simply put on the CD and enter the world of Jane Austen." Isis Records has three CDs in their Jane Austen Music Collection: "Enjoy Jane Austen's Favorite Music." A company advertising on the World Wide Web offers a set of Jane Austen bookmarks: "The Jane Austen Book Companions," with all the characters conveniently listed. But topping them all is Mattel, which is now advertising a set of *Clueless* Barbie dolls on the Cartoon Network.

5. The *Los Angeles Times* reports a more modest 9 million (December 9, 1995); Laurie Winer makes the claim for A&E's highest rating in "Colin Firth's Sexy Sensibility," *Harper's Bazaar* 34 (May 1, 1996): 171. CNN Online (January 14, 1966) claims that "the last episode drew 40 percent of the United Kingdom's total television audience; the home video sold more than 100,000 copies and a companion edition of the novel sold out."

6. See also M. Casey Diana, "Thompson's S&S," in *Jane Austen in Hollywood*, ed. Linda Troost and Sayre Greenfield (Lexington: University Press of Kentucky, 1998), 145: Penguin reports a 40 percent increase in sales.

7. One way Austen is being stitched into the present is evident in *Entertainment Weekly's* photograph of "Jane Austen" lounging by a pool in Hollywood.

8. The 1995 minutes of the Annual Meeting of the Jane Austen Society of North America note that their mission is "to foster among the widest number of readers the study, appreciation, and understanding of Jane Austen's works, her life, and her genius." In 1995, membership was 2,247.

9. In his essay on the recent popularity of Austen, "Jane's World," Martin Amis notes a certain adaptability or negative capability to the novels: "Jane Austen is weirdly capable of keeping *everybody* busy. The moralists, the Eros-and-Agape people, the Marxists, the Freudians, the Jungians, the semioticians, the deconstructors— all find an adventure playground in six samey novels about middle-class provincials. And for every generation of critics, and readers, her fiction effortlessly renews itself" (*The New Yorker* 71 [January 8, 1996]: 34). In contrast, Barbara Everett suggests that this "second Janeite movement" may be antiacademic in character: "The academic Jane Austen is conservative or radical, significant as she represents her period or not. It may be that the great new fashion in Jane Austen is a protest by ordinary readers, buying her fiction in staggering numbers, that the writer is not like this: she is only definable as a presence supremely capable of giving large pleasure" ("Hard Romance," *London Review of Books* 8 [February 1996]: 2).

10. *Jane Austen in Hollywood* (Lexington: University Press of Kentucky, 1998), 62.

11. Equally important but not examined here are the sequels and continuations; the sequels page at www.pemberley.com lists sixty-six sequels. Marilyn Sachs takes a dark view of such unrestrained proliferation: "Jane Austen would certainly not approve, but it appears unlikely that devoted admirers will ever stop luring her characters into sequels" (*The Jane Austen Companion* [New York: Macmillan, 1986], 376). For overviews, see Heidi Ganner-Rauth, "To Be Continued? Sequels and Continuations of Nineteenth-Century Novels and Novel Fragments," *English Studies* 64 (1983): 129–143; Kathleen Glancy, "What Happened Next? Or The Many Hus-

bands of Georgina Darcy," *Persuasions* 11 (1989): 110–116. See also Garrett Stewart, "Film's Victorian Retrofit," *Victorian Studies*, 38 (1995): 153–198.

12. Gayatri Spivak, *Outside in the Teaching Machine* (London: Routledge, 1993), 259.

13. Slavoj Žižek, *The Sublime Object of Ideology* (London: Verso, 1989), 111.

14. Marvin Mudrick, *Jane Austen: Irony as Defense and Discovery* (Princeton: Princeton University Press, 1952), 169. See also Julia Kavanagh, who in 1862 writes thus of Anne Elliot: "Here we see the first genuine picture of that silent torture of an unloved woman, condemned to suffer thus because she is a woman and must not speak, and which, many years later, was wakened into such passionate eloquence by the author of *Jane Eyre.*" Quoted from B. C. Southam, ed., *Jane Austen: The Critical Heritage*, 2 vols. (London: Routledge and Kegan Paul, 1968), Vol. 1, 195. Hereafter referred to as *JACH*.

15. In Marcia McClintock Folsom, ed., *Approaches to Teaching Austen's Pride and Prejudice* (New York: Modern Language Association of America, 1993), 19.

16. Nina Auerbach, *Romantic Imprisonment: Women and Other Glorified Outcasts* (New York: Columbia University Press, 1985), 22.

17. Alisdair MacIntyre, *After Virtue: A Study of Moral Theory* (West Bend, IN: University of Notre Dame Press, 1984), 185, 243, 240.

18. Wayne Booth, *The Rhetoric of Fiction* (Chicago: University of Chicago Press, 1961), 265. In a critique of this celebration, Fredric Jameson observes that such celebration often disguises a longing for the historically specific way of life and class structure Austen's novels represent: "The fact is that the implied or reliable narrator described by Booth is possible only in a situation of relative class homogeneity, and indeed reflects a basic community of values shared by a fairly restricted class of readers: and such a situation is not brought back into the world by fiat. . . . Thus the ultimate value of Booth's work is that of the conservative position in general: useful as diagnosis, and as a means of disengaging everything that is problematical in the existing state of things, its practical recommendations turn out to be nothing but regression and sterile nostalgia for the past" (*Marxism and Form* [Princeton, NJ: Princeton University Press, 1971], 357–358).

19. James Thompson, *Models of Value: Eighteenth-Century Political Economy and the Novel* (Durham, NC: Duke University Press, 1998), 188–192.

20. Ian Watt, *Rise of the Novel* (Berkeley and Los Angeles: University of California Press, 1957), 297.

21. In Ian Watt, ed., *Jane Austen: A Collection of Critical Essays* (Englewood Cliffs, NJ: Prentice-Hall, 1963), 134. This is a commonplace in Austen studies. Compare Jane Nardin: "A character's social behavior, in other words, the standard of propriety by which he lives—is, for Jane Austen, the external manifestation of his internal moral and psychological condition" (*Those Elegant Decorums: Propriety in Jane Austen* [Albany: State University of New York Press, 1973], 23).

22. For a recent version of this argument, see David Kaufmann, "Law and Propriety, *Sense and Sensibility*: Austen on the Cusp of Modernity," *ELH* 59 (1992): 385–408.

23. Julia Prewitt Brown, *Jane Austen's Novels: Social Change and Literary Form* (Cambridge: Harvard University Press, 1979), 15.

24. Alistair Duckworth, *The Improvement of the Estate* (Baltimore: Johns Hopkins University Press, 1971), 26.

25. F. R. Leavis, *The Great Tradition* (New York: George W. Stewart, 1950), 7.

26. For a fine overview of Austen criticism, see Philip Goldstein, "Criticism and Institutions: The Conflicted Reception of Jane Austen's Fiction," *Studies in the Humanities* 18 (1991): 35–55. Focusing on the politics of Austen's reception from Whatley through the second wave of feminism, Goldstein underscores the heterogeneous character of Austen criticism.

27. Clifford Siskin sheds considerable light on this phenomenon in his exploration of the division of disciplines across this period and its accompaniment by a privileging of the "narrow but deep" constraint of knowledge; Austen may very well offer an aesthetic and emotional counterpart to this stage of professionalization (*The Work of Writing: Literature and Social Change in Britain, 1700–1830* [Baltimore: Johns Hopkins University Press, 1998], 54–99).

28. Barbara Everett captures this effect in her title "Hard Romance," "a balance between what is romantic in itself, and what is hard": "There is a Janeite in every reader, even the most technically sophisticated, an aspect of the mind that reads the deft and light symbolism of feeling; for this reason we respond to the simple romance of Jane Austen's novels. We need these books to end with happy marriage, as we don't need thousands of trivial love-fictions which were written contemporaneously or before or after her" (12). In part this comes down to an acknowledgment in Austen of "how to reconcile her perceived extremes—love and money" (13), a thematic more than a generic contrast. At times, however, she seems to be contrasting pleasure and morality, as here, of *Emma*: "A moral dimension, often taken to be the story of the novel, satisfactorily deepens this supremely pleasure-giving affair" (14). Similarly, in an interview with *Salon* (December 2, 1995), Lindsay Duran, producer of Ang Lee's *Sense and Sensibility*, claims that "satire and romanticism are usually mutually exclusive. . . . Trying to find both things in one person—that's what makes Jane Austen such a great writer" (2).

29. See also the *People* review of *Persuasion* by Leah Rozen: "If you've never read Jane Austen, this movie is a swell introduction. If you're already a fan, it's like visiting old friends and discovering that they are still as good company as you remembered" (http://people.aol.com/people/movie-reviews/95/persuasion.html). An article by Laura Miller in *Salon* (December 2, 1995) is entitled "Austen-Mania": Austen's social climate, she argues, "isn't far from our own. Authority rests in the hands of a dubious elite, prosperity seems precarious and, most of all, parents are just not doing their jobs. Not a single Austen heroine enjoys the influence of a fully functional family. Their mothers and fathers prove negligent, over-indulgent, cynical, shallow, neurotic or simply absent." And yet they triumph into good marriages (making her novels sounds like the television show *Friends*, in which the protagonists find com-

fort and pleasure despite neurotic parents): "Austen had an idea of how to live in this imperfect world that comprised balance, moderation and consideration—all sorely undervalued in our sensation-mad society or, for that matter, in her own" (2). She concludes, "Austen's novels displace the serene conviction that decency, civility, and common sense will be rewarded."

30. Compare Anthony Lane in *The New Yorker* (September 25, 1995): "Anyone who knows "Persuasion" tend[s] to know it well, perhaps because it's all about renewing of acquaintances, the stoking of old flames: it somehow sets an example to the reader, who comes back to the story in the hope of further bliss, as the hero does to his beloved." (107).

31. Maggie Lane captures this sense of the pastness of Austen in her volume *Jane Austen's England* (London: Robert Hale, 1986), the latest edition (1996) of which announces on the cover, "The essential background to the award-winning film *Sense and Sensibility* with Emma Thompson and top-rated TV series *Pride and Prejudice*": 'She was indeed fortunate to live in an age when not only was England at the peak of its physical beauty, improved but not yet desecrated by human activity, but when cultured people were learning to appreciate the natural world after centuries of indifference or fear'" (13).

32. René Balibar, "An Example of Literary Work in France," in *1848: The Sociology of Literature*, ed. Francis Barker (Essex, UK: University of Essex, 1978), 27–46.

33. R. W. Chapman, ed., *Jane Austen's Letters* (Oxford: Oxford University Press, 1952), 452, 469.

34. Susan Stewart, "The Miniature," *On Longing: Narratives of the Miniature, the Gigantic, the Souvenir, the Collection* (Durham, NC: Duke University Press, 1993): 37–69. She explores the topos of *multum in parvo* much in little (52ff). See also her discussion of the dollhouse, whose two dominant motifs are "wealth and nostalgia" (61). "The reduction in scale which the miniature presents skews the time and space relations of the everyday lifeworld, and as an object consumed, the miniature finds its 'use value' transformed into the infinite time of reverie" (65).

35. A cover story in the *Boston Globe Magazine* (May 4, 1997) by Laura Pappano is entitled "The Crusade for Civility," but nonetheless is packed with one example after another of rudeness, as if we are experiencing a crisis of incivility.

36. Amy Heckerling herself sees *Clueless* as the opposite of *Kids* in her *Rolling Stone* (August 22, 1996) interview. Susan Lee, writing oddly enough for *Forbes* (November 4, 1996) rejects such an apposition: "Needless to say, this line of commentary finds our society distinctly uncivil in comparison. The way we live now is denounced as vulgar, our language seen as degraded and our daily social intercourse informed by brutality and shamelessness. Gimme a break." She goes on to find "the quiet acceptance required of Austen's heroines rather repellent" recommending instead the aggression of the heroines in *The First Wives Club* (391). In *Premiere* (March 1996), Libby Gelman-Waxner amusingly compares *Waiting to Exhale* with *Sense and Sensibility*, both of which are obsessed with "trying to find husbands." Earlier, Gelman-Waxner reviewed *Clueless* and *Kids* together (*Premiere* [October 1995]). She found *Kids* repulsively pedophilic, but "*Clueless* understands that America is a teen par-

adise and that trying to buy your children's affection with deluxe consumer goods is a very workable concept" (66).

37. Terence Rafferty in *The New Yorker* (December 18, 1995) writes, "The movie is, in most respects, an ideal rendering of Austen's down-to-earth manner. It is handsome but not vain, witty but not cruel: a gracious and unfailingly pleasant entertainment, which moviegoers—who are conditioned to low expectations—will probably embrace with wholehearted, we-did-not-dare-to-hope relief" (125). Anthony Lane writes in his *The New Yorker* (September 25, 1995) review of *Persuasion*, "You look at Amanda Root and you see how patience has shifted into neurosis, how niceties have condensed into suffocation; the battle of wits is now a fight to the death" (108). Elayne Rapping's column in *The Progressive* ("The Jane Austen Thing," July 1996, 37–38), works an extended comparison between Austen and *Melrose Place*.

38. *The New Yorker* (September 25, 1995): 107.

39. Regarding nationalism in Austen, note the connection between literary studies and the rise of nationalism: literary studies still dominated by the categories of nationalism, and the novel, as Timothy Brennan argues, plays a historical role in the emergence of nationalism "by objectifying the 'one, yet many' of national life"; the novel works by "objectifying the nation's *composite* nature" ("The National Longing for Form," pp. 44–70 in *Nation and Narration*, ed. Homi K. Bhabha [London: Routledge, 1990], 49, 51).

40. Francis Mulhern, "English Reading," 250–264, *Nation and Narration*, 253, 252.

41. Donald Lyons, "Passionate Precision," *Film Comment* 32 (1996): 36–41 writes of *Sense and Sensibility*, "[F]or the most part we are just shown a variety of capable women and feckless men, and left to draw our own, properly feminist, conclusions" (36). *People* magazine's On Line Chat (September 16, 1996), with Cathryn Michon and Pamela Norris, authors of *Jane Austen's Little Advice Book*, quotes Pamela Norris: "the heroines [of Austen's novels] are very thrillingly modern in that they speak their minds AND get the handsome rich guy to marry them." Judith Lowder Newton, *Women, Power, and Subversion: Social Strategies in British Fiction, 1778–1860.* (Athens: University of Georgia Press, 1981), 55–85.

42. *Reflections*, ed. Peter Demetz, trans. Edmund Jephcott (New York: Schocken Books, 1978), 154.

43. Jacques Lacan, *Four Fundamental Concepts of Psycho-Analysis*, trans. Alan Sheridan (New York: Norton, 1981), 253. Cf. "When, in love, I solicit a look, what is profoundly unsatisfying and always missing is that—*You never look at me from the place from which I see you*" (103).

2

Popular Culture and the Comedy of Manners

Clueless and Fashion Clues

Maureen Turim

"Of all the Austen film adaptations, *Clueless* is my favorite one to teach," a feminist eighteenth-century scholar whose specialization extends through the Regency period told me recently. "Maybe it's the contrast between the film and novel that makes it the most useful in getting students to think about what is at stake in *Emma* and for women during Austen's lifetime."[1]

Such sentiments seem readily understandable when one considers the problems presented by the other Austen film adaptations. To the extent that such adaptations attempt to illustrate directly Jane Austen's writerly voice with images meant to embody her prose, so much of the discussion focuses on the adequacy of the transposition. To the extent that such adaptations simply borrow Austen's settings and plots to tell a subtly different story, the differences and their purpose become the focus. In either case these films' contemporary reenactment of the historical inevitably shifts details. It may become difficult to extricate readings of the novel from the visual interpretations that begin to color it. Rewriting for film introduces patterns of glance-object or shot-reverse editing, for example, where they are deliberately absented from Austen's narrative design.

Consider the end of chapter 6 in which Mr. Elton watches Emma paint the portrait of Harriet, a situation that confirms for Emma Mr. Elton's fascination with the friend with whom Emma has decided to match him. In fact, Emma is mistaken, which we learn later; Mr. Elton is attracted to the artist,

Emma, and not the sitter. Austen's task as author is to narrate this event in such a way as to allow the reader to adopt Emma's speculations, while still setting up the elements of reversal that will be revealed latter. Mr. Elton's gaze is an object of the description. The scene is in some ways quite cinematic:

> The sitting began; and Harriet, smiling and blushing, and afraid of not keeping her attitude and countenance, presented a very sweet mixture of youthful expression to the steady eye of the artist. But there was no doing anything, with Mr. Elton fidgeting behind her, and watching every touch. She gave him credit for stationing himself where he might gaze and gaze again without offence; but was really obliged to put an end to it, and request him to place himself elsewhere. It then occurred to her to employ him in reading.[2]

The delight of this passage is in many ways retrospective and established for rereading. The phrase *watching every touch* gives a hint of Mr. Elton's preoccupation with Emma's activity. Another phrase, *she gave him credit for stationing himself* in fact is an interpretation by Emma of a skillfully hidden voyeurism, but she is mistaken about the object of Mr. Elton's visual fascination, as the object of the gaze is not Harriet so much as herself. For all its apparently cinematic preoccupation with the voyeuristic pliers connecting artist and model, a trope that began in early silent film history in such films as Georges Méliès' 1900 *L'Artiste et le mannequin* (*Artist and Model*) and continues through Jacques Rivette's *La Belle Noiseuse* (1991), we have in Austen's narration a twist of voice that belies any configuration of mise-en-scène. Adaptations tend to supplant the provocatively distant writing with a more accessible substitution, staging the scene, but evacuating the voice. *Emma* continues with recounting a second day of sitting without such attention to placement at all. Then there is a typical dialogue passage, in which numerous characters debate the verisimilitude versus the invention evidenced in the portrait of Harriet that Emma has painted. The dialogue is given without any indication of spatiality, no fullness of representation of bodies in space interacting with glances, movements, and gestures, but rather a chorus of competing voices articulating their respective positions. Austen's writing thus has its whim with spatiality, with the fullness of corporeal representation, presenting it ambiguously or ignoring it altogether when authorial purpose is elsewhere.

It would take a far different sort of adaptation to foreground Austen's writing; think perhaps of the film techniques Robert Bresson chose to adapt Georges Bernanos to the screen in *Journal d'un curé de compagne* (*Diary of a Country Priest*) (1952) and *Mouchette* (1967). Forceful, deliberately framed images, combined with a voice-over citing directly and selectively from the language of the text encourage the viewer to listen to the film as a reading of its source. While the Austen adaptations take a range of approaches, few dare to frame or edit with a similarly rigorous style, rebuffing familiar continuity editing in order to invoke extra attention to language. Instead, lines of written dialogue are presented as naturalistically as the highly written verbal exchanges in Austen allow, in those cases in which the formality of the 1816 language is left intact. As a result of efforts to make the films successful for audiences used to Hollywood-style filmmaking, updating in such traditional adaptations takes many forms. Subtle aspects of filmic representation transform the very sensibilities Austen's writing reveal. Her voice is lost. The adaptations are different from the late-eighteenth and early-nineteenth-century works, but they tend to hide these differences. Film simulation of the past intrudes upon Austen's very rendering of a perspective on social life addressed through her very studied form.[3]

A film set in the present, making no pretense of capturing the past, may stimulate a discussion of what the students actually discern of that past from the novel as cultural artifact. The displacements and transpositions in a film such as *Clueless* are far more revealed than are similar processes in either Douglas McGrath's *Emma* (1996) or Diarmuid Lawrence's *Jane Austen's Emma* (1996). Many university students are familiar with the social context of mid-1990s U.S. privileged high schools. This combination of familiarity of setting in the adaptation and revealed transformation simplifies numerous daunting pedagogical tasks that teaching an adaptation should pose for professors. Many students find the film fun, and some remember it from previous viewings in theaters or on video; that very circumstance awakens the student's desire to examine its source. Ultimately, *Clueless* may focus attention on the specificity of Austen's *Emma* in a manner period adaptations do not.

I wish, then, to explore how this work might be seen comparatively with the novel that served as its source, not simply as a point-by-point comparison of adaptation, but rather as a means of looking at issues surrounding a two-hundred-year history of narrative formations in the novel and film, in high and popular culture, and in the history of female adolescence and women's authorship. To do so, I have emphasized in my title the filiation of Austen's *Emma* in a lineage of novels linked to the Restoration comedy of manners, a genre that Pat Gill in *Interpreting Ladies: Women, Wit, and Morality in the Restoration Comedy of Manners* defines as directly addressing "the manners, wit, marriages, and morals of the author's present-day homeland."[4] She characterizes it as configuring its heroine as follows.

> Restoration comedy's witty, unrelenting attack on female hypocrisy thus needs a heroine who can be as charming and clever as any experienced sophisticate but who is nonetheless innocent of dissimulation and secret amours. The heroine's role as a formal and moral counterpoint to the rest of the female population serves as a locus, albeit a problematic one, for the play's tenuous moral underpinning.[5]

Gill goes on to say, "Restoration comic satire revolves around the female figure as prototype of problematic signification"(19). She examines how "in Restoration comedy, the moral indeterminacy and slippage in satiric language is both metaphor for and a metonymy of male uneasiness about female honesty and the related discomfort with the discursive components of social identity" (19).

We can see how Austen might be seen as an heir to this genre, configuring Emma as a locus through which to draw contrasts as the author addresses "the manners, wit, marriages, and morals" of her own environment. Other intertextualities of course inflect Austen's writing, and her own take on women and feminism is different from Restoration writers, though fruitful comparisons can be made to Aphra Behn.[6] Further, existing studies of influence do supply material that we might consider in our own investigation of intertexuality: *Emma* and *Clueless*. Rachel R. Mather suggests in her *The Heirs of Jane Austen: Twentieth-Century Writers of the Comedy of Manners* that Austen's intertextual reinscriptions of Restoration comedy have echoes in contemporary literature[7]; indeed, I am suggesting that *Clueless* usefully demonstrates how these shared aspects cross over into film comedy and television situation comedy, two media that are closely linked.

In pursuing such a comparative reading, the situation just described of combating a naive reflection theory becomes complicated by the need to grasp the specificity of each work. Inevitably voice, mimesis, and representation need to be understood theoretically and historically in all cultural texts, in Austen, in a period film adapted from Austen, and in the contemporary displacement of elements of Austen's plot and characters in *Clueless*. Attunement to structure and discourse within fictions needs to be honed as antidote to a tendency to read or view transparently these works as direct images of social reality. The adaptations that retain the Regency setting insist on just that transparency by meticulously giving us the details of clothing, decor, and architecture, even if some of the choices dress the scenes "inaccurately."

The question that I often pose to students is relevant here: What contemporary film would you chose as accurately rendering your life? Although some offer a particular film with which they identified greatly, say in 1999, James Mangold's *Girl, Interrupted* from Susanna Kaysen's book (despite its historical setting) or Sam Mendes's *American Beauty* from a script by Alan Ball (despite its exaggerated typage and stylization), they soon realize that what attaches these films to their sense of self is a sentiment of alienation rather than a depiction of their daily lives. If scholars viewed these films to investigate who contemporary Americans were from a perspective centuries from now, they would have to perform readings that could make such differentiations.

The students soon realize my question is meant to induce them to investigate the very mirroring of reality they assume any film must have to its period of production. Viewing Michael Curtiz's *Mildred Pierce* (1946), for example, they tend to take as cinema verité documentary the portrait of postwar-bungalow motherhood offered in the first flashback sequence that establishes Mildred before her divorce and class ascension. One must work to open recognition of this scene as construction and commentary, but here the predisposition to believe representations reflect reality at least allows for comparative examination of sociological sources concerning postwar working-class motherhood. Eventually they may ask how race might have determined class expectations, or now misogyny might enter into Mildred's portrayal in this scene, or conversely how this scene might represent a trenchant critique of a way of life rather than merely presenting it. Assumptions that such scenes simply reflect the times limit such investigation. The film noir twists of *Mildred Pierce* create entirely different problems given the students' tendency to read films as accurate and direct reflections of historical situations. The elements of psychoanalytic and ideological symbolization proposed by film noir call for a more complex deciphering. So the exercise of attempting to select "the film that tells my life" allows students to understand that mimesis does not equal sociological and historical veracity. Ultimately, one realizes that one's life escapes representation by a fiction film, and for many reasons. Hollywood-style commercial production is more distant from a nuanced sociological view than other forms of representation.

This exercise allows one to fully appreciate imitatio, as well as identification and projection, stylization and exaggeration, tone and voice. One may then return to a concept such as chronotyping prepared to see how complexly texts reveal their moment of production. One sees that reading a film or novel in its historical context means understanding the distance a text may represent from *social history*, a term that itself becomes open to investigation. It also enables discernment of those elements one might deem, through outside research and theoretical evaluation, more valid as descriptions of or commentary on social life in the historical period represented.

Clueless is easy to see as a text full of spirited exaggeration and license. One might compare its representation to life in the Beverly Hills of 1995, or to other middle- to upper-middle-class U.S. enclaves, but the film's style discourages us from assuming that it gives us an unmediated grasp of any reality. One becomes interested in the elements of genre and intertextuality that feed *Clueless*'s construction. One asks how the expectations of form determine its shape. By analogy, one can see that *Emma* as a creation displays similar distance from its setting, despite Austen's being of the class and place whose manners inform her stories. We can use this notion of distance to sharpen our hearing of Austen's voice, even as we understand how the observation of locale and the specificity of a period both color her novels.

In *Clueless*, social interaction and computer interactivity are contrasted with social activism as a major structuring device. For all its reveling in the superficiality of "Beverly Hills Bettys" and the fashion discourse of E! Entertainment television, the film must be seen as drawing a contrast between two modes of existence in contemporary U.S. culture, one purely consumerist, and the other engaged and aware. Like Emma, *Clueless* is a female coming-of-age story, but the manner in which it draws its contrast between the sheltered assumptions of adolescence and the realizations of womanhood contain both similarities and differences from the novel.

Clueless has already received much discussion as *Emma* adaptation. Suzanne Ferriss in "Emma Becomes Clueless" offers a detailed comparison of characters and situations transposed from the novel into updated equivalents. She highlights the cleverness of transposition:

> *Clueless* is most faithful to *Emma* in its recreation of the plot involving Mr. Elton, Harriet Smith, and Emma. Determined to find a match for the clergyman, Mr. Elton, Emma fixes on Harriet Smith. To orchestrate their involvement, Emma sketches a portrait of Harriet, intending the exercise as a ruse to draw Mr. Elton's attention to Harriet's beauty. Instead, Mr. Elton's praise of the portrait is not meant for its subject, but for Emma's artistry, a fact that Emma discovers, to her horror, only after he reveals his passion for her during an intimate carriage ride. This scene is exactly duplicated, though modernized, in *Clueless*. Cher takes Tai's photograph and mistakes Elton's request for a copy as evidence of his attraction to her protégé. As in the novel, Elton arranges to drive Cher home alone, and shocks her with his attempt to kiss her. Significantly, both Eltons object to the protégé's class. Mr. Elton exclaims, "I need not so totally despair of an equal alliance as to be addressing myself to Miss Smith!"(Austen, E 843). His cinematic counterpart asks incredulously, "Don't you know who my father is?"[8]

Ultimately, Ferriss wishes not only to appreciate the wit of the updating but also to explore, comparatively, the ideology of both works, particularly their discourse on women's place in society. She finds that despite a greater multiculturalism, *Clueless* is perhaps the more "conservative" text, as the film ends with sixteen-year-old Cher catching the bouquet at a wedding of her teachers brought together by her matchmaking, a device Ferriss takes as predicting her own future marriage; such an ending is seen as partially due to comedic genre conventions, but perhaps these are at present no longer necessary. In contrast, the ending of McGrath's version is seen as a daring break with *Emma* and an attempt to have an update culminate with a more empowered heroine. In fact, insofar as Knightley's agreement to move to Emma's family estate—Hartfield—already gave the novel a concession to female self-determination, Ferriss finds *Clueless* symptomatically retrograde. She indicates in her closing sentence that *Clueless* exemplifies how "contemporary consumer culture has sold women a distorted image of feminine achievement" (129).

Devoney Looser, in her essay estimating "Feminist Implications of the Silver Screen Austen," on the other hand, sees the film differently, especially the wedding scene ending. Looser notes that Cher catches the bouquet only after hearing that the respective boyfriends of Cher and her two best friends have a $200 bet on which girl will catch it, each betting on their own "Betty." While previously reluctant to join the others in this ritual, being apparently in no hurry to get married, Cher rushes into the competition on this admittedly materialist dare. Although Looser does not say so directly, she seems to be reacting to the way spunk substitutes for a more considered feminism in *Clueless*, a point I would like to develop at length. She is mostly supportive of *Clueless*'s embrace of Cher's energy as a dynamic of contemporary feminism, although she embarrassedly cautions against taking a lightweight film such as *Clueless* too seriously. The irony of Austen once having been disregarded as serious literature seems at this moment to have escaped her.

I propose to take *Clueless* quite seriously, and I think the very intertextual and formal elements that create diverse readings such as those mentioned challenge our critical skills. The constraints on Cher as a young female character may be seen in part as coming from genre conventions, in light of the film's screwball-comedy heritage as well as its sitcom intertextuality. *Clueless* may be seen as a self-conscious amalgam of screwball and situation comedy in parallel to *Emma* as innovative comedy of manners that invites metacritical readings of the process of writing. Screwball comedy is the highly verbal comedic form based on battling odd couples that was part of the renovation of comedy during the 1930s, with deep debts to the romantic comedy of Broadway theater. If much of the energy was sexually charged, verbal repartee, the narratives were characterized by such pairings as Claudette Colbert and Clark Gable in *It Happened One Night* (Frank Capra from a Robert Riskin screenplay, 1934), Irene Dunne and William Powell in *My Man Godfrey* (Gregory La Cava, 1936), and Cary Grant and Katharine Hepburn in *The Philadelphia Story* (George Cukor, from a Philip Barry play, 1940). In fact all three of these examples feature spoiled heiresses negotiating romance and/or marriage in relationship to class expectations, paternal control, and the appeal of men who at first seem inappropriate choices—screwball borrowed from slapstick silent comedy. Urbane sophistication never lets screwball shy away from deliriously broad humor in which the bodies of the protagonists came under the unsettling spell of objects determined to rage against them, or for that matter, each others' attack. Verbal and visual wit–tested sexual parity and satire was capable of skewering the pretensions of class even as attire and demeanor (especially that of the females) made elegance part of the attraction.

The heritage of screwball is quite evident from the beginning of the film in the relationship of Cher to her father and her stepbrother Josh. In fact

Cher's interactions with her father are more like Ellie Andrews' (Colbert) interactions with magnate father Alexander Andrews (Walter Connolly) in *It Happened One Night* or Irene Bullock's (Carole Lombard) negotiations with her rich father Alexander Bullock (Eugene Pallette) in *My Man Godfrey* than they are like Emma's interactions with Mr. Woodhouse. The novel's father figure, in contrast, is older and more self-absorbed; he seems entirely preoccupied with his own health rather than either estate management or business deals, or even regulating patriarchically the appropriateness of his daughter's suitors. The screwball comedies use the patriarch roles to showcase famous character actors Connolly and Pallette who each give performances as blustery, controlling dads whose corpulence signifies the inappropriate wealth attained by hard-driven and well-placed businessmen in the Depression. Yet from the start we get hints of their adoration of and devotion to their daughters that serve as precursors to softening to their daughters' whims. Pointedly, Mr. Horowitz in *Clueless* allows the film to take aim at corporate lawyers, mocking his purely instrumental and competitive lack of ethics. Alicia Silverstone does begin to approach Colbert's rendition of spoiled charm, standing up to her "Daddy" with perseverance, using his corporate lawyer's logic to argue her various cases against his opposition, an appeal that seldom fails to win him over. So, for example, Cher explains to her dad that the low grades inscribed on her report card "are just a jumping off point to a future bargaining position." After an elaborate campaign, the tactics of which we will look at shortly, she returns a changed series of grades to her astounded father. "Cher, I couldn't be prouder of you than if you actually worked to earn these grades," Mr. Horowitz intones. The elder Horowitz then is blamed as the source and abettor of his daughter's connivances; he raises her under the assumption that the upper class operates under its own laws that she, like he, should protect and justify. The lightness of the film does not foreclose the satire, but lawyer jokes are pretty safe fare in contemporary U.S. culture. Only when one considers how the film structure mimics the films of the 1930s does this satirical critique gain a certain historical force of memory.

Josh (Paul Rudd) enjoys a special status as adopted son of Cher's widowed father's interim failed marriage. He reenters their household as annoying older faux brother to Cher, critical of her ever-superficial gesture, disdainful of her carefully chosen clothes, and is able to tersely articulate his opinions as a series of quips in skillfully delivered put-down exchanges. Ostensibly, Josh is a figure parallel to Mr. John Knightley, the older friend of the family who acts as surrogate-father figure to Emma, trying to urge her into a maturity and self-awareness that she lacks, but perversely fascinated by her social machinations. These hardly disinterested males function as critical observers, voicing a perspective on Emma and Cher, respectively, that the voice of narration, aligned with their point of view, would be unable otherwise to articulate. Yet if Josh is like Knightley, his repartee aligns him with

Peter Warne (Clark Gable) the smart-allecky reporter following Ellie Andrews' escape from her father in *It Happened One Night* for the sake of breaking the story, with Godfrey (William Powell) who plays out a role of rescued-bum-turned-butler in order to observe and disapprove of Irene Bullock's (Carole Lombard) chic set in *My Man Godfrey*. In *The Philadelphia Story*, this role is divided between two men: former husband C. K. Dexter Haven (Cary Grant) and reporter Macaulay (Mike) Connor (James Stewart), both of whom critically observe socialite Tracy Lord (Katharine Hepburn) on the eve of her second marriage. These critical observers are given enough sophistication to make their critiques piercing, as the male–female not-yet-couples exchange jibes as an elaborate courting game. By its nature, screwball turns on a dime. The acerbic banter is prelude to a kiss. This is a genre of transformation, of softening, of opposites playing out all their antagonisms until they melt away. If *Clueless* navigates at a pace that is far more rapid than *Emma*, it is a measure of the modernist pacing of its screwball heritage.

Slapstick enters mainly in actual navigation, in the driving sequences. Certainly the fact that Cher's comic driving catastrophes take place in Los Angeles reminds us of the heritage of "The Keystone Cops." Vehicular clowning is a subgenre of silent comedy, extended by the deadpan antics of Buster Keaton and the attitude of continual astonishment governing displacement of Harold Lloyd. We might also think here of Cher as Lucy (Lucille Ball) of the classic sitcom *I Love Lucy* and especially of the film *The Long, Long Trailer* (Vincente Minnelli, 1954), the comedienne who plays expertly a woman overwhelmed by the machinery and circumstances of everyday life because her attention is elsewhere. Situation comedy repetitively explores character flaws or quirks. It places a defined character in situations that create havoc or discord, and allows us to enjoy the combustive energy that ensues. It is indeed hard for female-centered comedy to escape from under the mysogyny that gives credence to the ditzy, the easily distracted, and hysterical female. Bad women (or teenage girl) driver jokes are a feature of a culture that historically only reluctantly allowed women to venture behind the wheel.

With that in mind, we can see that the various driving mishaps present specific opportunities to exploit a portrait of the teenage girl as not so much too dumb to drive but as too distracted to focus and too bent on fabricating her own rules to bother with conforming to those of the road. First, Cher careens her white Jeep through a wide turn that hits a stationary object: a garbage can. "Where'd that come from?" she asks. Later, she defends herself as her father admonishes her for a series of unpaid traffic tickets. When her father insists that she drive only with a licensed driver, this motivates a sequence in which Josh substitutes for her father, chiding her reckless driving while Cher defends her mistakes. In one of several shoe jokes found in the film, she protests, "You try driving in platform shoes." In fact, Cher argues against the validity of even acquiring certain driving skills, such as parallel parking, when "everywhere is valet." Finally, Cher's driver's test, on the very day Cher is beginning to doubt her perceptions of the world and entertain her own attraction to Josh, has her sideswiping a parked car, yet unwilling to concede defeat to her astounded driving examiner. Cher thus displays in these sequences a perseverance in pursuit of a logic all her own; her universe has its own rules and she applies her intelligence defending them against an environment that she sees as absurd and coldly punishing.

I am reminded here of the strategic characterization of Lorelei Lee (Marilyn Monroe) in Howard Hawks's *Gentlemen Prefer Blondes* adapted from Anita Loos' novel. I wrote that "Lorelei's desire to marry for money, . . . is merely explained in practical terms as good business sense, the female parallel to any male commercial transaction."[9] In fact Amy Heckerling seems to be thinking of Monroe's portrayal of Lorelei. The film flirts with awkward stock expressions such as "Thanks, ever so," and Anita Loos' play with malapropisms when she has Cher's prodigy Tai employ the new word Cher has taught her to flirtatiously respond to Josh's "Be seeing you," with a tilt of her head and hips and the phrase, "I hope not sporadically." Lorelei's representation as a "dumb blonde" is a surface manifestation that enables Loos and the film to use her to establish another logic that exposes the exchange value that rules the larger culture. Lorelei explains to the wealthy father of the man she as a golddigger has snared in marriage, "A girl being pretty is like a man being rich, . . . If you had a daughter, you'd want her to marry a rich man." So while I began my analysis of *Gentlemen Prefer Blondes* by acknowledging "The line which separates celebration from satire in American culture is perniciously thin," I explore how insofar as satire survives in the film as well as the novel it does so by looking at Lorelei as a tool rather than as simply a reified object. Cher similarly can be read as a tool by which to skewer the values of the culture surrounding her. Her superficiality and distraction is precisely that of an ideal consumer attached only to acquisition of embellishing commodities; that such postures have dangerous consequences for society then become illustrated by her disastrous driving. Still, the satire is perniciously thin in the sense that it is possible to consume this film in entirely other ways as a celebration of a postfeminist reinstatement of 1950s' values, or turn it into a rather sappy conversion story in which Cher simply becomes a moral adult.

Careful attention to the music track makes either of these moves difficult. The music, which may be mistakenly heard as pop teenage anthems, figures in the film as relatively brief inserts of longer pieces from a wide range of contemporary groups, many of which express in their punk, funk, or rap an edgy critique of the very culture Cher represents. True, white middle-class American teens appropriate as their own music that is nourished by the discontents of the ghettos, of British working-class towns, and of New York's Lower Eastside. Thus, it is not unrealistic on the one occasion that music is presented diegetically as music played at a Valley party, that the song is "Rollin' with my Homies" by Coolio who grew up in Compton, a neighborhood that would grant him at least memories of homies who are quite different from the privileged children of wealth that populate the party. His rhymes are humorous, but he is calling the plays as he sees them from an alienated perspective. The two sequences that define Cher's friends as a group—both the opening montage of their habitual activities, which Cher acknowledges in voice-over as having the aesthetic look of a Noxema commercial, and the later posing for a group photo—have teen anthems subtending them: The Muff's "Kids in America" (sung by lead guitarist Kim Shattuck) and Supergrass' "Alright." However, given the context for teen anthems created by Kurt Cobain's 1991 Nirvana song "Smells Like Teen Spirit," one might suspect that neither of these is as straightforward a celebration of wholesome group adventures as surfer songs were for an earlier generation. These songs consciously mock the innocence of past generations of teenagers, and enclaves that try to retain that innocence, with self-consciousness and a flippant irony.

Jill Sobule's "Supermodel" provides the most obvious form of this, as the lyrics mock the very desires Cher articulates and embodies in the film. The lyrics are written in the voice of an aspirant teenage model who insists "My hair will shine like the sun!" and "Everyone will envy me!" while Sobule's New York punk delivery broadcasts her disdain of such posturing coupled with a certain empathy for the traps this fictional girl finds herself in. Cher, walking with her high school girlfriends, obsessively catalogs her three bowls of "Special K" and chewing gum diet; if we were ever to think that Cher is simply being celebrated, Sobule's song disabuses us of that notion. Similarly, World Party's "All the Young Dudes," written by David Bowie, mixes an air of sadness into its irony to deflate male bonding rituals.

Other songs with edges harder than they might first appear include Lucious Jackson's "Here," the Beastie Boys' "Mullet Head," and Radiohead's "Fake Plastic Trees." Granted, the film's soundtrack sold well as a CD party mix, and all the irony I have located in the musical cuts depends on contextual knowledge, as well as familiarity with more complete versions of the songs rather than just their brief use in the film. In fact "Fake Plastic Trees" only occurs in an instrumental version in the film, so good ears or possession of the soundtrack CD is necessary to discern the reference. Still, a good portion of the teenage audience sees soundtrack plus video or DVD ownership of films as adjunct activities to spectatorship.

Compared to earlier teenage high school sagas scored by rock music, this film uses its music less to establish the period and tastes of the teens depicted than to offer other perspectives, some that even comment critically or ironically on their rich enclave. George Lucas's 1973 *American Graffiti* (with a memorable soundtrack of hits from the 1950s) and Amy Heckerling's 1982 *Fast Times at Ridgemont High* (with a GoGos, The Cars, Tom Petty, and

Oingo Boingo studded soundtrack) established the prototype. *Clueless* uses its soundtrack more subversively than either of the other films from which its form derives.

Notably, Lucas's and Heckerling's earlier films explore high school and graduation as male coming-of-age stories, while *Clueless* breaks with this male pattern, focusing on Cher and her female friendships. Some have suggested that Heckerling goes all the way back to Austen for inspiration because Hollywood was so resistant to a female-centered story. It is true that Heckerling, in interviews, details resistance to financing this project.

Such hesitancy apparently occurred despite a contemporaneous reemergence of the female-centered narrative and particularly the group of girlfriends as forming the core of a multiple-protagonist narrative. Karen Hollinger's *In the Company of Women: Female Friendship Films* details the trend ranging from *Julia* (Fred Zinnerman, 1977) to *Steel Magnolias* (Herbert Ross, 1989) to *Fried Green Tomatoes* (Jon Aunet, 1991) to *Mi Vida Loca* (Allison Anders, 1994); many of the films Hollinger addresses do have literary or theatrical antecedents.[10] While she focuses primarily on films concerning adult women, her chapter on "The Female Friendship Film and Women's Development" (83–105) links *Desperately Seeking Susan*, (Susan Seidelman, 1985), *Housekeeping* (Forsyth, 1987) and *Mystic Pizza* (Donald Petrie, 1988) as exploring issues of adolescent bonding.

Looking for precedents to *Clueless*'s focus on female teenagers, we might note Molly Ringwald as the connecting force in a high school love triangle in *Sixteen Candles* (John Hughes, 1984), and Ione Skye as Diane Court in *Say Anything*, (John Cusack, 1989). Neither of these films sustains a focus on female friendships. In fact Molly Ringwald in *The Breakfast Club* (John Hughes, 1985) is isolated in detention with a group of teenage boys, a plot device symptomatic of a tendency to cut off a singular female protagonist from a female environment. Still, Sarah Jessica Parker as Janey Glenn and Helen Hunt as Lynne Stone share a passion for dancing in the 1985 *Girls Just Want to Have Fun* (directed by Alan Metter from a script by Janis Hirsch and Amy Spies). Yet, given the intensity of female friendships for high school girls, it is striking that teenage-oriented films are so apt to avoid that bond as a focus. The television series *Sabrina, The Teenage Witch*, which credits the Archie comics as a plot inspiration, has at times given Sabrina a best friend as well as a female nemesis: Libby. On many segments, however, Sabrina struggles with teachers, aunts, her boyfriend Harvey, his male competitors for her affections, and various visiting witches of both genders, in isolation from a group of girlfriends.

Cher's friendships with Dionne and Tai would therefore be worthy of our attention as a more concerted focus on teenage female friendship than in other contemporary texts, even if Heckerling did not intensify the difference of *Clueless*'s take on high school female friendship by the way she handles race, in the case of Dionne, and class, in the case of Tai. Given that in

Dionne's case her African-American heritage is coupled with economic and social standing presented as equal to Cher's, the film represents their strong and easy camaraderie as an idealized transcendence of racial division. Parallels between the two teens present them almost as twins. In one of the oft-cited quotes from the film, Cher tells us in the voice-over introduction of her friend, "We are both named after famous singers from the sixties who do infomercials." When Dionne appears, her suit jacket and short kilt skirt coupled with pastel knee-highs echoes the outfit we have seen Cher select for that day from her computerized guide to her closet. Once Dionne appears in her version of the same outfit, we retrospectively can speculate on Dionne's previous hours of preparation; however, the point here is that for all the parallelism Dionne is a secondary character whose life we see only when she enters Cher's car, Cher's house, or Cher's schemes at school. So if the film breezes past racial divisions and stereotypical expectations in certain respects, it sustains a long tradition of the white female protagonist seconded by her black female companion, as for example, in both film versions of *Imitation of Life* (John Stahl, 1936, and Douglas Sirk, 1959) in which the inability for the female friends to attain equal social status despite their close friendship becomes a commentary on structural, societal oppression. *Clueless* offers an alternative founded in idealized fantasy, that even so seems based in the best aspirations of the generation it depicts. In some contexts for this generation, racial divisions can melt away if class values are the same. Dionne does not have to be stripped of her cultural identity; her sassy retorts, while matching the banter of Cher, have a distinctly drawn edge of African-American female assertiveness. In fact, Dionne is allowed to be more black than Cher is allowed to be Jewish; the name Horowitz is the only signifier that suggests Cher's ethnic identity.

Yet, perhaps more racial nervousness surfaces in the comedy than one might first suppose. Jokes aimed at Dionne and her boyfriend seem to cluster around hair: first her "Cat-in-the-Hat" millinery, then later her questioning her boyfriend about a "cheap Kmart hair extension" she found in his car, which she denies could be hers since "I don't wear cheap polyester hair, unlike some people I know like Shawana." Finally, the joke turns to his head, when Dionne discovers his head being shaved by an equally shorn black male friend in the bathroom at the Valley party, much to her dismay. Here the jokes seem racially overdetermined, the humor fixing on the preoccupation with hair styling and hats that bears a complex link to hair as a marker of difference. Obviously what lies behind such referential humor is LA's ghetto black culture, the very funk context of the Coolio song played at the Valley party to the crowd's crossover delight. Dionne is seeking the same class ascendancy as Cher (think of Cher's remark that parallels the hair extension jibe on the cheap imposter perfume worn by her rival). Yet, somehow here the parallelism seems unconscious of how race might determine a difference in how we read the implication that Dionne is a snob about class.

This tension dissipates as Dionne plays an increasingly less significant role in the film, reemerging primarily to prepare Cher for her first sexual encounter, an event that never occurs. The focus shifts to Tai, the new girl who has moved to Beverly Hills from Brooklyn, replete with accent, street manners, a grunge wardrobe, a liking for recreational drugs, and a concomitant attraction to the "loadies" (drug users). Tai's makeover is the second in the film; prior to this project, Cher and Dionne together performed a similar Pygmalion transformation on their teacher, Miss Geist, by ambushing her in the mailroom to collectively perform a series of instantaneous ameliorations. This attack, presented as a favor, is preceded by a shot that borrows from a classic cinematic trope of the tilt down or up that surveys the woman's body, here accompanied by Cher's assessments of her egregious faults for which the makeover will serve as antidote: "Sure, there were runs in her stockings, and her slip is always showing, and she has more lipstick on her teeth than on her lips."[11] Given that Cher is preoccupied with footwear,[12] it is perhaps not surprising that the subjective shot of the teacher, Miss Geist, begins as a high angle on ill-fitting black pumps slipping off her heels and continues up over the other fashion faults that make the teacher such an appropriate target of their skills at transformation.

Makeovers, as presented in twentieth-century magazine culture, have come to inform teen female friendship. In fact, makeovers have migrated from the pages of women's magazines to magazines aimed at ever-younger audiences, as well as to television talk shows where they have become a staple. The makeover of the teacher, in fact, mimics a common talk show motif in which children request that the talk show staff makeover their mothers (alternatively to be more fashionable and sexy as is the case in the film, or to be more presentable and less sexy so as to not embarrass the child).

The work performed to makeover Tai closely parallels Emma's education of Harriet, a parallel that allows comparison of the function of fashion and manners in forming group identity in both the Restoration and at present. As Leslie Stern notes in "Emma in Los Angeles: Remaking the Book and the City," much of this makeover, like the referential coding throughout the film, is specific to LA culture, to Hollywood rituals[13]; though despite how the locality satirized in *Clueless* as a comedy of manners can be seen in this way as intensely specific, and despite the specific contrast drawn here to New York, I would argue rather that a different optic sees the Los Angeles references as undergoing constant slippage. Beverly Hills, the Valley, and Los Angeles here function as a 1990s updating of the Beach Boys anthem to "California Girls" in much the same way that Moon Unit Zappa's "Valley Girls" song references speech patterns that are at once local and national, since they represent how manners in contemporary consumer culture are immediately subject to media dissemination. Actual loci of fashion almost instantaneously give way to reestablishment in and as virtual realities. Grunge no sooner develops in Seattle than it becomes characteristic of Brooklyn, and of course, sectors of Los Angeles.

Stern also argues for reading the makeover as intrinsic to the particular inflection the film gives the female friendship film, though we might take issue with her comment that treatment of Cher as a female Zvengali has little precedence in films and therefore clearly owes its inspiration to *Emma* (232–233). In fact, the specifics of Tai as subject of the makeover becoming Cher's competition and turning on her guide, specifics that Stern notes are departures from *Emma*, echo narrative patterns in a multitude of 1930s' films. Like the competition among the would-be actresses in *Stage Door* (Gregory La Cava, 1937), the competition between Cher and Tai intersperses personal discord with class difference and resentment, all the while struggling to resolve these conflicts through the trope of nascent, and later renewed, friendship.

So as much as we may embrace the fun and the feminist potential of the female friendships *Clueless* celebrates, as much as we might enjoy aspects of the utopian transcendence of racial and class differences they suggest, it behooves us to recognize alongside this appreciation that all of this only becomes possible in a virtual space that a fantasy enclave of wealth inspires. African Americans of wealth, whether absolute or relative, still face cultural barriers. Perhaps no scars are deeper than those borne by the working-class or even middle-class kids zoned or bused into wealthy suburbs. The girls' friendships in *Clueless* shield us from that social reality, and this certainly underlies some of the pleasure to be gained through participation in this fantasy.

Cher's obsession with fashion might well be seen as both an ironic acknowledgment of recent feminist embrace of self-fashioning components of consumer culture as a claim on self-determination, and as a satire on the misplaced values of the rich who mark their privilege by their status as an upscale consumer class.[14] In Cher's world of exacting consumerist fashion expertise, a designer red outfit (named in the dialogue as the creation of Azzedine) becomes the perfect object for sabotage. First the red heels and later the dress fall victim to circumstantial assaults. At a Valley party, Coke is spilled on the heels, which causes Cher to shriek "Ruin my satin shoes, why don't you," as she rushes to the sink to repair her fashion emergency, and then lament, "This is *so* not fixable." Later that same evening, Cher is mugged at gunpoint, and this time it is the designer dress that is threatened by the thief's insistence that she lie down on the ground while he escapes. As objects subject to the abuse of a larger world that is less pristine and privileged, the designer clothes not only display Cher's desires but are also so emblematic of her self that their desecration serves as metonym for her threatened privileged being, and this on levels that the film both treats ironically and reproduces unconsciously. For as reflexive and satiric as the film may seem on issues of class privilege, it, like Austen, needs to take such privilege for granted at many levels. Perhaps these works suggest that female prerogatives may be in some ways more open to upper-class women, a possibility that poses considerable trouble for feminist appropriation, except insofar as we read this implication in a historical light, telling us something of the interaction of class and feminism.

To explore this further, consider how yet another dress, a white Anna Sui slip dress (in the film dialogue it is credited to Calvin Klein, perhaps because it is a more recognizable name)[15] becomes another focal point for discourse on fashion, consumerism, and a feminine rebellion to patriarchal constraints. Cher's father remarks on the dress by asking, "What the hell is that? It looks like underwear," to which she simply replies, "It's a dress." Her father persists, "Who says?" Cher counters, "Calvin Klein." Cher's father, urged on by her nemesis at this juncture, Josh, demands that Cher modify the outfit in the name of propriety. Our protagonist still must fight her otherwise indulgent, but in this case protective, father in order to fashion herself as in vogue, alluring, and sophisticated—signifiers that are themselves emblems of her class status.

As I note in "High Angles on Shoes: Cinema, Gender, and Footwear," Cher functions as a contemporary reincarnation of the flapper of the 1920s and the streamlined dance goddess of the 1930s. She provides at some level a similar celebratory image of youthful females as fantasy icons of either the success of capitalism and modernization or as the fond dream that such success will materialize or return. Yet, as emblems, images of the modern woman could sustain critical commentary or moralistic condemnation by intervening elements of narrative structure that create turns in the films' discourse. *Clueless* does suggest such a transformation of Cher, as I remark:

> By the film's end Cher has lost the red high heels of an adolescent rushing past youth into precocious consumerist adulthood. The film flirts with a comforting return to old-fashioned teenage romance, as she wears sneakers and jeans as she embraces Josh in the penultimate scene.[16]

As the film ends, at an elegant wedding of the successfully matched and wardrobe-reformed teachers, such casual, comfortable attire that bears little trace of class perhaps constitutes more of an interlude for Cher than a surrender to Josh's sartorial disinterest. If Cher displays a newfound social consciousness in line with Josh's, the film seems not to turn against its earlier nod to Cher's love of shopping as a female activity that feminism need reconsider.

Perhaps the function of closeted gay student Christian (Justin Walker), who becomes Cher's favorite mall companion, should be considered in its contribution here. Christian, as well as the gay gym teacher, whose Cher's voice-over describes as "in the grand tradition of P.E. teachers, Ms. Stover seemed to be same-sex oriented," display even better than Dionne and Tai some of the ironies that remain unconscious, rather than voiced, in *Clueless*.

Consideration of its representation of homosexuality will eventually return us to discussion of the films' matrimonial ending.

The film has tremendous fun with elaborating Christian through a series of visual references to 1940s and 1950s suave masculinity, unrecognized by many at the time as queer. The queerness of these images, either by virtue of the actual actors embodying this persona or by virtue of their appropriation by a gay subculture, now has overwhelmed our ability to recover a period reading of them as desirable heterosexual ideals. Sexual performativity is represented here as less multidirectional than as one might hope, a symptom of the moment perhaps not limited to the film or its comedic strictures. As he swivels and preens, as his "too cool" attitude outclasses, and therefore abolishes, even Cher's "above high school boys" forbearance of sexual attraction, Cher falls for Christian, even as the audience is given ample clues that this man wants to be the shopping partner, an alternative, fourth "girlfriend." The unconscious irony here is that which assumes the self-evidence of homosexuality, its absolute constitution and constitutive function, an assumption revealed in its exaggeration into the all-gym-teachers-are-lesbians joke. Of course, all pretty boys are not gay, nor are all gym teachers lesbians, but something of absolute categorization at the basis of comic typing and indeed all stereotypage would have distinctions be clear, inherent, and able to be revealed once and for all. *Clueless* plays with manifold questions of individuation and group filiation, not able to shake up entirely the class privilege or the heterosexuality it describes. This makes it the present-day parallel of the comedy of manners, a satire bent at holding certain aspects of the culture firmly in place.

The question of participation here is crucial. *Clueless* as a film text became also a popular audio CD, as we have discussed, and intriguingly, a CD-ROM game aimed at preteens, as well as a television series that ran for one season. These incarnations of the text are far more participatory than is the film alone and have consequences for our estimation of the functioning of satire in the context they provide. We can read each of these incarnations as a text, but not without considering how they become spaces one lives, acts, and plays within. If the scene in which Cher selects her wardrobe on a computer screen that has indexed all possible matches in her wardrobe delights at first in its outlandishness, and subsequently in its predictive register as signal to how all consumers were already or would soon be shopping, as Internet sales of clothing zoom in on just such virtual clothes closets, the CD-ROM of *Clueless* lets young cyber children makeover the *Clueless* characters or themselves. The game helps us understand that the film *Clueless*, like so much of popular culture, is about participatory pleasures that indeed go beyond voyeurism and identification into the formation of virtual group identities.

Returning to *Clueless* and *Emma* from the vantage point of pedagogy, we see that what we potentially learn when we use such pairings in the classroom is how to disclose many of the theoretical understandings central to

cultural studies. We retain much that earlier criticism and histories of literature and film taught us about the specificity of context and the historical
transformations of form, and we add to that the layered questions posed by
intertextuality conceived as transhistorical. The very specificity of *Clueless*
helps us place *Emma*, and vice versa.

Notes

1. I thank my colleague Patricia Craddock for permission to quote her here.
Thanks also to colleagues Alistair Duckworth and Elizabeth Langland for equally
stimulating conversations concerning Austen adaptations.

2. Jane Austen, *Emma* (*The Novels of Jane Austen* Vol. IV, London: Oxford,
1933).

3. See Linda Troost and Sayre N. Greenfield, eds., *Jane Austen in Hollywood* (Lex-
ington: University of Kentucky Press, 1998), especially the essays by Devoney Looser,
"Feminist Implications of the Silver Screen Austen" (159–176); Nora Nachumi, "As
If! Translating Austen's Ironic Narrator to Film" (130–139); and Suzanne Ferriss,
"Emma Becomes Clueless" (122–129).

4. Pat Gill, *Interpreting Ladies: Women, Wit, and Morality in the Restoration
Comedy of Manners* (Athens: University of Georgia Press, 1994), 21. See also Mar-
garet Lamb McDonald, *The Independent Woman in the Restoration Comedy of
Manners* (Salzburg: Institut für Englische Sprache und Literatur, Universität Salzburg
and Young, 1976); Douglas M. Young, *The Feminist Voices in Restoration Comedy:
The Virtuous Women in the Play-Worlds of Etherege, Wycherley, and Congreve*
(Lanham, MD: University Press of America, 1997).

5. Gill, *Interpreting Ladies*, 14.

6. See Alistair M. Duckworth, *The Improvement of the Estate: a Study of Jane
Austen's Novels (*Baltimore: Johns Hopkins University Press, 1971); James Thomp-
son, *Between Self and World: The Novels of Jane Austen* (University Park: Pennsyl-
vania State University Press, 1988); Roger Sales, *Jane Austen and Representations of
Regency England* (London: Routledge, 1994); Margaret Kirkham, *Jane Austen:
Feminism and Fiction* (Atlantic Highlands, NJ: Athlone Press, 1997); Devoney
Looser, ed., *Jane Austen and Discourses of Feminism* (New York: St. Martin's Press,
1995); Richard Handler and Daniel Segal, *Jane Austen and the Fiction of Culture*
(Tucson: University of Arizona Press, 1990); Jocelyn Harris, *Jane Austen's Art of
Memory* (Cambridge: Cambridge University Press, 1989); David Monaghan, ed.,
Jane Austen in a Social Context (Totowa, NJ: Barnes & Noble Books, 1981).

7. Rachel R. Mather, *The Heirs of Jane Austen: Twentieth-Century Writers of the
Comedy of Manners.* American University Studies. Series IV. English Language and
Literature; vol. 180 (New York: P. Lang, 1996).

8. Suzanne Ferriss, "Emma Becomes Clueless" in *Jane Austen in Hollywood*, ed.
Linda Troost and Sayre N. Greenfield (Lexington: University of Kentucky Press,
1998), 122–129.

9. Maureen Turim, "Gentlemen Consume Blondes," in *Movies and Methods*, ed. Bill Nichols (Berkeley and Los Angeles: University of California Press, 1985), 2: 369–378.

10. Karen Hollinger, *In the Company of Women: Female Friendship Films* (Minneapolis: University of Minnesota Press, 1998).

11. See Maureen Turim,"Seduction and Elegance: The New Woman of Fashion in Silent Cinema" in *On Fashion*, ed. Shari Benstock and Suzanne Ferris (New Brunswick, NJ: Rutgers University Press, 1994), 140–158, for a discussion of how this trope of the once-over look by the subjective camera is used to present women in relationship to discourses of fashion.

12. In my essay "High Angles on Shoes: Cinema, Gender, and Footwear," in *Footnotes: On Shoes*, ed. Shari Benstock and Suzanne Ferris (New Brunswick, NJ: Rutgers University Press, 2001), 59–90, I place Cher's fashions and especially her shoes in the context of a history of women's representation in the cinema.

13. Leslie Stern, "Emma in Los Angeles: Remaking the Book and the City," *Film Adaption*, ed. James Naremore (New Brunswick, NJ: Rutgers University Press, 2000), 232–233.

14. See David Desser and Garth S. Jowett, ed., *Hollywood Goes Shopping* (Minneapolis: University of Minnesota Press, 2000), especially Angela Curan's essay "Consuming Doubts: Gender Class and Consumption in *Ruby in Paradise* and *Clueless*" (222–250). For more general recent debates on the relationship of feminism to consumerism see Anne Friedberg, *Window Shopping: Cinema and the Postmodern* (Berkeley and Los Angeles: University of California Press, 1993); Simone Weil Davis, *Living Up to the Ads: Gender Fictions of the 1920s* (Durham, NC: Duke University Press, 2000); Jennifer Scanlon, *Inarticulate Longings:* The Ladies' Home Journal, *Gender, and the Promises of Consumer Culture* (New York: Routledge, 1995); Sarah Berry, *Screen Style: Fashion and Femininity in 1930s Hollywood* (Minneapolis: University of Minnesota Press, 2000).

15. The white dress in question is indeed a white Anna Sui slip dress chosen by costume designer Mona May. The discrepency between Sui and Klein may stem from the greater recognition value of Klein's name due to the advertising campaign and popularity of his ready-to-wear line, but Cher's tastes run to Sui, Alaia, and Klein's more exclusive line.

16. Turim, "High Angles on Shoes," 81.

3

Love at the Hellmouth

Buffy the Vampire Slayer

Kristina Straub

Buffy the Vampire Slayer, one of the most enduringly successful shows of the WB (Warner Brothers) prime-time "teen" lineup, draws on many previous treatments of vampires in novels, film, and theater, taking them into the hopelessly hip world of California youth culture. This modernization of a nineteenth-century text, even of the nineteenth-century-vampire text, is not unique to the show; Anne Rice's Vampire Lestat as rock idol is only one instance of the "ancient ones" survival into a presentist youth culture. Vampire stories invite anachronism, the jarring juxtaposition of past and present. In *Buffy*, vampires, as well as a wide array of demons, embody the monstrous persistence of a past ineffectually wished away by the teenagers of Sunnydale, California, the show's fictional setting. Sunnydale just happens to be located at the "Hellmouth," the portal to a vaguely defined netherworld, and it is the job of the Slayer—high school and, later, college student Buffy Sommers (Sarah Michelle Gellar)—to defend the "world as we know it" from vampiric and demonic scum. *Buffy* puts an unusual twist into horror conventions by framing the Slayer's fight against these anachronistic monsters as a problem in learning history. Like many students, Buffy and her "Scooby Gang" of demon-hunting friends would understandably prefer to ignore the past; but not only will it not be ignored, its demonic intrusions into their world demand that they become its students. *Buffy* self-consciously thematizes learning about the past as the students' embodied struggle to engage—so as not to be destroyed by—"a history that is not of their own making."[1]

The show's depiction of learning as embodied struggle complicates pedagogical models in which learning takes place through a sort of implantation, the means by which, as Michel Foucault theorizes it, human subjects enter discourse. Bodies become part of discourse, according to this theory, and there is little room for the subject's agency.[2] Student discussion and writing suggests that, for better or worse, something very different happens when students enter the discourse of history. *Buffy the Vampire Slayer* complicates the model of pedagogy informed by discourse theory. While it is certainly true that the lessons of the past help Buffy defeat the vampires, demons, and other evil beings that threaten her and the world's existence, the show puts pressure on the notion of teaching as a kind of cultural relay and learning as cultural implantation. The result is a retheorization rather than a rejection of historical pedagogy.

  Buffy articulates a particularly complex and, for teachers, heartening model for how the pedagogical process can be imagined in the popular media. It reminds us that pedagogy is part of historical change, not just a mechanism for bringing the lessons of the past to the present. And it suggests that this translation of past texts might be usefully thought of as collective, creative, and always open-ended, incomplete. Expecting my students to read Jane Austen or Bram Stoker as I read them, "to get it right," is rather like expecting a film adaptation of a novel to repeat the experience of reading it. Neither teaching nor adaptation is innocent of their historical conditions, and *Buffy* suggests that this caveat is not just the property of a few academic theoreticians. *Buffy* complicates Foucault's disciplinary thesis about the "putting of sex into discourse" by invoking the relevance of embodied desire to the translation of the past into the vernacular of the present.

The Monstrous Pedagogue

Like many other popular texts for teens, *Buffy* parodies and critiques teachers, mentors, and every other adult who sets up as a pedagogue. The show's central premise turns pedagogy into a life-or-death practice, however. Into every generation, a voice-over in the opening sequence tells us, a Slayer is born, one girl who is destined, whether she wishes it or not, to do battle with the demons and vampires who are remnants of the earth's prehistorical past. Every Slayer, the myth continues, has a predestined Watcher, a mentor who trains and assists the Slayer in her work.

  When not benignly boring, *Buffy*'s pedagogues frequently turn into the demonic embodiment of history, the threat of the past turned literal. The pedagogue's dual potential for mind-numbing tedium and life-threatening danger is most persistently embodied in Rupert Giles (Anthony Stewart Head), the British, scone-consuming librarian, who turns out to be Buffy's Watcher. The teaching of history saturates interactions between Buffy and Giles and generally pervades the show's first season. "Welcome to the Hellmouth," the pilot episode, begins, appropriately enough, with a history lesson on the "Black Death." The lecturer's attempt to engage her students in a question-and-answer session on the topic is cut short by the urgent ringing of the bell for changing classes, setting a pattern that also organizes Giles' dual role as Buffy's Watcher. He is both the pedant of history and her most constant reminder of the urgency, indeed, the threat, of the present. Giles alternates between teaching Buffy the lessons he culls from a library of old books and reminding her of the relentless attacks of anachronistic but all-too-present demons. Buffy's resistance to Giles' teaching is greatest in response to Giles' history lessons. Even in the first episode, she accepts that she will have to kill vampires and demons from time to time, and she aces Giles' lessons in the use of arms and hand-to-hand combat. On the other hand, Buffy is presented as historically challenged; she often does not "get" what Giles is attempting to translate to her from his books. Indeed, she does not "get" history in general. In "Nightmares," for example, her worst fear, horrifically realized, is taking an exam for a forgotten history class. In a sequence that anyone who has been a student can identify with, Buffy stares at a blank exam sheet while the clock hands race ahead hours, in minutes' time. History is frightening, even when not embodied in an ancient demon or centuries-old vampire.

The first season of *Buffy* makes historical pedagogy central to its horror plot. Giles' tutoring of Buffy is paralleled by the attempts of an old and powerful Vampire called the Master to kill the Slayer. Teaching history, in *Buffy*, takes a textual form; in the first season's episodes, Giles and the Master both menace Buffy with books. Her first day at Sunnydale High, Buffy finds herself without the required text and goes to the school library, where she encounters Giles, the new librarian, fresh from "a British Library—or the British Library, I forget which." Her request for a book on "Perspectives on Twentieth Century . . ." is cut short by Giles proudly flinging down on the desk between them a huge, leather-bound, gilt, embossed volume with the title *Vampyr*. Understandably, Buffy runs away from this intrusion of a horrific past on her attempts to make a new present at Sunnydale. But old books keep coming back at Buffy in the hands of both good and evil mentors. The librarian's old books, with their prophecies about vampiric plans at world conquest, are doubled in the dustier, more sinister copies read aloud by the Master to his evil minions. Both Giles and the Master brandish old books, and speak the lessons of the past in full, shapely sentences, unlike the hip sound bytes of the younger characters.[3] The literature presented to students by both good and evil teachers is, quite literally, threatening to the students' already tenuous sense of control over the present. Buffy's fears that Giles' "lessons" will ruin her attempt to rebuild a "normal" teenage life at Sunnydale High are paralleled by the vampire pupils who fear the Master's physical "lessons" of mutilation and death by staking. The comically inept pedagogue's tendency to override, ignore, or discount his female, teenage pupil's needs and desires constitutes a kind of assault on her sense of safety and bodily integrity.

Buffy battles many nightmarish reflections of the boring pedagogue who is oblivious to his students' embodied experience. Besides the Master, Sunnydale is populated by a biology teacher/praying mantis who wants to mate with Xander, Buffy's friend and confidant (Nicholas Brendan), and then bite off his head, and a hygiene lesson–spouting Mayor who turns into a giant, devouring serpent while giving the high school commencement speech. However, unlike popular culture texts such as *Teaching Mrs. Tingle*, which also indict abusive pedagogical power, *Buffy* is far from dismissive of pedagogy's goals. In fact, the teacher's failure to make the lesson clear is itself metaphorically realized as a mortal threat to the student's body.

Dusty books aside, the show affirms, over and over again, the importance of doing research, of knowing the past in order to survive the present. Willow Rosenberg (Alyson Hannigan), Buffy's computer-nerd friend, asks Giles, "How is it you always know this stuff? You always know what's going on. I never know what's going on." Giles replies, "Well, you weren't here from midnight until six researching it." Giles' function is providing the Slayer and her friends, "the Slayerettes," with the historical background they need to understand—and therefore intelligently fight—the demons and vampires that threaten their present. Books may be scary or dusty old objects, but they are also necessary to the world's survival, as is the online research that is the specialty of Willow, Giles' most valued research assistant. Buffy depends on Giles for the specific information she needs to defeat evil and she quite clearly realizes this dependence, despite her resistance to Giles' lessons. For instance, in "The Pack," Giles uncharacteristically lapses into ahistoricism by dismissing Xander's aberrantly aggressive behavior with a naturalizing "testosterone" comment. Buffy, who knows that there must be some cause for the behavior, thrusts a stack of books in his face and demands that he "look stuff up"; when Xander and his hyena-souled friends, the victims of an obscure spell, devour raw the porcine school mascot, Giles speedily complies. Gender and sexuality are not, the show insists, ahistorical, natural phenomena to be accepted as such, but the results of a specific history that must be learned if horrible outcomes are to be prevented. Pedagogy is the means by which that learning takes place and the pedagogue is more important—and more complex—than the dithering high school librarian or his literally monstrous doppelgangers.

Buffy's most important pedagogical relationship, between the Slayer and her Watcher, retheorizes the pedagogue as a part, as well as a teacher, of history. The show's depiction of pedagogy embeds it in power relations; the pedagogue is never "above it all." For all his dusty books, Giles has the personal history of many progressive-thinking forty-somethings, is self-critical in his teaching of Buffy, and is even eroticized in ways that bring him into relations of power and desire. The publication *American Libraries* made Giles their September 1999 cover story in an article that holds him up as having "done more for the image of the profession than anything in the past 50

years, with the possible exception of Katharine Hepburn in *Desk Set*."[4]
Giles, despite his stereotypical tweediness, is powerful, even sexy. (Head's
previous television credits include the "Taster's Choice" commercial, featur-
ing romance between coffee-drinking, flirtatious neighbors.) While the show
evokes, from time to time, the stereotypical wooden lecture machine, full of
information but unresponsive to students, it is usually to discount or at least
complicate it. For instance, when a ventriloquist's dummy takes over the role
of providing historical background in "The Puppet Show," Giles comments
wryly that it is nice to have someone else explaining for a change. The
wooden lecturer in this case, however, proves to be a tough-talking, sexy
demon hunter trapped in the wooden body of a puppet. He emerges as
human in his interchanges with Buffy, even sharing with her his memories of
a tasty Slayer with whom he had a fling in the 1930s. When he dies in his
last quest to destroy the demon who entrapped him, Buffy holds his wooden
body tenderly in her arms, signifying a human, even erotic, connection between them. Teaching and the getting of knowledge—when they work—engage history in embodied, physical ways.

One episode in the show's first season most extensively elaborates on the
ongoing theme of pedagogy's relationship to embodied power relations. In "I,
Robot, You Jane," a demon named Moloch the Corrupter is released onto the
Internet by being scanned into a computer from an old book that Giles (who
must have an amazing acquisitions budget) has purchased for his collection on
the occult. In an opening flashback sequence, we are shown the embodied
Moloch (think horns and scaly green skin) seducing and killing a beatific and
smitten young man. The setting and costuming are indeterminate but signal
"old." In a crosscut sequence, a group of robed, ecclesiastical, male figures
(monks?) perform the spell that binds Moloch by transforming his body into
the writing that then fills the pages of the same old book that Buffy, in the next
shot, unpacks in Sunnydale's library. Freed onto the Internet when Willow
scans this text into Giles' computer, Moloch repeats the flashback's seduction
sequence with Sunnydale's high school students, including Buffy's computer-
nerd friend Willow. He persuades them to work with him on a "project,"
which pretty much comes down to world domination. His seduction is a complex, Foucaultian knot of power, knowledge, and desire. He attempts to lure
one student into committing murder with visions of "a new world, Dave.
Knowledge, power. I can give you everything. All I want is your love." As
Giles explains to his "technopagan," computer science teacher colleague,
Jenny Calendar (Robia LaMorte), Moloch is a "deadly and seductive demon,"
who "preys on impressionable minds" with "promises of love, power, and
knowledge." Moloch joins the ranks of Sunnydale's many monstrous mentors,
adding to the mix an erotic cocktail of information, power, and seduction. He
is, of course, destroyed through the combined efforts of Buffy, Giles, and the
rest of her Scooby Gang, but the episode leaves in the viewer's mind a strong
connection between pedagogy, sensual embodiment, and power.

The demon on the Internet who preys on the desires of lonely, introverted students such as Willow exemplifies the power of the disembodied pedagogue over his all-too-embodied students. Moloch's disembodiedness on the Net makes him all-powerful, limitless in his control over his young lovers and able to be everywhere, paradoxically, because he is nowhere. Giles and Calendar realize that trapping the demon in some physical location is the only way to stop world domination. The demon–pedagogue unknowingly facilitates this plan by giving way to his own desire. Moloch longs for a body, for "touch," and has a robot made in which form he plans to meet Willow, whom he loves for having released him from his textual imprisonment. When Moloch enters his robot body in order to meet Willow "in the flesh," Giles and Calendar are able to cut off his access to the Net and trap him in the metal body that, though powerful, can be defeated by the Slayer.

The pedagogy that *Buffy* critiques is the legacy of Enlightenment, viewed through a feminist lens. This legacy is the construct of knowledge as somehow outside of and therefore more authoritative than embodied experience. Modes of teaching and learning knowledge that try to abstract themselves from bodies fail, or, in the case of Giles and Buffy, they become increasingly grounded in embodied relations of power. The body is not represented as a recalcitrant other to knowledge in the show, but is the site upon which knowledge is realized—that is, where learning really takes place. The lessons of the past can be internalized, made a part of the experience of Buffy and her Scooby Gang of friends, only as a knowledge of body and desire as well as of intellect. It is this embodiment of historical knowledge that makes it both relevant and deadly dangerous to the young learners on the show.

Sex and Pedagogy

If, as I argue, much of the show's critique of pedagogy is directed at teaching which does not account for the embodied quality of learning, sex is a significant factor in this embodiment. Willow is easy prey for Moloch because of her self-acknowledged desire for a boyfriend. The fact that Xander falls in love with his praying-mantis biology teacher is unsurprising in the context of his general horniness; as he wryly comments, "I'm a teenage boy. I look at linoleum and think of sex." (He also remembers an attractive female teacher's tight sweater but not the assignment she gave when wearing it.)

Sensual experience translates into sexual experience all too readily for Buffy and her friends. This slippage is marked at the end of "I Robot, You Jane" by parallel scenes, one between the pedagogues Giles and Jenny Calendar, the other between Buffy, Xander, and Willow. Both scenes comment on the embodied nature of knowledge and the ways in which lessons are incorporated into the learner's experience. In the first scene, computer science teacher and technopagan Jenny Calendar asks the cyber-phobic Giles, "What is it about computers that bothers you?" Giles responds, "The smell." When

Calendar points out that computers do not have one, Giles assents, "I know. Smell is the most powerful trigger to the memory there is. A certain flower or a whiff of smoke can bring up experiences long forgotten. Books smell. Musty and rich. The knowledge gained from a computer is, it has no . . . no texture, no context, it's there and then it's gone. If it's to last then . . . then the getting of knowledge should be tangible, it should be, uh, smelly." The acquisition of knowledge is not, at its best, disembodied, but a lesson learned in and through the body as well as mind. Learning involves a collapse of the artificial distance between the past and the present through the agency of embodied experience. The scene between the two teachers is sexually charged by their mutual attraction; Calendar responds to Giles by huskily replying, "Well, you really are an old-fashioned boy, aren't you?" Sensual experience, the scene reminds us, is never far from sexuality.

The slip from sensually experienced knowledge to sexual knowledge is completed in the second scene, the closing one of the episode, in which Buffy, Willow, and Xander discuss their disastrous love lives: Buffy is in love with Angel (David Boreanaz), a 240-year-old vampire, Xander has just (barely) lived through his crush on a praying-mantis biology teacher, and Willow has narrowly survived her online infatuation with Moloch the Corrupter. Xander laughs, "That's life on the Hellmouth." Buffy agrees, "Let's face it, none of us is ever going to have a happy, normal relationship," to which Xander rejoins, "We're doomed." As the scene fades, the laughter resolves into silence, each face registering the reality of the situation, that they are on the Hellmouth, and that love cannot be separated from the harsh realities of high school, for which the Hellmouth is metaphor.[5] The embodied "getting of knowledge" means that the past comes home to the present, but not always in the safe and pleasant form of Giles' "musty and rich" old books. The fact that Jenny Calendar is murdered in a later episode, her corpse turning up in Giles' bed in a horrible parody of the romantic tryst, reinforces the sense of doom that saturates the Scooby Gang's experience of embodied learning.

The sometimes horrific, always powerful, way in which the past invades the tactile—sensual reality of the present—is most poignantly depicted in the love affair between the teenage Buffy and the centuries-old vampire Angel. The relationship between Buffy and Angel mirrors, in many respects, the relationship between the Slayer and her Watcher. Both involve Buffy, a young person who is learning how to survive at the Hellmouth, and an older, more knowledgeable mentor who quite literally watches over her. Since Angel is not a formal mentor but a beautiful young man, not much older in appearance than the Slayer, learning in this relationship is fraught with sexual tension, and ultimately translates into sexual initiation. In Angel, Buffy confronts the embodiment of history, not in the demonized form of the show's many other evil intruders from the past, but as her lover.

In the first-season episode, "Angel," Buffy learns that the hunky, college-age-looking guy is, in fact, a vampire over 240 years old. Given the show's penchant for metaphor, Angel is a hyperbolic version of the sexually experienced "older man," who is destined to initiate the virginal Buffy. He is also the means through which Buffy learns the importance of the past in a "tangible," embodied way. In Angel, history is neither a demon to be exorcised from, nor a lesson to be assimilated unproblematically into, the present. He is not, we discover, a killer like the rest of his vampire kind as the result of a gypsy's curse. The narrative that emerges from flashback sequences in later episodes is that the vampire Angelus regained his soul in the nineteenth century when his "maker" and lover Darla (Julie Benz) brought him the daughter of a powerful gypsy clan as a "present." The girl's kinsmen curse Angelus with a soul that he can lose only if he ever experiences "a moment of pure happiness." The fact that he has a soul essentially means that he has a historical conscience. He not only remembers the past (all vampires do this), he feels its significance, and seeks to atone for his past by helping Buffy. But Angel cannot be simply Buffy's boyfriend any more than he can be reduced to the horrific title "Vampyr."

Angel, in other words, is ultimately the most effective pedagogue in that he destroys for Buffy the neat separation of present from past. As I argued earlier, Buffy is presented to us as historically challenged; the episode "Angel" dramatizes the binarism of past and present that ordinarily organizes her thinking. Buffy and her young friends, like many students, tend to divide the world into "now" and "then," a present and a past that operate on entirely different levels. Joyce Sommers (Kristine Sutherland), Buffy's mother, asks Giles about Buffy's "trouble with history": "is it too difficult for her or is she not applying herself?" Giles replies that Buffy is "very much in the now" and history is "very much about the then." "Now" is dating, a social life, going to classes, trying to keep one's grades up, the aspects of everyday life that point toward the future. "Then" is a dry lesson from a book, something that adults think students should learn. At worst, it explodes from the page as a demon or vampire, but these are forms that are easy enough for the Slayer to annihilate as alien bodies to be othered and destroyed. The Scooby Gang's approach to the literal study of history gives form to this binary approach. Willow and Buffy study together after school. Willow asks, "Are we going to talk about boys or are we going to pass history?" A rhetorical question, as she claps the book shut and proceeds to talk about her crush on Xander. Given the choice (though she rarely is), Buffy will always "talk about boys," but in the case of Angel, she learns that talking about boys and talking about history cannot be separated.

The show's writers impishly intertwine Buffy's struggles with the subject of history with her struggles over what to do about her growing attraction to Angel. Buffy introduces Angel to her mother as a student at the local community college who is tutoring her in history. Later in "Angel," Darla—the vampire who made Angel in the eighteenth century and his former lover—seeks access to Buffy by telling her mother that she is there to help Buffy study history. Teaching Buffy history, in Darla's case, means killing her. History is a threat to Buffy, and not just in terms of boring her to death. The history lesson that Buffy learns through her love for Angel is far more devastating, however, in that it changes the Slayer and therefore challenges her sense of autonomy in the present. The relationship between Buffy and Angel recapitulates the truism, theorized by Foucault, that *the* knowledge, since the eighteenth century, is sexual knowledge.[6]

After over a season of sexual tension between the Slayer and her vampire mentor, Buffy and Angel consummate their relationship in "Surprise." In the final scene of the episode, Angel runs from their bed, clearly in pain. In the next episode, "Innocence," we discover that Angel has lost his soul and become "a textbook example of the Insensitive Male After Sex,"[7] ending a searingly painful session of Buffy-baiting with "I'll call you." Without his soul, Angel reverts to Angelus, the evil vampire originally made in the eighteenth century. The history lesson that Buffy and Angel learn through painful experience is that if Angel ever experiences a "moment of pure happiness" he will lose his soul, which he has done, apparently in the "pure happiness" of orgasm. For Buffy, this history takes the form of the bitterest kind of sexual knowledge. "Knowing" Angel means incorporating the truth that she cannot be with him in any "healthy, normal" way.

Garden-variety romance is clearly out of the question for the two lovers, even when Angel reacquires his soul after being sent to Hell by the devastated Buffy at the end of the second season. History impinges on the present as surely as the undead return from the grave, a lesson that Buffy learns through physical and emotional pleasure and pain. Sexuality is the vector through which historical knowledge becomes *tangible*, to use Giles' word. "Knowing" Angel means knowing the inevitable impact of the past upon the present, and means knowing history in an immediate and embodied way. This conceptualization of knowledge cuts against the grain of the teen characters' attempts to reduce the past to "then," a dry and irrelevant lesson. Buffy learns, through her sexual initiation, that history cannot be reduced to a textbook, a class—or a monster.

Buffy learns the past in ways that inevitably and critically shape her present, but this learning is itself a transformative and creative process on her part. The past is not merely revisited or implanted in the student's head. Buffy's agency in history, her transformative capacity, probably has roots in Joss Whedon's, the show's creator, explicitly feminist agenda. He traces the origins of Buffy to his early fascination with horror movies, and, in particular, his discomfort with the inevitable scene in which the blond ingenue is isolated and annihilated by the monster.[8] Wouldn't it be satisfying, Whedon muses, if the blond girl faced the monster and kicked its butt?[9] This scenario is precisely what happens when Buffy first meets Angel in "Welcome to the Hellmouth/The Harvest." Prefiguring her agency in acquiring sexual knowledge, Buffy jumps the would-be stalker Angel in a scene fraught with physicality and sexual tension.

Buffy's agency is similarly critical to her other confrontations with the past. Accepting the past, taking it in as unmediated truth, is tantamount to victimization, to allowing herself to be jumped in dark alleys.

Buffy's versions of the past are conditioned by a variety of discourses, most notably feminist, which have drawn attention to gender and sexuality as historical, as opposed to biological, phenomena. Even the crudest historical notions of gender roles circulating in U.S. popular culture contribute to our students' awareness that maleness, femaleness, and the rituals of heterosexual coupling have changed over the course of the last two hundred or so years. A dominant cultural narrative affecting the sexuality of our "post-feminist" students is the story of liberation from corseted femininity and steely jawed masculinity into a brave new world of aggressive women and sensitive men. It is this narrative that the episode "Halloween" presents to the Slayer, asking her to incorporate it into her psychosexual experience. Instead of struggling with this "truth" about the past, Buffy nostalgically embraces it, and it nearly gets her killed.

Looking at an old Watcher's diary that she and Willow have purloined from Giles, Buffy sees drawings of women, their elaborate, feminine clothes and hair, from the eighteenth century, the age of Angel's "making." She reflects critically on the athletic gear appropriate to her slaying duties, and decides that, for Halloween, she will embrace the "feminine" image that she thinks will romantically engage Angel. Meanwhile, Giles' old schoolmate and former colleague in black magic, Ethan Rayne (Robin Sachs), has opened a costume shop in Sunnydale with just the outfit she covets. Unknown to Buffy, Giles, or any of the Scooby Gang, Rayne has cast a spell that will turn his costumes' wearers into the personae they represent. Buffy goes from kickboxing Slayer to helpless, screaming femme, precisely the victim against which the character of Buffy is a reaction. (Willow comments, "She couldn't have dressed up like Xena?"—a reference to another WB kickboxing heroine, Xena the Warrior Princess.) The wimpy, almost effeminate Xander, who has chosen a soldier costume, turns into a Sylvester Stallone/Arnold Schwarzenegger clone whose masculine military skills prove useful, but, significantly, inadequate by themselves. Spike (James Marsters), a punk/goth vampire who has killed two past slayers in his long unlife, sees the chaos created by Rayne's costumes as a fine opportunity ("This is . . . neat!"), and is on the verge of "doing" the helpless Buffy when Giles manages to beat the counterspell out of Rayne and reverses the charm. Buffy turns on Spike with "Honey, I'm home," renewed martial-arts prowess, and pummels the surprised vampire into flight. The uncritical reception of nostalgic versions of the gendered past is clearly as dangerous as the Slayer's failed attempts to keep past and present in separate, never-touching categories. The kind of learning that keeps the Slayer alive is not implantation, a process by which the body enters a discursive terrain that determines its meanings. The learning that helps Buffy survive takes place in a fluid process of exchange or struggle between the discourse and the embodied learner.

The Death of the Pedagogue

As a result of this emphasis on learning as a process that changes institutions as well as the individuals who are "hailed" by them, the show's critique of pedagogy shows decreasing tolerance, in the third and fourth seasons, for the rigidities of institutionalized instruction. By the end of the series' fourth season, *Buffy* has dispensed—in some cases violently—with most of its pedagogues. The 1998/1999 season could have been titled the "Death of the Pedagogue." In the season finale, Principal Snyder (Armin Shimerman) is eaten by the Mayor/Giant Serpent, who, along with Sunnydale High, is destroyed by a bomb at Buffy's commencement ceremony. Giles and Buffy both turn their backs on the vaguely institutional Watcher's Counsel at the end of a horrific parody of academic rites of passage in which the Counsel forces Giles to test Buffy's survival skills by injecting her with drugs that rob her of her superstrength. Buffy is reduced, again, to helpless feminine victim in a sequence that plays out like a nightmare version of female initiation into a male-dominated educational system. (She still manages to outsmart her adversary, a psychotic vampire.) Buffy rebels against this sadistic "training" by refusing the Counsel's authority, and Giles, who participated reluctantly in the test, resigns from the Watchers' Counsel to become a mere member of the Scooby Gang, albeit one with better research skills and greater knowledge than his younger colleagues.

The pedagogical relationship between Buffy and Giles has evolved, over the fourth season, from a negotiation between institutional authority figure and rebellious student into a more complex exchange between older and younger members of a sometimes contentious, sometimes collaborative team. When Sunnydale High School is destroyed in the third season finale, Giles loses his job as librarian and decides to stay unemployed. The fourth season shows us a Giles detached from educational—or any—institutions. And though he occasionally still lapses into talking like a "textbook with arms," he has become less and less a cardboard parody of the stuffy British tutor and more and more complexly human. He has an off-and-on sex life with Olivia, a beautiful woman of African descent, and the Scooby Gang has become more like his family than his students, with all the attendant irritations and endearments. Giles' fall from institutionalized pedagogy is not simply about making him more human, however; it entails a distinct redefinition of his power. In the penultimate show of the 1999/2000 season, he is reduced, in Buffy's words, to a "drunken clown" when Spike manages to set the gang against each other by sending them into their respective squirrel cages of self-doubt and mutual distrust. This development plays on, and takes to greater heights, the deeply unstable nature of pedagogical relations as they have played out since the first season. Even though Giles had previously played a more stereotypical teacher's role, the relationship between Buffy and Giles often tended to reverse "normal" pedagogical relations, with the Slayer frequently rescuing, even sometimes out-thinking, the Watcher.[10] Without the institutionalized authority of the library or the Watcher's Counsel, this instability is more pronounced, laying bare the ways in which the student's agency, not just the teacher's, determines the lesson to be learned from history.

The fourth season's episodes seem to be groping for ways to represent the pedagogue outside of educational institutions. The unemployed Giles has taken up singing in a local club, a role that the fourth season finale oddly conflates with that of pedagogue. In a sequence drawn from Giles' dreams, he sings his Watcher's directives while the Scooby Gang joins a cheering young audience holding up lighted matches. *Buffy*'s primary pedagogue has gone definitely counterculture, in an early 1970s way appropriate for the forty-something Giles. This reference to the period of Giles' youth is not a new development, but a logical outcome from previous plot elements. In "Band Candy," for instance, a show from the third season, Giles and Joyce Sommers revert to their teenage selves as the result of enchanted candy bars. The giggling, entranced Giles listens to 1970s heavy metal while getting it on with the equally "hip" Joyce (much to the horror of Buffy). The pedagogue, like pedagogy, is portrayed, at best, as a part of history, not the detached embodiment of Enlightenment technologies of education.

I read this critique of pedagogical hierarchy as going beyond the teacher-bashing so popular in texts that appeal to teen audiences. The radical destabilization of pedagogy is integral to the show's theory of learning as an embodied process of struggle. The 1999/2000 season continued this distrust of institutionalized pedagogy; at the same time it explored more deeply the relationship between pedagogy and the body in this process of embodied learning. In college, Buffy encounters a new pedagogue in the character of a psychology professor, Maggie Walsh (Lindsay Crouse). Initially, Buffy and Willow are attracted by the brilliant, charismatic lecturer, an interest that is erotically supplemented by Professor Walsh's handsome graduate assistant Riley Finn (Marc Blucas). The fourth season spent very little time on the college classroom, however, as the show mounted a new attack on institutionalized knowledge. Professor Walsh is found out to be the head of an undercover government/military operation called "The Initiative" that captures and does research on demons and vampires. Riley is a graduate student by day whose "real" job is that of an Initiative soldier. When Buffy first learns of the Initiative, she is impressed and attracted, not only to Riley, but to the promise of unlimited resources and colleagues in her fight against demonic evil. It quickly becomes apparent, however, that the independent and unconventional methods of the Slayer are not a good fit with the military discipline of the Initiative, and the rest of the season engages in a critique of institutionalized knowledge as a sort of

Frankensteinian enterprise, an exercise in building monsters it cannot ultimately control.

Professor Walsh is secretly building "Adam," a monstrous composite of demonic, human, and electronic parts. Adam, however, who seems to have developed his own initiative, murders his human "mother," and escapes to set up his own shop in world domination. The theme of embodied knowledge is taken a step further: Sex and the body, so critical as vectors for learning, are radically de-essentialized. The body is explored not as a last bastion against institutionalized knowledge, but as the creation of such institutions. While the previous seasons' treatment of embodied pedagogy often ran the risk of romanticizing sex and the body as privileged sites of "true" knowledge, the 1999/2000 season proliferated with bodies that are themselves reconstituted as monstrous by-products of Enlightenment technologies of knowledge.

The physical distinctions between vampire, demon, human, and technology are eroded by institutionalized quests for knowledge that are, in turn, exposed as thin covers for imperialist domination. The line between hero and villain is simultaneously blurred as bodies lose their boundaries. Most notably, the vampire Spike is captured by the Initiative and implanted with a chip that prevents him from doing harm to humans, though he can still damage demons. Buffy's former nemesis becomes a dissident member of the Scooby Gang, who protect him from the Initiative even though they know he is a loose cannon. Even the good guys are not proof against technological tampering. Riley is first discovered to be on strength-improving drugs that the professor has been slipping her soldiers, and then finds that he, too, has been chip-implanted to do the Initiative's bidding. Finally, the hybrid creation Adam converts the people and demons he slaughters into more or less sentient robots, starting with Professor Walsh who has been turned into an animated corpse. Bodies are constituted by institutionalized knowledge and its pedagogical representatives; they are not defenses against history, but its products. At times, they are even themselves the enemy, as is painfully illustrated by Riley digging out the chip from his shoulder with a piece of broken glass.

Nonetheless, the Slayer triumphs over Adam and his postmodern, pastiche bodies in the season's penultimate episode. The institutionalized search for knowledge embodied in the Initiative is revealed to be yet another imperialist power play. The show ends with a group of men, seated at a paper-strewn conference table, apparently concluding an investigation of the bloody events that ensue when Buffy and the Scooby Gang successfully defeat Adam's attempt at creating a master race of human/demon/techno hybrids. One concludes, "It was an experiment. The Initiative represented the Government's interest in not only controlling the other-worldly menace, but channeling its power for our own military purposes. The considered opinion of this Counsel is that the experiment has failed. . . . The demons cannot be harnessed, cannot be controlled." The university's pursuit of knowledge proves to be a cover for a Department of Defense–style pursuit of power.[11]

Buffy defeats this monstrous form of institutionalized knowledge not through her individual efforts, however, but through a mystical collectivity that grows out of the show's theme of unbounded bodies. Buffy finds the means to defeat Adam through an "enjoining spell" that brings the Scooby Gang's collective energy together in the body of the Slayer. The problem that the Slayer must solve is how to remove Adam's uranium energy source. Willow suggests a spell; Giles turns to his ubiquitous books; but it is Xander who comes up with the solution: "So, no problem. All we need is Combo Buffy. With her Slayer strength, Giles' multi-lingual know-how, and Willow's witchy power." While Buffy faces Adam, the Scooby Gang sits in a circle; Willow chants, "Power of the Slayer and all who wield it. Last to ancient first, we envoke thee. . . . Because mind and heart and spirit join, let the hand encompass us." Buffy, the "hand," is filled with a collective power that deflects Adam's bullets, turning them into flying birds, and enables her to wrest the power source out of his body. Knowledge becomes power in an embodied collectivity with cultural feminist overtones. The opposition between femininized, "alternative" means and masculine institutional power is impossible to miss. In one scene, a crew-cut, heavily armed military officer pulls the Scooby Gang's "weapons" from a bag. He stares in mystification at what Willow explains is a gourd; Giles sheepishly clarifies, "A magic gourd." In another scene, Professor Walsh, now an animated corpse, wields a nasty-looking bit of high-tech medical equipment at the Slayer: Enlightenment technologies square off against two ancient female powers, witchcraft and the Slayer.

The show's cultural feminist heroics are complicated, however, by the fourth season finale's theme of learning as a collective and always incomplete struggle with the past. Buffy and her friends fall asleep into a history that is, indeed, not of their making when the first Slayer, angered by being evoked in the previous episode's "enjoining spell," tries to kill Buffy and her friends in their dreams. The aboriginal-looking first Slayer attacks Buffy for not operating solo: "No friends. Just kill. We are alone." The force of a mystical past that had previously worked to defeat the monstrosities of military/industrial, technological knowledge is cast as the enemy within, the denizen of dreams. The question of knowledge is not, finally, resolved by turning to a reified past, as Buffy retorts, "You're not the source of me." But the episode's ending leaves the question of knowledge open. As Buffy stares into her darkened bedroom, focusing, I think significantly, on her bed,[12] Tara—Willow's lover—who had spoken for the first Slayer in Buffy's dream, speaks in voice-over: "You think you know, what's to come, what you are. You haven't even begun." Despite Buffy's spirited assertion of her independence from the legacy embodied in the first Slayer, her knowledge is presented as tentative, incomplete, a work-in-progress. She thinks she has made her bed, but her agency is as embedded in historical process as is her knowledge of the past.

The 2000/2001 season, the last before this book's completion, posed the radical suggestion that the past itself, as object of knowledge, is unstable. Buffy suddenly acquired a younger sister whose abrupt appearance goes unremarked by the show's characters because Buffy, her mother, and the extended family of the Slayerettes all inexplicably "remember" her. Dawn, the irritating but beloved little sister, is part of a "real" past that actually never happened. Learning that even intimate, familial memories are unstable parts of larger forces beyond the individual's reckoning seems to be the lesson that Buffy learns. The quest for embodied knowledge has, in the show's past, required the death of the disembodied pedagogue of the Enlightenment and any attendant illusions about institutionalized power and knowledge. The show seems, at the point of this writing, to be working toward an equally devastating critique of the student's ability to treat the past as her personal property, however worked for or dearly bought. In any case, *Buffy*'s models of historical pedagogy refuse to leave either teacher or student on high or even stable moral ground. Teaching and learning are locked together in an ongoing negotiation of the past through the embodied experience of the present.

Notes

1. I wish to thank Danae Clark for reminding me of these words and for a careful reading of an early draft of this chapter. In addition, Carol Goldburg and Jad Smith gave me many helpful suggestions. The quote from Karl Marx is appropriate. The show incorporates Marxist themes and imagery in several episodes, including one in which Buffy defeats a demonic version of workers' oppression while wielding a hammer and a sickle. See David Graeber, "Rebel without a God," *In These Times* 23 (December 27, 1998): 29–30.

2. I am thinking of early Foucault, in particular *The History of Sexuality: An Introduction* (New York: Vintage Books, 1990), although the move to "self" in his later work does not necessarily make much more room for theorizing the body's role in discourse.

3. Rhonda Wilcox, "There Will Never Be a 'Very Special' *Buffy*: *Buffy* and the Monsters of Teen Life," *Journal of Popular Film and Television* 27 (Summer 1999): 16–23.

4. Graceanne De Candido, "Bibliographic Good vs. Evil in *Buffy the Vampire Slayer*," *American Libraries* 30 (September 1999): 48–51.

5. Joss Whedon, Buffy's creator, is explicit about this aspect of the show in interview after interview. For high school, think Hellmouth; for a tough high school gang, think a pack of hyenas who eat the school principal; for a Celine Dion-loving roommate from Hell, think a Celine Dion-loving roommate from, well, Hell. The mythical characters and events of the show always resonate with the very human experiences of adolescents moving into maturity.

6. See Foucault's reading of Denis Diderot's *Les Bijoux indiscrets* in Foucault, *The History of Sexuality*, 77–80.

7. Christopher Golden and Nancy Holder, *Buffy the Vampire Slayer: The Watcher's Guide* (New York: Pocket Books, 1998), 105.

8. Whedon replays this scenario again in the 1999 episode "Hush" in which Buffy reenacts the ingenue's scream with a vengeance. The evil Gentlemen who come to steal, quite literally, hearts, can only do their work in total silence.

9. Interview with Whedon about the episodes, "Welcome to the Hellmouth" and "The Harvest."

10. I owe this point to Jad Smith.

11. This critique hits close to home as I write in the English Department at Carnegie-Mellon University.

12. One of the notable changes from high school to college is an exponential increase in the show's amount of sweaty sex. The theme of sex as imbricated with knowledge and power takes even more explicit forms.

Part II
In the Nation

4

Clueless: About History

Deidre Lynch

[T]he Hollywood epic shows us that the people—most particularly, the women—living History almost always wore extravagant clothes and spent a good deal of History changing them. Although no one in the audience is inclined to such accountancy, we are nonetheless told that Linda Darnell in *Forever Amber* (1947) wears "eighteen evening gowns, twenty daytime dresses, three negligées, and a wedding gown as part of the effort to recreate the seventeenth century England of Charles II."
—Vivian Sobchack, "'Surge and Splendor':
A Phenomenology of the Hollywood Historical Epic"

Emma Woodhouse, handsome, clever, and rich, with a comfortable home and happy disposition, seemed to unite some of the best blessings of existence; and had lived nearly twenty-one years in the world with very little to distress or vex her.
—Jane Austen, *Emma*

Following are the first questions I wish to address to the last decade's "Austenmania" and to the period films manifesting it. Do these remakes of classic texts from the past present us with opportunities to think historically—to perceive an organic and necessary relation between the bygone worlds they depict and our lived experience? Can we learn history—can we regain that capacity for retrospection ostensibly lost in a postmodern age—when Jane Austen is ghostwriting History's screenplay? This chapter seeks to reopen a consensus prematurely established around these questions. To remind you of the answer that others have decided on already, I would like to draw on the wisdom of *Clueless* and quote Cher Horowitz, who (handsome,

clever, and rich like Emma Woodhouse her prototype) has lived sixteen years
in the world with very little to distress or vex her: "As if!"

Media coverage and academic assessments of the "Austen Phenomenon"
have, with rare exceptions, concentrated on adjudicating between legitimate
and illegitimate ways of being true to Austen. In the background of such turf
wars over who truly owns Austen is a long-standing debate over who truly
owns "history." On the one hand, the reception given over the last seven
years to the Austenian adaptations seems frequently to recycle older approaches to Austen's novels that stressed their sub-historicity. According to
William Dean Howells, "This quiet little woman, who wrote her novels in
the bosom of her clerical family" was "*in her way* . . . asserting The Rights
of Man"—she could not help but breathe in the "stormy air of the time."
But, Howells confesses in 1901, he himself remains unsure whether little
Jane was conscious of writing the history of her epoch.[1] The premise that
Austen was incapable of knowing anything of "the world," that scene of action to which the opening sentence of *Emma* refers, has persuaded many of
today's film reviewers that blockbuster historical phenomena such as imperialism or revolution represent burdens too heavy to be supported by Miss
Austen's "narrow shoulders." Witness the grumpy reaction when Patricia
Rozema's 1999 adaptation of *Mansfield Park* spotlighted the slave trade sustaining the Bertrams' gentry domesticity.[2] On the other hand, much of the
distaste for the costume drama adaptations of Austen's works seems informed by a long-standing mistrust of the filmic (and, more recently, the
televisual) medium's ways of materializing the past. We are suspicious of
what happens when the historiographical enterprise goes public. As Vivian
Sobchack's account of the conspicuous consumption distinguishing the Hollywood version of history suggests (cited in the opening epigraph of this
chapter), that response might well bespeak our anxiety over what happens
when history, reformatted, solicits the female consumer in particular.[3]

It seems telling that what disqualifies the costume drama as history is in
the first instance its defining, feminine or feminizing emphasis on costumery.
And telling, too, that a standard putdown directed at the Austenian films is
the one we encounter when we read that the essence of one adaptation lies
in "scenery and costume display interrupted by actors" or read of "BBC 2's
customary round of swirling flounces and furbelows."[4] Such complaints are
often filed on Austen's behalf, in the belief that fidelity to the original entails
an acknowledgment that the novels can easily dispense with being decked to
the hilt. However, it is important to notice the parallel here. If there is a gendered logic at work within those conceptions of the historical (of the "real
world") that marginalize Austen's contribution to the realist tradition and
that make her enduring presence within realism's canon seem more "an act
of gallantry" than an index of her artistry, those who seek to be faithful to
her novels should notice that a comparable logic operates through these oppositions between being in fashion and being genuinely historical.[5]

Certainly, at stake in such oppositions is the recognition that, even as it plugs bodies into the codes of consumer culture and so adds a collective dimension to our experience of self, fashion does not tell time as we wish it to be told. What passes for historical change in fashion is a repetitive cycle of recirculation. (*Passes for* is the key term: Walter Benjamin found in fashion's ascendancy as the modern "measure of time" an explanation of why the concept of progress had forfeited its critical power in modernity, why, while industrial technology had advanced, exploitative social relations had stayed exactly the same.[6]) And certainly there is little to celebrate in the way that the spectacle of Regency dresses and furnishings that the Austen Phenomenon brings to our screens makes the privatized sphere of consumerism into the primary ground of historical continuity—little to celebrate in the fact that it is "our attraction to . . . the familiarity of the commodity [that] make[s] the trip into the eighteenth century a smooth one."[7] Still, I wish here to dispute the preconceptions about the "faux" (the commodified or the nostalgic) historicism of the period film that have shaped the reception of the Austenian adaptations. I wish to use Austen's novels and the 1990s Austen-inspired films—Amy Heckerling's 1995 *Clueless*, in particular—to argue instead for pluralizing the concepts of "true" history and of the "genuinely" historical.

The old myth of Austen's detachment from history has made it difficult to acknowledge that her writing career coincides with a far-reaching transformation in the protocols of historical representation: with, for instance, a turning point in history writing's relationship with a set of formal precedents and protocols of politeness formulated in the ancient world, and shaped by that world's rigid demarcation of public from private; with a moment when historians sought to enlarge the traditional province of historiography to include what Austen's own favorite, Robert Henry, author of the *History of Great Britain from the Invasion by the Romans under Julius Caesar* (1771–1793), called "the more permanent and peaceful scenes of social life"[8]; and so with a moment when modern novels and modern histories exerted new sorts of pressure upon each other as they competed for the favor of the book-buying public. And yet Austen's works—those particularly that postdate both the Battle of Waterloo and Sir Walter Scott's inauguration of a new line in historical fiction—constitute an extended commentary on this reframing of history-writing and on the gender politics that it entailed. Quite deliberately crossbreeding the costume drama with the teen comedy genre, Heckerling in *Clueless* remembers more than the directors of the ostensibly more historical remakes of Austen do about that commentary. Heckerling is just as self-conscious as a Roger Michell, an Ang Lee, or a Patricia Rozema about what is at stake in filming a "classic," about coming to grips with the temporal relations inscribed in that concept; but her self-consciousness takes a different form than that of her fellow adapters of Austen. This is because she remembers more about the protocols that dictate what kinds of knowledge will count as "historical capital" or what kinds of experience will count as experience of the "real world"—and so more about why the claims to historical knowledge that might be tendered by Cher Horowitz's history teacher—stand-in for Emma Woodhouse's governess—lack validity within the very historiographical framework that this Miss Geist's oh-so-Hegelian name evokes. (In *The Philosophy of History*, Georg Hegel identified *Geist*—Spirit—and its coming-to-consciousness as the motor force of historical progress. But what happens, Heckerling appears to be asking, if *Geist* is ascribed a feminine gender?)

To initiate this historicizing of the idea of history, the route to Austen's (as well as Hegel's) age of historicism that I shall pursue in this chapter begins in the classrooms of Bronson Alcott High School, site for the social life and, more rarely, the history lessons of Cher and her clique. The pedagogic setting—which in *Clueless* finds its mirror image in the shopping mall—has in the last century ended up housing a critical function that first became important in Austen's lifetime, that (never altogether successful) work of gate-keeping that discriminates the authentic from the market-driven version of the past. The reading I develop here will conclude with a return to fashion, which, when placed in the context of what Catherine Morland of *Northanger Abbey* calls "real, solemn history," frequently operates as a virtual synonym for the transient and trivial and for false consciousness and the faux. I shall be suggesting that fashion apparel's significance for historical thinking (for the retrospective dimension) may lie precisely with fashion's eschewing of referential power and its cultivation of the untimely.

To say that *Clueless* remembers anything may be already to invite your skepticism. Heckerling is very much a local colorist, minutely annotating the particular customs and lingo of the little white corner of Los Angeles that Cher calls home. And that city, notoriously, is the first place that Fredric Jameson goes to describe "an age that has forgotten how to think historically in the first place."[9] In *Postmodernism, or, The Cultural Logic of Late Capitalism*, Jameson describes and deplores the spatializing of time that is a symptom of this loss, outlining how the postmodern city pastiches the imagery of all times, reduces historical difference to differences in style, "ignor[es] the natural laws of transition and renewal for the sake of a compulsive accumulation, [and] exchang[es] diachronic sequence for the synchronic coexistence of different cultural layers."[10] *Clueless's* mise-en-scène bears out this account. In the opening sequence, for instance, in which Cher, as voice-over narrator, introduces herself and welcomes us to her home, Heckerling makes sure that we notice that this Beverly Hills mansion comes equipped with that perfect postmodern architectural accessory, the (neo)classical column: the acme of the decontextualized sign, able to stand in, in a promiscuous array of locations, for any variety whatsoever of good-looking antiquity.[11] As she plays tour guide, Cher tosses in a word that will prove crucial to the rest of the script—"Isn't my house *classic?*"—and notes that those columns date "all the way back" to 1972. History has been foreshortened in Cher's Los Angeles. What was, when adorning the porticoes of courthouses and public libraries, the symbol of the legacy of classical Greece and of an authoritative civic humanist tradition derives now from the epoch of *The Brady Bunch*, the TV program whose graphics have just been quoted in the film's opening credits.

On the one hand, Heckerling elaborates a citational aesthetic for *Clueless* that takes her beyond merely remaking a "classic" novel. This aesthetic involves, in addition, a cornucopia of visual and aural allusions to the cinematic prehistory of the teen film genre itself. (At one point we hear the theme from *The Summer of '42*; and when, on her first big date with Christian, Cher makes her dramatic descent of the staircase in the front hall, the sequence reworks countless Hollywood renditions of the debutante's first ball, and unfolds to music from *Gigi*. Christian for his part not only reincarnates Frank Churchill, but is decked out in ways that recreate the James Dean of *Rebel without a Cause*.) Heckerling's love of the quotable also means that *Clueless* boasts a sound track that cannot get enough of the 1990s covers of 1970s hits—including Jewel's cover of Eric Carman's "All by Myself," which almost three decades ago secured its bona fides as "classic rock" when Carman sampled the composer Sergey Rachmaninoff. Yet all this bricolage seems tailor-made, on the other hand, to manifest precisely the frenetic historicism that Jameson associates with the nostalgic mode of postmodernity, a mode that for him is "incompatible with genuine historicity" (10). The saturation in the signs of the historical that Jameson observes in the postmodern city bespeaks (because it compensates for) the contemporary de-authorization of that very category of knowledge. That time is speeded up (so much so that the 1970s seem retro) tells us that "real" history is at an end. Heckerling self-consciously responds to such diagnoses (it is a good bet that we would find a copy of Jameson on her bookshelves). Right on cue, she shows in her dialogue that she knows how she is meant to point the moral. She accounts for the end of history by pointing the obligatory accusatory finger in the direction of fashion and the fashionable: Cher's standard way of recommending that bygones should be bygones is to quip, "That's so last season."

As evidence of her cluelessness, this way of telling time (telling it with reference, that is, to the seasonal refurbishing of her designer wardrobe) is wholly of a piece with Cher's performance both in her debate classes at Bronson Alcott High and in the arguments she makes when called on to defend her preferences in TV viewing. These scenes at home and school work together in two ways: first, to elaborate a series of oppositions between domestic life and public life, between the private life of "manners" and public policy; and, second, to reveal how these oppositions between the home and the world correlate in their turn with another gendered opposition, that pitting fiction against real, historical life. The homework assigned by Mr. Hall, the civics teacher, requires Cher to work up a speech on U.S. immigration and refugee policy, but as an envious classmate complains, "the topic is Haiti, and she's talking about some little party." Whereas Cher opts to watch a cartoon show on MTV (*Beavis and Butthead*), Josh, the film's stand-in for Mr. Knightley, casts his vote for the latest news of war (in the Middle East, in Yugoslavia), as broadcast on CNN. The rationale behind Cher's choice of a fiction over a show that tells it as it is becomes clear when we next watch her perform in debate class, the subject this time being the censorship of the media. Why, Cher asks, pondering the priorities of the attorney general, worry about the violence in the shows that "need it for entertainment value" before one worries about the violence reported on the news?

While they pit Cher against Josh and against the civics teacher grading her debates, these scenes rehearse what *Emma* says about the gendering of epistemology. About to lose control of the remote control and watch cartoons against his will, Josh, who at the start of the film would prefer for Cher to leave the TV room and head for the shopping mall, observes to her sardonically that in some places, "it's cool to know what's going on the world." However, readers of Austen may be prompted to wonder exactly whose world he has in mind. As Austen's narrator tells us when she begins the story, Emma Woodhouse "live[s] in the world."[12] But, as it turns out, this heroine has never seen the sea. Indeed, the category of things Emma does not see is a large one. The round of social calls that preoccupy the female inhabitants of Highbury, and which readers of the novel witness, is counterpointed by a round of business meetings, which involve the local men of property, and which remain invisible to heroine and audience alike. Mr. Knightley officiously informs Emma—who indeed is much too certain, as Cher will also be, that she has her finger on the pulse of the "real world"—that the flaw in her matchmaking schemes lies in the fact that she is a stranger to such meetings on parish business. Emma cannot know, Knightley says, how men talk among themselves in "unreserved moments" (66).

But rather than merely arranging for Emma to get her comeuppance at the hands of a man more connected than she is, Austen seems repeatedly, in *Emma* and her late works generally, both to be demonstrating that knowledge—or the scheme that determines which aspects of the real world will count as important to know—is a gendered affair, and to be hinting that these men doing their parish business may be as liable to fall into self-involved parochialism (and not solely in the strict sense of that term) as those women whom they have excluded from civic life. (What are we to make of the fact that discussion at those parish meetings concerns matches being made—or so Knightley's hint to Emma indicates—as often as it concerns issues of property boundaries, footpaths, and rights of way?) Think of how, for instance, in an episode in *Northanger Abbey* to which I will return, Catherine Morland blows the cover on the universalist pretensions of history's reports on the real world (albeit without realizing she is doing so): "the men all so good for nothing, and hardly any women at all" (108). Think of how, for instance, *Persuasion* discusses the difficulty of moving from the local to the global— the lesson that Anne Elliot learns and relearns is, it is hinted, one from which all might profit:

> Anne had not wanted this visit to Uppercross, to learn that a removal from one set of people to another, though at a distance of only three miles, will often include a total change of conversation, opinion, and idea. She had never been staying there before, without being struck by it, or without wishing that other Elliots could have her advantage in seeing how unknown, or unconsidered there, were the affairs which at Kellynch-Hall were treated as of such general publicity and pervading interest; yet, with all this experience, she believed she must now submit to feel that another lesson, in the art of knowing our own nothingness beyond our own circle, was become necessary for her. (42)

Needless to say, I cast my lot with those readers who have found in *Emma* a simultaneously satirical and affectionate reflection upon the Highburians' solipsistic readiness to conflate Highbury and "the world." I part company with those readers who charge Austen's work with itself enacting such a conflation, as I do with those viewers who misunderstand *Clueless*'s Austenian preoccupation with the local, by misunderstanding how Heckerling calls on us simultaneously to identify with her heroine and identify her callowness.[13]

I would like to push these observations a bit further. Granted, even at the end of *Clueless* Cher's naivete remains intact: She still lacks that driver's license that might give her a broader purchase on the world, and she continues to believe that there's nothing a makeover cannot solve. Subsequent to what she herself calls a "makeover of the soul," she still conceptualizes change in those troublingly individualistic, private, and commodified terms, terms that could easily function to obscure large-scale struggles for social transformation. Yet there are ways in which Cher's clueless debates might nonetheless be taken seriously as models of the thinking woman's response to public policy in "the real world"—the latter being, after all, a term that not only designates the world that starry-eyed teenagers are meant to move into when they reach maturity, but also names a program on MTV. (Reminding us of this title, Heckerling shakes up our certainty that there is a difference between Cher's viewing preferences and Josh's more worldly ones.) When required to weigh in on the plight of the Haitian boat people, Cher recalls the story of how she surmounted an etiquette disaster. She points out that she did not turn away the guests who showed up at her father's birthday dinner after failing to

RSVP, and she wonders why "the government" cannot likewise rise to the occasion. If it would just "get to the kitchen, rearrange some things, we could certainly party with the Haitians"; "it doesn't say R.S.V.P. on the Statue of Liberty." Her analogy is trivializing, but it would be churlish to deny that the political message it delivers reframes the responsibilities of the state in ways that appeal.

In fact, understood as a stage en route to what Lauren Berlant calls "citizenship competence," such an analogy might be considered a cognitive instrument that enables those who deploy it to apprehend, however provisionally, the meaning of the conjunction in that enigmatic phrase "History and You."[14] Viewers of *Clueless* glimpse this phrase on a poster affixed to the wall of Miss Geist's history classroom. Throughout the school year it counterpoints the less-enduring exhortations that get scrawled on and erased off the chalkboard and that educate these budding historians in the virtues of linear chronology ("Study the time line") and imperial history ("Describe the areas Rome conquered"). Movie fans who remember *Fast Times at Ridgemont High* (1982) will know that for Heckerling this represents a repeat engagement with the history classroom and the question of how the public idiom of history becomes personal and so memorable. (The pothead surfer and his history teacher contribute to the happy ending of the earlier film when they come to a rapprochement about the class requirements by coming to a rapprochement about the meaning of Thomas Jefferson's violation of the rules: Jefferson, Spicoli the surfer offers, was saying that we "need some new cool rules of our own.") In his account of the postmodern annihilation of memory, Jameson discusses how nowadays the effort of coordinating local knowledge and lived experience with the impalpable, abstracted modes that yield access to a totality—the time line, for instance—proves impossible (53). What he is discussing is the difficulty of coordinating "History" with "You"—of getting from everyday, personal ways of marking time to the objective time of event-full history and back again, of mediating between domestic and public life.

For Jameson, this "crisis" of historical memory is the product of recent history: of, for example, the alliance between the media and the market; the tendency of television's ontology of liveness to immerse us in a perpetual present tense. But, remembering Catherine Morland's explanation of why she prefers novels to histories, one wonders whether this crisis is not old news (and less critical than banal) for women, who for a long time had to think of themselves as historical incompetents, unable to claim "the immortalizing impersonality" bestowed on those who could successfully situate their lives within the framework of public history and see themselves as living the past's sequel.[15] Catherine's complaint about history's emphasis on "popes and kings . . . wars or pestilences" and good-for-nothing men suggests that for her history constitutes the more fictive genre, that for her it is histories, not novels, that are estranged from what actually "pass[es] under one's own observation" (*Northanger Abbey*, 109). And, in fact, Eleanor Tilney, who is usually viewed as Austen's spokeswoman in this scene and who speaks in favor of history-writing, favors it because of its fictive dimensions: "If a speech be well drawn up, I read it with pleasure, by whomsoever it may be made—and probably with much greater, if the production of Mr. Hume or Mr. Robertson, than if the genuine words of Caractacus, Agricola, or Alfred the Great" (109). It is worth recalling, too, that the mock-heroic poetry of the eighteenth century devoted itself to precisely the question of how (or whether) one might document a modern commercial society and yet still use the protocols of representation and expectations about decorum bequeathed by classical antiquity. The experiments in scaling down the epic (but also in fitting out the domestic in a new, supersized format) that pervade that poetry are reprised in Austen's satire. For an instance of that reprise, consider the passage in *Emma* that recounts how, as if prescient about the power of the makeover, Frank Churchill buys himself a pair of gloves from Ford's—"the very shop that every body attends every day of their lives." Having refashioned himself as a "native" of Highbury, he feels certain he now possesses credentials of his *amor patriae* (200). The Latin catchphrase moves the reader into the territory of the mock epic. With it, Austen invites us to take the measure of the parochial and to size up just how diminished a *patria* might be.

To determine why Jameson must cast history's crisis as a new, postmodern thing, we might consider periodization in his scheme: how the opposition between modernism and postmodernism "obeys a discursive rather than a descriptive necessity," and how in this guise as a logical operator, a kind of machine for establishing categorical dichotomies, proves capable of generating in self-justifying fashion an almost infinite number of further oppositions, the opposition between genuine and pseudo-historicity included. Jameson's is a way of telling time, John Frow argues, that enlists binarism as "mode of historical explanation." Such a practice leaves no room for a more complex causality. When we chart oppositions, we construct "an idealist representation of a historical time which proceeds by the epochal succession of spiritual totalities." We also edit out the elements of discontinuity and heterogeneity within any one epoch. Not knowing what to do with these indications of how the past, far from arranging itself into sealed-off, synchronized periods, is instead a matter of multiple temporal strands, we relegate such elements to the expendable category of the anachronism. Historiography in another mode might opt instead to activate "the power of the anachronism as the potent icon of the past's incapacity to coincide with itself."[16]

If I go so far as to anachronistically clear a space for Austen within the Jamesonian picture of postmodernity, this is because I seek to complicate (and thereby de-idealize) that picture, and aim to do so by de-idealizing the time of genuine historicity that his *Postmodernism* locates in the past. That time is, implicitly, Austen's lifetime. (Implicitly, because reading *Postmodernism* is like reading history over Catherine Morland's shoulder: one encounters "hardly any women at all.") Explicitly, this epoch of genuine historicity is the one to which Jameson time-travels by remembering Georg Lukács' work on the historical novel and on the ascendancy of realism in the novel tradition. Lukács's 1937 study opens by commending Austen's contemporary Sir Walter Scott for securing, as no one had before, "an artistically faithful image of a concrete historical epoch." Within Lukács' *The Historical Novel*, the significance ascribed to Scott's "Waverley Novels" lies with the way in which, by revealing the human consequences of vast historical trends and by interweaving personal destinies and the determining context of a historical crisis, these books gave the readers of the early nineteenth century access to how society moves. "At the time of Sir Walter Scott," Jameson writes, as he remakes Lukács's case, "a contemplation of the past seemed able to renew our sense of our own reading present as the sequel of . . . [a] genetic series" (284–285). Jameson finds himself in his time, however, able only to invert Lukács's narrative of ascent. *Postmodernism* puts into reverse the latter's account of how "the historically faithful" triumphed "over the peddlers of bad faith"[17]—the latter personified by "a long list of second and third-rate writers" whose inconsequentiality is marked when Lukács refers at this point to only a single proper name. (It is not a surprise, given his investment in dissociating Scott from his novel-writing predecessors and casting him as a truly self-made man, that the name Lukács cites—Ann Radcliffe's—is a feminine one.) At other moments in this success story, what is vanquished is described as an understanding of history in which change means "merely a change of costumes"[18]: Lukács is far from prepared to deal with the fact that Scott's career as a novelist began when he completed a pseudo-medieval romance that had been started by an expert in costume history.[19]

And because, intent on theorizing realism, Lukács takes little interest in the fictionality of historical fiction; he likewise fails to deal with how Scott in conjoining history and the novel may have been addressing a pervasive anxiety in his lifetime about the fate of the historiographical enterprise. Jameson, too, engaged in his quest for a time and space of genuine historicity, overlooks how in the Britain of the turn of the nineteenth century, history-writing was undergoing a definitional crisis—a legitimation crisis, as well. What or who was history to be true to, in order to be true? Classical conceptions of "history" that refused that value-term to all but political narrative—accounts of the public affairs of public men—were, it was agreed, perceptibly deficient in "interest." This, at a moment when historians were conscious of needing to accommodate a reading audience, increasingly middle class and oriented toward commercial concerns, that had no equivalent in the time of Plutarch and Tacitus and of needing to accommodate in addition that audience's sense of "the importance of private life, considered in both its social and its inward dimensions: the everyday world of work and custom, as well as the inner one of sentiments."[20]

Historians needed to retailor historiography to ensure its applicability to life in modern civil society and to ensure that history, while retaining its antique dignity, would win recognition as a polite subject, appropriate for a mixed company that included the ladies. (These new, modern protocols of politeness might make the commission of anachronism a venial sin. In the conversation that she has with Catherine about history's pleasures, Eleanor Tilney in *Northanger Abbey* proves herself delightfully aware of the motives that would impel David Hume and William Robertson to substitute their own refined and stylish voices in the place of the less-polished and doubtless indelicate tones of the "real" Alfred or Caractacus. And indeed, as Jayne Lewis observes, some eighteenth-century commentators did fault modern historiography for cultivating an excessively intimate acquaintance with the softer, "overly accessorized" side of commercial society. A reviewer of Robertson's *History of Scotland* [1761] noted with a sneer that this acquaintance was the reason Robertson's volumes would "grace the toilet of the fair, and adorn the shelf of the macaroni."[21])

Men such as Robertson, Hume, and Adam Smith registered the problem that is at the heart of the Miss-Geist-ian "History and You" as a problem of genre. In his *Lectures on Rhetoric and Belles Lettres* (1762–1763), Smith, for instance, sought to maintain the privilege traditionally accorded to history's ancient, stately decorums and resisted many of the innovations distinguishing eighteenth-century historiography precisely because they lacked that classical authority. At the same time, Smith also spoke up for the social benefits to be gained when the reader's passions were moved, an end best achieved through representations of the inward dispositions of the individual mind. The result of this balancing act within the *Lectures* was a rereading of Tacitus that turned the Roman historian, whose hardheaded tolerance for realpolitik was notorious, into a sentimentalist, indeed a prototype for Smith himself in his demotion of outward acts and public occasion and his emphasis on invisible (and hence unrecorded and unverifiable) dramas of inner feeling. Like Eleanor Tilney, but without being able to admit it, Smith found that historiography would work just as well at its most fictive as it did at its most factual. Indeed, because of its attention to the affective, and its acknowledgment of how "private calamities . . . concentrate the passions," Smith's lecture on the writings of the ancient historian has been cited as providing "generous theoretical accommodation" for the rise of the novel.[22] Smith even compares Tacitus's historical narratives with the sentimental fiction that Crébillon and Pierre Marivaux were producing across the Channel in eighteenth-century France.

Such discipline envy can be detected elsewhere in eighteenth-century writing: the period's historians were increasingly aware of the kinds of advantages in narrating common life and in raising sympathy that could with impunity be claimed by their "less encumbered neighbours," the contemporary novelists. That awareness suggests why the memoir became recommending reading in this era, lauded for supplying insight into the hidden, personal life of the past. It suggests as well why the early-nineteenth-century editor of Lucy Hutchinson's seventeenth-century *Memoirs of the Life of Colonel Hutchinson* (1806) would promote his ancestress' work in these terms: "The ladies will feel that it carries with it all the interest of a novel strengthened with the authenticity of real history."[23]

Reread against this context, the arrangements that Scott's Waverley Novels make in order to connect everyday life in the past to that past's political narrative—arrangements that cast a new object, "culture," as the proper content of history—seem less surefooted, less an opening up of a new territory of truth-telling, and much more something on the order of a compromise formation. (Lukács's work on realism registers the compulsive pas de deux between High Modernism and mass culture that was a feature of his era; there is accordingly something both predictable and wishful about how he makes the era of the Waverley Novels seem a time that had not yet been obliged to acknowledge the expediency of such accommodations.) Indeed, to hearken to what was anxiety producing as well as anxiety resolving about the brokering between idiomatic and institutional life that produced this "cultural history," we might note that for each of the Waverley heroes the process of growing up culminates in the realization that history is for all intents and purposes already over and that what has succeeded it is "the end of history"—a concept that was as much bandied about after the Battle of Waterloo and the close of decades of war, Jerome Christensen demonstrates, as it is at the "postmodern" outset of the twenty-first century.[24] The Waverley hero discovers himself to be living (as we have recently rediscovered ourselves to be living) in a time of aftermath in which, as per the requirements of commercial society, remediation replaces revolution and conquest, conflict is routinized, and in which the future holds the promise of nothing more robust or eventful than "normal change." We might note too that for each of these heroes this realization coincides with his absorption by daily routine and domesticity, and note the resemblance that this era of aftermath bears to the time of plot in Austen's novels. Admired by Scott, she responds in turn to his project by beginning in just the place, at just the point of tedium, where he leaves off, and by examining at length the proposition that living in time means, as well, realizing that history can also be that which fails to happen. (A typical sentence in *Emma*: "Mr. Frank Churchill did not come."[25])

Let me do a bit more to complicate my account of how the relations of gender organized the cultural field within which historiography sought to claim its place and define itself as the culture's vehicle for the authentic.

Julius Hutchinson's spotlighting in the quotation just mentioned of the female and therefore the novel-reading portion of the *Memoir*'s audience recalls the sort of gendering of genres that Hume models, when, in his essay "Of the Study of History," he deplores his female readers' "aversion to matter of fact and . . . appetite for falsehood."[26] This gendering is also of course what Austen is talking back to in *Northanger Abbey*. She slyly complicates it by assigning to both Tilneys, the brother and the sister alike, a familiarity with novels; she has Eleanor Tilney take notice of Hume's own skirting of matter of fact; and she makes historians, in their proclivity for copying one another (the narrator counts nine hundred abridgments of *The History of England* [37]), sound as quixotic as novel-loving Catherine Morland in her proclivity for imitating Radcliffe. In the late eighteenth century, when the cultivation of sensibility was viewed as a national priority for Britons, the historiographer had to reconcile his own enterprise with the affective—and thus in his mind with the feminine.[27] Hence, the new priority that was given to scenes of domestic pathos—scenes, for instance, in which soon-to-be-executed Stuart monarchs pay their last farewells to their loved ones—within the era's Histories of England and of Scotland; hence, too, the attempt to engage scenes of lived experience as well as narratives of action and write histories of private, daily life. (One of the seven parts of Robert Henry's *History of Great Britain*—a history written, as Henry averred, on an entirely new plan—was devoted to the narration of the history of "manners, virtues, vices, remarkable customs, language, dress, diet, and diversions"; other sections included one that supplied a parallel linear history of "learning," while others engaged the rather more familiar subject matter of constitutional history and military history.[28]) The insistence that, after all, history and fiction were as different as the two sexes is constituted as a way of legitimating efforts like those. The gender binary provided historians with a means of firming up the boundaries that sustained the extant generic hierarchy, while behind the scenes giving themselves the room to maneuver.

And yet Catherine and Eleanor remind us of something important about the fortunes of the historiographical enterprise at this time, the latter by recalling her pleasure in reading Hume and Robertson, the former by, outrageously enough, not feeling over-awed by such historians in their guise as the "subjects-who-know" but instead pitying them for having to write only in order to "torment" the denizens of the schoolroom (109). What their conversation reinforces is the curious fact that in Austen's lifetime the study of history was a central component of the curriculum for girls—deemed pedagogically useful for those who were "debarred from the severer studies, by the tenderness of their complexion," those who were required, because in theory they were confined to the home, to get both their "experience" and their "materials for conversation" from books and not life.[29]

Novels were a woman's subject, then, while history was and remained— notwithstanding flamboyant exceptions such as Hume's dramatizing of the rivalry, and the psychological warfare, between Elizabeth and Mary, Queen of Scots—an account of male activity. And, with few exceptions, history was authored by men (authors who, even while they made the concessions man- dated by that new notion that one might read history in one's capacity as a private person, still made it clear that they wielded the authority accruing to gentlemen carrying out public responsibilities in the church or the state[30]). One way to engage such contradictions in the way the emergent discipline of history formulated an accessible past is to ponder how, under such circum- stances, women's acquisition of historical knowledge was arguably a matter of "tactics"—John Frow's designation (derived from the work of Michel de Certeau) for the tactful manner in which unauthorized ("debarred") users make culturally valorized discourses that are not really theirs serviceable all the same. Such doings, Frow writes, exemplify "a logic of momentary occu- pation without ownership."[31]

Frow's discussion seems relevant to the breezy manner in which, within *Clueless*, mall-rat teens encounter the past and make a place for themselves within culturally valorized modes of remembering its legacy. In this connec- tion we might also consider the manner in which Amy Heckerling, adept of the Hollywood teen comedy, stakes her claim to classic literature, the man- ner in which she enlists alongside the professorate as a guardian of Jane Austen's memory. One allusion her film makes to the "classics" occurs in the video clip that we see from *Spartacus*, Christian's favorite Tony Curtis movie. The character Curtis plays explains to the Roman aristocrat interro- gating him that he taught "the classics" to "the children of his master." If survival of enslavement and fidelity to the canon of the dead are coupled here, the message is not in any straightforward way that a pedagogic grounding in the "Great Books" will set you free because this devotion to the classics is coupled, too, with the devotion that Christian as gay viewer (and so as another unauthorized user of culture) brings to Tony Curtis. That is, it is coupled with a mode of reading that one does not learn in school and that prises style away from content to convert *Spartacus* into a campy vehi- cle for queer solidarity.

When Los Angeles and the postmodern are at issue, the classic as a site of value that deserves to endure is often represented as betrayed or disappear- ing. It is often the trigger for melancholy and nostalgia. (Think of the place of ruins in the futuristic Los Angeles of *Blade Runner* or of "classic" Holly- wood cinema in *L.A. Confidential*.) Heckerling arranges, however, to rep- resent classics (books, music, artworks) in different terms, whisking them into a nostalgia-free zone, not leaving them alone in solitary grandeur. When Cher remembers Shakespeare—first writing about the "darling buds of

May" on the greeting card that she sends as the first salvo in her match-making enterprise, and then knowing that Hamlet did not speak the line "To thine own self be true"—she is able to do so, first, because she knows her *Cliff Notes,* and, second, because she knows her Mel Gibson.

In this chirpy rendering of the postmodern commodification of art, the classic is assimilated into an intertextual network woven out of a diversity of cultural practices. Cher's range of cultural references defeats efforts to segregate now from then or high culture from low—efforts to move "along vertical paradigms that grant a hierarchical position as opposed to moving along a more integrative horizontality."[32] However, this description of the textual tapestry that is *Clueless* also does nicely as a description of the mix-and-match negotiations with both classics and trash—in *Emma,* with both Shakespeare and the mainly female-authored, Minerva Press novels on Harriet Smith's top-ten list—that is characteristic of Austen's work. Critics who find in Austen confirmation of their own absolutism on the issue of cultural quality and assume that she would find in our screen adaptations of her novels evidence of cultural decline overlook the "postmodern" code-switching that her intertextuality models. But, since she was likely aware of the gendering of these categories, it should not surprise us that (predicting Heckerling's ecumenical allusiveness) she shows more interest in collapsing the boundaries that segregate the canonical from the popular than in patrolling them.[33]

It is not evident to me, in fact, that Austen would dislike even the glitz (even the flounces and furbelows) that inevitably distinguish the period adaptations of her novels: notwithstanding the frequently heard assertion that as a novelist she is "cerebral" and really very "niggardly" in her "descriptive dealings with food, clothes, . . . weather, and landscape."[34] The materialization that the novels undergo in adaptation often does entail their conversion into vehicles for asserting Britain's film and TV production teams' monopoly on "quality"—the term that has come to denote the filmmakers' scrupulous attention to period detail and finish. Custodians of quality have a commitment to accuracy that moves them to research even the bywaters of the history of material culture (that is, they get the details right even for the period corset that no one will see); they tend to conduct themselves in bygone worlds as if they could afford to be genteelly unassuming (that is, they eschew all bright colors in their cinematography)—as if they really were, in short, to the manor born.

Why are the results of their efforts so often depressing? Certainly the thickness of texture that results when quality is a byword has on occasion made these films feel claustrophobic—lush but leaden. It is as if a movie can be weighed down by too much re-creation. (The way that the opening of Ang Lee's *Sense and Sensibility* [1995] recreates the atmosphere at Norland Park following the death of Mr. Dashwood comes to mind—the chill of damp marble is almost palpable, and as the family members hold their hushed conferences they are dwarfed by the crowd of painted people peering down at them from the portraits and conversation pieces that adorn the walls above. In director Roger Michell's *Persuasion* [1994], the dustcovers that shroud the furnishings at Kellynch Hall produce an analogous effect, and Anne Elliot the heroine also appears, if not shrouded, at least bowed down by the weight of the dowdy pinafores, shawls, and cloaks that muffle her.) Mary A. Favret comments on how the fidelity with which *Persuasion* re-creates domestic interiors "only propels a desire, shared by the heroine with the camera itself, to flee"; "The problem for [*Persuasion*] is finding a way to spring its heroine from the mortifying world it has, with exactitude, recaptured."[35] So absolute, she implies, is the sense of living *in* time that Roger Michell simulates, that there seems in this world to be a shortage of opportunities for simply living.

Nonetheless, such fidelity to the past produces in *Persuasion* at least one shot that to me seems a powerful refutation of the arguments against movie-made renditions of the past that historians have mounted since the beginnings of film: arguments that (as in the complaints Britain's Historical Association made against the costume dramas of the 1930s) attempt to quarantine the authentically historical against an emphasis on the decorative that threatens both to commodify history and—as the undertones of gender-panic in these contexts suggest—to feminize it.[36] At one point Michell trains the camera on the startlingly delicate boots—really, little booties—that Anne Elliot and the other female members of her party are wearing as they clamber about on the Lyme breakwater. Encountering this vivid documentation of the material constraints on the nineteenth-century lady's mobility, we see how, for a feminist historiography especially, film might be possessed of pedagogic resources that could trump those of written history. I want to note this; but, by way of speculating a bit further about why Austen might not have objected to the accessorizing of history that this shot of footwear supplies (even if, watching it, we cease to wonder about Wentworth's feelings for Anne and begin to think instead about the Regency woman's lack of sensible shoes), I also wish to make another, slightly different point. A fashion's relation to the time that creates it, and hence to authentic rather than ersatz recollections of the past, is a more complex and unruly one than can be assessed through notions of period accuracy.

If, as studio publicists have repeated for decades, the costume design in period films is the product of the most expensive and extensive research (Heckerling remembered this convention when she put the word about that *Clueless* was based on her fieldwork at the "real" Beverly Hills High), such research often seems to lead to an ironic result. It is costume that regularly incites historians to become a branch of the police and file charges of inauthenticity. However, the essence of fashion—which can in itself serve as a medium of a culture's reminiscences about bygone times—is a kind of temporal, as well as geographical, bricolage: Victorians trimmed their skirts in ways that recalled the panniers on eighteenth-century hoop petticoats; Regency ladies wore turbans. The fashions of any one era are a heterogeneous amalgam of styles and periods, and that heterogeneity makes the quest for exactitude in film something of a lost cause.[37] Furthermore, the intimacy between our clothes and our bodies overdetermines fashion's responsiveness to desires and dreams, and in this respect as well the collective script of costume, whether worn in life or represented on film, can introduce anachronism. To dress, or more particularly to dress up, can express one's desire to go in masquerade—an unseasonable desire to be someone else, somewhere else. Fashion encourages fantasizing. An article of dress can register a woman's desire to flee the era by which she is captured.

In fact, fashion in period film might be of consequence for the historically minded precisely in its capacity to remind us of what is wayward about individuals' relation to the time. It can preserve a sense of what is *untimely*— and so the resources with which to disrupt the foreclosed and fossilized sense of historical finitude we confront when we fall in with the notion that life in time arranges itself, in linear fashion, into a series of perfectly self-enclosed and perfectly synchronized historical periods, the Jamesonian era of postmodernity that ends history and time's cavalcade of periods included.[38] In her defense of costume drama, Pam Cook notes that while "[o]fficial historians . . . find it difficult to accept a notion of history as oscillating between reality and fantasy," feminist cultural historians are often less wary of "travesties of the past, perhaps because official histories have generally served them ill."[39] One might look to Austen herself for an instance of feminist cultural historian's openness to travesty, since in 1791, at age seventeen, she joined forces with her sister so that together (Jane supplying the words and Cassandra the pictures) they might produce a miniaturized *History of England* ("By a partial, prejudiced, and ignorant historian"). Bespeaking its status as a protest against the torments of the schoolroom, their history is "overly accessorized"—with a vengeance. Cassandra's illustrations make kings and queens into clotheshorses on which to hang apparel and trumps even Jane's wickedly Whiggish narrative in its insistent anachronism. As rendered by Cassandra, Henry VIII sports a Jacobin cap of liberty.

When she pays homage to Austen's classic status, Heckerling eschews the fixation on historical detail that Ang Lee, Roger Michell, and Patricia Rozema bring to that task, but it is arguable whether she does so precisely to deflect the mortifying demands of historical reenactment (mortifying as in embarrassing, mortifying as in death dealing) that Favret describes. Admirers of *Clueless* sometimes write as if Heckerling chose to do *Emma* in modern dress because the updating would allow her to prise the substance of Austen's novel away from the frill of Regency style (in which Austen = aristocrats + dancing) and so repair the costume drama's way of prising that style away from that substance. But this is not the whole story.

Heckerling's way of being true to Austen's sense of what history should be true to also entails a generous homage to the costume drama as a genre. Tacitly she seems to know that her postmodern makeover of *Emma* will be compared to others' period pieces. Yet this does not occasion her one-up-manship, but rather motivates a set of allusions to historical costume that, in their self-consciousness, match her reflexivity about moviemaking that aims to cope with the "classic." It seems just right that when the teenage girls of *Clueless* make their daily "costume decisions" (Cher's term), it's often empire-waist dresses that they pull out of their closets. (I use the plural because both Cher and her rival Amber favor this Regency fashion silhou-ette: a coincidence that in making both vulnerable to the charge of being fashion "clones" works to underline how Heckerling's mimicry is also at issue here.) Heckerling seems at such moments to remember all those movie scenes that have shown us a nineteenth-century ingenue dressing up for the ball. (Rozema engages in a comparably arch remembering of that conven-tion in a sequence in *Mansfield Park* in which her camera peers inside the windows of the Bertram manor house to reveal one family member after an-other—six in total—primping before their mirrors as, separately and collec-tively, they deck themselves out to impress the visiting Crawfords. Even Aunt Norris is glimpsed in this unwonted posture, trying out the winsome effect of a rose in her hair.) It seems just right, too, that the pens that Cher brings to history class at Bronson Alcott High come topped with feathers (pink ones) and so resemble the quill pens that in our imaginations we install in the hands of bygone women writers. Certainly, the visual idiom of *Clue-less*, with its pop-art color schemes, is not that of the quality versions of Austen—but it does share something with the 1930s and 1940s costume ex-travaganzas that so upset the British Historical Association. Heckerling's viewers cannot help but conclude, as audiences for earlier period films such as the MGM big-hair *Marie Antoinette* (1938) must have, that the actors are in masquerade; that when the characters of *Clueless* are being themselves in the highly stagey world of their high school, they are playing at being who they are. Such are the effects produced by the lampshade hat and tutu sported by Cher's best friend Dionne or the feather boas favored for class-room wear by Amber.

When costume drama is at its best, its costumery is more than a vehicle for re-creating the feel of the past. Costume drama can also reveal that cos-tumery is part of the content of that past—a content that reveals how we are subject to history, but which simultaneously keeps open the play of identity, keeps open what is theatrical, ambiguous, or mutable about the ways in which we make our selves through our clothes. (Rozema's *Mansfield Park*, for instance, manipulates differences in millinery and hairdressing to mount an argument about the potential for pathos in Regency women's class iden-tifications: fixated on appearances and apparel, few viewers notice that the same actress has been cast as both Lady Bertram—the sister who married up—and as Mrs. Price—the sister who did not.) I stress this to underscore the lesson brought home to us when we learn history from *Clueless* or from Jane Austen—a lesson that we may use to counter the charges of faux historicism that have been prompted by our "return" to her novels. Our quests for and our attachment to what appears to be "authentically historical" can prompt us to remember history, but they sometimes lead us to forget it.[40]

Notes

1. William Dean Howells, *Heroines of Fiction* (New York: Harper, 1901), 1:49; emphasis added.

2. In his *Guardian* review of Patricia Rozema's *Mansfield Park* (March 31, 2000, available online: http://www.guardian.co.uk/Archive), Peter Bradshaw complained of how Austen's "poor narrow shoulders" had been forced to "bear the weight of twenty-first century analysis and guilt."

3. Vivian Sobchack, "'Surge and Splendor': A Phenomenology of the Hollywood Historical Epic," *Representations* 29 (1990): 37.

4. See Stanley Kauffmann's review of *Persuasion* in *The New Republic* (October 9, 1995): 27; Jonathan Romney's review of *Clueless* in *New Statesman & Society* (October 20, 1995): 35. See also Jocelyn Harris's avowedly testy response to the film/TV adaptation of *Persuasion*: "Were Lady Russell's ravishing silk taffetas and toques, I thought crossly, to be the real protagonists?" (Review of four Austen adaptations in *Eighteenth-Century Fiction* 8 [1996]: 427).

5. Claudia L. Johnson, *Jane Austen: Women, Politics, and the Novel* (Chicago: University of Chicago Press, 1988), xiv.

6. Susan Buck-Morss, *The Dialectics of Seeing: Walter Benjamin and the Arcades Project* (Cambridge: MIT Press, 1989), 98.

7. Erin Mackie, *Market A-la-Mode: Fashion, Commodity, and Gender in* The Tatler *and* The Spectator (Baltimore: Johns Hopkins University Press, 1997), 105. Vivian Sobchack cites Janet Staiger to similar effect: "[T]he film implies [through its defining emphasis on spectacle] that what's historical is a physical reality. It is the mise-en-scène, the props, the costumes, and the people that are historical" ("Surge and Splendor," 37).

8. Henry is quoted in Mark Salber Phillips, *Society and Sentiment: Genres of Historical Writing in Britain, 1740–1820* (Princeton, NJ: Princeton University Press, 2000), 4, a study to which this chapter is extensively indebted. For Austen's response to Henry's *History*, see *Jane Austen's Letters*, ed. Deirdre Le Faye, 3rd ed. (Oxford: Oxford University Press, 1995), 59 (letter to Martha Lloyd, November 13, 1800).

9. Fredric Jameson, *Postmodernism, or, The Cultural Logic of Late Capitalism* (Durham, NC: Duke University Press, 1991), x. Subsequent references in my text to Jameson's writings are to this book.

10. Celeste Olalquiaga, *Megalopolis: Contemporary Cultural Sensibilities* (Minneapolis: University of Minnesota Press, 1992), 56.

11. Ibid., 20–21.

12. Jane Austen, *Emma*, ed. R. W. Chapman (Oxford: Oxford University Press, 1933), 5. Subsequent references to this edition will appear in the text. For quotations from the other two Austen novels that I cite in this piece, *Northanger Abbey* and *Persuasion*, I draw on the *Oxford Illustrated Jane Austen*, ed. R. W. Chapman (Oxford: Oxford University Press, 1923).

13. Lesley Stern notes how critical response to both Austen and Heckerling has been torn between lauding their ethnographic attention to what Austen calls "the daily happiness of private life" and deploring this narrowness of focus ("Emma in Los Angeles: *Clueless* as a Remake of the Book and the City," *Australian Humanities Review* [August 1997], at www.lib.latrobe.edu.au/AHR).

14. Lauren Berlant, *The Queen of America Goes to Washington City: Essays in Sexual Citizenship* (Durham, NC: Duke University Press, 1997), 25.

15. The phrase *immortalizing impersonality* is Berlant's: *The Queen of America Goes to Washington City*, 33.

16. John Frow, *Time and Commodity Culture: Essays in Cultural Theory and Postmodernity* (New York: Oxford University Press, 1997), 36; Jerome Christensen, *Romanticism at the End of History* (Baltimore: Johns Hopkins University Press, 2000), 3.

17. Angela Keane, "The Importance of Elsewhere: Romantic Subjectivity and the Romance of History," *The Wordsworth Circle* 27, no. 1 (1996): 17.

18. Georg Lukács, *The Historical Novel*, trans. Hannah and Stanley Mitchell (Lincoln: University of Nebraska Press, 1983), 30, 28.

19. Lisa Hopkins, "Clothes and the Body of the Knight: The Making of Men in Sir Walter Scott's *The Talisman*," *The Wordsworth Circle* 27, no. 1 (1996): 24.

20. Mark Salber Phillips, "Adam Smith and the History of Private Life," in *The Historical Imagination in Early Modern Britain: History, Rhetoric, and Fiction, 1500–1800*, ed. Donald R. Kelley and David Harris Sachs (Cambridge: Cambridge University Press, 1997), 319.

21. *Monthly Review* lxxviii (January 1788), 13, cited in Jayne Elizabeth Lewis, "Mary Stuart's 'Fatal Box': Sentimental History and the Revival of the Casket Letters Controversy," *The Age of Johnson* 7 (1996): 461. The phrase *overly accessorized* is Lewis's.

22. Ian Duncan, "Adam Smith, Samuel Johnson, and the Institutions of English," in *The Scottish Invention of English Literature*, ed. Robert Crawford (Cambridge: Cambridge University Press, 1999), 49.

23. See Phillips, *Society and Sentiment*, 100.

24. As well as drawing here on Christensen's *Romanticism at the End of History*, I rely on Ina Ferris's account of the historical turn of the early nineteenth century: *The Achievement of Literary Authority: Gender, History, and the Waverley Novels* (Ithaca, NY: Cornell University Press, 1991), esp. ch. 7.

25. On the necessity of expanding our definition of history to include emptiness and tedium, see Patrice Petro, "Historical Ennui, Feminist Boredom," in *The Per-*

sistence of History: Cinema, Television, and the Modern Event, ed. Vivian Sobchack (New York: Routledge, 1996), 197: "[G]ender and sexual difference are central to [the] experience of time in modernity—the time between the event and the uneventful, between that which happens and that which fails to occur. If as Fredric Jameson has claimed, 'history is what hurts,' then, as . . . women modernists have shown, history is also about what *fails to happen.*" See also Meaghan Morris on how this temporality of eventlessness is also the characteristic temporality of feminism, which is ill adapted, she observes, to heroic progress narratives, and whose task is thus to act "to bring about concrete social change while at the same time contesting the very bases of modern thinking about what constitutes 'change.'" (*Too Soon, Too Late: History in Popular Culture* [Bloomington: Indiana University Press, 1998], xv).

26. "On the Study of History," in *Versions of History from Antiquity to the Enlightenment*, ed. Donald E. Kelley (New Haven, CT: Yale University Press, 1991), 458. Of course, Hume goes on to demonstrate rather archly that nothing guarantees the veracity of the male historian either, for he devotes the passage succeeding this one to a story about how he seduced a female companion into an attentive reading of Plutarch by assuring her in advance that the *Lives* was "really" a novel.

27. See Lewis, "Mary Stuart's 'Fatal Box.'"

28. Phillips, *Society and Sentiment*, 3.

29. Hume, "On the Study of History," 459. See also Christopher Kent, "Learning History with, and from, Jane Austen," in *Jane Austen's Beginnings: The Juvenilia and Lady Susan*, ed. J. David Grey (Ann Arbor, MI: UMI Research Press, 1989), 59–72.

30. For an account of the eighteenth-century historian's strategies of self-authorization and of his cultivation of a gentlemanly identity, see Karen O'Brien, *Narratives of Enlightenment: Cosmopolitan History from Voltaire to Gibbon* (Cambridge: Cambridge University Press, 1997).

31. John Frow, *Cultural Studies and Cultural Value* (New York: Oxford University Press, 1995), 51; Michel de Certeau, *The Practice of Everyday Life*, trans. Steven F. Rendall (Berkeley and Los Angeles: University of California Press, 1984).

32. Stern, "Emma in Los Angeles"; Olalquiaga, *Megalopolis*, xvi.

33. Judy Simons, "Classics and Trash: Reading Austen in the '90s," *Women's Writing* 5, no. 1 (1998): 27–39.

34. I quote, as many recent discussions of Austenmania have, Martin Amis, "Jane's World," *New Yorker* 71, no. 43 (January 8, 1996): 31.

35. Mary A. Favret, "Being True to Jane Austen," in *Victorian Afterlife: Postmodern Culture Rewrites the Nineteenth Century*, ed. John Kucich and Dianne F. Sadoff (Minneapolis: University of Minnesota Press, 2000), 73. See also Kerryn Goldsworthy, "Austen and Authenticity," *Australian Humanities Review* (July 1996), at www.lib.latrobe.edu.au/AHR.

36. For an account of these arguments, see Pam Cook's suggestive *Fashioning the Nation: Costume and Identity in British Cinema* (London: British Film Institute,

1996). For a broad-ranging account of the vexed relations between historians' historical world and filmmakers', see Robert Rosenstone, *Visions of the Past: The Challenge of Film to Our Idea of History* (Cambridge: Harvard University Press, 1995).

37. Cook, *Fashioning the Nation*, 67.

38. Roger Michell, as Mary A. Favret explains in her discussion of his *Persuasion*, has to take advantage of the fact that the very precise chronology Austen supplies for her novel locates its plot within the short period of false peace and premature demobilization that preceded Napoleon's definitive defeat at Waterloo. It is this temporary reopening of hostilities that licenses him to give Anne Elliot that opportunity for mobility that he symbolizes with his closing shot of her leaving the harbor aboard Wentworth's ship. The film needs a means of eluding the petrifaction induced by the postwar settlement and, in Favret's reading, induced by the finitude that Michell's historical fidelity in re-creating period furniture and clothing ascribes to the past. I am suggesting that on a local scale costume can work to similar ends, projecting alternative, "virtual" histories in comparable ways. Arranging for a troupe of circus performers in outlandish costume to parade by Anne and Wentworth during the scene of their culminating kiss—a scene that proved equally outlandish for period purists—Michell is making just this point. See Favret, "Being True to Jane Austen," 78.

39. Cook, *Fashioning the Nation*, 71.

40. I am indebted to Goldsworthy's "Austen and Authenticity" for this point. There are other debts I would like to acknowledge: thank you to Robert Devens and Eliza Robertson for assisting me with the research for this chapter; to Stacy Carson Hubbard for conversations about fashion; to Suzanne Pucci, James Thompson, Paulla Ebron, Bruce Grant, and Tom Keirstead for their careful readings; and another thank you to Tom for sharing his own work on history and film.

5

"It Can't Go on Like This"

Dangerous Liaisons in the Reagan–Thatcher Years

❧※❧

Sarah Maza

In the late 1980s, the West was in a prerevolutionary mood. France was gearing up to celebrate the bicentennial of its 1789 Revolution, and further east the opening up of the Soviet Union held the promise of momentous changes. With the benefit of hindsight, the late 1980s of this century can look downright Dickensian, with neosocialism and popular anticommunism flourishing on the European continent while the Anglo-American elites flaunted obscene amounts of wealth: the 1980s were the age of Ronald Reagan and Margaret Thatcher, of Donald Trump and Leona Helmsley, of the novels of Tom Wolfe and Jay MacInerney. In retrospect again, it seems inevitable that the period from 1985 to 1989 saw the revival of what is arguably the best novel ever written about a depraved and doomed aristocratic culture. In 1985, the British playwright Christopher Hampton adapted for the stage *Les Liaisons dangereuses*, the 1782 libertine classic and the only novel written by Pierre-Ambroise-François Choderlos de Laclos. Hampton soon after modified his play to serve as the script for the movie *Dangerous Liaisons*, directed by Stephen Frears and released by Warner Brothers in late 1988.

It is not my intention to deplore the betrayal of Laclos's text in these successive recastings. For one thing, as adaptations go, the play and the movie were both exceptionally good at capturing the interest of twentieth-century audiences while remaining faithful to their source. I would also argue, in the spirit of reception theory, that texts of enduring interest

93

through their depth and complexity survive in part by being simplified and widely circulated, absorbing new meanings from each different incarnation and environment. A successful re-creation of the past, whether or not its vehicle is a work of literature, depends on some combination of preserving the past's strangeness and making it familiar. Hampton, working alone and then with Frears, preserved a large measure of the novel's remoteness—its formality and opacity, the constraints that rule the lives of its characters. But in bringing to stage and then screen a novel written in letters, Hampton and Frears also clarified the novel's meanings in subtle ways that make the story more recognizable and more palatable to a modern audience. Less subtly, the film evoked some of the central obsessions of the 1980s: wealth, moral corruption, and female ambition.

The bare plot of Laclos's novel is so cleverly titillating it is surprising it has inspired comparatively few adaptations. The story is powered by the rivalry between two master libertines who are former lovers—the Marquise de Merteuil and the Vicomte de Valmont—and it unfolds, as the carefully dated letters indicate, over the course of less than six months. The plot opens with Merteuil's challenge to Valmont to seduce a fifteen-year-old virgin fresh from the convent, Cécile Volanges; Merteuil plans this as revenge on her former lover Gercourt, to whom Cécile has been promised in marriage. Valmont at first refuses because the task is too easy and he has set his sights on the married and famously virtuous Madame de Tourvel. In the process of pursuing Tourvel, however, Valmont discovers that she resists him in part because of letters from Cécile's mother warning Tourvel against the rake. Furious, Valmont agrees to deflower and debauch Cécile to get back at her mother, while still besieging Tourvel, and Merteuil promises him a night with her if he can prove success with Madame de Tourvel. Valmont has no trouble ravishing Cécile, an amoral and guileless creature, but only after considerable struggle can he convince Tourvel, who appears to have deep feelings for him, to forsake her principles and become his mistress. When Valmont tries to claim his reward, however, Merteuil taunts him and challenges him to break up with Tourvel in an extremely cruel manner. Driven by vanity, Valmont complies but appears distraught at the consequences, as Madame de Tourvel goes into a sharp decline and dies from the shock and shame of how she has been used. Open war finally breaks out between the master-libertines, resulting quickly in their mutual destruction: Valmont is fatally wounded in a duel but manages before he dies to ensure the publication of Merteuil's letters. Merteuil ends up a complete pariah, banished from society, financially ruined, and disfigured to boot.

No summary can begin to do justice to the dazzling symmetries of Laclos's plot, which unfolds in four parts with victories evenly distributed between the two protagonists. Valmont and Merteuil are evenly matched: she is the stronger and smarter of the two, but is handicapped by having to maintain appearances of virtue because she is female (the pair bring to mind the famous remark that Ginger Rogers did all the same things as Fred Astaire, but she did them "backwards and wearing high heels"). Merteuil is the one initially driven by revenge, but Valmont soon has his vengeful reason for raping Cécile. After Valmont becomes Cécile's lover, Merteuil sleeps with Cécile's young suitor, the Chevalier Danceny. Relationships echo one another in the mode of irony: Valmont's involvement with the sentimental Tourvel is satirized by his trysts with the courtesan Emilie; and the novel contains three relationships on the mother–daughter model, of which the most vacuous by far is the one between a real mother and her daughter. The novel is built around a series of parallels, each with a twist to it that unbalances the edifice and keeps the plot careening forward.

There have naturally been countless critical interpretations of the novel since its publication in 1782. Over the decades it seems as if every French writer has felt impelled to provide a quotable tag to this *enfant terrible* of French literature, from Charles Baudelaire's comment that Laclos's novel "burns like ice" to André Malraux's description of it as an "eroticization of the will." Modern readings have fastened onto three issues, all of which have significant implications for anyone trying to adapt the book for another medium: the closed and theatrical "classical" properties of the novel, its epistolarity, and the author's stance and intentions. (These aspects are, in practice, all closely connected.)

Despite the length of Laclos's novel, approximately four hundred pages in most editions, its kinship to classical theater is what makes it adaptable to the stage. Among all of the many different traditions and influences at play in the text, its main models are the masterpieces of seventeenth-century French classicism, Madame de Lafayette's *La Princesse de Clèves* and the tragedies of Pierre Corneille and Jean Racine.[1] The novel involves only seven characters (Merteuil, Valmont, Tourvel, Cécile and her mother, Danceny, and Madame de Rosemonde), plus a small number of minor characters. Very much in the tradition of classical tragedy, the book opens in mid-crisis, even if that crisis is fabricated by the libertines rather than inflicted by the gods: Cécile must be seduced before her upcoming marriage, and Tourvel must be conquered soon lest Valmont appear a fool.

If the time frame is not the regulation twenty-four hours of classical drama, it is certainly compressed, as I have noted, with a profusion of events crammed between August 1 and January 15. As Michel Delon suggests, the compression of time not only highlights the virtuosity of Merteuil's and Valmont's libertinism, which is predicated on speed, it also points to a very classical disinterest in the sort of psychological change and maturation Jean-Jacques Rousseau had already portrayed in the expansive duration of his *Nouvelle Héloïse*. Laclos's libertines are who they are; they may make fatal mistakes, but change comes only in the form of destruction.[2] They do not have time to mature. As Delon puts it, *Les Liaisons* portrays "a yearning for passion in a world without love, a yearning for time in a world without history" (70).

The novel, finally, is theatrical in the spatial confinement that governs its world. This is true literally, in that most of the action takes place in a few drawing rooms and the occasional bedroom. But it is also true in the deeper sense that the libertines and their victims live in a strictly confined world from which they cannot escape: Madame de Tourvel cannot hide from Valmont, and when Merteuil is banished from the only social world that counts, she is as good as dead. Classic readings of the novel emphasize the claustrophobically limited nature of the high society in which these characters move and the literary consequences of this confinement. *Les Liaisons* is an exemplary "novel of worldliness" set in a universe that is both closed and excruciatingly public to those who inhabit it.[3] As in a court society (and here again the legacy of classicism is important), the characters expend all of their energies performing a role, hiding their motives, and "penetrating" others in order to manipulate them.[4] As Susan Winnett observes, it is precisely the closure of this universe that engenders the proliferation of meanings within it.[5] In a small world from which there is no escape, the best way to hide is under the veil of convention, but the very opacity of "manners" in turn ensures that a person's words and deeds will be scrutinized and endlessly interpreted by others.

A closed world, a small cast, a tight time frame make work easier for a theater director seeking to adapt this novel for the stage. The major stumbling block for translation into another medium will always be that aspect of the novel most treasured by literary critics: its epistolarity. Much has been written about the technical virtuosity of this letter novel, whose author is sometimes accused of having killed the genre by exhausting its possibilities: the dazzling polyphony of different voices; a variety in lengths and tones that ranges from Tourvel's long Rousseauean love letters to Merteuil's famous three-word screed: "Very well: war" (reply to letter 153); the many letters about a single event, or the single letter read differently by several readers; the clever choreography of dated missives; and the fact that letters are the main agent and end of the plot because every significant development happens through them and because of them.[6]

The problems this dimension of the novel poses for anyone adapting it to a visual medium are obvious. The least of it is that it is not very exciting to watch somebody writing a letter. (Laclos provides what must be a unique exception to the preceding statement with the famous instance of Valmont's letter-writing on the bare back of the prostitute Emilie—a scene Hampton happily appropriated for both the play and the movie.) Like Roger Vadim before him, Hampton alone, and then in collaboration with Frears, opted simply to abandon the epistolary dimension of the novel, replacing the letters with face-to-face encounters. (Initially Frears had intended to restore epistolarity to the film version by having letters read in voice-over, but the plan was dropped.[7]) Eschewing letters arguably improves the novel's plausibility in some respects, since, as Samuel Richardson's critics loved to point out, recording everything you do is inherently implausible, if not downright silly. For instance, Laclos has to expend considerable authorial cleverness in convincing the reader that Merteuil and Valmont have good reasons never to be in the same place; it makes far more sense for them to confide in one another verbally, as they do in the play and film. Elsewhere, however, the shift in medium makes for implausible situations. It seems right that Valmont would use a letter to break off his relations with Tourvel, since the act bespeaks his fear of his own feelings and of the pain he knows he will inflict. It is both implausible and awkward for him to parrot "It's beyond my control" in the presence of his jilted and hysterical lover, as he does in Hampton's two versions of the story.

More generally, the absence of the letters as material artifacts from the story profoundly affects the nature of the work. Most of the letters making up the novel are extremely compromising; they reveal shameful thoughts and intentions or deceitful actions on the part of nearly every character. Not only does this make the reader into a voyeur, it also means that the very medium of the tale is a constant threat to its characters. Most of these letters, if they fell into the wrong hands, could damage or destroy their writer—which does, in fact, happen in the novel, most cataclysmically at the end.[8] For Valmont and Merteuil the consignment of so much to paper is another dimension of the calculated risk-taking that is the sign of their virtuosity because all of the characters' letter-writing weaves through the plot a strain of constant danger, much like the wearing of a wire in a modern police drama: the slightest misstep could have the direst consequences.

Ultimately, though, the epistolary medium governs the truth-status of what is conveyed in the text, and hence one's entire reading of the novel. We are explicitly warned, as readers, that the letters making up this novel are not to be trusted. The warning comes in the famous "dual preface" of *Les Liaisons*: the editor's preface, the standard opening for this sort of novel, presenting the work as a collection of authentic letters, is undermined by the preceding "Publisher's Note," which in tones dripping with irony assures us that the manuscript must be a fake because the behavior it depicts would be unthinkable in contemporary France. Other more specific warnings are tendered in the course of the novel, such as Merteuil's pointed instructions to Cécile about letter-writing: "You will agree, I am sure, that when you write to someone it is for his sake and not for yours. You must therefore try to say less what you think than what you think he will be pleased to hear."[9]

Since we know that even allies and lovers lie to each other in the novel, since we have been warned that the purpose of a letter is to conceal rather than to reveal, how can we presume to settle on any interpretation of this text? How can we know for sure, Michel Delon asks, that Valmont really is a libertine and that Danceny is not? If an event is described in several different letters, how can we know that one version is truthful?[10] In a highly self-conscious epistolary novel such as this one, there can be no such thing as a neutral description, and therefore we never know the truth of any feeling or action described.

Joan DeJean, in one of the most acute recent readings of *Les Liaisons*, describes it as the archetypal "defensive text," a novel whose very purpose is to defeat any attempt by the reader at ultimate "penetration." Through the use of letters whose authorship is often unclear and whose writers are deceitful, and by building into the novel a pastiche of other texts, Laclos erects "literary fortifications" against attempts to subdue his work into meaning one thing.[11] Better still, DeJean argues, the center of this highly defended work is as hollow as the exploding *boulet creux* invented by Laclos the artilleryman. The dual preface warns us that this text has no author to take responsibility for it, as does the famous refrain in the letter Valmont sends to Tourvel to end their affair: "*Ce n'est pas de ma faute*" (nobody did this, nobody is to blame) (252–262). DeJean's reading of the novel challenges the widespread assumption that, despite Laclos's ambivalent moral stance toward his libertine characters, the plot revolves around a kernel of emotional truth: Valmont's passion for Tourvel, unacknowledged until it is too late. The latter, what DeJean calls the "romantic thesis," is the view shared by many readers along with eminent critics such as Laurent Versini and Peter Brooks.[12]

The novel's dizzying indeterminacy is largely the result of the letter form. In the absence of any narrator or point of view, guided only by letters whose purpose is explicitly to mislead and deceive, the reader can never be certain, notwithstanding all clues, that Valmont is really in love with Tourvel, or that Merteuil is really jealous of that love. When the novel is adapted to a stage or screen medium, however, its epistolary dimension is all but lost, and at least in the instances we will examine here, the romantic thesis becomes the key to the story's meaning. As adapted, intelligently and tastefully, to the stage by Hampton, and then to screen by Hampton and Frears, *Dangerous Liaisons* became a tale invested with much clearer moral and historical meanings. The Hampton and Hampton and Frears versions of Laclos also gave Euro-American audiences a parable that spoke to many of the central concerns of the social elites in the economically and ideologically volatile 1980s.

Hampton's play, opening in Stratford-upon-Avon, England, in September 1985 to a chorus of critical praise, took advantage of the novel's essential spareness. (Some of the visual paring-down was accidental, Hampton having been denied access to the Barbican to make way for a lavish staging of what he referred to sarcastically as "some other French thing": *Les Misérables*. The theater in Stratford—the Other Place—allowed for no scene changes.[13]) Hampton's greatest triumph, as critics on both sides of the Atlantic noted, was his play's verbal brilliance; he retained much of the novel's epigrammatic wit, while subtly updating it for the twentieth century. Epistolarity in general is well suited to dramatic adaptation, since it offers the characters' voices at length, unbroken by authorial intrusion.[14] As reviewers noted, Hampton had the good sense to avoid creating an explicit imitation of eighteenth-century speech (no embarrassing "Egad!"s or "Zounds!"s here), choosing instead to have the characters speak a language that is formal and witty without sounding archaic.[15]

Just as Laclos wrote his novel as a pastiche of the moralists and dramatists he knew well, Hampton devised his own dialogue as pastiche of Laclos. For instance, the play echoes Laclos's abundant recourse to aphorisms, and while many are lifted directly from the novel ("[W]hen one woman strikes at the heart of another, she seldom misses; and the wound is invariably fatal"[16]), others are invented ("[I]t's always the best swimmers who drown"[17]). Hampton occasionally has a good time devising swashbuckling ancien régime-isms, as when the dying Valmont says to Danceny: "[I]n this affair, both of us are her creatures."[18] His occasional recourse to twentieth-century psychobabble is no doubt legitimate if this is a pastiche, but it still sounds jarring to historicist ears. When Valmont asks Merteuil why men always chase the women who resist them, she comes back at him with a twentieth-century cliche: "Immaturity?"; elsewhere she speaks of their being able "to trust each other implicitly," using an adverb that is surely redundant in a culture based on the implicit.[19] In the end, though, Hampton's triple translation of Laclos (French to English, page to stage, eighteen to twentieth century) has to be admired. Who else would have rendered the novel's crucial phrase *"Ce n'est pas de ma faute"* as "It's beyond my control," thus avoiding the English "It's not my fault," which sounds much too guiltily defensive, while cleverly signaling to a modern audience the story's central issue of "control."

In the context of a different medium, the novel's epistolarity can be a downright hindrance. Hampton was, for instance, understandably reluctant to give up one of the novel's bravura pieces, the famous letter 81 in which Merteuil describes her self-education as a hypocrite and predator. Wishing to respect the letter's length and importance, however, Hampton has Valmont awkwardly prompt the Marquise like a seminar leader: "I often wonder how you managed to invent yourself" . . . "Yes; but what I asked you was how" . . . "Describe them" . . . "These principles are infallible, are they?"[20] Other transpositions of the letter dimension are more successful. Where in the novel much of the tension, and indeed of the comedy, comes from the juxtaposition of letters by the same character in two totally different voices (typically, a deceitfully "sincere" one and a candidly cynical one), Hampton is able to reproduce this by a combination of dialogue and stage direction. In the first scene, we are introduced to Merteuil in company, and then see her for the first time alone with Valmont. When her guests leave, her worldly politeness ("I approve of your aunt. She takes such an intelligent interest in the young") melts away and she asks, *"in quite a different tone,* 'Your aunt?'"[21]

Letters survive in the play inasmuch as they serve a central function in a plot that exploits voyeurism and moves forward through the regular exposure of characters (Valmont still gets his hands on Madame de Volanges' letters to

Tourvel, Madame de Volanges still discovers her daughter's letters to Danceny). But instead of responding on paper to information conveyed on paper, the characters now have to react on the spot to what they are "told," and the playwright has to, or in this instance chooses to, make that response legible.

Hampton presumably could have preserved the novel's ambiguity as to its social and moral message, but he chose not to. Where Laclos's text remains hermetic to the end, the playwright opted to impose a reading, framing the story as both melodrama and historical drama. Hampton's *Dangerous Liaisons* qualifies as melodrama in that it culminates, in the end, in the revelation of a concealed truth, and a sentimental one at that. Not that this comes as a total surprise to the viewer. The hidden truth of the story has already been telegraphed to the audience in a few somewhat clumsy exchanges, such as this one, in the first scene:

> VALMONT: Take care, now, you're speaking of the woman I . . .
> MERTEUIL: Yes?
> VALMONT: I've set my heart on.

Hampton nonetheless stages the revelation carefully, building up to Merteuil's pronouncement at the play's climax: "You loved that woman, Vicomte. What's more you still do. Quite desperately."[22]

It is true that Merteuil writes almost exactly the same words to Valmont at the end of Laclos's novel[23]; and Hampton's reading, which assumes that Valmont's authentic love for Tourvel is tragically thwarted by his own vanity and Merteuil's hold on him, has probably always been the most popular understanding of the story. Hampton leaves absolutely no doubt in the audience's mind, after the Marquise's words follows the stage direction: "*Valmont is very shaken. He's forced to make a great effort before he can resume, his voice a touch ragged with strain.*"[24] The duel scene that immediately follows includes Valmont's dying request to Danceny to go to Tourvel and "[t]ell her her love was the only real happiness I've known."[25]

The novel, on the other hand, includes no such scene. All we are told, by the minor character who describes the duel, is that Valmont behaved like a gentleman and that he entrusted some papers to Danceny, presumably the letters that are used later to discredit Merteuil (letter 163). After Merteuil's taunt, Valmont does not attempt to write to Tourvel, and the novel ends on a flurry of questions about what really happened, as Volanges and Rosemonde trade gossip and speculation. Laclos dangles the possibility that true love might be the key to the story, then carefully covers his traces. Hampton, conversely, fully embraces a melodramatic narrative in which love is tragically apprehended only when it is too late. Merteuil's "You loved that woman" takes on the familiar gasp-inducing function of Scarlett O'Hara's belated realization that she does love Rhett Butler, or Max de Winter's dramatic avowal to his second wife that he didn't love Rebecca.

Reviewers still worried, at least in the United States, that the play lacked redemptive meaning, that it showed refined nastiness for its own sake—a criticism that has also dogged Laclos's novel since its publication. The *Wall Street Journal* (May 6, 1987) portentously asked: "Are the duplicity, the perverseness, the cruel degradation of the innocent by the main characters to be condemned or reveled in? 'Les Liaisons' avoids a clear answer" (8).[26] But Hampton also supplied his play with a meaning that the novel could not have had: To his cautionary melodrama of love destroyed by vanity, he adds an element of historical retribution.

Here again Hampton must be admired for his restraint and subtlety. His historical reading of the story is conveyed mostly by the way in which he changes its ending. In the novel Merteuil is exposed and suffers multiple punishments: She is publicly humiliated at the opera; catches smallpox, which disfigures her; and is ruined by the loss of her lawsuit. In the play, Valmont does not expose her before dying, and the last scene shows her playing cards with Volanges and Rosemonde, still securely entrenched in her world (a card game also opens the play). The drama ends with her words: "I suggest our best course is to go on with the game." It is a shame that the stage direction also has the shadow of the guillotine flash across the back wall at this point (a ham-fisted touch the different productions I saw fortunately omitted) because Merteuil's survival is eloquent enough on its own. By allowing Merteuil and "the game" to go on, Hampton suggests that this is a world that fails to learn from its mistakes or deal with its moral shortcomings; no wonder it was headed for the abyss.

Hampton succumbed in the end (quite literally) to the convention whereby "any representation of the lives of the French aristocracy in the 1780s should be viewed through a guillotine-shaped frame."[27] Reviewers of the play on both sides of the Atlantic eagerly seized upon this tradition, producing in the process some of their purplest and most cliche-ridden prose. For the *Daily News* (New York) this was a "study of an increasingly depraved and inventive upper-class society soon to be swept aside by the French rabble." *USA Today* described the play as the two libertines' "personal Armageddon on the brink of the entire aristocracy's destruction." Even in England papers such as the *Daily Telegraph* produced the phrase "putrescent pre-revolutionary France," while the *Times* (London) was mercifully more blunt: "a privileged society shortly due for the chop."[28]

It never seems to make a difference that historians have been pointing out for decades that the vast majority of the French aristocracy were not at all depraved, that the guillotine claimed far more plebeian victims than noble ones, or even more obviously that "the entire aristocracy's destruction" makes their return in 1815 very puzzling.[29] The force of the Dickensian myth is irresistible, and Hampton, for all his deftness, succumbed to it: His version does away with Laclos's indeterminacy, anchoring the story between the twin pillars of tragic love and historical armageddon. Injecting postrevolutionary hindsight makes the story a lot more morally comfortable, since the misdeeds of this population will be soon punished by the forces of history.[30]

In rewriting *Les Liaisons Dangereuses*, Hampton delivered a product perfectly suited to the high end of the 1980s entertainment market, which was beginning to be receptive to a certain "postmodern" style. In the 1980s, film directors such as Jean-Jacques Beneix in France, Jonathan Demme in the United States, and Pedro Almodovar in Spain offered sophisticated urban audiences movies in which brightly colored retro charm (spike heels, red lipstick) and knowing wit were wrapped around an ultimately sentimental core. (Such films adopted the commercial trappings of postmodernism while generally shying away from its most disturbing nihilistic implications.) That *Les Liaisons* offered a similar package of sensuality, irony, and sentiment, to a roughly similar audience, must in part account for its success, and for its rapid metamorphosis into movie form.

Much of what I have presented of the play can be said of the movie *Dangerous Liaisons*, which opened late in 1988. Director Frears worked closely with Hampton, who adapted his own play as the script with rather few changes (Frears and Hampton were both older baby boomers, then in their forties, and Oxbridge graduates). The shift in medium made for some obvious differences, especially after the decision was made to shoot on location rather than in a studio. The movie featured sumptuous shots of French chateaus, scenes set in formal gardens, and a few episodes merely described in the play, such as visits to the opera and a famous incident involving a peasant family. Where the play opted for a stylized representation of eighteenth-century trappings with monochromatic white-and-cream colored costumes and sets and a few symbolic items of furniture (a highboy, a chaise longue, a screen), the movie follows the conventions of its own genre in going for a more naturalistic reproduction of historical costumes and interiors.

Although it is common for intellectuals to denigrate Merchant-Ivory trappings of this sort, it seems churlish to deny the film medium its quintessential strength: the providing of sensual experiences. *Dangerous Liaisons* does this in abundance: from the Jean-Honoré Fragonard–inspired visuals[31] (shot by Philippe Rousselot) to the casting of gorgeous actors such as Michelle Pfeiffer and Keanu Reeves to the period music on original instruments under the baton of Neville Marriner. All of these are far from irrelevant to the way in which the story is retold. A crucial turning point in the movie is an added scene: a concert at Madame de Rosemonde's chateau.[32] Merteuil, Valmont, and Tourvel survey and react to one another wordlessly while a countertenor sings a heartbreakingly beautiful Handel aria and the camera circles around them; Tourvel's body language suggests that this is when she decides to yield to Valmont. In no other medium is such a scene possible. Throughout the movie, the cinematography reinforces the script, with perfectly symmetrical perspectives (rows of servants, mirrored halls) underscoring the verbal decorum, and swirling overhead shots (a coach rushing through the night, a bloody death) signaling the characters' loss of control.

Here again, Frears and Hampton are to be admired for their restraint. The greatest temptation offered by the film medium, in this instance, would surely have been to use it to show a broader social world to reinforce the story's historical meaning. Frears and Hampton did indeed debate whether to include references to the Revolution and shot various scenes to that effect. In the end they decided to dispense with them, reasoning that, "if the film was strong enough it would work in the same subliminal way as the book did, and just indicate a society on the brink of collapse."[33]

The final product works extemely well in this implicit fashion. The scene in which Valmont stages his own "rescue" of a peasant family for the benefit of Madame de Tourvel's spy could have been an excuse to linger on the actual condition of the French peasantry. Instead, Frears re-creates the scene in a very "painterly" manner, pitching the style somewhere between Fragonard and Jean-Baptiste Greuze. Rather than trivialize poverty, however, the decision to aestheticize it transposes to film the damning social commentary of the novel: For Valmont, rural misery exists only as a picturesque backdrop, a contrived setting for his libertine enterprise. Similarly effective is the decision to focus the film very heavily on the protagonists, with only as many extras as strictly necessary—a priest here, a few anonymous footmen there. What is thereby conveyed is the radical isolation and solipsism of this upper class, its refusal to take account of anyone outside its own group.

But what of the film's recasting of the story? Did the screen version mostly reproduce the Hampton play, did it bring the narrative back closer to the original novel, or did it add new dimensions of its own? Hampton considered his screenplay to be a quite different item from his stage play, since he had considerably reworked the sequencing of the scenes, if not the play's actual dialogue. He spoke thoughtfully, in an interview to the *Los Angeles Times* (December 25, 1988, 40), of the difference between the media of novel, film, and theater. In Hampton's view, film and prose fiction share the same "open" possibilities, and he therefore saw it as his task, when rewriting for the screen, to go back to the novel.

Hampton was not very specific, but Graham Holderness, in an analysis of the novel, play, and movie, has developed the point. Unlike the play, he argues, the movie is able to restore to the work some of its epistolary dimension through techniques such as crosscutting. Where the play reduces each episode to a single dimension—if not a single meaning—the film medium, through such techniques as crosscutting, can preserve more of the novel's instability of meaning. He cites as an example the famous scene in which Valmont writes a sentimental love letter to Tourvel on the naked back of the courtesan Emilie: In the play, the episode becomes pure one-dimensional farce, while in the movie the scenes with Emilie are crosscut with scenes of Tourvel reading the letter and weeping over it.[34]

While not disputing the general point that the film medium may be better suited than the stage to the adapting of most novels, I would nonetheless disagree with the view that in this instance the film's reading of the text was more open than that of the play. One feature of the film noted by a number of reviewers was its unusually heavy use of closeups. Portraying a world in which even nominal allies such as Valmont and Merteuil routinely deceive one another, Frears opted to have the actors' faces and bodies reveal the "truth" of the characters feelings at critical moments, even as their words belie those emotions. This is often very well done. When Valmont, in bed with the young Cécile (Uma Thurman's first notable role), tops off a string of sexual gossip about her mother with the revelation that he was once that lady's lover, we get a closeup of the girl's loud hilarity twisting briefly into a grimace of pain.

But Frears's use of closeups, and of his principals' skills in general, like Hampton's play, does impose a definite reading of the story. Take the scene in which Valmont (John Malkovich), having finally bedded Madame de Tourvel, comes to announce his triumph to Merteuil (Glenn Close). The conversation begins with Merteuil looking delighted as she anticipates some good gossip and her ex-lover's expected dismissal of the conquered woman. But Valmont, here as in the novel, goes on to reveal that he felt ecstasy for the first time and had feelings for Tourvel that outlasted the act itself. When Malkovich delivers these lines he is in the background and Close faces the camera in closeup: We see her face fall and her devastation show briefly before she resumes her self-control.

Valmont's passion for Tourvel is even more clearly signaled in the film. In the breakup scene with Tourvel, Malkovich delivers the "It's beyond my control" speech with clenched face, voice, and fists, and is shown staggering after he leaves the room. As I noted, Hampton added a duel scene in which Valmont appears to commit suicide and then delivers a dying declaration of love for Tourvel; lest the point be at all unclear, Frears punctuates Valmont's halfhearted dueling with his flashbacks to lovemaking with Tourvel. The movie's original score further cues the reader to the dynamic on screen. Where the classical score serves mostly for historical color (the opera, the concert at Rosemonde's) or as sprightly accompaniment to comic moments (the beginning of Valmont's early-morning "hunt"), the overall tone of the movie is given by George Fenton's dark, pulsating original music. When Tourvel finally yields to Valmont, the music swells romantically to let us know beyond a doubt that rapturous consensual sex is going on here.

There is no question that an excellent film adaptation such as Frears' can add dimensions to a text that neither page nor stage afford. The duel scene, which crosscuts between Valmont's violent death and Tourvel's being bled by hospital nuns, effectively shows physical mutilation as the inevitable extension of the preceding verbal and emotional cruelty. Where Emilie's back had been used as the locus of a nasty sexual prank, the back of the dying

Tourvel is now the site of painful and useless medical treatments. But the movie, even more than the play, repackages Laclos's text to build its meaning around Malkovich's dying words, which are not that different from Leonardo DiCaprio's at the end of *Titanic*.

Viewers will remember well, of course, that Valmont's death is not the end of the movie because there is another story alongside romantic love, one that belongs more quintessentially to 1980s filmmaking. After Valmont's death, the movie cuts to Merteuil having what can only be called a fit of hysterics, hurling objects to the floor as her maids cower in the distance. There follows a scene borrowed from the novel in which Merteuil bravely appears at the opera and is booed by the audience (as in the novel but unlike in the play, the dying Valmont urged Danceny to make public her self-incriminating letters). The final shot is of Merteuil at home, a lonely and socially ruined woman, shedding tears (presumably of rage and self-pity) as she wipes off her makeup before the mirror.

This is the film's most significant departure from both the novel and the play. Eschewing any kind of overall commentary, the movie ends with the spotlight clearly and exclusively trained on the dangerous woman punished. Hampton, discussing the film, insisted that this ending was chosen serendipitously. Several were shot, but when the rushes came in they revealed in one version "a minute and a quarter of such consummate acting by Glenn Close that any other ending would have been an anti-climax."[35] If this is indeed what happened, Warner Brothers, who distributed the film, must have been relieved. Just two years earlier, in 1987, Close had broken through to stardom in Adrian Lyne's *Fatal Attraction*, which established her not only as a leading actress but also as the decade's icon of the villainous female. It was at the time widely reported that the ending of *Fatal Attraction* had to be reshot after the movie was shown to test audiences in the United States. Originally, Alex, the vindictive harpy, had committed suicide after ruining her married lover; however, because of audience protests that there was not enough "emotional payoff," the ending was rewritten to have her killed by the wronged wife.[36] Using *Fatal Attraction* (titled *Liaison Fatale* in France) as the obvious intertext will allow us to suggest in conclusion some of the meanings Laclos's text took on in the Anglo-American world of the 1980s.

The politics of both Hampton's play and Frears' movie are interestingly ambiguous. Both men, postwar British intellectuals shaped by the 1960s, identified themselves as belonging squarely to the Left. Hampton's view of Laclos's and the novel's politics was clear-cut, not to say simplistic: that Laclos was an Enlightenment liberal and his novel an all-out attack on the aristocracy from a "bourgeois" perspective.[37] (Notwithstanding his support for the early phases of the Revolution, Laclos was a nobleman well connected to the highest court circles, and Madame de Tourvel, whom Hampton identifies as the bourgeois victim in the story, is in fact a member of the high judicial aristocracy.) Lest there be any doubt, Hampton used as an epigraph to his play a 1939 quote by André Malraux: "As before so many products of our time—and not just works of literature—, the reader of *Les Liaisons* might have said: 'It can't go on like this.'" (Hampton, *Les Liaison Dangereuses*, 5)

As for Frears, his political and cultural proclivities were such, in the late 1980s, that a colleague learning of the project was heard to exclaim: "Why is Frears doing the eighteenth century? He *hates* the eighteenth century."[38] After training as an assistant to Karel Reisz and Lindsay Anderson in the 1960s, Frears had worked for two decades in television before breaking through as a feature film director in the 1980s. Filmgoers in that decade remember him as the director of movies that damned the British social and cultural establishment from the perspective of racial and sexual minorities: *My Beautiful Laundrette* (1985), *Prick Up Your Ears* (1987), and *Sammy and Rosie Get Laid* (1987). (The move to *Dangerous Liaisons* is less surprising in light of what these earlier films reveal of Frears' fascination with both sexual intrigue and narrative symmetries.) In the glare of publicity generated by the Oscar-nominated *Dangerous Liaisons*, Frears made it a point to reiterate his hostility to the Thatcher government, and to Thatcher herself.[39] He even commented to *Le Monde* (December 21, 1988, 18) (revealing in the process his own elitism) that Margaret Thatcher would have made an excellent Merteuil if she had any of the Marquise's brains and class.

This last comment may help us understand how it came about that two self-defined members of the intellectual Left produced a movie that fed into 1980s antifeminism. Hampton was fully aware of Laclos's reputation as a protofeminist (Laclos wrote a progressive treatise on women's education), and in both play and film he showcased the famous letter 81 and Merteuil's statement, drawn from the original, "I was born to dominate your sex and avenge my own."[40] Yet Frears and Hampton accepted the casting of Glenn Close with all that it implied at the time, and chose an ending that exclusively focused on Merteuil/Close's humiliation as the final outcome of the story. This can only have been because the powerful, perfectly coifed, steely eyed, and rather humorless Merteuil they created in Close was a stand-in for Margaret Thatcher.

How unaware could Hampton and Frears have been of the intertextual resonances of having Close in the lead role? The director of *Fatal Attraction*—Adrian Lyne—is also British and of the same generation as Hampton and Frears. Reading *Fatal Attraction* as a forerunner to *Dangerous Liaisons* is not much of a stretch. There are sharp differences, to be sure, between the psychotic single woman Close portrayed in the first film—a weak and self-destructive character—and the strong, supremely controlled Merteuil. Yet Merteuil's final tears make her look as pathetically lonely as Alex waiting by the phone for her married lover to call. Both movies are set in a moneyed upper class and both play out a triangle of an evil independent woman, weak man, and a sexy but conventionally virtuous woman. Both plots revolve around the danger of sex, although *Liaisons* is unusual in that the hero's destruction results from his having slept with the virtuous woman.

Both Close's presence in the film version of Laclos's novel and the movie's ending transformed the story's sexual politics from ambiguous to retrograde. In the novel, after a declaration of war and a bravado visit to the opera, the Marquise escapes abroad, severely damaged but not necessarily vanquished; in the movie, we see her hysterical and then defeated. Whether or not as a result of pressure from their Hollywood backers, Frears and Hampton fell in line with the 1980s antifeminism exhaustively documented in Susan Faludi's *Backlash*.[41] Even though the movie's (and play's) overall cultural commentary on issues of class and wealth is no clearer than its sexual politics, one can safely surmise that it partook of the fascination with wealth, glamour, and their attendant evils that was rampant in the decade of Donald Trump and Leona Helmsley. Hampton told ruefully of taking his ten- and eight-year-old daughters to see the play, asking them at the end whether there was anything that shocked them. "Daddy, don't be silly," one of them replied, "we watch 'Dynasty' every week."[42] The *Daily News* (New York) reviewer wrote of the play that the characters showed a cynicism and ambition that modern viewers would find recognizable: "Their careers are in 'love' rather than business, but the same ruthlessness seems to apply."[43] Reviewers picked up on the modern class implications of Bob Crowley's ostentatiously "tasteful" monochromatic sets and costumes. The point was presumably not lost on the *Wall Street Journal*'s designer-happy readership: "The color scheme is off-white to suggest understated wealth and elegance."[44] (In *Fatal Attraction*, Alex Forrest's trendy downtown loft apartment is decorated in shades of white.)

Not all re-creations of the Age of Enlightenment were as understated as Crowley's sets or as restrained as Frears' movie. In fact, as Debora Silverman has convincingly argued, the French eighteenth century became one of the central tropes whereby a new aristocracy of money and power in the United States represented itself to the world (others included Imperial China and Ralph Lauren's re-creation of the English country house).[45] The decade opened with a 1981 show at the Metropolitan Museum, titled "The Eighteenth-Century Woman," curated by Diana Vreeland. The prototypical "woman" of this lavish exhibition of costumes was of course not the ordinary Frenchwoman but the high aristocrat, the royal wife or mistress. For these women, Vreeland wrote, the eighteenth century was "a world of promise, optimism and possibility" that "burst like a rose and spent itself lavishly" and was therefore "very close to the way we live today."[46] Behind several such cultural extravaganzas in New York were the connections among a coterie of the very rich and powerful, including women like Vreeland, Nancy Reagan, and Betsy Bloomingdale (the three were close friends): the Merteuils of their own age.

By the end of the decade, in part because of the success of Frears' movie, the eighteenth century remained a significant cultural commodity, but with the fraying of the culture of heartless glamour embodied by the likes of Trump and the Reagans, it took on a more ironic motif. Witty, over-the-top young fashion designers such as Vivienne Westwood, Christian Lacroix, and Gianni Versace decorated their stagy outfits with snippets of Fragonard paintings. Madonna performed her hit song "Vogue" for the 1990 MTV awards as "eighteenth-century Vogue," wearing a copy of one of Michelle Pfeiffer's costumes for the film.[47] The eighteenth century's brief resurrection was coming to an end.

Frears and Hampton's stance toward the world of rich, clever, and profligate characters portrayed by Laclos could only be as ambiguous as Laclos's own attitudes toward his libertine creations. Through the Vicomte de Valmont and the Marquise de Merteuil, men from the aging generation of the sexual revolution cast a last nostalgic glance at their own fading prowess, using Madame de Merteuil as the scapegoat: "*Ce n'est pas de ma faute.*" It could not go on like this, and it did not, though twentieth-century libertinism was felled not by social revolution but by the threat of AIDS and the lure of domesticity. Rewriting *Les Liaisons dangereuses* for upscale cultural consumption, Hampton and Frears could not resist a sentimental and antifeminist reading of the story. For all of the intelligence and restraint presiding over it, this decision was ultimately as much of a capitulation as the saccharine images of domestic happiness on which *Fatal Attraction* closes.

Notes

1. Joan DeJean, *Literary Fortifications: Rousseau, Laclos, Sade* (Princeton, NJ: Princeton University Press, 1984), 3–18.

2. Michel Delon, *Pierre-Augustin Choderlos de Laclos:* Les Liaisons Dangereuses (Paris: Presses Universitaires de France, 1986), 66–70.

3. Peter Brooks, *The Novel of Worldliness: Crébillon, Marivaux, Laclos, Stendhal* (Princeton, NJ: Princeton University Press, 1969).

4. Norbert Elias, *La Société de cour*, trans. Pierre Kamnitzer (Paris: Calmann-Levy, 1974).

5. Susan Winnett, *Terrible Sociability: The Text of Manners in Laclos, Goethe, and James* (Stanford, CA: Stanford University Press, 1993), 6.

6. Laurent Versini, *Laclos et la Tradition: Essai sur les sources et la technique des* Liaisons dangereuses (Paris: Klinksieck, 1968), pt. 2, ch. 2, 3.

7. Kathryn Carson, "*Les Liaisons Dangereuses:* On Stage and Film," *Film Literature Quarterly* 24 (1996): 36.

8. Examples include Valmont's appropriation of Madame de Volanges' letters warning Tourvel against him, and more dramatically Madame de Volanges' discovery of Cécile's letters to Danceny. In neither case is the "discovery" accidental.

9. Pierre Ambroise Choderlos de Laclos, *Les Liaisons Dangereuses*, trans. P.W.K. Stone (London: Penguin Books, 1961), letter 105, p. 252.

10. Delon, *Pierie-Augustin Choderlos de Laclas*, 49–51.

11. DeJean, *Literary Fortifications*, intro., ch. 5.

12. Ibid., 214–217. This reading identifies Madame de Tourvel as the novel's only strong and authentic character, and Rousseau as a dominant and positive model for Laclos.

13. Graham Holderness, "Dangerous Les's Liaisons," in *Novel Images: Literature in Performance*, ed. Peter Reynolds (London: Routledge, 1993), 23, pp. 17–33.

14. Ibid., 21–22.

15. See the reviews in the *New York Post*, 1 May 1987; and *New York Newsday*, 1 May 1987; cited in *New York Theatre Critics' Reviews* 48 (1987): 258–259.

16. Laclos, *Les Liaisons Dangereuses*, letter 145; Christopher Hampton, *Les Liaisons Dangereuses* (London: Faber and Faber, 1985), act 2, scene 16, 93.

17. Hampton, *Les Liaisons Dangereuses*, act 2, scene 16, 95.

18. Ibid., act 2, scene 17, 97.

19. Ibid., act 2, scene 10, 70; act 1, scene 1, 16.

20. Ibid., act 1, scene 3, 31–33.

21. Ibid., act 1, scene 1, 11.

22. Ibid., act 2, scene 16, 94.

23. Laclos, *Les Liaisons Dangereuses*, letter 145, p. 340: "Yes Vicomte, you were very much in love with Madame de Tourvel, and you are still in love with her; you love her to distraction."

24. Hampton, *Les Liaisons Dangeureuses*, act 2, scene 16, 94.

25. Ibid., act 2, scene 17, 98.

26. *New York Theatre Critics' Reviews* 48 (1987): 258; See also the review in *Women's Wear Daily* (May 1, 1987): "What is missing from the play is a point of view. One doesn't get a sense of why Hampton is retelling Laclos's tale and what, if any, importance and relevance he thinks it has in the age of AIDS" (260).

27. Holderness, "Dangerous Les's," 24.

28. *Daily News* (New York), 1 May 1987; *USA Today*, 1 May 1987; *New York Theatre Critics' Reviews* 48 (1987): 257, 260; *Times* (London), 26 April 1985, p. 14. The *Daily Telegraph* review is quoted on the back of the Farber and Farber paperback edition of the play.

29. See, for instance, Guy Chaussinand-Nogaret, *La Noblesse au XVIIIe siècle: de la féodalité aux lumières* (Paris: Hachette, 1976); Donald Greer, *The Incidence of Terror during the French Revolution* (Cambridge: Harvard University Press, 1935); or

for a synthesis, see William Doyle, *Origins of the French Revolution* (Oxford: Oxford University Press, 1980), ch. 6.

30. Bill Overton makes this point, as cited by Holderness in "Dangerous Les's," 25.

31. On the Fragonard inspiration, see Stephanie Hull, "*Dangerous Liaisons* from Film to Fashion," *The Spectator* 12 (Spring 1992): 46.

32. See Hampton's discussion of this scene in the interview he gave to the *Los Angeles Times* (December 25, 1988), sec. C, 40.

33. Hampton as cited in Holderness, "Dangerous Les's," 25.

34. Holderness, "Dangerous Les's," 30–31.

35. *Los Angeles Times* (December 25, 1988): 40.

36. Susan Faludi, *Backlash: The Undeclared War against American Women* (New York: Crown Publishers, 1991), 122.

37. Holderness, "Dangerous Les's," 18–21.

38. Kathryn Carson, "*Les Liaisons Dangereuses* On Stage and Film," *Film Literature Quarterly* 24 (1996): 35.

39. See the interview he gave to *Revue du cinéma* 448 (April 1989): 75–78.

40. Holderness, "Dangerous Les's," 20; Hampton, *Les Liaisons Dangereuses*, act 1, scene 4, 32.

41. See note 36.

42. *Newsweek* (May 11, 1987): *New York Theatre Critics' Reviews* 48 (1987): 261.

43. *Daily News* (New York, May 1, 1987): *New York Theatre Critics' Reviews* 48 (1987): 257.

44. *Wall Street Journal* (May 6, 1987): *New York Theatre Critics' Reviews* 48 (1987): 257.

45. Debora Silverman, *Selling Culture: Bloomingdale's, Diana Vreeland and the New Aristocracy of Taste in Reagan's America* (New York: Pantheon Books, 1986).

46. Ibid., 57.

47. Hull, "*Dangerous Liaisons* from Film to Fashion," 46–47.

6

Placing Jane Austen, Displacing England

Touring between Book, History, and Nation

Mike Crang

In this chapter I want to think through the popularity of Jane Austen by linking her work to two sets of places. The first is the imagined geographies produced through the text, or perhaps more accurately through its reading, which speak of a vanished English society. The second is the present geographies of tourists who visit Austen-themed locations in contemporary England. The juxtaposition of these imagined cartographies raises three issues that this chapter tries to unpack: first, a nostalgic geography of a lost English society that has a specific appeal and specific political implications; second, the effect of this imagined landscape on the reshaping and marketing of the current landscape as a tourist product; third, the need to then interpret that tourism as part of a disseminated practice of reading—where the action of reading is to connect disparate worlds from the text to home, to tourism, and so forth. To coin a phrase, this chapter discusses the worldliness of the text and the textuality of the world. It considers the geo-graphy of reading Austen as literally writing the world. I want though to suggest that doing so reframes both the conception of the world used in tourism and of writing in literary studies.

I am less concerned with interpreting Austen's works than with engaging in what we might call "reading at a distance." That is, I am more interested in what others actively make of her writings than in the writings themselves.[1] It is not a matter of assessing how well Austen depicts a place, nor how accurately her fictive places are mapped onto supposed inspirational sites, nor for that matter of how well readers and visitors can recall and understand her work. It is not about the accuracy of any of these representations. Rather, it is about interpreting reading and visiting as doing, as shaping real and imagined landscapes—creating what J. Hillis Miller has called "atopical space," or as James Donald glosses that space which is "less the already existing setting for such stories, than the production of space through that taking place, through the act of narration."[2] The production of space in this manner involves two issues: First, it avoids creating an assumed reading in which the interpretations and actions of readers are drawn from immanent patterns in the text; second, it means that judgments about what is "authentic" do not stand above the practices of reading but are part of the currency within them. What it focuses on is how Austen's work is appropriated and circulated to produce senses of "hereness," which inscribe identities into places. To illustrate this, I begin with critiques of "Austenmania" as part of a "heritage industry" in the United Kingdom, that suggest her work is used to sustain a reactionary and deeply conservative vision of Englishness. I then examine literary tourism as a practice by which key texts are mapped onto what becomes or is transformed into a mythical landscape. However, I suggest we move from metaphors of textualized landscapes to ideas of reading practices that open up a pluralized version of the geographies created. I thus try to suggest a disseminated landscape comprising different, multiple places and times of reading and multiple stories told by the linking between times and places.

Think of England

From the 1980s in Britain there has been an expansive celebration of the national past and a growing intellectual critique of that celebration. This seemed to be occurring at a range of levels, from official political discourse to a plethora of new museums to a burgeoning tourist industry to local history societies to period costume dramas on screens big and small to conservation districts in towns and villages. Critical accounts looked at this and, invoking the Frankfurt School, heralded the birth of a heritage industry. The promotion and manipulation of the past was argued to provide a compensatory nostalgia for a time when Britain was "Great," in, for instance, the rash of films adapting classic imperial fiction.[3] Critics pointed out that part of this was the recovery of a "traditional England" in the face of a multicultural Britain, an Englishness that invoked history to both cloak and set a purported Anglo-Saxon ethnicity against other Celtic, Asian, and African Britons.[4]

One of the most cogent criticisms located a "cult of the country house" as creating a symbolic heartland for this nostalgic English nationalism.[5] The country house was a favored symbol for conservative commentators who could use it to stand for a stable, hierarchically ordered society that symbolized the "English character." In the country house, the Right promoted a set of "virtues" as intrinsically English and associated them with a period of national "success." Various analyses indicated the symbolic centrality of the country house, which forms a disproportionate amount of preserved (and subsidised) landscape,[6] archetypically located in a rural lowland landscape. This lowland idyll has long been used to suggest a controlled, and we might say domesticated, country, which was well ordered and carefully managed—in sharp contrast to upland British landscapes, which tend to suggest wildness and uncontrolled emotion.[7] In terms of landscapes typically associated with certain authors, the southern county of Hampshire (where Austen's home of Chawton is located, although none of the main sites of her novels are explicitly based in that county[8]) and the country house geography have become linked with Austen.

Austen calls forth a specific type of landscape that in turn authorises a particular version of English history. Country-house landscapes support an essentialized English identity through a static, enclosed sense of the past, in terms of both geography and history. In terms of geography, it is an enclosed English landscape that is divorced from contemporaneous imperial dominions. It takes the shrunken little England of the present and projects it back to find an essence in rural, elite society. But at that time England was inextricably bound up with wider imperial processes. Most famously, Edward Said has pointed to the exclusions in *Mansfield Park* in which oblique references to plantations point to a hidden history of England.[9] In Derridean terms this is the constitutively excluded outside that allows the textual creation of polite society and that forms strategic silences and absences through the novel.[10] The extent to which this polite society was dependent on plantations for its income was often empirically small,[11] but that is hardly the point. What is of concern is how this sense of a discrete and self-contained world offers a discrete and self-contained England for contemporary political appropriation.

Let me illustrate the political stakes by thinking through two moments centered on Caribbean sugar plantations. First, let us turn to contemporaneous campaigns over the abolition of slavery. In one of the earliest consumer boycott campaigns, abolitionists urged the British public not to use Caribbean sugar. The terms of this argument linked themes of domesticity and femininity, mobilising fears of morally and literally contaminating the body politic and the bodies of female consumers with the blood and sweat of black slaves working on sugar plantations. It drew its rhetorical force from the linking of female bodies and the national body-politic, both being contaminated by soiled produce.[12] Let us jump ahead now to contemporary multicultural England. When we look at Asian and Black British groups, we find they are written out of "our island story" (as former Prime Minister Margaret Thatcher called it), which reads current national space back into the past. A ruefully mirthful Stuart Hall perhaps best expressed this when he spoke of his arrival from the Caribbean:

> [P]eople like me who came to England in the 1950s have been there for centuries; symbolically, we have been there for centuries. I was coming home. I am the sugar at the bottom of the English cup of tea. I am the sweet tooth, the sugar plantations that rotted generations of English children's teeth. There are thousands of others besides me that are you know the cup of tea itself. Because they don't grow it in Lancashire you know. Not a single tea plantation exists within the United Kingdom. This is the symbolisation of English identity—I mean what does anybody know about an English person except that they can't get through the day without a cup of tea? Where does it come from? Ceylon—Sri Lanka, India. That is the outside history that is the inside history of the English. There is no English history without that history.[13]

Austen, through the landscape and enclosed society drawn from her novels, has been appropriated by discourses that support this insular notion of English identity. Her works bring to life a particular form of society, in Austen's famous phrase: "Three or four families in a country village is the very thing to work on." Not only is this, thus, a spatially contained world, but a world socially focused around the institutions of country-house life. Most readings, for instance, see this point expressed in the opposition of stability and politeness at Mansfield Park to the rowdy, turbulent life of Portsmouth.[14] The politics of a celebration of rural stability thus becomes entangled with the modern experience of her work. In temporal terms, the world of the country house forms a timeless past, a static cameo, rather than an ongoing historical process.[15] This moment is essentialized as authentically and unchangingly English, a period before the fall into a modern world of mass culture and state regulation. This is not entirely a modern reading since Raymond Williams noted that nineteenth-century literature offers a "receding escalator" of nostalgia in which truly authentic rural society is always located some thirty years before the then writer.[16]

A closer reading of Austen's work suggests a landscape that, far from being an unchanging rural scene, was shifting and developing. So recent commentary has suggested that Austen is using Portsmouth to literalize the hidden reality of Mansfield Park as full of contention and jealousy.[17] Indeed, in terms of rural life Austen charts changing landscape tastes through her main heroines.[18] In *Sense and Sensibility*, she provides an elegant picture of the different moral and aesthetic visions behind picturesque and Rousseauist versions of nature.[19] However, the dominant frame is spatial and social exclusion where country houses reshaped the landscape around them, to both reflect and reinforce the exclusivity of the owners. Indeed, far from being a symbol of rural harmony, they symbolised and materially enacted divisions in rural society:

> The mansion thus lay in the midst of an insulating sea of turf, hidden from view by encircling belts [of trees]. And once established as a sign and symbol of exclusivity, the patterns of social contact which the park engendered could only serve to perpetuate the emerging divisions in rural society.[20]

The rather enclosed world of Austen reflected power relations that enabled the wealthy to physically and socially distance themselves from the rural poor. That said, it should also be noted that her works, in gender terms, are often marked by leaving home and a more itinerant role for leading female characters that suggests a certain instability.[21] It is also true that, punctuated by departures and absences associated with naval duties, something Austen knew from her own family life, novels such as *Persuasion* and the unfinished *Sanditon* situate her apparently isolated estates rather more critically in the theater of imperial geopolitics.[22]

My concern though is not how a fixed geography of class, gender, and empire may be reflected or destabilized in her texts themselves, but how these geographies are interpreted in the twentieth century. Indeed, critiques of imperial connections in *Mansfield Park* are now incorporated into film versions, such as Patricia Rozema's in 1999, with abolitionist sentiments ventriloquized into characters—much to the horror of purists such as Edward Mullan, who decries "film-makers and literary critics . . . [who are] in cahoots. The film of *Mansfield Park* is full of references to slavery. Fanny Price even discovers a sketchbook of horrors perpetrated by Sir Thomas Bertram on the slaves who work his Antiguan plantations. These clearly echo the way the novel has been 'reinterpreted' by critical postcolonialist academics such as Edward Said."[23] So also the National Maritime Museum of London uses "a Jane Austen-like figure sipping tea, with a sugar bowl on the table. On the floor below her, a black hand stretches in supplication through the hatch of the slave ship," drawing upon Austen's father's slave connections and the known issue in *Mansfield Park* to try to explicitly open up British history.[24] What is notable is that it still seems that the conjunction of a canonical woman writer (and both terms seem important) with empire can be used for shock effect. Susan Fraiman argues that this effect of "[the] yoking of gentle Jane to sex and slavery"[25] animates Said's choice of targets, and it certainly provoked such a row in the National Maritime Museum that the exhibit has since been replaced by an exhibition of the carved wooden figures from the bows of ships, emphasizing the banning of slavery in 1807.[26] It is how Austen gets appropriated and fixed in the current landscape that I want to turn to now.

Locating Pemberley

Although Austen does not set any major scenes in Hampshire, using for instance her brother's manor but transposing it elsewhere, it is clear that her work is informed by that landscape. Her books are not though regional novels—say like Thomas Hardy's are. That Hardy provides a fairly direct transliteration of Dorset and its surroundings into his Wessex is clear.[27] However, literary Wessex cannot be judged on how closely it corresponds to "real" Dorset. The relationship of fictive and real landscape is complex[28] but the model of mapping literature onto landscape (or vice versa) has proved enormously appealing to the tourist industry, to such an extent that most of England is now carved up into different literary zones—until in 1988 the British Tourist Authority produced a literal map of "literary England."[29] "Literary Hampshire" focuses on Austen (with walk-on parts for Gilbert White and Charles Dickens, and notwithstanding the absence of novel settings in the county); Haworth is the center of Brontë Country; Stratford-upon-Avon is Shakespeare Country; North Devon is Lorna Doone Country; and so on. As the last begins to suggest, it is not just the classic canon because we have Herriot Country in Yorkshire through to South Tyneside and Cleveland boasting Catherine Cookson Country. Mundane and otherwise unremarkable scenery is invested with significance (and revenue-generating potential) by the magic of literary association.[30] Tourism is thus, as George Hughes argues, "a spatially differentiating activity which has the potential to realize different 'geographies' in a semiological way."[31] Of course, associations are often not clear-cut, since various sites are over-coded by multiple associations—thus the Cobb at Lyme Regis is both a place of Austen pilgrimage and the setting for the final scene in the film of the *French Lieutenant's Woman*. The British Tourist Authority currently runs promotions listing settings for various films. The cycle of movies, video releases, and TV reruns (and international syndications) means that, even aside from classic novels, the effect of screen adaptations is marked and long-running.[32]

The relations of fictive and real are complicated even by Austen's style, which rarely used direct references to existing places. So if we take Pemberley (*Pride and Prejudice*), it "is a fictitious literary landscape created in the same way that Gilpin said he composed his picturesque landscape; ideas are taken from the general face of the country not from any particular scene. . . . [T]he Pemberley chapters had almost certainly been written based on her concentrated reading of Gilpin."[33] Austen thus based a fictional place on a textual composite made by a writer who himself developed amalgams of key places. Austen also studied Humphrey Repton's "Red Books" for planned improvements, as well as his actual work at Stoneleigh, alongside William Gilpin's writing. It is not merely then that her landscapes are open to multiple interpretations, but that they are themselves compound forms in which text and landscape are not distinct categories. The landscape itself was a vehicle for expressing a range of ideologies of ownership, improvement, modernity, and, not least, sensibility.[34] Moreover landscaping had changing fashions as people emulated other places.

The way Austen is linked to places reminds me of Jacques Derrida's analysis of James Joyce—where he speaks of traversing the haunted work of the text, where the authorizing signature is permanently displaced.[35] Derrida suggests that disseminating the work, and reciting it, in the name of the original, inevitably buries and displaces that original. Perhaps a resonant example is in the marketing of "Proust's Normandy"; indeed, that proprietorial naming of it can be found on a 1930s tourist map, where "Proust's identification with Illiers is important today not because it has made it possible to create a local shrine to the writer but because it encourages a convenient, idealized identification of reality with fiction, which always makes for easier reading."[36] For Austen we have not merely fictive landscapes founded on theoretical landscapes but films and series that then seek approximations to those landscapes—looking for sites that offer both the right scene setting and resonances. A number of times the original site (if it is known) is not suitable, so a new site is introduced. Of course this site has its own history that is thus drawn into the story. So, for instance, Pemberley is widely regarded as inspired by Chatsworth—though Cottesbrooke Hall and the grounds, but not the building (Ilham House), also have their supporters. However, its most recent filmsetting is Lyme Park, but with Sudbury Hall being used for interiors. Thus, putting Austen on the map is not a simple task.

However, that is exactly what a growing form of tourism endeavors to do. Faced with overseas competition and changing tastes, the English tourist industry has turned to specialist tourism as a means of selling places. In a world in which people are increasingly mobile, distinguishing each locality becomes evermore important. Alongside this goes the popularization of high culture, what Scott Lash calls the structural de-differentiation of mass and high-culture distinctions.[37] It is in this moment that literary tourism can grow as a form of specialist tourism: touring sacred sites of secular saints in a modern-day reverential ritual that shares features of pilgrimage. Indeed, discussing this with a friend, she produced the self-description of "a Jane Austen Pilgrimage to Bath" at the age of seventeen. We may, for instance, look at the relationship of texts and itineraries as conforming to that most venerable of spatial narratives: the lives of the saints.[38] In classic terms this involved tracing the sites of events derived from the text onto the terrain of a saint's life. Jane Austen tours likewise comprise visits to and the reading of scenes from novels in particular locations. As a practice it echoes narration, as each individual site becomes part of a larger itinerary binding them together in a spatial story, with an almost Aristotelian structure of beginning, middle, and end.[39]

Here I want to pick up on the spatial stories this process suggests. The Hampshire tourist department, for which Austen serves as a lure for getting people to spend time in Hampshire, advertises that "Exploring 'Literary Hampshire' is one of the most pleasant ways to discover our traditional English countryside, romantic stately homes, historic cities, bustling market towns, picturesque villages and delightful coastline."[40] This description not only draws on intertextual connotations (stately homes are always romantic, the countryside is always traditional), but it also "bundles" attractions together. So one of the "sites" of literary Hampshire is the New Forest— whose association with Austen goes as far as the occasional boat trip— while, of course, the cafe in Chawton is called "Cassandra's cup."

Meanwhile, the literature on tourism highlights a quest for authenticity[41]— one in which the spatial story marks out and stages what is to be treated as authentic. Tourism is seen as a semiotic system that writes significance onto the landscape through markers, often quite literally signs. So sites that would be unnoticed are brought to notice by being marked out: by plaques, guidebooks, and so forth. In an effect familiar from structuralist interpretation, then, the signifier has only a conventional or arbitrary relationship to any "reality." In literary tours this implies that defining the markers of sites thus shapes what is experienced very strongly. In this reading, the content of sites becomes hollowed out and mapped in terms of empty difference: "The marker itself can become a sight, and the sight is inevitably seen as a marked site, one which, like the Saussurian sign, exists only because it is different from any other."[42] This is the transformation of a *site* into a tourist *sight*, something to be seen, witnessed, and possibly recorded on film.[43] In other words, although tourism seems to be looking for evidence in the landscape, it is shaped by markers and invisible elements. Thus, brochures point to the Austen house in Castle Square in Southampton, which no longer exists. We are guided to its location next to the city walls, which also no longer exist, and we see the contemporary "Castle Inn." And at Steventon only a historically doubtful, and hardly inherently distinctive, pump is left of the rectory. The interpretative landscape depends crucially on invisible markers. As Barbara Kirshenblatt-Gimblett suggests, "Increasingly we travel to actual destinations to experience virtual places. This is one of several principles that free tourism to invent an infinitude of new products."[44]

The combination of visible and invisible landscapes is mediated through a range of texts and objects. Thus, "Regency Bath" plays up its Austen associations (and downplays her unhappiness there). Regency Bath is itself, of course, impossible to visit,[45] but the tour through contemporary Bath takes each street and accompanies it with a more or less specific and authorizing quote from one of the novels. From the injunction "to discover the Bath of Jane Austen, walk! Just as Jane did," we are led to retrace Isabella Thorpe's shopping itinerary in Milsom Street (from *Northanger Abbey*) or to find Mrs. Croft's drawing room in Gay Street (from *Persuasion*). The National Trust "Pemberley Trail" at Lyme Park restages scenes of the film—making the location of Austen's fictional site more solid.

So far I have suggested that we have textual universes created through the books for readers—imagined and depicted places of Regency life that are fictional, to state the obvious—overlain on "real" sites—though these may be the filmed settings of later screen adaptations or the half-erased traces of the author's life. Tourist sites connect these as signifiers and signifieds. And around this we have the intertextual associations that both reinforce this pattern—genres of literature and period drama—and pluralize it as sights become over-coded with multiple and indeterminate literary references. However, to persuade someone to actually visit somewhere, the experience of being there has to be important. Something has to be offered there, not elsewhere. So Kirshenblatt-Gimblett goes on to note that it is not the real-world site that authenticates fiction but the other way around: "The production of hereness in the absence of actualities depends increasingly on virtualities."[46] So if we look at a travel diary entry of Lauryl Lane, on a tour of Bath, she writes, "The Assembly Rooms were really neat. I felt pretty proud of myself—recognized exactly where Anne Elliot/Captain Wentworth/Lady Dalrymple scene was filmed from *Persuasion*. Could just imagine how wonderful it would be to try to have another REAL ball there."[47] Not only signs but also prior knowledge and anticipation produce an expected landscape, and visitors often come prepared to see, to have knowledge confirmed rather than changed.[48]

However, the actual place does play a role in authenticating tourist knowledge in an accumulatory economy in which sites are "done" and "ticked off." Indeed, part of the exchange among groups of readers involves lists of places to visit and debates over their "authenticity." But, rather more, the practices at these sites create a range of numismatic rituals in which objects suggest a connection to an imagined place. So, at Sudbury Hall one of the attractions is a gallery of costumes worn in the film *Pride and Prejudice*. Meanwhile, at other "Austen sites" there are explicitly encoded souvenirs on sale, from badges and guidebooks to postcards and tea towels, alongside generic products made special solely because they were acquired while at that site.

Purchasing an object may be a vital part of the "successful" visit, as it will allow the site to be enjoyed in later times and other places—and authenticate the visit to other audiences. Some souvenirs, then, seem striking in this context; for example, Chawton offers Austen paperbacks for sale when the majority of visitors have already read them. Possibly these are intended to introduce the novels to those who have come after having viewed Austen films because alongside them are both BBC (1997) and Gwyneth Paltrow (1996) versions of *Emma*. In part these objects are meant to provide a wide range of "Austen" products to an interested audience, but Chawton imbues them all with material links to the author. Passing through the house, a visitor reaches beyond the ropes to touch the desk on which Austen wrote. Although they know it is forbidden to touch the desk, and knowing why too much contact could damage the artifact, nevertheless the compulsion to physically touch, to make contact, comes through. As well, forbidden photographs are taken when custodial eyes are turned elsewhere.

This sense of contact, then, comes through original artifacts, such as Austen's writing box unveiled at the British Library or the opportunity offered to the tour by the Jane Austen Society of North America to read from and hold original manuscripts, but the magic also extends to replicas and souvenirs, right down to admission tickets or other ephemera that may be kept as souvenirs. These are numinous objects offering contact with other worlds—both that of the authors and the place–time specific to the experience of visiting. The latter is too often missed by academia's "rigorous exclusion of all that may awaken the emotional response of personal association,"[49] and we are reminded that many tourist memories are not "semantic-based" knowledge about places, but episodic memories that are time and context dependent (framed in terms of remembering what the group was doing at a particular point).[50] Too often linguistic analogies lead to a focus on tourists as sightseers, as "all eyes, no bodies (and sometimes no brains)."[51] In the next section, I take a different linguistic approach that highlights performative and active reading practices.

Placing Reading

In the tourist literature there is a large subfield devoted to visitor responses, as managers have become increasingly concerned with what visitors make (or do not make) of their products. A concern with who visits, and why, follows from this. It should also be noted that there has been a growing concern with those who do not visit, and why they do not. Thus, for instance, visitor surveys to museums report favorable reactions, but the sample is selective. Extending research to non-visitors found a negative reaction to museum ambience and displays.[52] Putting it bluntly, museums preach to the converted.

Austen books and heritage are social and cultural artifacts that have specific gendered, ethnic, and class appeals. Surveys of heritage use and nonuse in the United Kingdom show over and again an upper- and middle-class visitor base. The limited data on Chaworth and other Austen sites also suggest that 60 percent of visitors are social class A/B.[53] The implications of this are that we cannot treat Austen's works as floating free of current class understandings and positions—their audience is located within a particular class fragment. To think this through we might usefully draw from the interpretations of reading as a practice and from the notion that that practice varies between different interpretative communities.[54] One helpful starting point has been to see communication in terms of a circuit of culture[55] that moves us from one-way processes to viewing discourse as circulation—and I shall suggest dissemination. Communication in this sense moves from transmission models, which involve a more or less fixed message more or less successfully delivered to waiting receivers,[56] to a model that involves interpretations being made available to a public that then reinterprets them through various of their own ideas and backgrounds. So the experience of places is not fixed but, rather, is open to wider cultural values and varying intertextual sources brought into play by the visitors. It therefore becomes important to trace the social and spatial trajectories that frame different readings.

I do not want to create typologies of people; I prefer, rather, to think about different practices that may be combined in a variety of ways by people.[57] The practices may range from a passing interest, to "cultural tourism" involving visits to places of historic or cultural interest, or to what Robert Stebbins calls "serious leisure"[58]—that is, people who work at their hobby, attending classes and lectures and joining dedicated literary and study tours about Austen, weighing in at a hefty $3,500 or so. Indeed, we might revisit Walter Benjamin's distinction between auratic objects that draw in the involved spectator and modern life dominated by a culture of distraction, in which the spectator indifferently passes by more or less interesting objects. As Meaghan Morris put it, "The past-in-the-present is now a look, not a text" for the casual visitor.[59] Or the very "visibility" of history marked out for the tourist glance—where past times are more "naturally" absences—distinguishes tourist places, an example of what Paul Virilio calls the aesthetics of appearance.[60]

However, rather than opening a debate about the authenticity of sights, I want to think about modes of experience for the audience. Box Hill (*Emma*), for example, is a National Trust property that attracts something over one million visitors per year, of whom very few are on tours doing reading scenes from Austen. Detailed semiological examinations far too often omit this range of practice. Museum studies have indeed come up with a colloquial typology of reading practices—streakers, strollers, and students (in declining order of speed)—to refer to the pace with which people interact with material. So when I have wandered about and made field notes on exhibits, the two things that strike me are that, first, as I linger over labels and ponder their theoretical interpretation, I am likely to be run down by people walking through at a steady pace; and, second, I am one of very few solitary visitors. The experience of touring is basically social. Far from quiet reading in a solitary room, here people discuss, reenact, and indeed play out various moments of film and book. Thus, visitors, a little illicitly, pose against the mantelpiece used at Chatsworth by Mr. Darcy/Colin Firth. Few silently contemplate without a guide, be that someone a member of a family group (perhaps the only one to have read Austen), or a member of a formal tour. In this sense the story is narrated.

I draw on the idea of reading as a literal and figurative practice to suggest that the "identity of the text, as distinct from the work, lies in its destiny not its origins, in the moment of its consumption not of its production."[61] Or as Stanley Fish would suggest, reading involves a notion of text considered as a series of temporal—and here I shall add spatial—operations[62]; that is, to see Austen as being read in a series of encounters linking episodes and places together. Thinking of tourism as a practice like reading that involves traveling, assembling, and interpreting an itinerary of sites highlights three sorts of wanderings through Austen. First, there is the sense of wandering through her texts; second, the travels—real and imagined—between the reader and the text; and, finally, the real and imagined travels around historic sites. In the first sense, Wolfgang Iser's evocative phrase "wandering subjectivity" suggests readers moving through the fictive worlds of the novels—with possible detours and maneuvers through films, "pass notes" adaptations, and so forth. More to the point in this chapter are the second and third wanderings, which locate the experience of Austen in terms of personal, class, gender, and national trajectories.[63]

Let me offer a personal positioning as a way into the second itinerary of encountering Austen. For me, her works, and period drama more generally, trigger memories of school or rather the Sunday evenings when period dramas seemed to infest the TV schedules. Thus, for me, they evoke that melancholy sense of the weekend ending and work looming. Meanwhile, I also saw the great wave of "period drama" to which I reacted with increasing skepticism through the 1980s—looking at the rightward drift of politics, the mobilization of ideas of a "past nation" and "our island story." Nor am I entirely alone in this as when in a discussion project a student confessed (or is that proclaimed?), "Period dramas. Hmmh... the very phrase sends unpleasant shivers down my spine." Furthermore, I was brought up in a strongly masculinized educational environment; so for me books were feminized, labeled as something boys did not enjoy. I would like to say that I sneaked off to enjoy them, but I was far too conformist for that to be the case. This may be symptomatic, since female tourists among Austen fans form a much more visible grouping than in other sectors. Whereas for me Austen is a melancholy half memory of school, for many visitors from North America, she is filtered through an imagined England—which frames her and to which she contributes. As Shelagh Squire has argued, in the context of Beatrix-Potter tourism, literary England conveys notions of countryside to North American visitors. As summed up by Ben, a librarian: "I think people have a very romantic view of England . . . and they expect [it] to be all a land of quiet life and countryside . . . and very nice gardens." Specific literary meanings get caught up in, appropriated, and linked to wider cultural values.[64]

Following from this then is the third journey through the real places, which trigger and enable these associations. Many tourists exhibit a strong sense of personal acquaintance—so the Austen center endorsements from ordinary visitors refer to her as "Jane" and mention her palpable presence. Sallie Wadsworth, a tourist, writing an account of a tour organized by Book Adventures for the Jane Austen Society of North America, describes how a select party gathered, in period dress, at "Jane's" death place and there read

Cassandra's letter before following what must have been the route of the cortege. "The tour director had thoughtfully provided a rose for each of us to add to an arrangement below the plaque to Jane's memory near her tomb, and not a few sobs punctuated the prayers and thoughts of those gathered."[65]

Reading Austen involves for these tourists not just the bedside, the school, nor wandering through textual Pemberleys, but trailing and touring around sites associated with her. In effect, a geography of Austen emerges through itineraries leading to key sites; thus, Chaworth, Lyme Park, Chatsworth, Sudbury Hall, Bath, and, to a lesser extent, Lyme Regis, Lacock, Box Hill, Southampton, and Winchester get bound into tours.[66] At its most formal, these are organized tours that restage the tradition of peripatetic reading groups—reenacting scenes at appropriate locations—while for others it may be just a gradual accumulation of visits as opportunity arises. Among fans it can also be a way of sharing the text through tourist practices—a sharing of enjoyment. Indeed, this can be a shared ironic engagement, as when Lauryl Lane describes Lacock (used for Meryton scenes in *Pride and Prejudice*): "It was cute, quaint etc. Very enjoyable."[67] This sense of a community of readers, for whom Lauryl and others are writing, suggests that we also need to unpack the experience of visiting.

Since the places mentioned are bound into these wider stories, I would suggest that they are "disseminated." Not only may they be "read" in terms of films or novels, but also of souvenirs, suggesting a "reading" practice that is distanciated and dispersed in time and space. So postcards tell distant others of the reading, while souvenirs allow the reading to be revisited later. The value of souvenirs lies in the context of their consumption; they are encoded by the narrative of the possessor, not just the authorial narrative. Indeed, the souvenirs act as metonymical markers of an extraordinary space and time in which normal patterns and practices need not hold. They speak of unique experiences: "We do not need or desire souvenirs of events that are repeatable. Rather we need and desire souvenirs of events that are reportable, events whose materiality escaped us, events that exist only through the invention of narrative. Through narrative the souvenir substitutes a context of perpetual consumption for its context of origin."[68] At a social level, interpretation and reading are thus fragmented and dispersed in space and time through a range of practices occurring not just at the site but later and in other places. Souvenirs are mementos around which stories get woven and rewoven.[69]

Overlaying this social interaction in places associated with Austen is thus a further geography of practices and conversations about her work. The Republic of Pemberley,[70] an electronic discussion and resource forum modeled on an imaginary territory of "Pemberley," with areas devoted to different aspects of her life, works, and times (and meditations around touring sites), makes these otherwise invisible conversations apparent. In this sense, one textual geography is folded inside another, both bouncing off a set of places that are fictive and real. The engagement with Austen can also be through non-textual practices, such as replica clothing, Regency dance events, and so forth. Thus, the Friends of the English Regency, who put on costumed events, invite us to join them: "Do join us, especially if you are at least reasonably frivolous." All of which should remind us that this is all about pleasure. Even though participants are "having fun," making costumes can require considerable skills and personal research on clothing of the period. I would also add that the knowledge gained by performance again creates different perspectives on Austen. For instance, wearing female costume can bring home what shifts in corsetry and design can mean in terms of freedom of movement and so forth, not just by representing femininity but in its lived practice. So other registers of knowledge and imagination are in play.

The Distanciated Subject of Austen Tourism

The reader and Austen are both located and mobile, present and absent in the landscape. Austen, as we have seen, is made present through a range of commemorative symbols, sites, and, indeed, shrines, and made mobile through the circulating networks of books and films. However, whereas conventional tourist studies look at the circulation of countable, touchable visitors, this chapter reveals a dispersed practice of reading Austen. What this leaves us with is, I think, a rather more interesting if less concrete sense of Austen as a phenomenon. She is present—"with us"—as her books circulate alongside "period" souvenirs and collectible items. She is used to produce what we might call senses of "hereness" in stories of identity ranging from the nation to tourism. And yet what we are depicting here is a geography of deferral and absence. We have visitors trying to connect personal readings (which may or may not be "accurate"), public representations, and specific sites. Each is marking the other, each forming a chain of signification.

Now, at one level traveling to see original sites just becomes a tour to see signs of tourism. Similarly, the sites are chained together as equivalent items and interchangeable items ("today is Wednesday it must be Bath"), each mediated by the sequence in which they are encountered instead of being self-fulfilling wholes. So while sites ostensibly make the past—Jane Austen's world—present, they are also more equivocal spots haunted by the invisible worlds of the past, as reconstructed in accounts and imagined versions of Austen's life, and by imagined worlds from her books. This, then, is a moment of uncertainty and openness in which meaning occurs between the various components. This is a geography of betweenness, less a fabric woven from significant sites than a stitching together of gaps. As Susan Stewart put it, "Whenever we speak of the context of reading, we can see at work a doubling which undermines the authority of both the reading situation and the situation or locus of the depiction: the reader is not in either world but rather hovers between them."[71] In the case of touring sites, I have tried to suggest that this rather more than doubles the complexity of the situation.

Let us look at one of the high points of Kaliopi Pappas's "Tour of Jane Austen's England" in 1997, during which, after visiting Wilton, with its many Jane Austen–related exhibits—costumes worn by actors in screen adaptations—she travels to Lyme Park in Cheshire:

> I did Lyme Park, the exterior location for Pemberley in [the BBC version of] *Pride and Prejudice* and Chatsworth—which some say inspired the REAL Pemberley in a single day. The sight of the great house nestled into the deep green hillside, surrounded by dark mist, was certainly a sight! It was a Marianne Dashwood moment.[72]

The complexities of presence and absence, in both temporal and spatial terms, of what is standing for what—the real house for a fiction, the comparison of real houses, the fictional character as a way of expressing experience, the evocation of landscape—run round and round each other. Nor is it simply a matter of defining "real" or "authentic" in terms of provenance, as Pappas's travel journal shows, she is aware of what are replicas, film sites, or originals.

All the readings and reenactments seem to try to make something concrete and present, but instead, they point to the absences and gaps. It gives us, then, a twin sense of the instability of meaning and creative work of interpretation that we need to take on board. The question is not so much whether the landscapes of tourism accurately represent Austen or whether tourists develop an accurate understanding of her work, rather, it is a performative sense of bringing together and articulating a range of imagined connections. This means that interpretation is a work of assembling and connecting that is always partial and bound to different geographies. Our interpretation of Austen's role today should not use metaphors of representation or mirroring, but conversation and language in action, a sense of representing, of making present. In that sense we can perhaps see the continuing appeal of her work through the way people connect with it, and connect it to their personal worlds. From politics to personal life, Austen is a vehicle through which people can articulate different cultural values.

Notes

1. I am aware here of J. Sharp's recent criticism of not only traditional geography mining literature for commentaries about places but, equally, of critical geography treating literature just as a cultural product. She argues cogently for a sense of authorial voice and textual structure to be a focus, to look at how novels shape textual landscapes, which I address in this chapter. However, I also wish to add a concern with how those novels are read. J. Sharp, "Towards a Critical Analysis of Fictive Geographies," *Area* 32, no. 3 (2000): 327–34.

2. J. Hillis Miller, *Topographies* (Stanford, CA: Stanford University Press, 1995), 7; J. Donald, "This, Here, Now: Imagining the Modern City," in *Imagining Cities: Scripts, Signs, Memory*, ed. S. Westwood and J. Williams (London: Routledge, 1997), 183.

3. R. Rosaldo, "Imperialist Nostalgia," *Representations* 26 (Spring 1989): 107–122.

4. One of the highlights of a series on race in England was to see a senior Right-wing politician cheerily inform the (black) presenter that while they were both British only he was English. D. Howe, *White Tribe* (2000), Channel 4.

5. P. Wright, *On Living in an Old Country: The National Past in Contemporary Britain* (London: Verso, 1985).

6. K. Walsh, *The Representation of the Past in the Present: Museums and Heritage in a Post-Modern World* (London: Routledge, 1992).

7. R. Shields, *Places on the Margin: Alternative Geographies of Modernity* (London: Routledge, 1991).

8. For a map of locations of scenes in the novels, see D. Herbert, "Place and Society in Jane Austen's England," *Geography* 76 (1991): 206.

9. E. Said, *Culture and Imperialism* (London: Vintage Books, 1993), 100–116.

10. Post-structuralist readings have also seen this as a deliberate ironic critique of social relations, in which Austen uses the relations of property implied in slavery to undermine Sir Thomas—for instance, in the "dead silence" of the response to questions on the plantation. See, for instance, M. Ferguson, "*Mansfield Park*: Slavery, Colonialism, and Gender," *Oxford Literary Review* 13, no. 1–2 (1991): 118–138. My point is not whether Austen is culpable in some way but rather how she is read by the population at large.

11. Recent work, for instance, suggests that we need some caution regarding claims that Mansfield Park would not have been possible without the slave trade—in terms of how common sugar plantation holdings were, or rather were not, in Northamptonshire, but even in terms of detailed analysis of the likely scales of investments, working from figures in Austen's text itself, which relate income to dowry sizes. See the painstaking calculations in T. Lloyd, "Myths of the Indies: Jane Austen and the British Empire," *Comparative Criticism* 21 (1999): 59–78.

12. C. Sussman, "Women and the Politics of Sugar, 1792," *Representations* 48 (Fall 1994): 48–69. While less clear in Austen, the high Victorian, nationalist, and heroic epic poetry of Felicia Hemans stressed again an "assumption of an intrinsic connection between the values of domestic sanctity and of imperial domination." See T. Lootens, "Hemans and Home: Victorianism, Feminine 'Internal Enemies,' and the Domestication of National Identity," *Publications of the Modern Language Association of America*, 109 no. 2 (1994): 238–253.

13. S. Hall, "Old and New Identities, Old and New Ethnicities," in *Culture, Globalization and the World System*, ed. A. King (Basingstoke, UK: Macmillan, 1991), 48–49.

14. Herbert, "Place and Society," 200.

15. E. Cromley, "Public History and Historic Preservation Districts," in *Past Meets Present: Essays about Historic Interpretation and Public Audiences*, ed. J. Blatti (Washington, DC: Smithsonian Institute Press, 1987), 30–36; D. Lowenthal, "The Timeless Past: Some Anglo-American Historical Preconceptions," *Journal of American History* 75, no. 4 (1989): 1263–1280; D. Lowenthal, "British National Identity and the English Landscape," *Rural History* 2, no. 2 (1991): 205–230.

16. Rosaldo, "Imperialist Nostalgia," 116.

17. S. Fraiman, "Jane Austen and Edward Said: Gender, Culture, and Imperialism," *Critical Inquiry* 21 (1995): 809–810. It has to be said that this chapter turns on a close reading suggesting that the phrase "If tenderness were ever wanting" (at Mansfield Park) is meant to convey to the reader that indeed it often was, and thus aligns it with the ensuing tumult described for Portsmouth.

18. M. Batey, *Jane Austen and the English Landscape* (London: Barn Elms, 1996), 8.

19. The Romantic movement itself has informed and been linked to literary tourism in the Lake District. See S. Squire, "Wordsworth and Lake District Tourism: Romantic Reshaping of the Landscape," *Canadian Geographer* 32, no. 3 (1988): 237–247.

20. T. Williamson, *Polite Landscapes: Garden and Society in Eighteenth-Century England* (Baltimore: Johns Hopkins University Press, 1995), 102.

21. See S. Morgan, "Adoring the Girl Next Door: Geography in Austen," *Persuasions On-line* 21, no. 1, np, www.jasna.org/pol02/morgan.html.

22. Though we might see this as a recuperative gesture wherein a naval meritocratic Austen played out a criticism of Regency politics by making "imperial war the arena in which the gentry could rediscover the manly authority necessary to govern effectively." T. Fulford makes this point in "Romaniticizing the Empire: The Naval Heroes of Southey, Coleridge, Austen, and Marryat," *Modern Languages Quarterly* 60, no. 2 (1999): 186. Fraiman also points to the naval characters and brings in the provincialism of the colonial core ("Jane Austen and Edward Said," 814); see also K. Kuwahara, "*Sanditon*, Empire, and the Sea: Circles of Influence, Wheels of Power," *Persuasions* 19 (1997): 144–148, for an argument that the instability posed by these outside forces seems to be finally overwhelming Austen's last, albeit unfinished, work.

23. E. Mullan, "Fanny's Novel Predicament," *The Guardian* (March 28, 2000): 16.

24. J. Ezard, "Empire Show Arouses Pride and Prejudice," *The Guardian* (August 23, 1999): 30.

25. Fraiman, "Jane Austen and Edward Said," 806.

26. J. Ezard, "Britannia Rules Are Waived," *The Guardian* (August 7, 2000): 9.

27. See, for instance, the early work of H. C. Darby, "The Regional Geography of Thomas Hardy's Wessex," *Geographical Review* 38 (1948): 426–443.

28. See the different mobilizations of landscape in J. Johnson, "Literary Geography: Joyce, Woolf, and the City," *City* 4, no. 2 (2000): 199–214.

29. R. Riley, D. Baker, and C. Van Doren, "Movie Induced Tourism," *Annals of Tourism Research* 25, no. 4 (1998): 920; see also D. Hardy, "Historical Geography

and Heritage Studies," *Area* 20, no. 4 (1988): 333–338. The ubiquity of this tactic is such that ironic postcards in the Lake District show a house with a plaque bearing the inscription "This house has absolutely nothing to do with Wordsworth" (R. Dilley, "Wordsworth and the Lake District: A Reply," *The Canadian Geographer* 34, no. 2 [1990]: 157).

30. G. Dann, *The Language of Tourism: A Sociolinguistic Interpretation* (Wallingford, CT: CAB International, 1996), 59.

31. G. Hughes, "The Semiological Realization of Space," in *Destinations: Cultural Landscapes of Tourism*, ed. G. Ringer (London: Routledge, 1999), 18.

32. N. Tooke and M. Baker, "Seeing Is Believing: The Effect of Film on Visitor Numbers to Screened Locations," *Tourism Management* 17, no. 2 (1996): 87–94; see also Riley, Baker, and van Doren, "Movie Induced Tourism," 920.

33. Batey, "Jane Austen and the English Landscape," 76.

34. See, for instance, S. Daniels, "The Political Iconography of Woodland in Later Georgian England," in *The Iconography of Landscape*, ed. D. Cosgrove and S. Daniels (Cambridge: Cambridge University Press, 1988), 60–75; S. Daniels, "The Political Landscape," in *Humphrey Repton: Landscape Gardener, 1752–1818*, ed. G. Carter et al. (Norwich, UK: Sainsbury Centre for Visual Arts, 1982), 110–121; S. Daniels, *Fields of Vision: Landscape Imagery and National Identity in England and the U.S.* (Cambridge: Polity Press, 1993).

35. J. Derrida, "Ulysses Gramophone," in his *Between the Blinds* (New York: Columbia University Press, 1991), 589.

36. A. Compagnon, "Marcel Proust's *Remembrance of Things Past*," in P. Nora, ed., *Realms of Memory: The Construction of the French Past*, vol. 2, *Traditions* (New York: Columbia University Press, 1997), 226.

37. S. Lash, *Sociology of Postmodernism* (London: Routledge, 1990).

38. M. Certeau, *The Writing of History*, trans T. Conley (New York: Columbia University Press, 1988), 280–282.

39. G. van den Abbeele, "Sightseers: Tourist as Theorist," *Diacritics* 10, no. 2 (1980): 9; M. de Certeau, *Heterologies: Discourses on the Other*, trans. B. Massumi (Manchester, UK: Manchester University Press, 1986).

40. Hampshire County Council brochure, nd, 3.

41. For example, D. MacCannell, *Empty Meeting Grounds: The Tourist Papers* (London: Routledge, 1992).

42. Van den Abbeele, "Sightseers," 4.

43. J. Urry, *The Tourist Gaze: Leisure and Travel in Contemporary Societies* (Beverly Hills, CA: Sage, 1990); M. Crang, "Picturing Practices: Research through the Tourist Gaze," *Progress in Human Geography* 21, no. 3 (1997): 359–374.

44. B. Kirshenblatt-Gimblett, *Destination Culture: Tourism, Museums and Heritage* (Berkeley and Los Angeles: University of California Press, 1998), 171.

45. To point out such time travel is impossible and is in one sense banal, but the jarring of periods does have impact on claims of "experiencing" Austen's world. So, whereas Austen was struck by the glaring whiteness of the newly built Bath, the same streets have now mellowed and possess an antique patina.

46. Kirshenblatt-Gimblett, *Destination Cultures*, 169.

47. Lauryl Lane published at www.lauryllane.com/england/england3.htm, last accessed November 4, 2001.

48. D. Pocock, "Catherine Cookson Country: Tourist Expectation and Experience," *Geography* 77 (1992): 236–240.

49. J. Glynn and R. Maines, "Numinous Objects," *Public Historian* 15, no. 1 (1993): 21.

50. P. McManus, "Memories as Indicators of the Impact of Museum Visits," *International Journal of Museum Management and Curatorship* 12, no. 4 (1993): 367–380.

51. O. Löfgren, *On Holiday: A History of Vacationing* (Berkeley and Los Angeles: University of California Press, 1999), 9.

52. M. Hood, "Staying Away: Why People Choose Not to Visit Museums," *Museum News* 61, no. 4 (1983): 50–57; E. Hooper-Greenhill, "Counting Visitors or Visitors who Count?" in *The Museum Time Machine: Putting Cultures on Display*, ed. R. Lumley (London: Routledge, 1988), ch. 10; N. Merriman, *Beyond the Glass Case: The Past, the Heritage, and the Public in Britain* (Leicester, UK: Leicester University Press, 1991).

53. D. Herbert, "Artistic and Literary Places in France as Tourist Attractions," *Tourism Management* 17, no. 2 (1996): 81.The figure is similar to most "heritage sites" in the United Kingdom.

54. S. Fish, "Narrative and Reader Response," *Critical Inquiry* 7, no. 1 (1980): 5–25; R. Scholes, "Is There a Fish in This Text?" in *On Signs*, ed. M. Blonsky (Oxford: Blackwell, 1985): 122–138; W. Iser, *Prospecting: From Reader Response to Literary Anthropology* (Baltimore: Johns Hopkins University Press, 1989).

55. See, for instance, S. Squire, "Accounting for Cultural Meanings: The Interface between Geography and Tourism Studies Re-examined," *Progress in Human Geography* 18, no. 1 (1994): 1–16.

56. For example, Herbert, "Artistic and Literary Places"; R. Prentice, "Measuring the Educational Effectiveness of On-site Interpretation Designed for Tourists: An Assessment of Student Recall from Geographical Field Visits to Kidwelly Castle, Dyfed," *Area* 23, no. 4 (1991): 297–308.

57. T. Edensor, "Staging Tourism: Tourists as Performers," *Annals of Tourism Research* 27, no. 2 (2000): 322.

58. R. Stebbins, "Cultural Tourism as Serious Leisure," *Annals of Tourism Research* (1997): 450–452.

59. M. Morris, "At Henry Parkes Motel," *Cultural Studies* 2, no. 1 (1988): 2.

60. According to G. Hoffmann, "the aesthetics of appearance asserts place identity and a sense of rootedness, creates spaces and times of individuation and of social or universal connection" (439). Although in this case these sites are a fragile balance between a promise of this and a feeling that they are manufactured or inauthentic (G. Hoffmann, "The Aesthetic Attitude in a Post-Ideological World: History, Art/Literature and the Museum Mentality in the Cultural Environment," *American Studies* 34, no. 4 [1989]: 423–479).

61. D. Bennett, "Wrapping Up Postmodernism: The Subject of Consumption Versus the Subject of Cognition," in *Postmodern Conditions*, ed. A. Milner, P. Thomson, and C. Worth (Oxford: Berg Publishers, 1990), 15–38.

62. I am wary that accounts that stress the indeterminacy of texts and the primacy of interpretative communities can either end up with a reader response determined by that community or return the "decentred subject to an imaginary autonomy and transcendence" (Bennett, "Wrapping Up Postmodernism," 31).

63. For one take on this national framing, and how British productions pick up on class, while those for a North American audience gloss over it, see C. Dole, "Austen, Class, and the American Market," in *Jane Austen in Hollywood*, ed. L. Troost and S. Greenfield (Lexington: University Press of Kentucky, 1998), 58–78. For a further discussion of the connections of tourism, gender, and heritage, see C. Aitchison, "Heritage and Nationalism: Gender and the Performance of Power," in *Leisure/Tourism Geographies: Practices and Geographical Knowledge*, ed. D. Crouch (London: Routledge, 1999), 59–73, where she recounts how many nationalist sites are overwhelmingly masculinized.

64. S. Squire, "The Cultural Values of Literary Tourism," *Annals of Tourism Research* 21, no. 1 (1994): 110–116.

65. Reported on the JASNA Web site: www.jasna.org/tour1997.html as accessed March 27, 2000.

66. Cf. M. Crang, "On the Heritage Trail: Maps of and Journeys to Olde Englande," *Society and Space* 12 (1994): 341–355.

67. Lauryl Lane, Web site.

68. S. Stewart, *On Longing: Narratives of the Miniature, the Gigantic, the Souvenir, and the Collection* (Baltimore: Johns Hopkins University Press, 1984), 4.

69. Stewart, *On Longing*, 135. See also Lury, "The Objects of Tourism," in *Touring Cultures: Transformation of Travel and Theory*, ed. C. Rojek and J. Urry (London: Routledge, 1997), 75–95, who looks at the circulation of objects that evoke memories of travel at home and evoke home while travelling; B. Gordon, "The Souvenir: Messenger of the Extraordinary," *Journal of Popular Culture* 20, no. 3 (1986): 135–146.

70. Its home page is http://www.pemberley.com/.

71. Stewart, *On Longing*, 44.

72. Kaliopi Pappas, Travel Journal, Austen's England: www.ocf.berkeley.edu/^licp/travel/journal5.html accessed 6 April 1999.

Part III
At Home

7

The Return Home

❦

Suzanne R. Pucci

The Republic of Pemberley is a haven for fans of Jane Austen's novels and the films adapted from them. It's mostly made up of places to talk—bulletin boards and a chat room. Everybody is welcome and we have all kinds of people here, though we all are bound by a common fascination. (If you don't like Jane Austen, or you don't know who she is, this place is not going to interest you.) In fact, the more obsessed you are the greater your enjoyment will be. *If you've no obsession at all, you just won't get it—like most of our "real" families and friends!"*

—Internet site, www@Pemberley.org (emphasis added)

Mr. Knightley, a sensible man about seven or eight-and-thirty was not only a very old and intimate friend of the family, but particularly connected with it as the elder brother of [Emma's sister] Isabella's husband. He lived about a mile from Highbury, was a frequent visitor and always welcome, and at this time more welcome than usual, as coming directly from their mutual connections in London.

—Jane Austen, *Emma*

Home and Abroad

At the Internet site dubbed the "Republic of Pemberley," we are welcomed into the fold of Jane Austen's world and given a strong hint of the reason for its popularity. Our "real" families and friends tend not to understand: "If you've no obsession at all, you just won't get it—like most of our 'real' families and friends!" All is said in these diacritical marks that challenge the authenticity of the bonds between family and friends existing outside these

133

enclosures. The intimacy that encircles members within this Web site creates bonds based in fiction and situated somewhere in cyberspace that supplement, even supplant, the "real" of one's own contemporary connections.

This Internet address designates a site where social, familial, and geographical space are interwoven. An "x" marks the spot of the Republic of Pemberley enclosed within a peninsula, on a crude map of some imaginary land where an enchanted domestic world occupies a space of its own, almost an island utopia. Visitors are instructed to follow the signposts that dot this virtual landscape of chat groups, information, news about Austen, her novels, or the film adaptations, and that always indicate a way to go "home." Indeed, you are never far away. At the bottom of the home page, we read this message enclosed within frames highlighted in bold: "No, you have not lost your way. You remain safe within the borders of the Republic of Pemberley." No one loses his way in this virtual world so clearly mapped with names and places that form the "secure sites" enclosing Jane Austen's world.

All the Austen film adaptations, with the exception of *Mansfield Park*, inscribe an attempted "return home" as a strategy through which spatial, social, and familial enclosures articulate the interconnections of domestic intimacy. This chapter explores the paradox implicit in the formation of a Web site that maps these spatial and social enclosures of domestic intimacy onto a virtual space without boundaries or borders of the ether-net or Internet.[1] Such an encounter between cyberspace and early-nineteenth-century domestic space dramatizes the issues at stake in the near mania of adapting Austen's fiction to the screen. What happens in mapping the very domestic concerns of these novels onto the social and familial and filmic space of contemporary culture? The conflation of family and friends, those real family and friends, operative throughout the cybersite, becomes, I suggest, an obsessive thematic and aesthetic preoccupation in the medium of film. To what ends does this seeming reproduction of nineteenth-century concerns take place? How does it relate to the pleasure of the contemporary viewer?

Austen's novels themselves, of course, repeatedly marry domestic with social relations. The narrative passage cited at the beginning of this chapter, which is from the opening pages of *Emma*, establishes domestic intimacy early on through full reciprocity between family and social ties.[2] Mr. Knightley who becomes at the end of the novel Emma Woodhouse's husband, is introduced into the story through connections that link him both socially and through family to Emma and her father. In effect, Knightley is formally presented in this passage through a series of relational terms that in their explicit and persistent redundancy (over)determine these bonds of social and domestic intimacy.

Mr. Knightley is a friend of the family who is himself family. The attributes "old" and "intimate" friend are qualified in the same sentence by still more substantial ties of kinship. Indeed, Knightley is the "elder brother of [Emma's sister] Isabella's husband" (vol. 4, p. 9). From an emphasis on the close familiarity of friendship we move to familial relations of sister- and brother-in-law. Furthermore, the ties of kinship lead metonymically in the following sentence to yet another connection, that of geographical proximity. Kinship finds analogy in the spatial intimacy of Knightley as close neighbor: "He lived about a mile from Highbury" (vol. 4, p. 9).

This redundancy of union enlists the terms of friendship, familial ties, and familiar proximate territory, repeating intimacy at each of these levels, thus duplicating the bonds that connect Knightley to the Woodhouse family, in particular to Emma. And while the thematics of friendship, family ties, and close neighbors are construed to signal intimacy in every phrase of the short passage, language itself reproduces such likenesses. In the description of Knightley, repetition of certain lexical items works to intensify this union of sameness. Knightley is not merely well received, being "always *welcome*" (vol. 4, p. 9) (emphasis added), he becomes on this occasion doubly so. A repetition within the same sentence of the exact same term, "welcome," intensifies the sense of Knightley's especially desirable company. This markedly special occasion is Knightley's recent visit with the married couple, Emma's sister and his brother, located sixteen miles away in London. Such additional familial contact as he carries back to Hartfield makes him "more *welcome* than usual" (vol. 4, p. 9). The spiral of duplicated connections knows no boundaries here as this family friend who is himself family returns from the family to be doubly welcomed into the fold of family friendship and intimacy. Each connection is reproduced in terms that are not just thematically and relationally similar but also linguistically identical. "Connection" as the key underlying assumption as well as explicitly stated term is employed in this passage first to describe how Knightley was "particularly *connected*" to the Woodhouse family, and then repeated in the next sentence to allude to Knightly's return from their "mutual *connections*" (vol. 4, p. 9).

The insistent resemblance between "intimate friend" and "family," between the usual "welcome" and the "more welcome than usual," between "particularly connected" and "mutual connections" of Mr. Knightley in such close textual quarters lays a foundation for semantic and thematic closeness, an intimacy between people that like the linguistic model repeatedly collapses into a union of the same. What appears to be a desired resemblance between friends and family members, between the friend who is family and family who is friend, leads to the formation of yet another union of the same. Emma marries Knightley at the close of the novel, thus further complicating the already interwoven strands of their kinship and friendship by repeating them yet again. The last words of the novel emphasizing such "union," which are echoed verbatim in the voice-over of the Douglas McGrath film *Emma*, reiterate the sameness brought now to further fruition: "the wishes, the hopes, the confidence, the predictions of the small band of true friends who witnessed the ceremony, were fully answered in the perfect happiness of the union" (386).

From the perspective of legal or religious codes and conventions, the marriage of cousins and/or in-laws such as Emma and Knightley was a complex and highly ambiguous matter both in the eighteenth and early nineteenth centuries when Austen was writing. As Glenda A. Hudson points out:

> The incest taboo applied [during the eighteenth century] as much to familial members related by marriage as to blood relatives. Forbidden degrees of marriage were rooted in the laws of Chapters 18 and 20 in the Old Testament Book of Leviticus. During the Reformation, the secular courts reduced the number of previous incest taboos from cousins in the sixteenth degree to close blood relatives according to the Levitical degrees (which excluded first cousins). But, at the same time, the courts added the prohibition (believed to be implied by Leviticus) that a man could not marry his deceased wife's sister.[3]

Yet it was also the case that "in Austen's time, first cousins and brothers/sisters–in-law were permitted to marry by law and the church, even though feeling against this practice, while certainly not as prevalent as in the late nineteenth century, was discernible" (Hudson, 31). The sense of taboo coexisted alongside practices that were legal and thus highly ambivalent. Hudson proposes several social as well as then current scientific principles, such as those of Charles Darwin, which militated against "in-family" marriages (30). At the same time, there were also important aspects of social practice that made these kinds of marriages almost a conventional norm.

Emma and Knightley are not related by blood, nor does their union infringe upon laws that would then or now actually prevent them from marrying. What prevails, however, is the insistent emphasis as in the preceding passage and elsewhere in Austen's texts on canceling, on collapsing, in story, theme, and language, all distance and difference between members of this small society. The text, as in the preceding passage, confuses domestic and social intimacy to such an extent as to negate precisely the notion of marriage as exogamous. These intimations of incest thus define members of such an enclosed world who did in effect dwell within the same social, familial, geographical, and linguistic circle. "And so it was that, at a time when sexual relations between affinal relatives were often regarded to be as incestuous as intercourse between blood relations, incest presented itself as a major concern in the lives of people living in close contingency with blood relatives and in-laws with little chance for geographical or social mobility" (Hudson, 15).

The incest taboo, in other words, conflicted both potentially and in reality with social, familial, and geographical conventions that encouraged the very intimacy this taboo formally prohibited. The society that regulated marriage customs, at least in attitude if not in law, so as to avoid in-family or endogamous relations is the same that on another level valued just this union between domestic and social alliances. Such complex but unresolved tensions likely constituted the very reasons why a concern with incest found its way into the thematics and, as I have shown, into the semantics of fiction.[4] But why would these topics interest us today when "geographical or social mobility" and the very opposite of "close contingency with blood relatives and in-laws" dominate our own social practices?

The late-eighteenth- and early-nineteenth-century landscape of proximity redoubled by intimacy now seems quite foreign, even exotic, to the current scenarios of contemporary American as well as British social and family life. We can hardly say that today "in the cloistered, insular familial world of the English upper and middle classes, intensely intimate ties between blood relations [are] forged" (Hudson, 13). On the contrary, the mobility of our society is endemic, particularly in the United States, in which family members tend to be so geographically scattered and where there is a fundamental difference and distance between social and familial life. Ours is a society in which peer pressure and networking at the social, commercial, and economic levels typically and increasingly tend to bypass the family scene. Television sitcoms such as *Friends* or *Seinfeld* illustrate this formation of close ties among peers in groups that at certain moments clearly seem to take the place of family ties that have clearly been loosened or even completely exchanged for peer group relations that themselves often appear tenuous. The family of the late twentieth and early twenty-first centuries is in effect redefined also because it is increasingly constituted by members who are not necessarily in a stable kinship or biologically defined relation: children from different marriages living under the same roof; children living with adults who through divorce, donor insemination, or adoption are not their biological or sometimes even legal parents. And here, as opposed to Austen's world, such groups are not self-sufficient, enclosed, and domesticated. Their very fragile configuration is potentially always in the process of changing. Austen's contribution to the treatment of incest in fiction according to Hudson is that "[u]nlike other literary works of the time, where incest increases horror or creates moral chaos and violence, Austen's novels present incestuous alliances that preserve order and reestablish domestic harmony" (25).

The complex ways in which the family has undergone profound change and fragmentation at the millennium relate to contemporary connections that are articulated specifically beyond the purview of the domestic sphere. Relations with global markets and networks today do indeed link us with each other across immense distances. That does not mean, however, that we are comfortable in this situation, or that these new kinds of links have anything to do with the domestic entity we call the family. Our world might indeed be shrinking through technology and a global market economy but increasingly this global entity cannot be reducible to, does not flow from, the dimensions of a single extended or nuclear household; nor can it be defined in terms of family values.[5] In contrast to the "moral vision" of domestic life, I would also contend there is much evidence that we look today with growing suspicion on the very intimacies and affinities of the contemporary household.[6]

Says the voice-over that opens the Miramax film *Emma*: "In a time when one's town was one's world and the actions at a dance excited greater interest than the movement of armies . . ."[7] This statement does not exist in the text of the novel, as might be guessed. Rather, in flagrant contrast with the vast networks of our own contemporary spaces, the narrative voice-over shrinks the world to the confines and concerns of a diminutive as well as intricately connected and thus anachronistic dimension. In fact, the world of Austen's novels and, as we shall see, in several of the film remakes seems even more confined and more enclosed than even the "town" might imply. Though several villages are associated with Austen's protagonists—Highbury where Emma and Mr. Woodhouse reside, or Meryton, the village near which *Pride and Prejudice* is situated—it is the country house that designates and delimits the material, familial, and social parameters of Emma's and most other protagonists' worlds. The estates of Longbourn, Netherfield, Rosings, or Pemberley define the living and dwelling places of Elizabeth and Jane Bennet as well as the rest of the Bennet family of *Pride and Prejudice*. It is the country estate of Mansfield Park that constitutes the focal point of Fanny Price's education, life, and identity. Even the heroines' permanent loss of an estate such as in *Sense and Sensibility*, or quasi-permanent loss such as in *Persuasion,* or threatened loss as in *Pride and Prejudice* structures their lives economically, and socially, as well as geographically, such that these country houses become and remain the implicit focus of the novel.

Raymond Williams notes this emphasis through Austen's seeming lack of concern with larger issues, specifically with the places and people of town or village, or with the countryside itself. Public places as well as the general population are ignored in favor of the enclosure of the country house with its select and intimate inhabitants: "And it is not only most of the people who have disappeared . . . [i]t is also most of the country which becomes real only as it relates to the *houses which are the real nodes*; for the rest the country is weather or a place for a walk."[8]

Austen's focus, according to Williams, ignores what of course always did exist. No matter how enclosed or intimate were the relations between kinship and social "in-family" members of these country houses, "most of the people," "most of the country," had to go unnoticed, had to "disappear" in order for Austen's world to exist. And it is not merely a question of ignoring all but the socially and economically privileged strata of England, it is also a question of excluding as well most of the world. According to Edward Said:

> In projecting what Raymond Williams calls a "knowable community" of Englishmen and women, Jane Austen, George Eliot, and Mrs. Gaskell shaped the idea of England in such a way as to give it identity, presence, ways of reusable articulation. And part

of such an idea was the relationship between "home" and "abroad." Thus, England was surveyed, evaluated, made known, whereas "abroad" was only referred to or shown briefly without the kind of presence or immediacy lavished on London, the countryside, or northern industrial centers such as Manchester or Birmingham.[9]

This dichotomy of "home" and "abroad" highlights an opposition basic to understanding Austen's appeal even as the notion of abroad might today seem an anachronism within postcolonial space and global discourse. Said, in *Culture and Imperialism*, fleshes out the shadow of imperialist structures that have always been lurking within and formative of the seemingly enclosed and independent domestic life both in and out of fiction. He reconnects Austen's world of home to the larger picture to which it belongs, that is, to the English expansion into the Caribbean and India, from where the production of, for instance, sugar and tea, become necessary ingredients of both domestic life and fiction (62–97):

> I am not trying to say that the novel—or the culture in the broad sense—"caused" imperialism, but that the novel, as a cultural artifact of bourgeois society, and imperialism are unthinkable without each other. Of all the major literary forms, the novel is the most recent, its emergence the most datable, its occurrence the most Western, its normative pattern of social authority the most structured; imperialism and the novel fortified each other to such a degree that it is impossible, I would argue, to read one without in some way dealing with the other. (71)

If colonialist expansion taking place abroad was necessary to the definition of intimate enclosed domestic space at home as well as to domestic fiction, then again, how does the emphasis on these anachronistic enclosed spaces operate in postcolonial, postmodern times? In particular, what is the relation of the complementary dichotomy home and abroad to the production of Austen in film remakes? Some potential answers to this question will become apparent in what follows.

Everywhere implicit in organizing the social and domestic space of Austen's fiction, the home, the country house as the site of domestic intimacy, becomes in all the Austen film remakes an explicit focal point.[10] Discursive sites of the country home in the novel acquire in the medium of film a striking and dominant visual presence. There is little substantive description of these places in the novels, as critics such as Roger Sale point out.[11] Nearly every Austen film remake, however, opens with the camera converging in the first few minutes and frames on carefully constructed views of a country house and estate. Film critics have curiously paid little attention to the striking importance of these material objects and physical sites. Norland Park, Barton Park and Barton Cottage, Longbourn, Rosings, Pemberley, Netherfield, Hartfield, Donwell Abbey, Mansfield Park, though lacking concrete material characteristics in the novel, become through the repeated litany of these proper names metonymically familiar and familial topoi, taking on attributes from those who inhabit them. Nearly every Austen film adaptation, on the other hand, converges in the first few minutes and frames on carefully constructed detailed views of a country house and estate. Discursive sites of domestic intimacy in the novel acquire in the medium of film a dominant visual presence through, as I will show, strategically constructed spatial enclosures.

The Parkland in the Picture

A "well-dressed, pompous individual" on horseback riding fast and furious opens Ang Lee's film remake *Sense and Sensibility* in the title sequence.[12] Norland Park is the rider's destination, an image pictured in the film's initial first scene. We arrive at this country manor whose imposing exterior is described in Emma Thompson's 1995 screenplay: "Silence. Norland Park, a large country house built in the early part of the eighteenth century, lies in the moonlit parkland" (27). From this scene, viewed from a great enough distance to provide a full shot of the large stately house, we move into the interior, into the bedroom where a dying Mr. John Dashwood anxiously awaits the arrival of his son John. Like travelers from afar ourselves, we are given entry into this country mansion to witness a most private domestic scene. The camera does not leave us on the threshold, distant from the intimate event taking place, but rather brings us, the viewer, in a series of close-ups to the bedside of Mr. John Dashwood. In this solemn scene of a family death, illuminated by the meager light of a candle, we are admitted into the dimly lit bedchamber to overhear the master of Norland Park issue in hushed tones his last words and directives.

At stake in this father's arrangements is the disposition of his fortune, and in particular of the family estate Norland Park, entailed to his one male heir, a half brother only to his sisters and no relation at all to his father's second wife. Says Mr. Dashwood to John: "Norland in its entirety is therefore yours by law and I am happy for you and Fanny" (30). Mr. Dashwood's last words also manifest great concern for the others in his family—his wife and three daughters—left with very little, and he extracts a promise from his son to provide for the other side of his, the father's, immediate family left penniless and without dowry. This constitutes the film's drama around which all events will revolve. The viewer is admitted into the Dashwood home, into the private and very intimate domestic scenes of life, death, and the succession of property, while simultaneously learning that this house and home is on the verge of being disrupted. The material site of intimacy emerges at the moment it has already almost become, like Austen's world itself, vestigial.

We then see the young Mr. Dashwood with his wife, the fortunate couple riding in their posh carriage toward Norland Park, which they are now about to appropriate. Then, in yet another arrival that for the film viewer is already denoted as a return, we again glimpse Norland Park, which, as in the opening scene, is first observed from afar, from a vantage point giving us a full view of the imposing house nestled amidst the lush green English countryside. Filmgoers get the same view as does Edward Ferrars, Fanny Dashwood's brother, whom we glimpse from the rear riding toward the house, like John Dashwood, fast and furious. During a momentary hesitation of his rearing white horse, he seems before entering the grounds to be taking in the imposing facade of Norland Park.

From the view provided the filmgoer, to the character Edward, to the land that surrounds Norland Park, all conspire to situate the country house as the central pivotal visual focus. Framed in the countryside, the estate is also framed by these figures on horseback, who in turn become part of the picture ultimately framed by us, the viewers. Each element—parkland grounds that surround the house, the more distant meadows, the figure on horseback that lends a distinct perspective from which to view Norland Park, the even more far-off film viewer—creates an evermore extended perspective and sweeping vista. At the same time, however, each of these elements serves in an opposite capacity as another frame that focuses on and encloses the country house, defining it as a protected and sheltered place. Camera shots, which in one sense appear to position the estate of Norland Park within a broad framework, a distant sweeping perspective, actually serve another objective: that of domesticating the landscape by enclosing the estate within several imbricated frames.

In *Sense and Sensibility*, as in all the Austen remakes, the film opens with riders and often inhabitants approaching the enclosures of the parks and country estates. In the first frames of the A&E *Pride and Prejudice,* we see Elizabeth Bennet out walking in the meadows. She witnesses two riders— Mr. Bingley and Mr. Darcy—as they gallop past Netherfield Park with an eye to renting it. The film audience watching Elizabeth watching Bingley and Darcy viewing the country estate of Netherfield Park nestled within two wooded copses constitutes a series of viewers forming a kind of bridge that not only links spatial planes along one continuum, but once again brings us in line with the other viewers. Such openings work to return us as spectators in our contemporary space to a time as well as place that have been strategically disposed along the same spatial and seemingly temporal continuum.

In the next scene, Elizabeth Bennet returns home to Longbourn. Here as well we move from the viewers and the outskirts beyond the estate to the park and to the foreground, finally to the interior of an enclosed and protected domestic space, complete with the animated discussion and the gentle disagreement of siblings and parents, all of whom become present, animating the entrance into the home and into the very first moments of the film.

In fact, this picture is completed by a representation in film quite different from that in the novel of the relation between an excitable and silly Mrs. Bennet and her more dignified, studious but also aloof and ultimately negligent husband. In the many household arguments that ensue, the serious tension in the novel between the husband who would rather hide in his study from his wife's tedious hysterics and from all family problems receives in the film little moral or psychological scrutiny. Here, seemingly good-natured arguments contribute to the often-comic all-in-the-family conflict between two people whose differences pose no real threat to a palpable domestic intimacy that predominates.

In these openings we do not move in the direction of the outward bounds of these sweeping shots. Rather, we travel with the camera from the outside in, from an approach to an arrival, from the meadow to the park in the landscape, to the façade, to the interior. With the exception of the ironic commentary of *Mansfield Park* on this very convention, each film begins, by staging through its camera work, a return home.

In the first five minutes of *Sense and Sensibility*, we have arrived not just once but three times at Norland Park, where we have penetrated to become acquainted with individual as well as family economic, social, and emotional tensions. Norland Park, Longbourn, Kellynch Hall, and many other country estates reside at the center of both family intimacy and tension, the material and symbolic object of wealth, social standing, and domestic intimacy. Within these walls, the family, it is implied, does, did once, or might again in the future, dwell in intimacy and happiness.

Mr. Dashwood's death in the novel *Sense and Sensibility* is actually recounted in one small paragraph and does not open the novel with the domestic scene pictured in the film.[13] In fact, the narrative dwells rather on specific legal aspects of the succession (ch. 1). Those legal aspects are carefully if dispassionately recounted in Austen's text without occupying any dramatic or descriptive space, whereas the camera lingers, one could say longingly, on the physical and geographical object of Norland Park. The country home is thus initially situated as primary focus of the characters and at the same time constitutes the principal vehicle through which the contemporary film viewer finds entry into this world.

The Douglas McGrath film *Emma* opens with just this trajectory of returning home. After the title sequence, we reside but a moment at the reception to celebrate the wedding of Emma Woodhouse's former governess, before repairing with Emma and her father to their own country estate of Hartfield. The return home is in effect the central thematic and symbolic event. Mr. Woodhouse, who in both film versions functions as a caricature of Emma's own propensity to keep things as they are—not to leave home—is always insisting on staying put, and comically pities all those, including Emma's sister and Miss Taylor, who marry. He does not like it when "people go away." Thus, it is fitting that this version opens with the Woodhouses leaving a festivity to return home. During their short trip—Hartfield being barely a half mile away—Emma's father laments the marriage that has taken "poor Miss Taylor" (actually the happy bride) from their own comfortable home.

In the first five minutes of the film, we move with Emma and her father in the Woodhouse carriage toward Hartfield, their family association already made intimate by comfortable chatter in the close quarters of their carriage. We come upon an imposing country home viewed from the exterior and then repair with its owners to the house, where, as in the opening shots in *Sense and Sensibility*, the scene is dimly but warmly lit. Domestic intimacy is carefully constructed in this scene of father and daughter quietly conversing at one end of the long dining table where the immense proportions of both table and room are visibly diminished, rendered in this shot small and cozy in the warming glow of selective partial lighting, which here as in *Sense and Sensibility* brings the viewer in close.

In the circumscribed world of this *Emma*, people, places, and events all tend to be framed visually by reassuring enclosures. The earth itself is symbolically reduced to a small, soft, multicolored globe that takes the shape of a decorative accessory, like a pincushion, that Emma dangles nonchalantly in the first scene at her governess' wedding party. This trinket shrinks the world into a diminutive sphere of manageable social, familial, geographical space. And in the opening credits of this film, festoons frame and link together several almost childlike sketches of each major protagonist and country estate: Emma, Mr. Knightley, Hartfield, Donwell Abbey, Randalls, et cetera. These likenesses have all become decorative medallions, miniaturized and enclosed in the bows and flower garlands that frame a seemingly childlike, protected bliss. In precisely another such enclosure we meet Mr. Knightley for the first time.

Into this circumscribed world ringed by the comical and somewhat preposterous, even caricatured, concerns of a doting father for whom all changes, any movement at all in the domestic circle, especially marriage, are treated as disasters, steps Mr. Knightley. He approaches the Woodhouses in an easy, familiar, and intimate way. Overhearing the conversation of Emma and her father through an open window, he stops to chat. In so doing, his entrance contributes to the spatial focus on enclosures. Unlike the novel and the epigraph that opens this chapter, it is not at the level of narrative that we learn of Knightley's close relation to the Woodhouse family. The passage that overdetermines Mr. Knightley's intimacy as family member, neighbor, and friend is transposed in the film into spatial terms. Knightley himself becomes a kind of family portrait as he drapes himself in the open window that frames him.

The film insists on intimacy through repeated devices that, as in the just mentioned example, visually illustrate a familiarity between the two families and simultaneously enclose Knightley as well as Emma within the domestic frames that define them. The overdetermined relations of brother and sister, of brother- and sister-in-law, and of friend and neighbor punctuate the dialogue at crucial moments in the film. During these first scenes in the McGrath version, Knightley justifies his chiding of Miss Woodhouse: "I'm practically a brother to Emma. Is it not a brother's job to find fault with his sister?" Instead of the subtle passage from the novel that suggests a confusion between kinship and friendship, between blood and legal relations, the film flattens these multiple registers into an explicit allusion to the most extreme affinity of sibling relations, if only a near ("practically") sibling relation. Allusions to sibling-like relations that are compounded by their actual legal ties as sister- and brother-in-law abound throughout this film in ways too plentiful to cite individually. Domestic intimacy is a persistent allusion and engine in the McGrath, as well as in the Sue Birtwhistle, *Emma*. In effect, this latter production puts additional emphasis on Emma's and Knightley's relation/non-relation as sister and brother, made explicit in conversation at several junctures throughout the film. Repeated emphasis on such remarks in these films illustrates an abiding tension between the conversion of domestic into romantic relations but also of romantic into domestic relations.

Negating Intimacy

These variations on the theme of simultaneously negating and also suggesting romantic sibling relations mark each stage of courtship in this in-family intimacy. Each time the denial is pronounced, we the viewers are treated to countless visual and verbal intimations of the repeated intermingling of social, familial, and familiar relations. The Birtwhistle *Emma* is constructed in a most explicit way on such apparent contradictions and negations.

The opening scene of this *Emma* shows another night sky where the moon moving out from behind the clouds casts light on the ample façade of a country house deep in silence. A huge ruckus shortly breaks into this tranquillity. This *Emma* opens with a closeup of squawking chickens and the noise of thieves breaking into the Woodhouse poultry yard, disturbing the quiet of the night, seemingly disrupting the enclosures of household and private property. The figure of a servant faithfully defending the yard with rifle in hand shoots in the direction of the villainous intruders. Chicken thieves threaten this enclosed world; they destroy the calm of the night and, worse, they break into another's world, a little like us who as viewers are also stealing moments that do not belong to us.

Yet, though such noisy assault seems to depart radically from the schema we have been tracing of the Austen remakes, the scene in fact constitutes a complementary version of returning home. Like burglars, we viewers are positioned beyond the servant planted in front of the country house where at gunpoint he wards off intruders from the outside world of strangers. Instead of gaining immediate entry into the privacy of domestic country space, we are for a brief moment kept at bay—another strategy to define, or rather to create, a sense of the private, separate and inviolate space of the country house. What lies within that protected space is revealed to us in the next shots in which Emma is awakened by the ruckus. The loud squawking gives way somewhat magically without break to the bright, cheery crowing of a cock announcing a new day. The threatening first scenes transform into their seeming opposite, where nothing seems really to be in danger or out of place.

In what seems yet another reversal of the opening scenes and credits of the McGrath *Emma* and the other Austen remakes, we see this *Emma* in the very next scene with her father and Miss Taylor in a carriage *leaving* Hartfield—as opposed to making an approach, to arriving, we seem to be departing. Instead of heading toward the house, the protagonists are moving away. They are of course leaving for the "distant" destination of Randalls, the country home where Miss Taylor, Emma's former governess, is joyfully to be married and to the great chagrin of Mr. Woodhouse to live there as Mrs. Weston. Emma's father laments: "There's still time to reconsider. Come back home with us. . . . Six good hens and now Miss Taylor . . . Randall's is such a distance." "Barely half a mile," reponds Emma. In the novel, a similar scene depicting the complaints of Mr. Woodhouse takes place, though not in the carriage that is leaving home. And at this particular moment in the book, no mention is made of an exact distance between Hartfield and Randalls (5–6). [14]

The minimal but unspecified distance mentioned in the novel becomes in the opening scene of the film a precise and at the same time so negligible a distance that, like the disruption of the chicken thieves, it cannot be truly threatening, certainly not to twentieth- and twenty-first-century viewers. Mr. Woodhouse does indeed "take it very ill when people go away," but for the contemporary viewer, this half-mile marker signals just the opposite function. It collapses the distance that Mr. Woodhouse so woefully bemoans, thereby creating for the viewer once again a diminished or miniaturized geographical scale and thus a sense of enclosure and immobility. For us, these protagonists never leave home. The scene, then, though it opens the film with a near violent disruption and departure, turns out to be constructing from the outset a thematics and a symbolics of returning home.

The same can be said for the inclusion of distances in most of the Austen remakes. In the many choices to exclude or to include elements of the novel made by screenwriters and directors, there seems to be an unspoken consensus to incorporate references to distance. This is the case even when and, I contend, especially *because* all these distances, whether mentioned in the *Emma* films or in *Persuasion* or in *Pride and Prejudice*, are minimal, even infinitesimal, in comparison to the global expanses of today. Thus, the outing to Lyme in *Persuasion* is considered a great event in the lives of the young people, who have never seen Lyme or the sea because it lies nearly thirty miles away. The A&E film *Pride and Prejudice* retains the discussion between Darcy and Elizabeth of what constitutes a sizable distance precisely when it is a question of measuring the separation between daughter and parents. Darcy refers to Charlotte Collins who he thinks must be happy that, being "only fifty miles away," she is so "close to her parents' home." But his comment only leads Elizabeth to disagree, since for her this distance is not negligible. Darcy in fact underscores the question of distance as being relative to personal sentiment. The way one experiences distance dictates a person's remoteness or closeness to the family left behind. Darcy might be testing Elizabeth as to the eventual distance he hopes might be established between her and her own family so that he might condescend to their union. Spatial distance is carefully and symbolically measured in terms of attachments to the home.

The cinematic world is orchestrated through strategies of "returning home" that engage not just the principal characters but viewers as well. Representations of the kind of "home" we find in the remakes, which never necessarily belonged to us, evoke a nostalgia for a world only seemingly lost, buried in past time and place, thus recuperable. And yet, the success of a strategy that marks a distance that really is not one depends for the most part on the dislocation of such markers from their position and value in the novel, on taking them out of their context, removing them from "home," relocating them in contemporary film where they are reassigned by the postmodern viewer a new and quite different function.

At the end of the Birtwhistle *Emma*, Mr. Woodhouse accepts the matrimony of his daughter to Mr. Knightley who has agreed to move to Hartfield. Reminding her father that the feared chicken thieves spotted again in their neighborhood might strike again, Emma convinces him that Mr. Knightley's presence is needed all the time. The threat of the outside world, in other words, can be held at bay, especially the dreaded chicken thieves' assault, so that everything might remain exactly the same. But in the last frames of the film we see reenacted the same break-in featured in the first scenes, which in the novel's opening passages play no role whatsoever. We are being treated here to an oppositional strategy that operates to reassure us that this world does not change.

Though Knightley will no longer reside at his Donwell Abbey, about a mile from Hartfield, he assures his tenants and farmers at the engagement celebration that despite such a move "there will be stability; there will be continuation." The commotion of the chicken thieves in the next scene fits neatly and indeed participates in this rhythm of "continuation," this union of the same. The very filmic repetition of the theft seen in the first scenes and now in the last domesticates its disruptive power by integrating it as a familiar event into the flow of quotidian continuity.

Even a theft can be successfully inscribed into this pattern of familiar and familial repetition. Repetition is conveyed, as we have seen in both *Emma* films, through a seeming insistence on the many though minute disturbances of the familiar, the quotidian, the same. Distancing, disruption, departure, even loss of one's own home, as in the case of Mrs. Dashwood and her two daughters in *Sense and Sensibility*, seem to break the continuity that each of these films is in reality constructing. Those disruptions work most often to achieve the very opposite objective and effect. Thus, when in the Miramax *Emma* Mr. Woodhouse, the symbolic embodiment of this strategy, complains that "[m]arriage is so disrupting to one's social circle," we take this remark as reassuring proof to the contrary, that indeed no such disruption will ever take place.

In surveying what appears to be the smooth, manicured, extensive grounds that form each estate in the Austen remakes, it is hard to believe that they are but bits and pieces of various sites—manors, cottages, rooms and grounds—stitched together. One has only to consult the list of properties used, for instance, in Ang Lee's *Sense and Sensibility* to understand how the visual impression of each estate or cottage is produced, most often not from any one home, meadow, or park, but rather from a variety of homes and topographical sites. Thus, Emma Thompson describes the partial use of the Flete Estate on location for Barton Cottage:

> Barton Cottage is located on the vast Flete Estate at Holbeton, south Devon. The cottage which appears modest from the front is actually a magnificent Edwardian residence when viewed from the side, a fact the filmmakers took pains to conceal.[15]

Or, while Mompesson House provided the scene for Mrs. Jenning's "sumptuous London town house," the setting for her drawing room, which "provided the backdrop for many important scenes in the film," was taken from another manor: Mothecombe House (according to Thompson 284). The extensive grounds that appear unified in every parkland and manor in these films are actually constituted through the camera from a variegated patchwork of sites whose representations are nowhere in reality to be found as an integral object. In symbolic terms, however, these places project through contemporary filmic techniques an insistence on continuity and homogeneity of the familial/familiar that everywhere inhabits these films.

Along with the continuity of family, estates and grounds, of lives lived in enclosed and persistently repetitive familiar and familial rhythms, even sharp distinctions of social class that were integral to creating these intimate domestic communities become at moments transformed in these films into markers of continuity. Emma's lesson in the McGrath version involved learning to accept persons of a different class, which blatantly contradicts the novel. At the harvest dinner in the film, Emma makes her way to the table of the tenant farmer Robert Martin, now engaged to Harriet Smith. For the first time, she recognizes his presence, allowing herself to be formally introduced, even inviting him and Harriet along with his sister to Hartfield. Although Mrs. Elton looks on scandalized, Emma's gesture brings the celebratory atmosphere of the harvest and her engagement to the entire community gathered there.

The Austen novel is remarkably different from its filmic counterpart. Once Harriet becomes engaged to the farmer Mr. Martin, Emma, as she warned Harriet at the outset of both films and novel, could not retain such a friend. The novel reads:

> Harriet, necessarily drawn away by her engagements with the Martins, was less and less at Hartfield; which was not to be regretted.—The intimacy between her and Emma must sink; their friendship must change into a calmer sort of goodwill; and, fortunately, what ought to be, and must be, seemed already beginning, and in the most gradual, natural manner. (384)

Harriet recedes "naturally" into the background as each class assumes in the novel its rightful place in the social hierarchy. The exigencies of liberal democracy emerge in the film, negating class distinctions by extending the family to the entire community. Yet, these films are constructed on distinctions between home and abroad that derive from class differences as well as from distinctions between the circumscribed world of our nostalgia, the past, and the open-ended fear of contemporary and future unbounded space.

If, as I have been suggesting, the technologies of film and cyberspace are deployed in the recent remakes of Austen's novels to create a new site where we might return "home"; if these techniques attempt to reassert the distinctions in our own postmodern times that Raymond Williams analyzed as crucial to the construction of domestic fiction in the late eighteenth and early nineteenth centuries, that is, the country manor as social and familial enclosure cut off and protected from the rest of the population and the rest of the countryside and country; if these films revisit an imperialist dichotomy identified by Said as the domestic fiction of "home" built on the exclusion of "abroad"—the most recent Austen remake, *Mansfield Park* (1999), asserts those very ruptures and exclusions that the novels and films have persistently denied. *Mansfield Park* reverses the paradigm we have been analyzing in the Austen remakes precisely by thrusting what was excluded— "abroad"—back into the midst of the family enclosure where it not only disrupts the plot but (re)converts social and domestic intimacy into the threat of incest and the dread of family itself.

"Abroad" (Be)Comes Home

Patricia Rozema's screenplay and direction (1999) are based on Austen's novel, her letters, and early journals. It is no coincidence that of all these remakes *Mansfield Park* has received the least publicity and fanfare because, instead of smoothing out the contradictions and anxieties of our contemporary rootlessness with Austen's comforting repetition of quotidian familial/familiar domestic enclosures, instead of involving the viewer and Internet user in a community through the visual acknowledgment of its loss, it confronts us with those very omissions that Williams, Said, Jameson, and others insist have always constituted the cornerstone of domestic fiction.[16] *Mansfield Park*'s major differences from the other remakes lie in its negation of the very reasons contemporary viewers have passionately returned to Austen.

Instead of a world enclosed, separated from the colonial world that supports and nourishes its very claim to social and familial self-sufficiency, the domestic world of the *Mansfield Park* film is plagued at home with the problems of abroad, specifically with the problems of Sir Thomas Bertram's sugar plantation on Antigua. The motif of slavery and the English investment in the colonies mentioned—but barely in the novel—cross the threshold into film, the English countryside, and right into the living room.

In the early scenes, the film provides an approach to the manor house like that of the other films, but which cannot be experienced as a "return home" either for protagonist or viewer. The manor is not invested as a site of domestic familial and social intimacy. A sense of distance is introduced in the opening scenes, this time precisely not as an insignificant measure to be contradicted by the ostensible intimacy of people and places. Distance and separation become here the very measure of relations between people and even between family members themselves. The one hundred miles separating Fanny Price from her real parents and her former home shown in the very first scenes constitute a departure that doubles as an emotional, social, geographic, and class distance from the Bertram aunts, uncle, and cousins whom she is going to join at Mansfield Park. On both ends of the journey there is estrangement.

Fanny arrives at Mansfield Park to find nothing but a dark night, and where she is forced to wait outside until morning. Someone is indeed there, sitting on a balcony above the entryway, oblivious to everything inside as well as outside the house; his back is turned to the front of the screen, to Fanny, to us. He marks, but in a negative way, the boundaries between the enclosure of the country manor and the rest of the world. Drunk and alone, the eldest son and heir of Mansfield Park, Tom Bertram, lends a forlorn, lonely, even debauched isolation to this first encounter with the darkened, uninviting home.

Instead of domesticated views of the parkland where manors are nestled within all-encompassing frames, viewers are first met in this film with broad sweeping vistas of the English coast that introduce Fanny to a strange place and the strange practice for her (and for us?) of slavery. As her carriage stops on a hillside overlooking the coast on her long trip to Mansfield Park, the far-off cries of suffering slaves imprisoned in ships offshore, referred to by the coachman as "black cargo," erupt into the verdant English countryside.

Rozema insists on the thematics of the slave trade as an ironic comment on its nearly complete absence in the novel. The colonialist enterprise of plantations and slavery that works an unacknowledged but major influence on what transpires at Mansfield Park is kept literally at an ironic distance from the English shore. We hear only muffled cries from the ships. Later in the film, we see only Tom Bertram's drawings of the atrocities carried out on the sugar plantation in Antigua, in part by his father Sir Thomas himself, though these are taking place at least geographically far from English civilization and the domestic scene. We never actually see slaves within the world of the English country manor, except in what the film designates as representations. The viewer receives representations of slavery in voice and in rough drawings as opposed to any "real-life" filmic reenactment. The world of early nineteenth-century domestic England remains intact as a smooth visual filmic surface whereas the rougher acoustic and visual sketches of slavery challenge, while not entirely displacing, what thus becomes a (de)mystifying image. Though remaining unseen and offshore—slaves were not allowed, were not to be seen, in England—the consequences of slavery and colonialist trade enter compellingly into the picture in which they mark every critical juncture of the film.

It is only later in the film that we see the drawings sketched by his son, in which Sir Thomas is represented with female slaves in sexual and sadistic activity. But this has already been anticipated by his earlier remark just before deciding to give a ball in honor of Fanny. He relates an unrealized decision to bring a young slave woman to England where she would have "helped out" in the house. Whether it would have been at all possible and within the realm of verisimilitude in terms of English laws at the time, this decided departure from the novel, along with several others, designates the slave as an obvious figure of Fanny herself.

Sexual intimations are ubiquitous in the *Mansfield Park* film. As such, they undermine the close family ties represented in the other films. The inherent ambiguity of domestic in-family intimacy emerges through its conversion here into incest, sexual abuse, licentiousness. Such realities impede the domestic continuity and familiarity that in the other films flirt with incestuous behavior only to translate them into a cozy intimacy that comforts the contemporary, weary, global traveler. If the tendency toward in-family marriages in Austen's fiction is emphatically underscored in film as "a way of fortifying the family"; if in Austen novels as we read them today and see them adapted in films "incestuous alliances [. . .] preserve order and reestablish domestic harmony"[17]—the film *Mansfield Park* rejects such an anodyne interpretation and brings the stigma of incest and other violations to the surface.

Members of the family in this film are either distant, unconcerned, or, if close, they are suspect. It is not only Harold Pinter's portrayal of Sir Thomas Bertram that suggests through his looks and general demeanor less fatherly concern than lecherous desires. Fanny Price's own father in greeting his daughter after many years holds her too close, takes a momentary and inappropriate interest in her development into a young woman, as the glances exchanged between Fanny, her sister Susan, and her mother corroborate. And though the relation between her cousin and surrogate brother Edmund and Fanny remain as companionate, bland and nonsexual as in the novel, their brother–sister counterparts—Henry and Mary Crawford—are too close, too familiar. They remain unconcerned by moral considerations or lustful tendencies, such as in Mary's obvious desire to look and touch Fanny when in one scene Fanny steps out of her rain-soaked clothes.

Instead of the intimate spaces, which in the other films quickly establish close physical and verbal contact and communication between father and daughter, husband and wife, sisters, and sister or sister-in-law and brother, *Mansfield Park* introduces the manorial home as a set of alienating and disconnected spaces. Furniture is placed in the middle of large empty rooms, arranged awkwardly and discontinuously as opposed to being ensconced with relation to each other, assimilated within comfortable and warm lived-in rooms furnished with the bric-a-brac of everyday living. The rooms themselves in Mansfield Park have unusual angles that prevent any spatial understanding of their relation one to the other. Lady Bertram sinks into a laudanum-induced stupor that counterfeits her perfect tranquillity and comfortable privileged laziness in the novel. Even the windows, which in all the other films play an important part in framing domesticity and the portraits of protagonists within its enclosures, have here lost their transparency. Their panes are cloudy, their images distorted.

And if this formal house has banned intimacy through the configuration of its large, imposing, uncomfortable, and unrelated spaces, the small impoverished home of Fanny fares no better as a site of domestic warmth or communication. Fanny's desire to "return home" from Mansfield Park to her own family and real parents in the second part of the book is frustrated by the reality of her ungracious, uninterested, and negligent parents and by the crowded living conditions. The ceiling, which is too low, weighs heavily on Fanny and the rest of this family in the first scenes of the movie and, later on, contributes to the sense of closeness that here suffocates privacy and negates the pursuit of any individual activity or freedom of movement. Such spatial and architectural enclosures, which are also economic and educational limits, confine Fanny, her siblings, and her parents to intimate contact that always threatens to be too close.

The family today, like its portrayal in the *Mansfield Park* film, is a constant object of concern and suspicion. Intimacy often and increasingly is seen as threatening disaster for children too closely monitored by adults, too closely held, touched, or looked at, even and especially by relatives, children too controlled by rules and regulations that impede their independence as individual and free agents. These complaints and others besides make "intimacy" a term and a concept fraught with negative implications and overtones that the Austen remakes have worked hard to cover over and to efface. At least all remakes except *Mansfield Park*, the exception that proves even more clearly the rules and strategies governing the other Austen films.

The *Mansfield Park* remake plunges us back into contemporary space and relations, tracing out the contrast between what we want to see in Austen and what we are attempting not to see. The principal purveyor of that contrast is Mary Crawford, the antagonist whom the viewer, along with the straitlaced upright Fanny and Edmund, comes to identify as evil, an evil that must be expelled. The scene of expulsion in which Edmund breaks off relations with Mary thus must take place in the film at Mansfield Park instead of, in the novel, at a London residence. Mary's sin is attempting to assuage the sorrow, outrage, and moral conscience of the family, especially that of Sir Thomas Bertram, in the scandal surrounding the already-married Maria Bertram, who has run off with Mary's brother, Henry.

This moral relativism on the part of the woman he had sought to marry leads Edmund to question not just her suitability as his partner but her very identity. Mary has become a stranger who as such no longer belongs at Mansfield Park; she is exiled to another world, abroad. That world is our very own. In front of the family, assembled in a drawing room at Mansfield Park to discuss the scandal, Edmund tells Mary that he does not "recognize her." The term carries the sense here of Edmund not knowing any more who she is and also implies, in its older social meaning, his complete personal and social rejection of her. These two meanings are intricately linked, since social conventions dictated that strangers are excluded from family/familiar society. Before the assembled family, Mary Crawford makes a final exit, expelled to the world beyond the familial spatial but also temporal boundaries of Mansfield Park.

Mary makes several references in the film to living in a "modern world": "we're living in modern times," she says at one point and, when trying to appease the family, "It's 1806 for heaven's sake." No such explicit references to modernity appear in the novel. But in the film Mary Crawford's repeated allusions to the world beyond Mansfield Park, her interest in and attachment to the world of ambition, moral ambiguity and to the "modern," place us viewers in a curious and ambivalent position. For, although Edmund does not "recognize" that world, we viewers do. While we have been strategically and securely positioned on the side of Fanny and Edmund, whose exemplary moral conduct dominates Mansfield Park, especially at the end of the film, we do recognize Mary's voice coming from a place we know only too well.

Even with the feminist conversion of the novel's Fanny, who in the film has magically turned into a writer with strong ambitions of her own, we, like Mary Crawford, cannot reside at Mansfield Park. Do we accept the companionate marriage between Fanny and Edmund that never did satisfy many readers and critics either in Austen's time or in ours? Can we reside in a place so ultimately disconnected from the structure of our lives? Mary's presence functions like the eruption of slavery into the lives of the Bertrams. Though it is she who is exiled, though we as identified viewers even participate in that expulsion, nevertheless, we find ourselves in that very same position: desirous of staying behind, but like Mary we do not belong.

The next to last scene, without equivalent in the novel, shows us Mary and her brother—each of whom has acquired a new partner—seated at a garden table. Married or not, the two spouses, or lovers of the Crawfords have formed barely veiled, intimate relations with each other, exchanging knowing glances, while Mary and her brother seem unconcerned and at ease. Looking straight at the audience, Mary comments matter of factly: "It could have all turned out differently, but it didn't." How "it all turned out" glosses more than the denouement of the plot and her and her brother's lost opportunity of marriage to Edmund and Fanny. Such a remark places her outside the borders of Mansfield Park, beyond the temporal frames of the story and is directed explicitly to the twenty-first-century viewer. The small, intimate, enclosed world of secure boundaries that Edmund and Fanny nevertheless construct was not to be the outcome for Mary Crawford and neither can it be for us.

Rozema's film brings out the reasons for Austenmania by underscoring the spatial and temporal virtuality of the contemporary viewer who, with the media of film, cyberspace, as well as with the novel, cultivates a fantasy of residing in a small, intimate world while living in a global society. Fredric Jameson describes a fundamental dichotomy already in the late eighteenth/early nineteenth century between individual experience and the structure in which this individual and so-called private, intimate experience was clearly embedded.[18]

> The phenomenological experience of the individual subject—traditionally, the supreme raw materials of the work of art—becomes limited to a tiny corner of the social world, a fixed-camera view of a certain section of London or the countryside or whatever. *But the truth of that experience no longer coincides with the place in which it takes place.* The truth of that limited daily experience of London lies, rather, in India or Jamaica or Hong Kong; it is bound up with the whole colonial system of the British empire that determines the very quality of the individual's subjective life. Yet, those structural coordinates are no longer accessible to immediate lived experience and are often not even conceptualizable for most people.[19]

Today, it is perhaps because we have become so acutely aware that the "truth of our experience does not coincide with the place in which it takes place" (Jameson, see above) that we look to the most open-ended virtual places of all, the spaces of video, TV, film and the Internet, to propel us into the world of Jane Austen, where we want to live the exotic, if identifiable, fictions of domestic intimacy.

Notes

1. Internet space also can be reconfigured from one moment to the next. Thus, the Republic of Pemberley site has already been redesigned and the former map described is no longer featured on the first page. In effect, it seems to have disappeared in the new design of the site.

2. Jane Austen, *Emma*, ed. Robert Clark, intro. J. M. Dent (London: Everyman, 1996), 6. Reference to this text throughout this chapter will be to this edition. R.W. Chapman, ed., *The Works of Jane Austen*, vol. 4 (1933; London and New York: Oxford University Press, 1988).

3. Glenda A. Hudson, *Sibling Love and Incest in Jane Austen's Fiction* (New York: St. Martin's Press, 1992, repr. 1999), 14. For further discussion of the laws regarding incest, see pp. 14–32.

4. Hudson seems to suggest this as well in speaking about the close proximity of siblings and family members: "Since siblings had fewer restrictions socially and emotionally, writers found it easy to dream about the erotic possibilities of such propinquity, such intimacy in their work" (Ibid., 16).

5. Fredric Jameson speaks of the family as the former basic building block of a society that is "hierarchized" ("Cognitive Mapping," in *Marxism and the Interpretation of Culture*, ed. Cary Nelson and Lawrence Grossburg [Urbana: University of Illinois Press, 1988], 355 [347–357]).

6. See Suzanne R. Pucci, "The Nature of Domestic Intimacy and Sibling Incest in Diderot's *fils naturel*," *Eighteenth-Century Studies* 30 no. 3 (1997): 271–287.

7. *Emma*, film version written and directed by Douglas McGrath, Miramax (1996).

8. Raymond Williams, *The Country and the City* (New York: Oxford University Press), 166 (emphasis added).

9. Edward W. Said, *Culture and Imperialism* (New York: Vintage, 1994), 72. See also Williams, *The Country and the City*, 165–182 passim.

10. See in particular Deidre Lynch, "At Home with Jane Austen," in *Cultural Institutions of the Novel*, ed. Deidre Lynch and William B. Warner (Durham, NC: Duke University Press, 1996), 159–192, in which she discusses the changing function in English history of the Austen staple of the country home and household. For a discussion of the country home in terms of domesticity, the household, and women, see Nancy Armstrong, *Desire and Domestic Fiction: A Political History of the Novel* (New York: Oxford University Press, 1987).

11. See Roger Sale, "Jane Austen," in his *Closer to Home: Writers and Places in England, 1780–1830* (Cambridge: Harvard University Press, 1986), 35–64.

12. Emma Thompson, *The Sense and Sensibility Screenplay and Diaries: Bringing Jane Austen's Novel to Film* (New York: Newmarket Press, 1996), 27.

13. The novel does not begin with a description of the death scene but rather with this description: "The family of Dashwood had been long settled in Sussex. Their estate was large and their residence was at Norland Park, in the centre of their property, where, for many generations, they had lived in so respectable a manner, as to engage the general good opinion of their surrounding acquaintance" (Jane Austen, *Sense and Sensibility* [Middlesex, UK: Penguin, 1995], 3).

14. The half mile is mentioned later (8), not in response to Mr. Woodhouse's complaints but in passing by Emma to Mr. Knightley.

15. Thompson, *Sense and Sensibility*, 284.

16. Jameson, "Cognitive Mapping," 347–360.

17. Hudson, *Sibling Love and Incest*, 25.

18. Jameson remarks "a growing contradiction between lived experience and structure, or between a phenomenological description of the life of an individual and a more properly structural model of the conditions of existence of that experience. Too rapidly we can say that, while in older societies and perhaps even in the early stages of market capital, the immediate and limited experience of individuals is still able to encompass and coincide with the true economic and social form that governs that experience, in the next moment these two levels drift ever further apart and really begin to constitute themselves into that opposition the classical dialectic describes as *Wesen* and *Erscheinung*, essence and appearance, structure and lived experience" ("Cognitive Mapping," 349).

19. Ibid. (emphasis added).

8

The Return to Repression

Filming the Nineteenth Century

Virginia L. Blum

Mythologies say what is being sought "in the image" because no one dares to
believe in it anymore, and often what *fiction* alone is able to give. They betray
at once hunger and action. They translate at the same time a refusal to lose and
a refusal to act. Thus, too many words or images tell of a loss and an impo-
tence, that is, the opposite of what they display.
—Michel de Certeau, *Culture in the Plural*

Somewhere a network TV–movie exec is probably saying, "Forget Danielle
Steel, we're doing Mansfield Park."
—Jeffrey Gantz, "Ageless Austen"

About Iain Softley's *The Wings of the Dove*, a reviewer for *The New States-
man* complained that the sex was not especially sexual: "Anyone searching
for the extraordinary reticence that characterises the prose of Henry James
would be sadly disappointed. The novel's great undescribed moment of
physical passion in a hotel room ends up in the film—as perhaps it might on
a holiday package tour—as a knee-trembler in the Venetian arcades."[1] This
reviewer remains committed to a notion of sexuality created through textual
indirection, through the omission of the actual sex scene. Indeed, what
would make Henry James worth adapting, for this reviewer at least, is such
a style of repressing the act. To film the sex in all its tedious and overwrought detail is simply not sexy, not Jamesian; rather, it is just more of the
same old pedestrian sex typical of this sex-for-fun-and-sale culture. Such a
reproach speaks simultaneously to our fantasy of what we might recuperate

via the adaptation of pre-Victorian and Victorian novels and our sense that we have lost the experience of desire that they had to struggle to repress.

From the perspective of the twentieth-century narcissistic subject, Richard Sennett observes, sexual repression could be among the worst threats to personal fulfillment. In *The Fall of Public Man,* he writes, "In rebelling against sexual repression, we have rebelled against the idea that sexuality has a social dimension."[2] According to Sennett, in refusing the distinction between the public and private, sexual intimacy risks becoming less "intimate." "Intimacy," he writes, "is an attempt to solve the public problem by denying that the public exists" (27). This loss of investment in what Sennett calls "the expressive life and identity of the public man" has led to "a new life, more personal, more authentic, and all things considered, emptier" (109). Because the sexual relation became the place of authenticity (as Stephen Heath puts it), "I may do this and that in society but I am only really me in bed," we are left with what seems to be an irreconcilable tension between the relationality of sex and an emphasis on personal experience.[3] The implicit contradiction in representing the sexual relation as merely a transiently social means to a narcissistic end suggests why the twentieth-century sexual relation, insofar as it has been represented, has not managed to fulfill its promise.[4] Moreover, our ongoing concern with sexual repression and sexual dysfunction is an attempt to seduce sexuality itself into reappearing in public, in private—it does not matter where. It is gone, and we cannot find it anywhere.

We have books to commemorate its passing. Different kinds of liberatory sex manuals. The "Kinsey Reports" of 1948 and 1953. Virginia Masters and William Johnson's heady investigations into the science of arousal. Alex Comfort's *The Joy of Sex* that graced the middle-class bookshelves of everyone who knew anything about the public promotion of one's private life. Shere Hite's and Nancy Friday's more recent steamy accounts of the netherworld of women's sexual fantasies. During the 1970s, the sex-therapy/narrative books assumed the importance of a category unto itself among booksellers.[5]

Where does sexuality happen—and how? Supposedly, the twentieth century has led us toward the increasingly liberated pursuit of pleasure for its own sake, unharnessed by restrictions such as reproduction (birth control solved that) or marriage (which is no longer the social form in which sex must take place). Evermore unrepressed, ever closer to the direct unmediated attainment of sexual gratification for its own sake, we peeled off all the excess clothing, modified and repealed out-of-sight obscenity laws and, most important, the oppressive social conventions that congealed our pleasures. John D'Emilio and Estelle Freedman quote Mary Quant's account of her invention of the miniskirt: "Am I the only woman who has ever wanted to go to bed with a man in the afternoon?" she asked. "Any law-abiding female, it used to be thought, waits until dark. Well, there are lots of girls who don't want to wait. Mini-clothes are symbolic of them."[6] Even the diurnal clock is construed as a rupture between desire and its satisfaction. The miniskirt decorates a body ever ready for sexual activity, freed up from the interdictions of daylight and work spaces.[7]

The 1990s version of the sex manual is the film adaptation of the nineteenth-century story of sexual repression. Of course, there is nothing especially liberatory about these narratives. Are we waiting for them to throw off their fourteen layers of undergarments and experience the unrivaled pleasures of their sartorially challenged flesh? Not exactly. Rather, we want them to keep their clothes on. Nothing, in fact, is quite so dismally unsexy as the final scene of *The Wings of the Dove* in which Helena Bonham-Carter's Kate Croy engages in explicit and torpid sex with Linus Roache's Merton Densher.

After all, it is repression itself we were after all along, the empty form that conveys with it a sense of the sexuality that we seem to feel ebbed with the passing of the Victorians. This is what we want from them, the secret of all that lusty sexual energy they kept under wraps so tightly that they wound up with various hysterical disorders as a result of too little to show for so much.

No such limits are placed on our bodies and souls. There is no firm boundary between the private and the public. We are under no such constraints. Is that because there is nothing left to constrain? Was there ever? "One of the vicissitudes an instinctual impulse may undergo is to meet with resistances which seek to make it inoperative. Under certain conditions . . . the impulse then passes in the state of 'repression.'"[8] Was Victorian repressed sexuality a figment of Sigmund Freud's imagination that was already merely a token to mark its fading?

It used to be that we would present quiet, civilized demeanors in public while in private we lusted. Now, we lust in public and in private often we are, well, as the sex therapists tell us, we are simply not functional. Indeed, low sex drive is among the top complaints patients bring to the therapist's office. We spend a lot of time curing this much vaunted problem. Moreover, one of the primary side effects of Prozac and other antidepressants is its suppression of the libido. Perhaps this would have been welcomed by one of Freud's overwrought guilty masturbators? Not so, today's depressives. Indeed, we talk about it quite openly; over lunch we bemoan the one little drawback of our cherished antidepressants. "So and so and I never" we confide to each other—but it is really no confidence at all because we tell virtual strangers and, anyway, you would learn as much from an article in *Good Housekeeping* or overhearing two women openly converse in the waiting room of the dentist's office.

Everyone knows that the Victorians suffered terribly for their repression. "Sex," writes Stephen Kern, "was less satisfying for Victorians than it was for the moderns because the Victorians had more to fear."[9] If so, then why are we wanting to know so much about them, why endlessly replay their cautious alliances that were forged through endless conventional defiles? If they were not having an especially good time of it, why do we think they were? It is as if we want to find out: Would they, if they could? Did they think about it? Let us strip them bare and watch (like the miserable lovers of *The Wings of the Dove*). But that is not what we want at all, in the end, which is what the scene is meant to illustrate. Indeed, the sex is no better for us than for them.

Why do we want to watch our Victorian lovers not doing anything? We wade through almost six hours of the 1995 BBC version of *Pride and Prejudice* just to get the final kiss between Darcy and Elizabeth. It is in the apparent "nothing" that we hope to locate their sexual secret—which for us is the secret of sexuality that eludes us as a culture. These Victorian adaptations give us the structure of repression as if the structure alone were enough to resuscitate what we imagine to be its content. Good post-Freudians that we are, we are more addicted to the idea of repression than we are to the sexual desire itself we imagine to be foaming at the bit.

If we revive the old strategy, the repressive regime, will we recover our desire as well? But what exactly do we imagine about this regime, its conventions? What do we think characterized the sexual as such, and finally, what is it we think we recognize in this prior social form that will function as antidote to our current sense of sexual malaise?

Kern's "history of love" shows us

> moving in the direction of greater authenticity as modern men and women become increasingly able to think about and experience the meaning of these new possibilities. For even though their authenticity was facilitated by changes that came about through no effort of their own, these changing circumstances enabled modern lovers, more than Victorian lovers, to act resolutely in the face of circumstance, reflect on the meaning of their love, and hence make it more their own.[6]

For Sennett, however, it is precisely this level of self-absorption that has made the love relation increasingly narcissistic—not object related at all.

If love is more our own, whence the divorce rate? Depression? Interminable and increasingly agitated discussions across the twentieth century of how to improve one's sex life? First manuals, then chemicals. What exactly is this authentic love relation we are told by Kern is ours for the asking? Kern's own account of the lifting of Victorian constraints perfectly illustrates the terms of our confusion.

Michel Foucault has convincingly and influentially argued that the so-called repressive hypothesis of the nineteenth century is part and parcel of the system of sexual surveillance. Sex was not repressed at all—just look at the plethora of antisex tracts, sexologists' lengthy tomes, and, ultimately, the psychoanalytic "confessional" where the secrets offered up are inevitably sexual in nature. No, Foucault insists, it is not that sex was repressed but rather that sexuality became a way of monitoring and cataloging modern subjects. As Anthony Giddens points out, however, in the face of clear evidence of repressed sexuality in the nineteenth century (including the very limited number of people who even had access to the works of the sexologists), it is difficult to argue, as Foucault does, for an undisrupted continuum between institutional power and the active forging of sexual discourse.[10] More important, for the purposes of what will become central to my discussion of the passion for adaptation, we need to distinguish between discursive and bodily forms of repression.

Even if there was a proliferation of a certain kind of "talk," as Henry James puts it in his novel *The Awkward Age*—circuitous, punitive, and confessional—there were most assuredly numerous restraints placed on bodies. It is exactly this structure, the intense innuendo with no apparent sex, that so many of these films recapitulate for us. It is important here to make a distinction between unconscious repression and social repression. While, as Freud noted frequently, a repressive social apparatus has the effect of intensifying unconscious repression by increasing the discrepancy between the imperatives of reality and the sexual drive, in order for any kind of social organization to be sustained, the sexual drive needs to be repressed to some degree.[11] Nevertheless, there is a curious overlap between his account of instinctual functioning and the movements of pleasure and constraint in the social order itself. Consider the following passage from *Civilization and its Discontents* in which he tells us that "intense enjoyment" can only be experienced by way of contrast: "What we call happiness in the strictest sense comes from the (preferably sudden) satisfaction of needs which have been dammed up to a high degree"(*SE*, 21:25). Like the spatial distribution of work and domesticity among the Victorians, whereby the joys of the home can only happen through being set at a remove from the workplace, the satisfaction of needs, indeed pleasure itself, is only achievable through being "dammed." This is a deeply economic account of Victorian modes of gratification that Freud replays both interior to and outside the human subject. Thus the repressive modality itself, while an interference to sexual pleasure when its claims are too great, is nevertheless constitutive of human desire.

If, as Foucault suggests, modern sexuality has been constituted by its increasing "putting into discourse," it is curious indeed that these adaptations—products of a putatively "sexually liberated" society—give us pleasure through suppressing sex or at least heavily circumscribing the ways in which sex can be deployed—this, in contrast to what became the almost agonizing process of undoing repression through countless 1970s cinematic celebrations of the sex act. Why keep looking (and looking again) at these pictures of nineteenth-century repression when we have liberated ourselves to see all the sex we want? It seems crucial that the discursive sex largely supplant bodily sex for the technology of desire to operate.

Low Sexual Desire

> "Hypoactive sexual desire is probably the most prevalent of all
> the sexual dysfunctions."[12]

"In fact," write Raymond C. Rosen and Sandra R. Leiblum, "hypoactive sexual desire (HSD) is a major focus of . . . the field of sex therapy generally."[13] Surprisingly, there are those (many in fact) who do not thrive in the wake of the sexual revolution. Bernard Apfelbaum laments that the "downside of the sexual revolution has been a virtual epidemic of response anxiety. It is now as if being good in bed is what sex is all about."[14] The trick for the therapist is to locate where and why in the chain of drive and arousal events. What reforges your sexuality, apparently, is *delay* and *abstinence*—two key words, we should take note, for the Victorian sexual imagination.

"The [stroking] assignment is done without clothes, using a bed. There should be at least enough light to see what you are doing, and the assignment should not be done unless the room is comfortably warm, since any chill blocks other sensations. Don't try to create a special mood with wine or music, since the idea is to get a kind of baseline impression."[15] The assignment should unfold according to strict procedure. In place of repression interfering with the unmediated flow of sensation, it could be the temperature of the room or romantic "aids." "Stroking movements should blend into one another in a slow continuous motion without losing contact with your partner's body. The idea is to do a teasing touch, especially in sensitive areas."[16] Here, in sex-therapy talk, are the two competing discourses of sexual desire—repressive and liberatory—summed up in what might be called two doctrines of sexual stimulation: continuous undisrupted stroking versus teasing touches.

"All other sexual activity should be avoided on the day the assignment is done."[17] The success of these assignments is largely dependent on postponing the very sex these poor couples only think they do not want. The longer they delay, as they are put through the inflexible steps of stroking exercises, the more likely it is that they will be reassimilated into the proper structure of desire. Again, recall Freud's insistence on the "damming up" in order to heighten the experience of satisfaction.

To understand the vicissitudes of sexual desire, "a distinction can be made between desire *for* sex and desire *in* sex."[18] It is equally important to distinguish between psychological defenses/conflicts and physiological response. According to Helen Kaplan, "Patients learn to have an orgasm even though the deeper layers of the sexual conflict remain untouched."[19] Like many other sex therapists, she believes that through controlled and distracting fantasy, the body can be trained to overcome sexually inhibiting psychological conflicts. In a radical reconfiguration of what was for Freud the conflict between instinctual impulses and the imperatives of civilization, here we find the social order actively soliciting those (still) recalcitrant drives.

Darcymania: The Look of Sex

"And yet, amid the tastefulness, sexual tension lurks."[20]

I recall a certain period of time, the late 1960s to the late 1970s, when you would be hard-pressed to find a movie without at least one obligatory sex scene. There was the inevitable question attached to each "adult" film: How much was going to be shown? Full frontal? Just women or, finally, men as well? It was all very exciting, this outing of private sexual practices in the movie theater where liberated middle-class couples could discuss over a post-film glass of wine the relative tastefulness of each sex scene before retiring to homes graced by Calder lithographs, where body paints and other "hip" sexual stimulants were openly stored in bathroom cupboards.

Asked to account for the public heat generated by his performance in the 1995 BBC production *of Pride and Prejudice*, Colin Firth explained his acting strategy: "I thought to myself: 'This is where he wants to go across the room and punch someone. This is where he wants to kiss her. This is where he wants sex with her right now.' I'd imagine a man doing it all, and then not doing any of it. That's what I did."[21] In other words, what he did precisely was to think instead of act. The trick is to assume the look of desire instead of acting upon it. It is the thought itself, the very illicit sexual idea, Foucault asserts, that in the seventeenth century overtook behavior as the central issue of sex. Sex was relocated from deeds to words and thoughts, "shifting the most important moment of transgression from the act itself to the stirrings—so difficult to perceive and formulate—of desire. For this was an evil that afflicted the whole man, and in the most secret of forms."[22]

In becoming the central site of knowledge, sex had to be at once hidden and traceable. Peter Gay describes the perceived relation between inner passion and somatic clues in the Victorian period: "a quavering voice, a trembling hand, a twitching face betrayed the anxious, often sexual, turmoil within."[23] That desire supplants the acts themselves makes sex something more pervasive, inevitable, and less knowable—thereby inciting a discourse of detection. It is no wonder that Foucault sees psychoanalysis as another "technology of sex" linked to the power–knowledge production of sex and the ubiquitous always already known "secret."

Homosexuality as well, for psychoanalysis, became less about practice than about desire. It was a kind of "interior androgyny, a hermaphrodism of the soul."[24] Where the nineteenth-century sexologists categorized homosexuality (or inversion) as a distinct perversion separable from those who were "normal," psychoanalysis traces homosexual predispositions and impulses in the most pristinely heterosexual of lives. Linking sexuality to desire instead of practice renders every sexual subject the subject of scrutiny and speculation (both inspection and introspection).

Ultimately, in the more sexually "liberated" late twentieth century, one's sexual desire is seen as one's "authenticity" just as previously, among the Victorians, it was identified as one's worrisome secret. "By the late 1960s," write D'Emilio and Freedman, "the belief in sex as the source of personal meaning had permeated American society."[25] To know one's true desire thus became the project of the sexually liberated subject, the route to self-knowledge. Relationships, as Giddens points out, thereby became the means to such self-expression instead of an end in themselves. He calls this a "pure relationship."

> A pure relationship . . . refers to a situation where a social rela-
> tion is entered into for its own sake, for what can be derived by
> each person from a sustained association with another; and
> which is continued only in so far as it is thought by both parties
> to deliver enough satisfactions for each individual to stay within
> it. Love used to be tied to sexuality, for most of the sexually
> "normal" population, through marriage; but now the two are
> connected more and more via the pure relationship.[26]

Giddens' account of an intimate relationship based on mutual profit is the natural consequence of a sexuality yoked to one's core self; when the other person stops giving one pleasure, including sexual pleasure, the relationship necessarily loses all benefit for "me." What seems apparent is that to tie love to marriage would endanger the narcissistic impulse with the demands of the social. In many of these adaptations (especially the Jane Austen films), we find the combination of the repressive plot with the marriage plot; in other words, just as they were for their original nineteenth-century readers, the conclusions are sexual inasmuch as they point to the marriage bed. While the tedium of the marriage bed in the postliberation world can seem to interfere with the ongoing unfolding of one's sexual truth, in fantasy we are drawn to the fixity of desire, love, and personal fulfillment.

The twentieth-century apotheosis of the relocation of sex from outward behavior to interior desire is the film closeup.[27] Here, character or inner substance is imagined to radiate through the surface we intensely scrutinize for this interiority. Leo Braudy writes that the "visible body is our only evidence for the invisible mind" and the closeup is the extreme example of the ways in which character is legible on the surface of the face.[28] Specifically, to read the desire of a film character during the film closeup is the twentieth-century instance par excellence of decoding sex.[29]

Cinematic Austen capitalizes on depicting repressed sexuality. We watch the repression take place, note its lineaments, the fierce looks, trembling mouths, shuddering eyelids, lighting meant to simulate pallor. Repression is the very thing we watch for. The longer it is sustained, the more gratified we are by its being overcome. Austen's characters perfectly enact what for us has become the essence of Victorian sexuality—this transcendence of repression. "My feelings will not be repressed," Darcy confesses to Elizabeth Bennet.[30]

Well, insofar as Colin Firth's Darcy is concerned, they will and they will not. Watching him struggle with his pent-up emotion is the centerpiece of the 1995 *Pride and Prejudice*.[31] Because she frequently shows women of modest means and matrimonial prospects vastly exceeding their class status through marriage, Austen is the perfect narrator of the repressive plot. It is through their desirability that these women dangerously tempt men away from their fixed social order. Overcome with passion, Darcy explains the battle between desire and class affiliation:

> You must allow me to tell you how ardently I admire and love you. In declaring myself thus I am fully aware that I will be going expressly against the wishes of my family, my friends and, I need hardly add, my own better judgment. The relative situation of our families is such that any alliance between us must be regarded as a highly reprehensible connection. Indeed, as a rational man, I cannot but regard it as such myself—but it cannot be helped. Almost from the earliest moments of our acquaintance I have come to feel for you a passionate admiration and regard which despite all my struggles has overcome every rational objection and I beg you most fervently to relieve my suffering and consent to be my wife.

This speech, written for the televised adaptation, spells out in detail the terms of Darcy's conflict. While in contrast to Austen's contemporary readers, most viewers of these films might find uncompelling the war between familial duty and personal interest expressed by Darcy. What we do feel most keenly is his capitulation to a desire that has shattered the hold of whatever name he attributes to the repressive social forces.[32]

The fact that the two principals—Jennifer Ehle and Colin Firth—of the BBC production of *Pride and Prejudice*, had an affair during the filming is an essential part of the story of our reception of this particular Austen adaptation that led to a phenomenon known as "Darcymania" among British and North American women. Women loved him. For a great part of the BBC's version of the story, he hung around in the background, not saying much. Firth did a lot of his acting with his eyes. Other characters talked a great deal about him while he was absent. Unlike a lot of male heroes, he was a mystery. He was in no way a feminized wimp. Late in the day, burning with passion and unfulfilled sexual desire, he jumped off his horse into a pond and emerged, his shirt dripping. What people remember is those muttonchop sideburns flying through the air. For the entire Bridget Jones generation, this was a superb antidote to the dull, whining, noncommittal "New Man of the 1990s"—and he did not drink lager and go on about football all the time.[33]

Firth claimed that the profound viewer reaction to Darcy's sexiness had nothing to do with him. "When I wore football shorts in *Fever Pitch*, for example, I think everyone could see that I was nothing out of the ordinary. My legs and arse didn't have the same effect on women at all."[34] But Colin Firth's beefcake version of Darcy has less to do with the attractions of his body and more to do with a series of sultry and meaningful "looks" spread over the duration of six hours. The not-said, the implied, the "certain" look captured in the cinematic closeup—these are the places of sexuality in the twentieth century. Not surprisingly, we go in search of sexual desire in what we imagine to be the most repressed context of all, Austen's pre-Victorian world of heavily controlled courtship, significant glances, and ever unstated agendas. Moreover, as William Leith writes, Darcy "is not remotely non-committal"[35]; in contrast to the inevitable transience of Giddens' "pure relationship," Darcy offers what seems to be a full-fledged object relationship—or at least what we imagine such a thing would look like.

In many ways, this particular version of Austen is a parody of our expectations. Darcy's meaningful looks stimulate all our erotic fantasies about the not-said, the repressed, the imagined—at the same time that we interpret it all quite consciously. But it is in the structure of repression as such that we hope to find the erotic morsel—the good old erotic as it was meant to be before it came out of the closet and bored us with its endless displays of what sex really looks like. As Firth commented during the making of the series:

> There is nothing exceptionally sexual about it all. Nudity? So far no one has even removed a shirt. In fact I go for a swim after a long ride in one scene and remain fully clothed. What happened, I think, is that someone said they wanted it to be sexy. What they meant was the kind of sexuality that's in the book, the sexuality of repression. When you read the book, you know that everybody's horny—all that flirtation and dancing and conversation, but nobody's going to get laid.[36]

But just this sexuality, the sexuality of repression, is where sex happens for the desire-starved late-twentieth-century viewer—as Firth was later to learn firsthand in the throes of Darcymania.

Scorching looks alone, however, would not do it for us. Rather, it is through the iconic and discursive juxtaposition of periods. The old repressive devices and vocabulary along with this twentieth-century "technology of sex," the closeup (perfectly devised to follow on the heels of the relocation of sex from outside to inside), yoked to the sexual revolution icon of beefcake bodies as well as the pivotal claim for female sexual agency—it is this particular mix that makes us all so feverish.

Originally intending to show Darcy naked,[37] this version of *Pride and Prejudice* caused a stir among some Austen purists.[38] A pre-televising narrative of a sexed-up *Pride and Prejudice* was ultimately bound up in its reception. Although Darcy is not naked exactly, we almost get a peek during a bath scene that expertly combines innuendo, the tension between the suppressed and liberated body, and the vicissitudes of the desiring gaze. Prior to this scene we have had the pleasure of witnessing Darcy's intense stares at Elizabeth Bennet. The constant tension between Darcy looking at Elizabeth and us watching Darcy, fuels a sense of longing, of looks that sweep back and forth, in a pattern of erotic identificatory shifts.[39] The scene in the bath is a good illustration of the ways in which the camera's movements tease our desire. The scene opens with Darcy in a bath. Next, we see Elizabeth fully clothed, outside the house. We cut to Darcy arising from his bath and donning his dressing gown (it is at this point that we just miss seeing his naked body). The camera trails Darcy as he moves to the window and gazes out on Elizabeth playing with his hunting dog. We bring to this scene our twentieth-century context of familiarity with the sight of naked bodies on screen (certainly we have been treated to an abundance of male bottoms)—which is now juxtaposed with the (also familiar) pre-Victorian prohibition on looking and touching. But this prohibition is not derived from the outside, from social law; rather, this time, in the case of these kinds of programs, it is we ourselves who install the impediment to our satisfaction.

It is precisely this knowledge of our own instrumentality in both delaying and interdicting certain kinds of sexual scenes that is pleasurably enacted in the anachronistic unfolding of the bathing scene. It is we, finally, twentieth-century sexually liberated subjects who choose to contain what otherwise would spill out rapturously. This is the proof of our desire—how hard we must work to contain it. About this production, Julian North writes: "Austen has been marketed as, at once, sexually restrained and sexually explicit, safely in the past and less safely in the present."[40] But it is precisely the dull safety of the present that this production is intended to unsettle through its metonymic troubling of the past. Importing into the present style of sexual relations the affective blockages of the past allows us to borrow the sense of desire evoked by repressed passions. The danger is not anywhere; in other words, this is the problem.

In considering the politics of Ang Lee's 1995 adaptation of *Sense and Sensibility*, North observes that in contrast to the novel's perspectival (and hence official) identification with the ideology of Elinor's restrained "sense," Emma Thompson's screenplay film identifies with Marianne's sensibility, the "authentic," unsuppressed, emotional life. "What is presented as Elinor's self-command in the novel is revealed by Marianne as her self-delusion in the film" (43). Moreover, North points out, the youngest of the three sisters, Margaret, assumes a role of prominence in the film, which is to speak aloud what others suppress in the name of social convention, female modesty and propriety. "The temptation in a film adaptation must have been to cut Margaret altogether, but Thompson chose not merely to retain her, but to develop her role to become one of the most significant in the film" (43). Since the process of constructing and overcoming repression is the central objective in bringing Austen to a postliberation audience, it makes perfect sense that the story should be strained into ideological complicity with the liberatory narrative.

Mary Reilly and the Joys of Repression

Peter Gay's *The Tender Passion* seems motivated by his powerful conviction that those Victorians are repressing something and he is going to find out just what with the aid of his psychoanalytic armamentarium.

> In this increasingly opaque, anxiety-provoking situation, it was only rational for the bourgeoisie to develop an almost desperate commitment to privacy and to mount a largely sincere, only partly conscious search for refined variants of earthly desires. This gives psychoanalysis its opportunity to assist the historian intent on discovering the farther reaches of love behind the smoke screens thrown up by purposeful propriety, diligent self-censorship, and tense moral preoccupations. . . . [Uncovering Victorian love] requires the programmatic suspicion of manifest surfaces that lies at the heart of Freud's investigative technique.[41]

Is his four-volume pursuit of what he calls "The Bourgeois Experience" really any different from our filmic attachment to the repressive plot? Consider Gay's own exuberant reaction to the repressive Victorian theme: psychoanalysis has an "opportunity," the historian is looking for "the farther reaches of love." This particular historian is nearly palpitating with the thrill of erotic discovery.

Stephen Frears' 1996 film *Mary Reilly* illustrates clearly how we process current repressive formulas through the Victorian plot. Robert Louis Stevenson's story of Dr. Jeckyll and Mr. Hyde is reframed through one of our culture's top-ten sexual stories: child sexual abuse. It is possible that the reason we are so interested in child sexual abuse, in fact, is because it so nicely acts out for us the repressive narrative—especially its formal investment in a particular relationship between surface and depth—exterior signposts to interiority.

From the opening scene of the film, we are taught to read the body for signs of otherwise secret and repressed sexual acts. Dr. Jeckyll, entering his house in the early hours of the morning, pauses to observe the servant, Mary Reilly, scrubbing his front steps. He notices scars on her wrists and bite marks on her neck. Later, we will find out that these are the physical traces of her father's abuse—both violent and sexual. The kindly and concerned Dr. Jeckyll (with his authorized medical gaze) wants to know the origin of her wounds. His alter-ego, the unrepressed Hyde, is overtly turned on by the scars that speak of Mary's sexual secrets. We are supposed to understand that both versions of this man read the body with the same intent: their desire lies in decoding and revealing the sexual truth that lies buried in Mary's mind but nevertheless remorselessly legible (for those who possess the right kind of insight) on the surface of her body.

Sexual desire and sexual repression go hand in hand, according to *Mary Reilly*, which throughout iconically tempts us with turning everything inside out. Even the skinning of an eel in the kitchen is meant to symbolize the anxiety aroused by unpeeling successive surface layers. Mary is horrified by the sight of the skinning, but what we learn is that underneath the surface layer are simply more layers, leading to an endlessly anxiety-inducing and sexually-arousing experience of archaeological discovery. Fog is the ubiquitous texture of the film, representing its titillating pursuit of clarity through obscurity. As Jeckyll pries into Mary's sexual secrets, so too is Mary wondering about the passionate man, Hyde, hidden within Jeckyll's tidy facade.

Deeply bound up in the logic of Victorian sexual repression, Jeckyll cannot manage to have a girlfriend so he visits brothels to satisfy his shameful sexual urges. It is precisely because of divorcing his public reputable life from his secret sexual and desiring life that such an element as "Hyde" can happen. It is repression that interferes with the integration of the public and private; but repression operates on two axes: one a spatial repression between the public life in his house and his secret life in the brothel, the other the repression of an "inner" desiring and aggressive self who is born, it seems, as a consequence of the massive effort at keeping separate the "two lives." This Hyde, the Hyde of *Mary Reilly*, is no distorted creature from Stevenson's short novel. Instead, this Hyde is the hyper-alluring, young, and attractive version of the older and grayer Jeckyll. Indeed, we cannot help but feel that an integrated doctor would not be nearly as stimulating as this heated-up creature who sinuously curves around Mary's trembling body. He is the object of her desire, the man in her dreams. Moreover, without the structure of repression, the outer shell describing the shape of a particular content, no such intense passion would be expressible.

According to Freud, under the influence of repression the instinctual representative

> proliferates in the dark, as it were, and takes on extreme forms of expression, which when they are translated and presented to the neurotic are not only bound to seem alien to him, but frighten him by giving him the picture of an extraordinary and dangerous strength of instinct. This deceptive strength of instinct is the result of an uninhibited development in phantasy

and of the damming-up consequent on frustrated satisfaction
(*SE*, 14:149).

Stevenson's Hyde is certainly frightening, a misshapen monster to mirror
the out-of-control "prolifera[tion] in the dark" of the instinctual representative so radically severed from consciousness. But Frears' version of Hyde
is actually quite "hunky," as one reviewer observes, suggesting that what
grows in the dark no longer seems quite so monstrous[42]; on the contrary, it
is where we go in search of passion that is missing from the manifest sexual landscape.

Let us return to Freud's economic explanation for this state of affairs:
"What we call happiness in the strictest sense comes from the (preferably
sudden) satisfaction of needs which have been dammed up to a high degree."[43] Thus "intense enjoyment" can only be experienced by way of contrast. It is all rather tenuous, actually, on the edge of too little and too
much—a well-timed oscillation between the state of damming up and the
rush of satisfaction—which is exactly the libidinous structure these films are
intended to induce in the viewer. The reason the film fails, however, is that
the rapid conversion of Hyde from grotesque monster to beefcake short-cir-
cuits the very repressive apparatus we were after to begin with. This repressed sexual content is the "good stuff" as we all know, and thus the
monster struggling from the repressive body of Jeckyll necessarily is the very
picture of our desire. Indeed, there is hardly any delay at all between the
film's libidinous urgency and the unveiling of its sexual protagonist. John
Malkovich's Hyde is the absolute image of the repressive plot reconfigured
through the late-twentieth-century appetite for the good old days.

While the film draws a parallel between Mary's father and Hyde (about
her father Mary reports, "It was like he carried another person inside him
and the drinking brought him out"), we are encouraged to long for what
would be overtly Oedipal contact between the glamorous Hyde and Mary.
A psychoanalytic reading of repressed Oedipal desire generally requires the
Oedipal to be, well, more repressed. Not so in this account that takes Oedipal lust as its origin and end. Hyde probes her about the relationship with
her father, asks how "far it had gone" and didn't she "look forward to those
evenings alone" with him? Directly after, Mary dreams of being seduced by
Hyde. The fun is in finding out about the "real" sexual abuse lurking beneath the signs of physical abuse (bite marks) just as Mary discovers the
"real" Hyde lurking beneath the repressed Jeckyll.

According to some drawings Mary discovers in the doctor's study, Hyde
is like a huge erect phallus escaping from the body's entrails. One drawing in
particular is simply a medical drawing with the cutaway of the body's interior. Superimposed on the flaccid penis of the medical drawing is an enormous erection, juxtaposing this form of scientific exposure (the successively
revealed layers of the body from skin to muscle to internal organs) with the

suppression/expression of the body's desire. At the same time, such imagery implies a never-ending search for the origin of desire that remains elusive— no matter how many layers of the body we medically excavate, the film (compulsively repetitive) repeatedly makes us watch the emergence of desire from repressed psyches and bodies.

The origin, it seems then, is in the very process of discovery itself. One drawing shows a tongue depressor inserted into the open mouth of a skull, as though one might find something further hidden inside the skeleton that by its very nature is the subject's remainder—the last layer exposed after all layers have eroded. To skin the eel, to explore the mouth of the skull, is to deny any ultimate truth or terminal point in the search for knowledge about the body. Incest sounds good—but is it enough? Or is it just another means for stimulating the bottomless appetite for knowledge about what was ostensibly repressed?

"Don't you know who I am?" Hyde coaxes Mary after cracking the teacup that is intended to recapitulate a childhood scene with her father. He is, of course, the "father." The "inside" of the father–doctor is the primal sexual man who cannot contain his baser impulses, even with his small daughter. Civilization, cultural imperatives, social law all are discarded like a dressing gown as Hyde (the primal phallic energy) rises up to have his way.

If Oedipal desire is so shocking it needs to be repressed, why does this film delight in putting it center stage? Moreover, doesn't the currency enjoyed by the story of child sexual abuse suggest that the Oedipal is anything but repressed?[44] In recent years, Freud has been vilified for mistakenly leading us to believe that it was children who fantasized about parents, not vice versa. The notorious reversal of his "seduction theory," supplanting with the Oedipus complex his original notion that hysterics were largely victims of childhood sexual abuse, was subsequently attacked as Freud's own suppression of the horrific cultural "fact" of the sexual victimization of children.[45] Both versions, of course, are repression narratives of sexuality. Either neurotics are repressing their early but real sexual experiences at the hands of lascivious adults or they are repressing their first experiences of sexual desire—Oedipal of course. *Mary Reilly* agonizes over and enjoys both versions: the repressed but real sexual abuse and the repressed but nevertheless powerful reciprocal Oedipal desire of the child. Hyde repeatedly suggests that Mary "wanted it" from her father, and Mary seems to confirm his theory. It is as if the film cannot get enough of the process of unrepressing the repressed materials—it is a sex act that continues to repeat its own self-stimulating formula. There is a secret, it is dangerous, there is pleasure to be had in the discovery.

Mary is excited by her discovery of the inner Hyde because she wants to learn more about what animated her father: "Where does it come from, sir?" she asks Hyde. "The rage?" To know what makes Hyde is to understand the origin of her own traumatic sexual awakening. She tempts the

"father" to see his rage/desire reemerge. She claims to have broken the cup
Hyde breaks. Henry Jeckyll cannot understand why: "After the story you
told me about your father, I can't understand how you could ever bring
yourself to say you had broken a cup—especially when you didn't do it."
Who "did" it—initiated the sexual act? The father in deed? Or the child
in fantasy?

Perversely, *Mary Reilly* monotonously restages different configurations of
Oedipal-style repression and its implosion to generate the very desire reported to be deliriously repressed by the Victorians. The undoing of repression becomes predictable, just another arousal machine—like the most
humdrum of pornography. But while the characters suffer from sexual repression, the film does not. As Freud observes, "*the essence of repression lies
simply in turning something away, and keeping it at a distance, from the
conscious*" (*SE*, 14: 147). There is a split in this film between its own frank
knowledge of the vagaries of sexual desire and its quiveringly repressed
characters. It is over trying to re-repress the Oedipal that the film obsesses.
To uncover a series of mysteries, it is necessary first quite self-consciously to
conceal them.

According to contemporary sex therapists, such as Garry McCarthy,
sexual dysfunction is often traceable to childhood sexual abuse: "The past
decade has seen an extraordinary upsurge of interest in the role of childhood sexual trauma as the core issue in sexual dysfunction, especially inhibited desire."[46] The low sexual desire syndrome, thus, stands for the
traumatic sexual secret. This squares neatly with the sexual repression
convention. What happens, paradoxically, is that low sexual desire is
made to stand for an early efflorescence of sexual experience. The seeming
absence of sexual desire is recuperated into sexuality by finding its decid-
edly sexual origins. The "cure" for such sexually traumatized subjects is,
first of all, to bring the secrets into the light of day. "[I]t [is] not unusual
for secrets and fears to inhibit sexual desire" (154). Sexual desire has to be
unimpeded, flow effortlessly through the liberated subject. There is "therapeutic power [in] revealing secrets" (154). As McCarthy puts it: "I spent
some time conveying examples of other clients, how shame over secrets
had inhibited their desire, and how problems had been resolved in therapy.
I gave Paul the option of writing out the secret or discussing it as part of
the sex history" (152).

There seems to be a structural congruence of the narrative of achieving
self-knowledge with that of sexual repression. As the sex therapists tell us,
we cannot achieve true intimacy with others without knowing ourselves better—what Sennett would link to mistaking our narcissism for object relat-
edness. Repressed memory syndrome, whereby one retrieves hitherto lost
memories of child sexual abuse, is a useful vehicle for fusing the two narratives. Not only do you learn the long lost truth about yourself and hence bet-

ter comprehend a whole life's worth of troubles and disappointments, you should also now be free to enjoy a happy sex life.

The Wings of the Dove:
The Delibidinized Aftermath of the Victorian Body

From the opening shots of Iain Softley's 1997 adaptation of Henry James' novel, we are prompted to await the eventual exposure of Kate Croy's (Helena Bonham-Carter) body. Kate and Merton Densher (Linus Roache) catch each other's eye in the underground train and within minutes ardently clutch each other in a caged elevator. The passion is captured all the more forcibly by the resistance of her thick daytime garments to his hands pressing against breasts and bottom. These clothes then stand for what both Merton and the camera long to rip from the woman's body. We cut from this scene to Kate wearing only her slip while making herself up at a dressing table. The metonymic movement from their fully clothed embrace to Kate half dressed illustrates the film's desiring trajectory to reveal the woman's body.

In many ways, *The Wings of the Dove* is James decked out in various hetero-masculine fetishistic contrivances of the contemporary cinema. Repeatedly, we are bombarded by the straight male fantasy around the possible lesbian configurations of two beautiful women. At one point Kate shows up in Milly's room: "It's freezing in my room." "Sleep here," offers the sensuously obliging Milly. The exchangeability/substitutability of the two women in the novel is more like having a bordello's worth of options in the film. The women comb one another's hair and Kate tenderly applies lipstick to Milly's mouth with her finger. For the festival scene in Venice, Milly is dressed as a princess, while both Merton and Kate are outfitted as men. It is unclear at a certain point whom Kate desires more—Merton or Milly. Rapidly, the film solves its own teasing question by having Kate and Merton steal away to make love in an alleyway (both still dressed as men!). Almost in the manner of sexual farce, viewers are kept wondering who will sleep with whom and how much will we see when they do.

It is the leading-lady's body, however, that stands for the repressed sexual desire that is ultimately exposed. By the time we finally see it, however, the accumulated tension has dissipated. The final sexual scene of *The Wings of the Dove* stops in its tracks the film's desire. Densher has greeted Kate with indifference; he has been in town for two weeks without contacting her. Kate undresses on his bed and turns to look at him, a look Densher returns quite coolly. She lies waiting for him. He is slow to arrive. The actual sexual contact is repeatedly disrupted by the emotional mismatch of the two. Although this is a scene that does not (and never would) make an appearance in the James novel, it nevertheless offers in late-twentieth-century terms a very Jamesian version of the ultimate impossibility of fulfilling the passion the characters talk and imagine to death. We have the sexual body promised to us from the film's outset now on full display. Yet we do not want this deli-bidinized body anymore than Merton; or rather, we are ambivalent about what we are getting: Is that all there is? This is the culminating lament of the film that offers up sex drained of both sexuality and love. That Merton's carnal love for Kate has been rerouted into spiritual desire for the dead Milly is presented by the film as the asymptote of desire. What comes to occupy the place of the repressed (in place of Kate's body) is Milly's memory, the memory he is now "in love with."

Although Softley's *The Wings of the Dove* certainly makes changes to the way in which sex happens in the novel (James writes simply, "[Y]et she had come, that once, to stay, as people called it," he nevertheless reproduces for a modern audience the novel's sensibility.[47] James' 1902 novel is in transition between the Victorian dispensation of repression and the modern commit-ment to being true to one's authentic sexual self; ironically, for a modern au-dience, the only way to express convincingly the end of sexual passion for this couple is to give us an explicit sex scene.

Aimlessly we carry on in the narrative logic of repression, it seems, with nothing especially left to repress. Because, under the repressive regime, re-pression is structurally central to the story of desire itself, without it there can be no origin of desire. Repression becomes the origin of desire insofar as "the thing" repressed is always the same old sexual desire. Repression is desire's public face, the very contour of the story of sexual desire. With-out repression, there is no sexual story to tell, no beginning and end, no original trauma, no Oedipal origin of neurosis, no conflict between primal urges and cultural imperatives, no secrets, no displacements, no final res-olution through unrepressing what had been for so long under the sea. These film adaptations offer us the old story that we are convinced they counted on, that worked on their libidos so perfectly that even marriage (the dullest form of sex for postliberation subjects) appears wildly excit-ing. Like the nineteenth-century readers of Jane Austen, we know what the marriage plot stands for: the marriage bed. Steven Heath claims that in the twentieth century the "big O"—orgasm—supplanted marriage as the cul-mination of plot: "As marriage is the end and resolution of the nineteenth-century novel, so orgasm—good, proper, authentic, real, successful, total, mind-blowing, truth-revealing, the moment when IT HAPPENS—is that of twentieth-century fictions, the point of representation."[48] Yet here we have the marriage plot making another appearance as corrective to the failed orgasmic plot.

Within the story of the resolution of repressed desire the marriage bed far exceeds all the desperate inventions of sexually liberated subjects: our sex manuals, our sexual aids, our strip clubs, our porno films, our daytime soap operas even, or for that matter our advertisements, all these routes toward symbolizing just how free, open, and satisfied we are. This is because the marriage plot is restored to the repressive narrative we continue to believe in—without its incentives.

Notes

1. Richard Gott, "We Must Stay True to the Real Henry James," *The New States-man*, January 30, 1996): 46.

2. Richard Sennett, *The Fall of Public Man* (New York: Alfred K. Knopf, 1977; reprint, New York: W.W. Norton, 1992), 8 (page citations are to the reprint edition).

3. Stephen Heath, *The Sexual Fix* (New York: Schocken Press, 1984), 101.

4. For a fascinating account of the narcissistic structure of Freudian object relations along with a way out of narcissism through Plato's *Symposium,* see Leo Bersani, "Sociality and Sexuality," *Critical Inquiry* 26 (2000): 641–656.

5. For a Foucauldian analysis of twentieth-century sexual liberatory discourses, see Heath *The Sexual Fix.*

6. John D'Emilio and Estelle Freedman, *Intimate Matters: A History of Sexuality in America* (New York: Harper and Row, 1988; reprint, Chicago: University of Chicago Press, 1997), 306 (page citations are to the reprint edition).

7. Central to the liberatory sexual practices of the twentieth century, D'Emilio and Freedman point out, has been the uncloseting and public tolerance of gay and lesbian sexuality. Indeed, part and parcel of male homosexuality was the promiscuity that intended to symbolize its "liberation." Yet, ironically enough, as D'Emilio and Freedman observe, it is gays and lesbians who now lobby for the reproductive and marital privileges discarded by heterosexual couples as outmoded shackles of sexual repression. Given that gay and lesbian sexuality in many ways has stood for sexuality itself in the modern imaginary, in part because of its radical split between sexuality and procreation, what might it mean to the location of sexuality as such that all the "old restraints" are being pursued by the most "liberated" of sexual bodies? In part, we can see here an ongoing pattern of the relationship between social practice, the body, and the law. The ways in which homosexuality imperils the heterosexual landscape seem to shift in relation to heterosexuality's own self-characterization.

8. Sigmund Freud, "Repression," in his *The Standard Edition of the Complete Psychological Works of Sigmund Freud*, trans. James Strachey (London: Hogarth Press, 1957 [1915]), 14:146. All further references abbreviated as SE.

9. Stephen Kern, *The Culture of Love: Victorians to Moderns* (Cambridge: Harvard University Press, 1994), 336.

10. Anthony Giddens, *The Transformation of Intimacy: Sexuality, Love, and Eroticism in Modern Societies* (Stanford. CA: Stanford University Press, 1992). For an excellent account of Foucault's historical misrepresentation of the repressive hypothesis, see Christopher Lane, *The Burdens of Intimacy: Psychoanalysis and Victorian Masculinity* (Chicago: University of Chicago Press, 1999).

11. See, for example, " 'Civilized' Sexual Morality and Modern Nervous Illness," *SE*, 9:181–204. Importantly, the prohibition against incest is central to the psychoanalytic account of repression. For psychoanalysis, the law is constitutive of desire (prohibition against incest) in contrast to Foucault's assertion that repression is a component of the "law"—which does not stand outside/preexist circuits of power.

12. Helen Singer Kaplan, *Disorders of Sexual Desire and Other New Concepts and Techniques in Sex Therapy* (New York: Simon and Schuster, 1979), 57.

13. Raymond C. Rosen and Sandra R. Leiblum, "The Changing Focus of Sex Therapy" in *Case Studies in Sex Therapy*, 4.

14. Bernard Apfelbaum, "Masters and Johnson Revisited: A Case of Desire Disparity" in *Case Studies in Sex Therapy*, ed. Raymond C. Rosen and Sandra R. Leiblum (New York: Guilford Press, 1995), 40.

15. Ibid., 25.

16. Ibid., 41.

17. Ibid.

18. Harold I. Lief, "Integrative Therapy in a Woman with Secondary Low Sex Desire" in *Case Studies in Sex Therapy*, ed. Raymond C. Rosen and Sandra R. Leiblum (New York: Guilford Press, 1995), 111.

19. Kaplan, *Disorders of Sexual Desire*, 149.

20. Ginia Bellafante, review of *Pride and Prejudice*, *Time* 147, no. 3 (January 1996): 66.

21. Linda Blandford, "Beware the Insidious Grip of Darcy Fever," *The New York Times*, Sunday, 14 January 1996, sec. H, p. 31.

22. Michel Foucault, *The History of Sexuality*, vol. 1, *An Introduction*, trans. Robert Hurley (New York: Vintage, 1980), 19–20.

23. Peter Gay, *The Tender Passion*, vol. 2, *The Bourgeois Experience: Victoria to Freud* (New York: Oxford University Press, 1986; reprint, New York: W.W. Norton, 1999), 333 (page citations are to the reprint edition).

24. Foucault, *The History of Sexuality*, 43.

25. D'Emilio and Freedman, *Intimate Matters*, 327.

26. Giddens, *The Transformation of Intimacy*, 58.

27. For an account of D. W. Griffith's invention of the closeup, see Alexander Walker, *Stardom: The Hollywood Phenomenon* (New York: Stein and Day, 1970), 17.

28. Leo Braudy, *The World in a Frame: What We See in Films* (Chicago: University of Chicago Press, 1976), 184.

29. Richard DeCordova offers a Foucauldian account of our fascination with the sex lives/scandals of movie stars. "The star system then exists in part as a kind of confessional apparatus. The confessions elicited lead us to the private, and, as I have

suggested, the sexual stands as the privileged, ultimate truth of the private." (*Picture Personalities: The Emergence of the Star System in America* [Urbana: University of Illinois Press, 1991], 142–143).

30. This statement is taken directly from the novel. The remainder of Darcy's declaration, however, is written for the screenplay by Andrew Davies.

31. The 1996 film version of *Emma* plays endlessly with the notion of repression. This version presents an Emma who is herself highly contained and tries (vainly) to contain her whole environment. Her matchmaking, thus, seems no more than an effort to still potential sparks. Arranging marriages is characterized by the film as containing what otherwise might be uncontainable: the overflow of sexual desire.

32. See Julie Shaffer, "Romance, Finance, and the Marketable Woman," in *Bodily Discursions*, ed. Deborah S. Wilson and Christine Moneera Laennec (New York: State University of New York Press, 1997), 39–56; Nancy Armstrong, *Desire and Domestic Fiction: A Political History of the Novel* (New York: Oxford University Press, 1987).

33. William Leith, "True Romance," *The Observer*, Sunday, 9 April 2000, p. 10.

34. Martyn Palmer, "Man of the Moment," *She Magazine* (February 1999): http://hem.passegen.se/lmw/she.html.

35. Leith, "True Romance," 10.

36. David Nathan, "An Upwardly Mobile Phoney," *Times* (London), 27 August 1994, Saturday Features.

37. Apparently the BBC would not allow the scene. Kate Lock, reporter. Leith, "True Romance," 100.

38. Kate Lock, "The Wait Is Over," *Radio Times* (July 5 1997): www.radiotimes .beeb.com/film/ "Most people would agree with that, although the 'no sex' part became controversial when writer Andrew Davies, who adapted the screenplay, rashly mentioned the words 'sex and money' in an interview, prompting 'Sex romp Jane Austen' headlines and whipping the Janeites into a lather. 'Tell me,' demanded a scandalised lady of a rather uncertain age when I attended a meeting of members of the Jane Austen Society, 'is it true that Andrew Davies is going to show Darcy in the buff ?'

"He didn't, of course—well, not entirely; you do see him in the bath, but it's impossible to tell whether make-up did a good job of Firth's chest hair, which was reputedly tinted for the shot, let alone anything else. (I made a point of checking carefully.) A party of Janeites who were invited to the preview were also monitoring very closely what they described as the 'erection scene'—they had heard Davies' script instructions had described Darcy as being particularly pleased to see Elizabeth when she turns up at Netherfield all flushed and muddy from her hike over the fields. 'I am notorious for this, but I think it's one of the nice things in life to write about,' admits Davies."

39. Lisa Hopkins writes that the central difference between this version and earlier cinematic versions of *Pride and Prejudice* is making Darcy the object of desire: "For

even as Elizabeth becomes the object of *his* gaze, he himself is clearly offered as the object of *ours*" ("Mr. Darcy's Body: Privileging the Female Gaze," in *Jane Austen in Hollywood*, ed. Linda Troost and Sayre Greenfield [Lexington: University of Kentucky, 1998], 114; emphasis in original). Although Darcy's being the object of the female sexual gaze is indeed central to this version, this was true of the other two filmed versions as well. Consider that Lawrence Olivier was the first cinematic Darcy! The difference here (in addition to the bathing and swimming sequences) is that Elizabeth is explicitly shown looking at him as a sexual object.

40. Julian North, "Conservative Austen, Radical Austen: *Sense and Sensibility* from Text to Screen" in *Adaptations: From Text to Screen, Screen to Text*, ed. Deborah Cartmell and Imelda Shelehan (New York: Routledge, 1999), 40.

41. Gay, *The Tender Passion*, 3–4 (1914. "Repression." *SE* 14: 141–158; 149).

42. In fact, insofar as Hyde seems primarily to be the sexed-up version of Jeckyll, his killings make no sense.

43. *Civilization and its Discontents*, 1930. *SE* 21:59–145; 76.

44. James R. Kincaid claims that we keep telling the horrific story of child sexual abuse because it turns all of us on, but we get to deny as much and scapegoat the bad guys. (*Erotic Innocence: The Culture of Child Molesting* [Durham, NC: Duke University Press, 1998]).

45. Freud's revision of the "seduction theory" has been widely debated. For the most interesting contributions to this debate, see: Jean Laplanche and J.-B. Pontalis, "Fantasy and the Origins of Sexuality," *IJPA* 49 (1968): 1–18; Jean Laplanche, *New Foundations for Psychoanalysis*, trans. David Macey (Oxford: Blackwell, 1989); Peter Gay, *Freud: A Life for Our Times* (New York: W.W. Norton, 1988); Jeffrey Moussaieff Masson, *Assault on Truth: Freud's Suppression of the Seduction Theory* (New York: Penguin, 1985).

46. Barry McCarthy, "Childhood Sexual Trauma and Adult Sexual Desire: A Cognitive-Behavioral Perspective," in *Case Studies in Sex Therapy*, ed. Raymond C. Rosen and Sandra R. Leiblim (New York: Guilford Press, 1995), 148–160.

47. Henry James, *The Wings of the Dove*, ed. John Bayley (New York: Penguin, 1986), 399.

48. Heath, *The Sexual Fix*, 101.

9

A Generational Gig with Jane Austen, Sigmund Freud, and Amy Heckerling

Fantasies of Sexuality, Gender, Fashion, and Disco in and beyond *Clueless*

Denise Fulbrook

It will surprise no reader of nineteenth-century literature to find in *Clueless*, Amy Heckerling's makeover of Jane Austen's *Emma*, a dead mother.[1] While not a pretty statement to make about the delectable candy land of bright tartan minis, cool retro chic, and leopard-spotted pants that comprises this fantastical wonderland of Austen in Beverly Hills, the dead mother is as central to the organizing fantasies of *Clueless* as she is to Austen's 1815 novel. Of *Emma*, the psychoanalytic critic Frances L. Restuccia writes: "*Emma* can be read on the model of [Julia] Kristeva's theory in *Black Sun*, as a melancholic/masochistic text, whose addiction to the 'maternal Thing' operates both at the level of the story (the fabula) and the level of the functioning of the narrative itself (the sjuzet)"[2]; "*Emma* fails to release herself from the mother's clutches;" or "Despite its apparently ebullient beginning and the hale body of its primary figure, *Emma* is bloated with mourning and the incomplete mourning known as melancholia" (451). While it will become clearer as this chapter progresses just how close *Clueless* is to *Emma* in its attachment to a fantasy of a mother, at this point the terms of Restuccia's critique hardly sound applicable. For unlike *Emma*, a novel in which heroines

179

and imaginations overtly fall ill, in *Clueless* actualities of sickness are few and far between.[3] Words such as "in the mother's clutches," addicted, or depressed scarcely leap to mind when thinking about *Clueless*. Bloated with the dead mother? *Clueless?* Sick?

Despite the fact that kitchens feature centrally, a kid vomits in the pool, Cher identifies with Mary Shelley just as "the chunks . . . rise up in [her] throat," and Josh eats in nearly every scene– despite this plethora of evidence that would lead to a depressive plot about the mother from the perspective of a psychoanalytic interpretation of *Clueless*, such a diagnosis would surprise the critics who made "fun" and "light-weight" tag lines for the film. Peter Stack entitled his review of *Clueless* "A Romp among the *Clueless.*"[4] Brian Hoffman declares, "'*Clueless*' is Plotless, But So What? It's a Lot of Fun."[5] Nick Madden, in a write-in review for the *Boston Herald*, states "'*Clueless*' shows teen-age life the way we like it in the summer; not deep and tragic but silly and sassy."[6] These words echo throughout reviews, as spectators of 1995 reveled in the brightly hued dreamscape of *Clueless*, cruising in fantasy with "white Barbie" Cher (Alicia Silverstone), "black Barbie" Dionne (Stacey Dash), and their Beverly Hills friends through the high school playgrounds of the rich and trendy.

Indeed, far from moodily melancholic, *Clueless* emerges through the words of fashion designers and media critics as a veritable galleria of fun, a moving clothes rack on which to hang the latest incarnation of an American generation in 1995. In the mid-1990s, the girl took a stroll down the catwalk of media print culture and emerged in a golden tiara as the princess of a new age of style and a fashion of alacrity. In the *Sunday Times*, Amruta Slee captures both the mood of *Clueless* and its involvement in a generational revolution of style and affect:

> In America, the hottest film of the summer is *Clueless*, in which 18-year-old Alicia Silverstone plays Cher, a spoiled Los Angeles teenager, whose live-to-shop image is about to usher in a new post-grunge age. Unlike slacker films such as *Reality Bites* and *Dazed and Confused* in which the smartest thing the teenage stars are seen wearing is a thrift-shop dress or a pair of jeans without obligatory rips, Cher and her friends dress only in expensive designer labels. In *Dazed and Confused*, when the going gets tough, the film's young hero retreats to his bedroom to don his headphones for a prolonged session of listening to heavy guitar music. Cher (motto: "Never trust a mirror; always take a Polaroid") on the other hand, gives makeovers to her high school friends when she wants to deliver "a sense of control in a world of chaos."[7]

For many, *Clueless* emblematizes the shedding of a "grunge" culture whose most popular media icon, Kurt Cobain, killed himself at age twenty-seven (the year before its release) and whose style in the mainstream media tended toward the unwashed and the depressed. Unlike the emblematically male, white Generation Xer, whose day in the media sun was dressed in heavy flannel and overcast with thick clouds of melancholy, the *Clueless* generation is by implication feathery free; rather than retreat to their rooms to sulk, the rich girls in pink platform pumps refuse to succumb to the melancholy fate imagined as having befallen the generation preceding them. Heckerling, director and writer, explains the affective feel of the film in these terms:[8] "I wanted to do a happy movie about a very optimistic young girl. . . . I really had her attitude in my head, and what I thought I needed was a strong structure in the style of comedy of manners. You see all these Merchant/Ivory movies and think, 'What if all this behavior was happening in a more lightweight kind of world?'"[9]

Happy, breezy, fashionably fun, *Clueless*'s dreamworld is positioned in the media as also and specifically anti-tragic, anti-melancholic, anti-plot, and anti-grunge, thus speaking to the fantasies of the dead mother with which I began this chapter—if only by sharing in similar plots of affective struggle. Indeed, *Clueless*'s anti-melancholic appeal is manifold, referring among other things to simultaneous triumph of the girl over grunge— particularly an older, grunge brother—and over psychological narratives that would lock her into a pathological embrace with a lost, injured, or dead mother. In both cases, I argue, *Clueless* reveals its investment in playing and replaying a generational metaphor and a generational narrative for sex, style, and violence and rescripts Oedipally imagined scenarios for gender and sexuality by crossing a narrative about the generation of a generation (the "Kids in America") with one about generations of mothers and daughters.[10]

Clueless begins with a scene of "jeepin'" and a generation of girls in motion and ends with a wedding; a movement that seemingly scripts narrative development as a linear progression from childhood to adulthood, from pre-Oedipal to Oedipal, from girls to boys, from jeep to house, from girl to the mother, and so on. But, even as the film drives this generation of teenagers into heterosexual romance, this cinematic trip down developmental candy land necessitates the development of other ways of thinking about this film than Oedipal. Those ways, I argue, turn upon understanding "jeepin'" as a primal fantasy of *Clueless*. The VHS version of *Clueless* that I own has a video for Supergrass' "Alright" following the credits. And, it is this video with which I will begin because despite the differing representatives for a "generation" it proffers, this video writes large the investment *Clueless* has in developing strategies for reading and responding to culture that are explicitly anti-pathological. This generation, as the video stresses, knows the diagnostic symptoms aforehand and rejects their force. On the screen, the band—all male, white, young, and British—rides along atop a large bed toward us. The lyrics play:

We are young,
We get by,
Can't go mad,
Ain't got time,
Sleep around if we like,
But we're alright!

Got some cash,
Bought some wheels,
Took it out,
'cross the fields,
Lost control,
Hit a wall,
But we're alright! . . .

While not necessary to understand the fantasies of sex, violence, and generation in *Clueless*, this video makes evident the pervasive convergence of moving vehicles and sex in *Clueless* and the role it plays in creating an anti-pathologizing metaphorics of a generation. By presenting Supergrass on the bed qua car singing "We're alright," it throws the metaphorical significance of the jeep throughout Heckerling's film into relief, because if in the video we find a bed where we would expect a car, in the film the jeep repeatedly appears where otherwise might be a bed, working as a crucial vehicle for figuring this "generation's" staking of a claim to being "Alright."

Although not visually represented as a bed, in *Clueless* "jeepin'" overtly means "vehicular sex." Dionne defines it in the first school-yard skirmish with her boyfriend Murray (Donald Adeosun Faison). With a camera shot that begins from behind, Murray enters with the words "What, have you been jeepin' behind my back?" "Jeepin'?" Dionne asks, miffed. "Yea jeepin'," Murray avers. Dionne rejects his accusation and says, in controlled calm, "No. But speaking of vehicular sex, would you explain to me how this cheap Kmart hair extension got into the backseat of your car?" Spectators gather as they turn to the subject of menstruation, establishing early the centrality of jeepin' to the film's means of projecting its fantasmatic of sex, generation, and violence.

From generational jeep to generational bed, *Clueless* revolves on primal fantasies that resist the realization of an Oedipal conclusion and work as a counterforce to the reinscription of the sexual and generational plots rendered legible by the legitimate laws of genital reproduction. Specifically, the film's fantasies of jeepin' turn the Oedipal bedroom into the "backseat" of sexual desire, coursing the film's journey toward heterosexual coupledom as a revolutionary upending of the rules of Oedipal narrative development, driving the film and the characters along through fantasies of anal and vehicular sex and through primal scenes of, what I will call following Sigmund Freud, "cloacal" generation. Indeed, *Clueless* offers a secular salvational plot for the girls of 1995 that works via fantasies of vehicular anal sex and cloacal generation to resurrect disco from the dead and help script an ending and origin other than the depressed mother–daughter pair for both itself and psychoanalysis. This jeepin'-generational scene begins the film, and it also, even if overtly absent, ends it, turning a wedding and a dead mother into a scene of "cruisin'" and "buggin,'" continuing the project set in motion by the jeep's wheels in the opening scene. When Dionne announces her fantasy of bridedom, she does so not with a whole lot of romantic sentimentality but by speaking her desire to wear a "sailor" dress and to redress her crew in "sailor outfits with the sailor caps." Murray responds, moreover, by saying she "must be buggin'." The combination of words, I argue, where sailors and "buggin'" converge, and the silent allusion to Christian (whose "outing" results in Cher's "totally buggin'") they carry, are less incidental than indicative of the queer generational games driving the generational jeep of girls downtown in *Clueless*.

In *Clueless*, when the girls enter into sexual, romantic relationships with boys, Heckerling ensures that they are well armed, well witted, and well dressed with a protective identificatory structure geared toward saving them from the dangerous violences imagined as the terrain of sexuality and gender in *Clueless*—psychoanalysis, domestic battery, date rape, and depression, for example;[11] in Heckerling, this identificatory structure includes primal fantasies of anal sex and cloacal generation as well as, and relatedly, primal scenes of disco. In *Clueless*, disco more than survives with the desires of the "next" generation, it thrives. In mainstream print media the romance between grunge boy Josh and "It-girl" Cher continues beyond the film, resulting in neither girl's nor mother's death but in a bloodless victory of the girl over grunge. In Heckerling's hands the sometimes-battered babes of disco take on a new face and a fantasy structure that envisions the girl as able to resist the more lethal and often gender-specific violences of a world shared with men. This is not to say that women in *Clueless* are nonviolent. Indeed, it seems, aptly enough that once the girls enter into the playground of anally erotic fantasy in *Clueless*, the gloves come off, so to speak. And the clogs? They fly, bringing down grunge, bringing up disco.

The Black-Eyed Cleopatra

One place to begin thinking through the ways *Clueless* simultaneously makes over the depressive mother–daughter dyad that Restuccia finds in *Emma* and participates in a remaking of the anti-melancholic face of the "Kids in America" is at the nexus between the beginnings of Heckerling's makeover of Jane Austen's *Emma* and H. B. Gilmore's novelistic remake of *Clueless*. In Heckerling's film, the visual text opens with a shot of a moving jeep filled with this text's version of the "Kids in America." But, Gilmore's book situates Cher's fantasies, identifications, and desires as tied from the start to her dead, wounded mother. The film offers movement, talking, and laughter; the book proffers a daughter fixated to a dream of the stilled, melancholic mother.

Even as media critics toasted the fabulous mid-1990s makeover of *Emma* that *Clueless* offered, another reading became available to its teenage viewers. Presenting us with a portrait of a dead mother, crying, with blackened eyes in its opening pages, Gilmore's book pops the balloon on Heckerling's no-strings shopping spree and cinematic joyride. In the title work of what became a series of *Clueless* novels (all written by different authors) for young teens, Gilmore steers Heckerling's film toward the uncanny from the get go, turning this "happy" film into a novel, tragedy, and domestic ghost story on the opening page. Gilmore begins in Cher's first-person voice:

> I had this dream . . . about my mom. She died when I was just a baby. A fluke accident during a routine liposuction is what I tell people. My mom was a seriously stunning disco babe. A real Betty. There's a portrait of her in go-go boots hanging in our living room, which is about the size of the Coliseum but done in polished pink Italian marble and ankle-deep cream carpeting instead of AstroTurf.
>
> Anyway, in this dream, I'm like catching her up on my life. I tell her about . . . Dionne . . . and how we ride around town with other cute kids in the cherry red Jeep my dad, the Litigator, gave me. . . . I paint her a picture of me and my pals striding through the high school halls, styled hair cleanly bouncing, makeup salon fresh, fat-free bodies aerobicized to sinewy perfection. We are the world, we are the in crowd.
>
> I want my mom . . . to know I'm okay. So I don't say how much I miss her. I don't even mention my childhood fantasy of us shopping Rodeo Drive together in these adorable mother–daughter outfits with matching Visa Gold cards. No, I keep it light and breezy so she won't get bored. So she'll stick around.
>
> "My life is so fun. It's like: Help! I'm trapped in a Noxema commercial," I quip to her. I feel like I'll hurl if she leaves me again. So I let her know that basically I'm beautiful, rich, and happy.
>
> Then I'm waiting for her to tell me how glad she is. Or proud. Whatever. Her hair's all poufed out in this total bouffant. It sways as she shakes her head sadly. . . .
>
> She gives me this deeply caring look. Suddenly, tears are spilling over her double set of false lashes and smearing the Cleopatra liner around her cat green eyes.
>
> Mom . . . strokes my cheek. Her hands are warm. They smell like bread. "Clueless," she says.[12]

For at least one significant reader and reinventor of *Clueless* all was not bubble-gum bright. In Gilmore's hands, the film's famous fashionability is pathological; the text fixates mother and daughter in a depressive and familiar psychological script from the start. Yet, while *Clueless*, the movie, could be read as fulfilling the demands of these scripts for feminine finery, it is worth a pause before doing so; not only does Cher laconically reject psychoanalytic readings that implicitly pathologize her behavior, but *Clueless* also begins with a jeep and not the mother, with a fantasy of generation which puts the emphasis on the disco half of the 'Disco Mom"—on the dancing, on the driving beat, on the fantastical revolving place in the history of American generations it represents.

Like the generation that emerges in the media along with *Clueless*, disco represents for many a fantasy of generation that points less to a singularly imagined mother and more to a scene of movement—of bodies, races, classes, genders, and sexualities—all driving along to the beat, much as Cher cruises to The Muffs' remake of Kim Wilde's teen anthem "Kids in America" in the first scene and No Doubt's "Just a Girl" in the second—both sound tracks that highlight crossings at the place of identity formation. "Kids in America" was written by the British musician David Bowie and No Doubt is known for its mixture of the traditions of Ska and Pop. As Walter Hughes argues:

> Implicit in early disco is the assumption that only a black woman can openly vocalize her sexuality, and that only a gay man would join her in a free-fall from rational self-mastery. But the evolution of disco is one of both appropriation and integration, both exploitation and empathy; the negotiation between usually straight black women and usually white gay men seemed to open up and make visible the various subject positions between these polarized identities. . . . The violence . . . [disco] does to fixed identity results in a doubling, slippage and transference of black and white, male and female, gay and straight subject positions. Grace Jones can sing of "feeling like a woman" and "looking like a man;" Donna Summer can plead . . . to "turn my brown body white." In their wake, many permutations of disco singer can appear: Jimmy Somerville, the gay white man as disco diva or Madonna, the omnisexual white woman as disco diva.[13]

While Hughes' project is to explore what submitting to the endlessly driving, disciplinary beat of disco means for gay male subjects, in particular, and as such differs from the project of *Clueless*—a text invested in screening its fantasies of disco through the eyes of a white, overtly straight girl— Hughes' remarks on disco nonetheless echo strongly with the kinds of crossings *Clueless* imagines for the staging of the "slippage and transference of black and white, male and female, gay and straight subject positions" it sets in action (153). Indeed, when the grunge boy's friend's party becomes a dance floor in which Cher and Christian (Justin Walker) dance with pleasure and the "classic" gay male who listens to Billie Holiday and dresses like Sammy Davis Jr. can cruise amidst the turning lights with abandon, we can begin to make sense of the project of *Clueless* as one about the resurrection of disco and its stagings of primal fantasies of identification and desire.

In many ways, it is Christian who provides *Clueless* a route to detour from an Oedipal set of road rules for fantasy and narrative and to resurrect a new "classic" world order. Christian, as his name implies, serves as a kind of Messiah in *Clueless*. Set in opposition to the "Messiah of the DMV"—a father type who tries to stop Cher's movement dead in its tracks—and "God's gift" Elton (Jeremy Sisto)—a snob who brings Cher into a dark parking lot of "Circus World," liquors and tries to kiss her against her will—Christian is a cinematic savior who helps Cher, Tai (Brittany Murphy), Dionne, and the film find a safe, "classic" space for their interest in refashioning the world, and, in playing the girl as a means to keep the terrain of gender and sexuality moving. Cher's desire for and identification with Christian works as one means by which to wrest hers and *Clueless*'s fantasies of generation from confinement to the Oedipally scripted bed and the tragic plots of motherhood it offers. He presents a means by which *Clueless* makes its own interest in generating anti-Oedipal scripts for history and creation itself visible as a "classic" tale of creation, and he helps indicate that part of the anti-melancholic appeal of *Clueless* lies in its resurrectionary fantasies. In the stylistic and linguistic traces at the fantasy of Dionne's wedding, we find not only Christian but the Disco Mom. In the relentlessly pink-and-white color scheme of this final scene, the luridly pink-and-white "Betty" hanging in Cher's father's hallway smiling like a "Charlie's Angel" with feathered hair and a silky, clinging white dress is resurrected as well.

If the film depicts Christian as the most overt Messiah of this film, it simultaneously dedicates itself to claiming for the girl a genealogy of identificatory scenes that would position the Disco Mom as herself a "classic" figure in history with whom these girls might identify directly, safely, and to signify their allegiance to an anti-Oedipal, anti-melancholic script for their development. In a scene of the film that begins with a behind shot of Cher at her vanity-table mirror, she reacts to stepbrother, lover-to-be, and grunge representative Josh's (Paul Stephen Rudd) arrival by complaining about his music. As Radiohead's "Fake Plastic Trees" plays, we hear her voice-over: "Yuk! Uh, the maudlin music of the University station." "Waa, waa, waa," she says to her mirror. Walking around the corner ready to do battle, she reemerges in the kitchen with the words: "Yuh, what is it about college and cry-baby music?" She asks, "So, the flannel shirt deal. Is that a nod to the crispy Seattle weather, or are you just trying to stay warm in front of the refrigerator?" While there is much of interest to note about this scene, Cher's costume certainly tops my list. She is dressed as Madonna of the "Like a Virgin"/"Like a Prayer"/*Desperately Seeking Susan* era, wearing white tank under black netted shirt, black pants, blond hair, and a big silver cross around her neck, offering herself as another anti-Oedipal Messiah. Madonna is, after all, a disco babe and pop icon that has moved and continues to move in anti-Oedipal motion. Like Dionne's reenactment of Tina Turner, this appearance of Cher as Madonna works to keep the big wheels of gender and sexuality "rolling on the river"—at the site of the mother, at the site of the text's imaginings of generational metaphors, at the site of the Jeep, and at the site of the sailor.[14]

Jeepin' and Buggin'

> Like the movie, [the soundtrack] is a breezy, lightweight treat that . . . fully captures the cruising-with-the-top-down vibe of summer vacation. The frothy mood is set with the Muffs' exuberant opening track, a cover of Kim Wilde's 1982 hit "Kids in America," and . . . continues through . . . infectious cuts by rapper Coolio, British buzz act Supergrass, and others. . . . The party comes to an abrupt halt when the producers try to evoke teen angst with tracks by Counting Crows and Radiohead—the kind of decidedly un-fun material . . . Silverstone astutely labels "complaint rock."[15]

Jean Laplanche and Jean-Bertrand Pontalis' essay on Freudian primal fantasy is worth revisiting when near *Clueless* because *Clueless* establishes a few structuring primal fantasies that go unnoted as such in the "classic" Freudian triptych of primal fantasies. "Jeepin'" is one of them. In "Fantasy and the Origins of Sexuality," they write: "Fantasy . . . is not the object of desire, but its setting. In fantasy the subject . . . appears caught up himself in the sequence of images. He forms no representation of the desired object, but is himself represented in the scene although . . . he cannot be assigned any fixed place in it."[16] These earliest forms of fantasy are called "primal" because they represent origins. Laplanche and Pontalis explain that like "myths, they claim to provide a representation of and a solution to the major enigmas which confront the child. Whatever appears . . . as something needing an explanation or a theory, is dramatized as a moment of emergence, the beginning of a history"(19). The three most common fantasies of origins they claim are the primal scene that pictures "the origin of the individual," the scene of seduction that figures "the origin and upsurge of sexuality," and the scene of castration that stages "the origin of the difference between the sexes" (19). As scenes, these fantasies assign no clear subject positions; however, as John Fletcher argues, their separation into discreet entities already presupposes an assumption of castration-as-difference. He writes: "The 'themes' of castration and seduction as primal fantasies are not explicable apart from the primal scene and the overall . . . Oedipus complex in which they figure."[17] In this respect, these scenes share an origin, arising from the retrospective dreams of a heuristic that subsumes narratives of sexual difference to genital difference and to the laws of legitimate genital reproduction.[18]

The metaphor of the Jeep in *Clueless* is perfect for considering in terms of primal fantasy and drives the revolutionary nature of the project of *Clueless* from the start. *Clueless*, and this generation, is out to reinvent the proverbial and symbolic wheel, turning repeatedly to scenes in which the Jeep sets in motion the text's primal fantasies of sex and gender, working as a privileged vehicle for the text to play out games of identification and desire that exceed the rhetoric of identifying with or desiring an object or subject of fantasy per se. It illustrates how one might identify with a verb in a sequence of fantasy or become part of the sequence of images, part of a movement of film and fantasy in which one is assigned no clear subject position. As an open-topped vehicle, a space in which people can readily switch places with others, and an auto associated with adventure and play, the Jeep charts a course for *Clueless*'s attempt to keep everything moving long enough to effectuate a revolution at the site of gender and sexuality by proffering to its spectators scenes of jeepin', buggin', and cruising with which to identify.

Heckerling's opening introduces one of the film's structuring fantasies. Before any image, Kim Shattuck's gravelly voice begins to sing, "Looking out a dirty old window, I can see the cars and they're moving, rushing by. I sit here alone and I wonder why . . ." The titles burst by in bubble-gum pink and white, a white-and-black Jeep drives onto the screen, and the camera pans to an overhead shot as Cher drives her Jeep full of teenage girls down the street. "Kids in America" provides soundtrack—"Friday night and everyone's moving; I can feel the heat but its soothing getting down; I look for the beat in this crazy town"—and scene after moving scene flashes to it: Cher and her girlfriends in the Jeep, carrying shopping bags, dancing, poolside, and so on. The shuffle between scenes quickens as the introduction to the fantasy world of *Clueless* nears its end and onto the screen spill and splash the pool, the soda shop, the girls' bodies, a boy eating a cherry from a girl's hand, and the Jeep's turning tires, celebrating the spirit of a generation in motion. The anthem to the "home movie" sequence hits its refrain and Shattuck's voice rises to a crescendo: "[D]owntown, we always are going. Downtown, we always are going. We're the Kids in America. We're the Kids in America."

While the irony of using a British songwriter's words to designate the "Kids in America" has more effects than I can recognize here, let's assume momentarily that the most salient function of this song is to do just that: to establish *Clueless* as a generational text, as about the making of a generation of "girls," while at the same time ironizing that construction, keeping even those fantasies moving. Indeed, as the Jeep, the succession of vignettes, and the convergence of Wilde's line about "moving" on a Friday night with the opening driving scene, *Clueless* recreates *Emma* for the 1990s by working to lift desire and identification from the more obvious subject positions that Oedipal plots make available. *Clueless* stages a visual and verbal fantasy of moving for the sake of it, for the thrill of turning oneself over, as Wilde lyricizes and The Muffs sing to the "beat."

Of disco, Hughes writes: "Disco forefronts the beat, makes it consistent . . . repetitive . . . disco 'turns the beat around, turns it upside down.' This troping and inversion . . . makes it the dominant element in the music, and attributes to it the irresistibility that is disco's recurrent theme. As the lyrics of disco songs make clear . . . in a characteristically redundant way, the beat brooks no denial, but moves on, controls us. . . . Dancing becomes a form of submission to the overmastering beat."[19] If the last shot of the series of images focuses on the wheels turning to the Muffs' search for the "beat"—this is one way in which Heckerling merges the plot of "jeepin'" with her project of resurrecting disco at the outset; the visual text and the musical text merge into a fantasy of irresistible generational motion. And, while Wilde's song might hardly be said to emblematize disco, as disco critics generally stress, through integration and repetition also comes change—and with it, in *Clueless*, a certain multiplicity of musical styles emerges (matching the multicultural stress). The scenes and fantasies *Clueless* incorporates as part of its resurrection plots are imagined as themselves already in motion, already turning around the ground on Oedipus. In this sense, disco represents one incarnation among many of the ways in which this text envisions formative scenes of identification as precisely that: as scenes—scenes fueled in this case by verbs of turning and generating, revolving and re-creating, scenes that cannot be reduced to a story about identification with a specific, solitary object–subject. In *Clueless* there are scenes to be replayed, resurrected, and re-created and verbs of movement with which to flirt. Disco is a privileged one of those scenes; it emblematizes a cultural site of historical movement and a fantasy of an esprit de corps that spins the space of the crypt right around into the stage for a party.

Hughes writes: "The power of disco to re-create the self lies in the always implicit parallel between the beat and desire. . . . The most common topos in disco lyrics, the exhortation to . . . 'get down,' suggests that the power of the beat to make us dance is commensurate with the power of desire to lead us into sexual acts, even those considered forbidden, unnatural, even unnamable" (150). As the song ("Change" by Lightning Seeds) accompanying Cher's curtsy to students applauding her successful "boink-fest" plot between Mr. Hall (Wallace Shawn) and Miss Geist (Twink Caplan) encourages: "Put your foot down and drive. Oh you're a pretty thing. Put your foot down and drive. Oh you're a silly thing. You don't know what to do, so you do anything you like. Put your foot down and drive. . . . You don't know what to do, but you're going out tonight." Whether jeepin' or dancin', the girls of *Clueless* are going out and getting down, adhering above all else to a principle of illicit movement. Indeed, Cher's Jeep joins Murray's and Elton's cars, the revolving clothes rack, Travis' skateboard, and the "homies" who go "rollin'" as one among many sites through which *Clueless* journeys these characters toward a smiling, technologized heterosexual coupledom *not* by moving them toward Oedipal fantasies of sex and generation per se, but by routing the text's journey toward the parental marriage bed in reverse, so to speak.

If we assume Wilde's looking through the window takes the place of the more familiar psychoanalytic child looking, then in the first scene of a primal fantasy the spectator already assumes the place of that child, looking not onto the parental bed but onto the moving Jeep of the girls qua "Kids in America." This framing scene prepares us for reading a pattern in the multiple primal scenes *Clueless* stages throughout: that it is not parents who most insistently occupy the primal stages of either sex or generation in this film but, rather, teachers, siblings, and friends, and that the girls have a directionality for their fantasies of jeepin' and moving already. As the song says, the girls are moving "downtown" in this film. If the spectator of the "Kids in America" as primal scene finds herself looking out of a specifically "dirty" window at cars rushing "downtown," we can see already that the trajectory *Clueless* imagines for staging a revolution via jeepin' will route the fantasies of this first scene of girls and their moving Jeep through, in part, the fantasies *Clueless* has of Christian and his sexuality. When Christian leaves Cher after their night at the frat house[20] turned disco to follow the boys in the band, he says, "You are a down girl"; and the fantasies of jeepin' *Clueless* stages to move these girls from the all-girl playground to the final wedding scene reach a crisis in a scene wherein a big, maroon truck threatens to run over Cher, Dionne, and Murray from behind, linking the Jeep to the scenes of dancin', cruisin', and buggin'.

In the final scene of the film, the women and girls of the wedding party are dressed in pink and white, the boys and men in tuxedos; around Cher's neck is a rose; Dionne's hair is studded with pink-and-white flowers and she is telling everyone what her wedding will be like. After Tai describes the "floral motif" she wants for hers, Dionne says "No, no, no, no. When I get married, I'm gonna have a sailor dress, but it's going to be a gown, and all my bridesmaids are gonna wear sailor hats . . . with veils." Murray responds by leaning toward Josh and saying, "Oh, my God. They're planning our weddings already. Could you all stop all that to death do us part mumbo-jumbo. I'm telling ya, man, I'm completely buggin'." Josh, unfamiliar with the lingo of this "next" generation, imitates him awkwardly with the words, "I'm buggin' myself." These fantasies of buggin', I would argue, bring the Jeep past its stopping point—with Cher's failure to gain a driver's license from the DMV Messiah—by going back to the climactic scene of jeepin' that leads to Dionne's change in hymenal status, where the status of jeepin' as a metaphor for sex becomes not only verbally but visibly manifest in a scene in which the unlicensed Dionne finds herself on the "freeway of love" with Murray beside her, Cher in the backseat, and a big truck behind.

While Freud would deem a primal fantasy of anal sex and a primal fantasy of cloacal creation indicative of pre-Oedipal fantasies of sexuality that are later displaced and rescripted according to the laws of legitimate genital reproduction, *Clueless* might be said not only to hold an allegiance to those pre-Oedipal fantasies but also to see those fantasies themselves as a means to rescript what it means to have an "adult" sexuality.[21] Because if one way of thinking about the narrative trajectory of *Clueless* is as a *Bildungsroman* and comedy of manners—as a text that moves the girl and the wayward plot of her desires toward marriage and an Oedipal conclusion—another way is as a text that works very hard to move simultaneously in what would seem an antithetical psychoanalytic direction. *Clueless* turns the very scenes that would support such critical fantasies of Oedipally scripted start or finish lines into a story about a girl's movement away from the laws and violences of the Oedipal family and its primal fantasies of sex and generation. When Cher calls "Psych 101" specifically "ugly"—in a text in which one of the primary goals is to look fabulous—this is because *Clueless* is deeply invested in prettifying and publicizing the "dirty" underside of Freud's theory of the primacy of the genitals and the laws of legitimate reproduction.

When Cher realizes that she loves Josh, she plays the role of Gaston (Louis Jordan) in *Gigi* and makes the discovery, like him, walking near a fountain that suddenly lights up. While the music Gaston sings as he walks and thinks emerged in *Clueless* a few scenes earlier, this scene provides its visual text and also rescripts the film. In the first scene, Cher descends the black-and-white stairwell toward Christian and their first date; "Gigi" plays, announcing Cher's movement toward a seemingly awakening sexual desire in audio. At the bottom of the stairs Christian awaits, kisses her on the cheek, and says, "Dollface." Cher responds, "Handsome," and the two ride off in Christian's "classic" convertible to the dancin' scene. While in this scene, Cher might be said to be in the position of the "girl" of that film, Gigi (Leslie Caron), and Christian in the place of Gaston—a coupling that already rescripts Gaston as gay and as identified with Sammy Davis Jr.—in the scene at the fountain some new casting decisions now allow the girl's verbalization of her own sexual desire. The scene of Cher walking and remembering scenes of her and Josh together replays Gigi, as in the scene with Christian, but also crosses gender lines to do so, enacting another reversal. Rather than Gaston walking and thinking a series of still photos of Gigi while singing "Gigi," or finding either Josh or Christian dreaming of stills of Cher, Cher walks past a fountain and imagines moving scenes of her and Josh together. In *Gigi*, Gaston sings, "Oh Gigi. . . . When did your sparkle turn to fire? . . . your warmth become desire? Oh, what miracle has made you the way you are?" In *Clueless*, Cher replaces these words with her own; and when her epiphany arrives, instead of a series of questions put to her, we hear in a combination of Cher as voice-over and as visible character, "And then it dawned on me. I love Josh. I am butt crazy head over heels in love with Josh." Trumpets sound and the fountain turns into a rainbow of light and mist. If the revolutions of *Clueless* turn things head over heels, they do so by returning the "butt" to the girl, so to speak—driving her on to crazy love in terms clearly indicative of a fantasy we would call "anally erotic," acceding to her the vocalization of her own awakening to desire, even while routing that vocalization, in part, through fantasies of the body and desires of a gay male.

When Cher discovers that she has tried to give her virginity to a gay boy, she is with Dionne and Murray in the car wondering for the first time if there is something wrong with her. Murray is giving Dionne a driving lesson and they are fighting as usual. Dionne who only has a learner's permit is at the wheel and Murray is gritting his teeth, trying to suppress his customarily staged anger at her. Dionne first mistakes the windshield wipers for the turn signal and then moves the entire car along with her head as she checks behind her before switching lanes. Murray criticizes her inability to drive at every turn, saying, "I swear woman, you can't drive for shit." From the backseat Cher wonders with Dionne why Christian did not want to sleep with her when Murray asks whom they are talking about. When Cher replies, "Christian," Murray responds, "Are you bitches blind? My man Christian is a cake boy." In unison both girls say, "A what?" The camera moves to capture the characters' expressions and interactions. Dionne continues driving as Murray explains, "He's a Disco-dancin', Oscar Wilde readin', Judy Garland lovin', Barbara Streisand ticket holdin' friend of Dorothy's." The girls mull it over and Dionne says, "Cher, the boy can dance and he does like to shop." Cher says, "I'm totally buggin', I can't believe I could be such a bonehead." Suddenly, the sexually/vehicularly inexperienced Dionne inadvertently drives onto the freeway as Heckerling propels a scene that begins with Dionne and Murray fighting and a discussion of Christian into a story about driving that ends in a shift in Dionne's virginal status.

It would not be difficult to read this scene of driving as an allegorical sex scene—the definition of "jeepin'" *Clueless* offers is, after all, "vehicular sex"—but this scene is more than one of many such scenes; it stages the climactic moment in the text's plot of jeepin'. Throughout the scene Dionne is screaming, while Murray is encouraging her by saying, "Just take it easy baby, I'm here with you." . . . "Just breath baby; just breathe. [You're] doing great, just take it easy, and whatever you do under all circumstances just keep your hands on the wheel!" With those words we see Dionne, her hands held to her ears, screaming loudly; cars, vans, and Hell's Angels on motorcycles fly from behind them, spreading out on either side of the car to the yells of the girls (much as the driveway and stairs of Cher's home split one thruway into two). The camera films mostly from the front of the car, moving sometimes atop to film what is coming at them from behind. As the camera shoots from the front, a big maroon truck looms in the background and Murray joins Dionne and Cher in the frantic screaming. The truck gets closer and closer, and larger and larger behind them, honking and blowing. Just as the visual and acoustic text reaches a frenzy, Dionne exits the highway, breathing heavily, unable to speak. Murray, also a bit breathless, sighs as they pull off, saying, "Oh. There it is. There it is." He then turns to the stunned Dionne, and asks, "Are you okay baby? You did great." The now more vehicularly and sexually inexperienced Cher, sitting in the backseat like a psychoanalytic child, chimes in with the words, "You did great De." The scene culminates with Murray and Dionne kissing and Cher's thoughts about the end of Dionne's virginity and her own desire for a boyfriend. They have arrived, it seems, "downtown" and while terrified, these girls and Murray clearly joy in this thrill ride of cinematic and sexual pleasure.

This is where jeepin' and buggin' converge—in this highly sexualized, terrifying, and disorienting fantasy of a car ride. For not only does the discovery of Christian's being gay set the climactic frenzy of this scene of buggin' in motion, but when Murray explains that Christian is gay he does so with a series of verbs of movement, verbs that match precisely the gerundive case of Cher's response: "I'm totally buggin'." Indeed, the multiplication of signifiers in Murray's description of Christian's sexuality and the repetition of "in'" not only indicate that Christian signifies a site of movement in terms of sexuality—one way the text moves downtown—this multiplication also carries a primal fantasy of reproduction, of a generational metaphor. This fantasy comes alive in car after car and horn after horn on the freeway, introducing another vehicle through which generational fantasies themselves multiply in *Clueless*.[22]

When Jane Austen writes in *Northanger Abbey*, "That a love of dirt grows into a love of finery" (1072), she tells us something over which we might pause for a moment when in the vicinity of *Clueless*—a text that shares as much, I would argue, with *Clueless*, as *Emma*.[23] In *Northanger Abbey*, a novel that also raises and refuses a melancholic mother plot, this love of finery manifests itself in the form of the effusions of Mrs. Allen. Of her, Austen writes: "In one respect she was admirably fitted to introduce a young lady into public, being as fond of going every where and seeing every thing herself as any young lady could be. Dress was her passion"(1075). Indeed, in Austen, Mrs. Allen's love of finery is more than just a passion, although it is importantly that; it is also presented as an alternative to motherhood. Of Mrs. Thorpe and Mrs. Allen, Austen writes, "Mrs. Thorpe talked chiefly of her children, and Mrs. Allen of her gowns" (1085). By putting Mrs. Thorpe and Mrs. Allen against each other, Austen juxtaposes

fashion and motherhood for more than satirical effect. By staging this encounter between this birth mother who talks about children as if they were
gowns, and this mother of fashion (dirt) who talks about gowns as if they
were children, she simultaneously aligns and opposes two fantastical
economies of reproduction, two economies we might name through Freud
"genital" and "cloacal," respectively.

While this aspect of Freud's thought is consistently overlooked, according
to him the first theory the child creates to account for the origin of babies is
the cloacal theory of birth; the theory that babies are born like excremental
"lumps" is what the child constructs in answer to the question "where do
babies come from?"[24] and it is this theory that I would suggest comes alive
in this jeepin' scene and in Austen's text. *Clueless*, like Austen, sets in play a
primal fantasy and generational sex scene that scripts that fantasy as one of
cloacal reproduction—the illegitimate parent and child of the genital theory
of reproduction in Freud. It is this fantasy, in particular, that fuels the multiple generational plots in this "plotless" film. An interest in fashion is an interest in dirt, linked in psychoanalytic theory to anal economies of meaning.
To couple a fantasy of maternal effusions with a fantasy of a mirror text to
combat, as Austen does, is to couple dirt and fashion in a fantasy scene of
filthy reproduction.[25] This is also the game of creation *Clueless* plays.

When Cher confronts the effects of her makeover of Tai, she echoes Mary
Shelley's *Frankenstein*, claiming that she has created "a monster." Now we
could think of this reference as just another allusion to the Oedipal or even ab-
ject mother of patriarchy, and, as is often done with Shelley, reduce Cher's reference to a story about a dead, genital mother. We could also limit Josh's
chilling suggestion of "sterilization" to a story about fantasies of genital maternity. But in either case such a reading will have done an injustice to the tire-
less work this text does to lift fantasies of sex, creation, and generation away
from the legitimately reproductive family. When Cher, for example, jabs at her
double and nemesis, Amber (Elisa Donovan), by calling her a "clone," she is
alluding in the first instance not to a biological, human mother, rather, she is
critiquing a practice of endless, repetitive, mechanical, and scientific reproduction—the reproduction of simulacra, of repetition without change—even
while refusing to relinquish an investment in the fashion system that seemingly
supports such fantasies of creation. In *Clueless*, we find a text invested in reproduction but of a reproduction of difference from within similarity.

Shelley famously describes her novel as a "hideous progeny," Frankenstein's workshop as a scene of "filthy creation" (50), the "monster" as an
"abortion" (219)—all words and phases, I would argue, indicating a fantasy
of cloacal creation at play.[26] As Freud writes to his friend, Wilhelm Fliess, for
example: "I can scarcely detail for you all the things that resolve themselves
into—excrement for me (a new Midas!). It fits completely with the theory of
internal stinking. Above all, money itself. I believe this proceeds via the
word 'dirty' for 'miserly.' In the same way, everything related to birth, mis-

carriage, [menstrual] period goes back to the toilet via the word *Abort* [toi-let] (*Abortus* [abortion])."[27] But while Shelley's story easily becomes a linear teleology that begins like most psychoanalytic narratives, and like this chap-ter, with a fantasy of a tragically dead, biological mother, Austen's relation-ship to a fantasy of the conflation of death and maternity resists ready conscription into this particular mother–daughter plot.

Austen not only has no dead mother through which we can contain these fantasies of cloacal creation, but her own bitchy fantasies of the convergence of the baby and death also read very differently from Shelley's—even if, I am trying to suggest, they relate. Famously, Austen in a letter to her sister Cas-sandra drops a reference to the stillborn child of her neighbor without a blink or an ounce of sentimentality. In the midst of writing about fashion, she interrupts with:

> I bought some Japan Ink . . . & next week shall begin my opera-tions on my hat, on which You know my principle hopes of hap-piness depend. . . . I had the dignity of dropping out my mother's Laudanum last night. . . . Our dinner was very good yesterday, & the Chicken boiled perfectly tender; therefore I shall not be obliged to dismiss Nanny on that account. . . . I have unpacked the Gloves & placed yours in the drawer. . . . Your letter was chaperoned here by one from Mrs. Cooke, in which she says that Battleridge is not to come out before January; & she is so little satisfied with Cawthorn's dilatoriness that she never means to employ home again. Mrs. Hall of Sherbourn was brought to bed yesterday of a dead child, some weeks before she expected, owe-ing to a fright—I suppose she happened unawares to look at her husband—There has been a great deal of rain here for this last fortnight, much more than in Kent; & indeed we found the roads all the way from Staines most disgracefully dirty—Steventon Lane has its full share of it.[28]

As a psychoanalytic critic, I cannot help but awe at the consistency of the fantasy set in play by Austen's seemingly random train of thoughts leading to and immediately following her mention of the stillborn baby. From the inky hat to the dropping of laudanum to the tender fowl to the Nanny, the Cook(e), a female author and her embattled ridge ("not to come out before January"), the fantasy of dilation carried by dilatoriness to a dead child, and an exploration of the "disgraceful dirt" from "Staines," a fantasy of cloacal reproduction travels through line after line, creating a scene awash with fan-tasies of anality and reproduction, a "Staine[d]"mise-en-scène of desire.[29]

When Cher's shoes are specifically "stained" at the "Val" party, she is walking down a cloacal lane of desire and generation imagined by Austen nearly two centuries earlier. If Josh (the grunge representative) suggests that something Cher could do to help humanity would be "sterilization," his comment is less random than a direct attack on the scene he has just witnessed between Cher and Tai in which Cher gives Tai pointers on how to have "buns of steel," how to speak properly, and how to plan one's reading, et cetera—a scene in which Cher metaphorically and literally reproduces herself by remaking Tai. Hence, he says to Cher in the kitchen in the subsequent scene, "You don't have a mother so you're acting out on this poor girl as if she were your Barbie." Cher flings back "Oh no, Psych 101 rears its ugly head," highlighting in one flip line the critique *Clueless* wages against psychoanalysis at the level of the mother.

A fantasy of "unnatural" qua symbolic reproduction haunts Josh's suggestion of sterilization, bespeaking a desire to unite Cher with her dead mother and to kill the value and practice of Cher's symbolic reproduction of herself; kill her rather than have her re-creating herself through Tai might be the subliminal message. For all the "tenderness" of Josh's gaze as he watches Cher giving lessons, his fantasy of sterilization carries as well a hostility against the scene of tutelage, against those reproductive scenes deemed undesirable, or, as the word *sterilization* implies, dirty. Indeed, for all Cher's stress on cleanliness, this text is invested in allowing the girl a certain claim to dirt, to, in fact, generative dirt. Which is why, contra Freud who sees menstrual blood as so noxious as to become automatically taboo once man evolves from olfactory to visual being, in *Clueless* menstrual blood is neither taboo nor representative of a stage of sexuality (whether phylogenetic or ontogenetic) to be surpassed. Menstrual blood itself generates movement and a generational metaphor rather than indicating simply waste, dirt, or wasted baby as Freud would make it seem. Indeed, in Mr. Hall's class Cher turns menstruation not only into a kind of sport but into a metaphor carrying life and movement. To explain away her tardiness, Cher says, "Mr. Hall, I was surfin' the crimson wave. I had to haul ass to the ladies."

If we seem to have traveled quite a way from the resurrection plot and Christian, we have only arrived here by another means, because for when Cher "hauls ass" earlier in Mr. Hall's class, it is in the context of a speech about eating and buggin' and immediately precedes her introduction of the absent Christian to the film as a victim of, specifically, the laws of legitimate genital reproduction. In a debate about U.S. immigration policy in Mr. Hall's class, Cher argues:

> So, OK, like right now the Haitians need to come to America. But some people are all "What about the strain on our resources?" But it's like, when I had this garden party for my father's birthday right? I said R.S.V.P. because it was a sit-down dinner. But people came that like, did not R.S.V.P. so I was like, totally buggin'. I had to haul ass to the kitchen, redistribute the food, squish in extra place settings, but by the end of the day it

was like, the more the merrier! And so, if the government could just get to the kitchen, rearrange some things, we could certainly party with the Haitians. And in conclusion, may I please remind you that it does not say R.S.V.P. on the Statue of Liberty?

This passage might quell doubts about the centrality of buggin' to the strategies of redemption and resurrection *Clueless* imagines for itself. If I have read Cher's "surfin' the crimson wave" and "haul[ing] ass" as evidence for this film's investment in fantasies of cloacal generation, then this particular "haul" reaffirms that interpretation of the wave of movement on which Cher and the text rides. The proximity of buggin' to haul(in') ass in Cher's debate indicates not only that "hauling ass" involves a fantasy of anal sex, but that buggin' is indeed a carrier of such a fantasy and that these instances of jeepin', buggin', and haulin' ass are knotted, pointing toward an Eden wherein eating constitutes one part of a primal fantasy of generational movement through which buggin' leads to salvation and in which the sexual, digestive, and creative body merge.

Two versions of the productive "law" coexist in *Clueless*. If the "Messiah of the DMV" represents an incarnation of the law as simply prohibitive and rigid, both Cher's father and Mr. Hall's classroom represent the law as a place of debate and change. After Cher delivers her speech she returns to her seat and extends her critique by invoking Christian, moving from the "domestication" of public policy to the laws of genital reproduction governing domestic disputes.[30] Distributing report cards for debate class, Mr. Hall asks, "Christian Stovitz. . . . Does anyone know a Christian Stovitz?" The camera cuts to Cher, hand raised, sitting at her desk amidst various students with nose jobs and cell phones. She answers, "The buzz on Christian is that thanks to an awful custody battle, Christian will spend half the semester with his mother and half the semester with his father. If you ask me," she continues, debating the point, "it is a travesty of the legal system." When Christian enters the scene via Cher, it is as an explicit sacrifice to a legal system mistakenly invested in upholding an outdated mode of family values even at the cost of the child, providing an occasion for Cher to protest this system and its effects, making a travesty of the law.

It is tempting to read the trajectory of *Clueless* as one that creates a salvation narrative for itself by incorporating Christian and the fantasies of sex, generation, and cultural history that go along with him. Christian is, after all, represented as edible: appearing in absentia in the mouth of Cher, described by Murray as a "cake boy," and the only male character over which Heckerling's camera lingers with explicit desire. As a way to help Tai recover from "God's gift," Elton, the girls also skip school to "have a calorie fest" and see "the new Christian Slater," and when Cher first sees Christian Stovitz, she looks at him like/as the camera with lust and says, "Yum." His involvement in the text's various salvation plots is also not in doubt.

In the scene following Christian's rescue of Tai from the boys who threaten to drop her over the railing at the mall, Heckerling offers a slow zoom to two girl's butts—next to each other in pink and white. When they part, we see Tai sitting at the lunch table, newly popular, describing her "spiritual" experience at the galleria, explaining, "Right before you die, your mind just sort of gets very clear. It's a very intense, spiritual thing." She continues, "It's spiritual . . . I can't . . . pinpoint the spirituality out for you, you know, if you've never experienced anything . . . It was spiritual." Christian is also the first person Cher imagines when she realizes she wants to "make-over" her "soul." Sitting in Miss Geist's class, Cher dreams of her and Christian in an art gallery, Dionne and Murray sharing a sandwich, and Miss Geist in a classroom; her voice-over plays,

> Later, while we were learning about the Pismo Beach disaster, I decided I needed a complete makeover, except this time I'd make over my soul. But what makes someone a better person? And then I realized, all my friends were really good in different ways. Like, Christian, he always wants things to be beautiful and interesting. Or Dionne and Murray, when they think no one is watching, are so considerate of each other. And poor Miss Geist, always trying to get us involved, no matter how much we resist?

Along with Dionne, Murray and Miss Geist, Christian presents a means by which the film creates a salvation narrative for Cher and for the strategies of the film itself.

Christian and the venerable history he represents is in a sense "trash" culture already redeemed, already "classic;" it is his character who most overtly moves popular culture in the film into the terrain of "high" or "classic" art.[31] To the stylish, Christian is the connoisseur of fashion. His character not only has a passionate knowledge of high art and an awareness of how one could capitalize on art; he loves movies now considered "classic" such as Spartacus, clothes that pay tribute to "classic" queer icons and music that identifies him with Billie Holiday, Judy Garland, and Barbara Streisand. Finally, he drives a "classic" convertible and calls Cher from art museums where cartoons hang, framed behind him. This last scene provides the film with a recognizable script for the movement of popular culture to the hallowed halls of high aestheticism.

If Christ turns the sinful flesh through transubstantiation into a route toward salvation, *Clueless* is engaged in a similar project to an almost opposite end, using Cher's and Heckerling's identification with and desirous consumption of Christian as a means not only to sublimate its dirty desires à la its investment in fashion and pop culture, but to highlight and stage a girl's "down" and dirty fantasies of anal sex and cloacal generation and make of them the fantasies from which art and creation spring. Under "generation" in the *Oxford English Dictionary*, the birth of Christ appears—Generation: "1.a. The act or process of generating or begetting physically; procreation; propagation of species . . . d. *Theol.* The origin of the Son from the Father." This definition highlights what I have been arguing throughout: that the multiplicity of the generational metaphors at play in *Clueless* intersect via a resurrectionary plot and a fantasy of cloacal creation. Moreover, it points to a fantasy structure for salvation plots that ultimately takes us well beyond *Clueless*. From Freud's famous patient, the "Wolf-man," for example, who says "God-shit" as part of his fantasies of resurrecting himself anally, we know that fantasies of Christ and anal rebirth may sit in close proximity, but we have yet to make much of this finding. While this is not the time to begin that project per se, *Clueless* also shares an allegiance to fantasies of cloacal reproduction and of anal sex that intertwine with those of resurrection—but this time of the girl. Thus, while we might say that Cher and Heckerling's camera devours Christian to stage their identification and investment in a fantasy of sex and generation that reverses Oedipus, we might also wonder if Christian's appearance is not already an aftereffect of the fact that the birth of God consistently appears in Western discourse through fantasies of cloacal creation. As Milton writes of the birth of the world, the birth that makes God, God so to speak: God "Dove-like sat'st brooding on the vast abyss/And mad'st it pregnant"(ln. 21–22, 32).[32] Or, as the Hail Mary reads: "Christ emerges from *'le fruit de sex entrailles.'*"

Although I have been implying otherwise, I would suggest that while Christian may most obviously bear the combination of fantasies of anal sex, anal reproduction, and salvation via incorporation *Clueless* offers, this film works concurrently to undo the association of buggin' with Christian by investing in plots that show girls and a woman film director who go buggin' regularly—with or without Christian. Rather than strictly imagining that the film incorporates Christian on Cher's behalf as a means to return girls to fantasies of anal sex and anal reproduction in discourse—from which we have been figured as absent—we might also imagine *Clueless* as being propelled by fantasies of anal sex and anal generation that then lead to the fantasy of a gay boy—an effect rather than cause of Oedipus—and to Christ, both privileged sites of identification and desire for the girl or the female film director invested in making such fantasies both visible and an active part of the textual strategies available for undermining the Oedipal scripts for gender and sexuality.

Christian is only one of many Messiahs of *Clueless*. At dinner, for example, Cher's father asks of Josh "Hasn't he grown since Easter?" And, then, there is Cher herself—as Madonna, as teen idol. In the Cher qua Madonna scene, Heckerling films Cher's cross-bearing self through a mirror from behind and, after Josh suggests sterilization, Cher's religion becomes verbalized as an alternative to one in which destroying a woman's reproductive capacity would share the same meaning as cleansing her of a desiring role in a "dirty" economy of meaning, sex, and reproduction. Josh and Cher's dialogue in the kitchen proceeds:

> "So what do you think?" Cher asks, skipping over to Josh with a grin.
> "I'm amazed, " he says, making a sandwich.
> "That I'm devoting myself so generously to someone else?"
> "No, that you found someone more clueless than you are to worship you."
> "I'll have you know that I'm rescuing her from teenage hell. You know the scars of adolescence can take years to heal."
> "And, you've never had a mother, so you're acting out on that poor girl as if she were your Barbie."
> "Psych 101 rears its ugly head." Cher quips back.
> "I'm not taking psych," returns Josh waving a rolled piece of sandwich meat.
> "Whatever," Cher says dismissively, "I'm going to take that lost soul in there and make her well-dressed and popular. Her life will be better because of me. How many girls can say that about you?"

Unsurprisingly Josh's fantasy of sterilization immediately precedes this scene; as he works hard to prevent Cher from creating herself into a God, from "generating" according to the theological definition of the term—even if she has other plans. For Cher, too, scripts Tai's makeover through the language of devotion and salvation, scripting a secular passion play in which she is the great redeemer of "lost souls," the savior of girls from "teenage hell"—in effect, a God.

If Cher and Christian both bear the cross in one way or another, as the film keeps rolling Heckerling proffers even more Messiahs, more fantasies of generating a generation. The scene of Cher's and Christian's first date, for example, also brings all of the major teenage characters together either in person or fantasmatically to create a scene of dancing, into the site of a collective resurrection. The band is playing a song called "Where'd You Go?" by The Mighty Mighty Bosstones—repeating Gaston's question in "Gigi," discussing its own plotlessness, and speaking of a man's journeying and questioning after one who would not sit still. On the dance floor, Christian and Cher "slide" together quite happily even if trouble for Cher's romantic plot emerges when Heckerling films the gaze of Josh watching Christian dance with another boy. A scene of resurrection enters the film again. As Christian cruises the dance floor, as Cher dances with him amidst flashing lights and the quick beat of the song, and as Tai and Josh get into the groove, Heckerling turns God Almighty into the lead singer of The Mighty Mighty Bosstones, filming Dicky Barrett as he falls into the crowd with arms spread as if he were on the cross. Of course, the doubling of Christian's "outing" by Heckerling on the dance floor with this staging of a resurrection helps to create him as *the* Messiah of the film. However, this scene also replays Travis Birkenstock's (Breckin Meyer) fall into an inhospitable crowd at the Valley party. When Travis, who worships the "Party Gods," does his sacrificial stage dive, the people he hopes will catch him let him tumble. Upon rising, he says "Thanks for the hospitality," sarcastically offering them gratitude for turning the "homie" (homey) scene he wanted into one of hurt, showing the way Heckerling uses the site of the dance party to resurrect the negotiable laws of good "hospitality," which Travis practices and in which the text believes.[33] It is perhaps crucial to understanding the resurrection of disco in the film, that while this scene of crucifixion/resurrection/incorporation *in* the 1990s dance party might be read as the film's way of psychologically mending the harm done to the sweet and kind "loadie" and 1970s peace-loving foot soldier, Travis Birkenstock, the significance of the spectacular and tender incorporation by the crowd of the Mighty One's crucifixion extends beyond Travis. The singer also reincarnates Murray, replaying the angry faces that Murray makes at Dionne throughout the movie and voicing issues about possession and Dionne emerges in this scene not only in her own dramatizing of a "Disco Queen"—Tina Turner—but in Christian's question to Cher. After Christian returns from flirting, he asks Cher to dance with the words: "Ready to slide?" replaying the dance lingo from Salt-N-Pepa's "Shoop," a song that appears elsewhere in the film as Heckerling opens a scene with a shot of a boy's butt.

If almost every song on the *Clueless* sound track includes the words turn or turning, then each gyration returns to the disco floor upon which a metaphorics of buggin' unites all of the plots of salvation, resurrection, and generation. Indeed, even "Gigi" reappears in the dance scene in which the lead singer falls and is gently incorporated rather than devoured by the crowd whose shape changes to accommodate him—Gaston's song echoes over and over again in the refrain "Where'd you go?" To put the girl behind the wheel of sexuality and on the road toward a revolution in gender relations, Heckerling deploys a metaphorics of anal sex and anal generation, ensuring that Cher's salvation fantasy in Miss Geist's class and the salvation of her Disco Mom and buddies begins with three fantasies of primal scenes that carry just such a metaphorics. If Cher's attachment to her "groovy" mom does not lead her to "ugly" fantasies of depression that is in part because the characters and the text do not incorporate objects per se but, instead, scenes and directionalities of movement. If Cher identifies with Madonna, she incorporates a fantasy of a mother who dances and rocks with gay men, white women, black men, black women, lesbian women, straight men, drag queens, with Christ, and in scenes of illicit pregnancy; she incorporates a figure who herself represents a revolutionary nexus for crossings of desire and identification prohibited by the white-ruled, Oedipally figured laws of legitimate reproduction.

When Heckerling introduces Murray she not only brings the camera into motion as one of the many vehicles through which the text's fantasies of anal sex and cloacal generation travels, she does so in conjunction with "Shoop," by hip hop artists Salt-N-Pepa, a song whose lyrics plot in mini form the overdetermined fantasy course of *Clueless*, providing in absentia verbal evidence to match Heckerling's visual project of using jeepin', dancin', and buggin' as a means to give voice to a girl's active desires and of resurrecting the evolving—revolving scene of disco for the 1990s. While "Shoop" plays for the briefest of intervals during *Clueless*, the words carry the reference to "sliding"—the word for Christian's and Cher's dancing—and plot a course parallel to *Clueless*, telling a story about a girl, her polymorphous sexual appetites, her car, and the voicing of those desires—hence, the presence of "Vox" in the pile of Cher's lesson books. If, that is, as Hughes argues, "Implicit in early Disco is the assumption that only a black woman can openly vocalize her sexuality, and that only a gay man would join her in a free-fall from rational self-mastery,"[34] then *Clueless* works as more of a permutation of those cross-identifications and conjoined, simultaneous movements of desire because even as *Clueless* draws on the words and desires voiced by a black female rap group, it frames those desires through a white film director's identification with them by joining the story they tell in absentia with Heckerling's film and camera.[35]

If there is a certain stress on the back and the butt in "Shoop," it is one that matches and magnifies by another means Heckerling's cinematic project. Just as "Shoop" plays, Heckerling's camera cuts from Cher and Dionne walking and talking to a close-up of Murray's butt. His boxer shorts hang out of his sagging jeans and while Heckerling differs from Salt-N-Pepa on the pleasing qualities of such attire, she nonetheless shares with them a desire to give women a claim to an active and discerning sexual desire through fantasies of ass shopping or shooping, butt loving, and public "coup[in']." This shot, like the largely absent lyrics to the song, offers salvation for the girls and for disco only insofar as they can, like Salt-N-Pepa and like Heckerling's camera, give voice to their "Scoobie-doo" desires.

This shot from behind is not a one-time deal. Aside from her games with Cher's mirror, Heckerling begins scenes with shots from behind when Cher's father first walks downstairs to Cher's voice-over saying that "he is a litigator . . . the scariest . . . of lawyers," when the line of walking high school boys enters with the same shot used to introduce Murray, and when the final wedding scene begins. Upon Cher's kiss with Josh atop the stairs, we hear Cher's voice-over, "You can guess what happened after that" and Heckerling cuts to the wedding scene. Cher says, "As if! I'm only sixteen" just as Heckerling's camera arrives at the back end of the aisle, offering a long shot of Mr. Hall and Miss Geist at the altar from behind. This shot, like the butt shots before it, works in conjunction with the thematic of "buggin'" in *Clueless* to redefine the laws of legitimate genital reproduction—the laws that help make both marriage and sex bound to and determined by plots about genital procreation—helping us to understand that this wedding stops none of the revolutions of sex, gender, and sexuality already set in motion throughout the film. If Cher Horowitz looks to Miss Geist for inspiration, then she identifies with fantasies of sexual movement and generation similar to the others offered as critical to Cher's makeover of her soul: Murray and Dionne sharing a sandwich, she and Christian in the art gallery. When Heckerling approaches the wedding scene of Miss Geist and Mr. Hall by filming them down the aisle, she focuses on the backsides of these two bodies and on Miss Geist who is wearing a clinging, bare-backed wedding dress for the occasion. In such a detail and in conjunction with Heckerling's camera direction, the text carries its illicit fantasies of jeepin' and buggin' right into the wedding scene and continues the revolutionary movement that begins with that first glance through the dirty window, making Cher's failure at the hands of the Messiah at the DMV more or less insignificant. Indeed Cher neither stops nor changes direction by making over her soul—only the vehicle through which she will continue buggin' along quite happily.

After her confrontation with a prohibitory law she elsewhere characterizes as a travesty of justice, Cher is metaphorically and spiritually reborn. Yet, this spiritual rebirth nonetheless adheres to the pre-transformational fantasies propelling the film. As we know, when Dionne fantasizes her wedding, she imagines a scene of sailing. But that scene has been afloat in the text all along: at the heart of Mr. Hall and Miss Geist's romance, driving the movement from the opening waterfall to Christian's "clam-bake" to "surfin' the crimson wave" toward Pismo Beach. Etymologically related to ghost, the name "Geist" leads directly to the subject of resurrection. The *Oxford English Dictionary* refers to "Ghost," and places the origin of "geist" in the nineteenth century, defining it as "Spirit, spirituality; intellectuality; intelligence" (419). And, by identifying with Miss Geist and serving as "captain" for her spirited projects of salvation by the sea, Cher finds another way to continue the generational fantasies that replay insistently: replacing the parental bed with the classroom, turning the classroom into a lesson about the multiplication of the loaves and fishes; because if an identification with Miss Geist means an identification with the scene of her desire, even Miss Geist is shown as quietly reveling in precisely the fantasy voiced by Dionne at the wedding table. Not only is her back bared at the wedding, she also enacts a fantasy of sailing and buggin' by uniting with Mr. Hall, whose name Cher turns into a verb about carrying one's "ass" somewhere and into a scene that involves sailing.

Cher, of course, uses the word *haul* as a crucial part of her participation in the film's cloacally generative plots: she "hauls ass to the kitchen" at her father's garden party and to the "ladies" on the "crimson wave" in Mr. Hall's classroom, but in doing so, she reminds us of the multiple and layering meanings of haul/hall.

haul. . . . n . . . 1. The act of hauling; a pull, a tug; spec the draught of a fishing net. . . . b. . . . a journey; *fig.* A project, a task. . . . 2a. A quantity of yarn for rope-making. . . . b (The quantity of) a draught of fish. . . . 3. The making of a substantial gain; an amount gained seized stolen, etc.

haul. . . . v. Also (earlier) **hall** [Variation of HALE . . .] 1. Naut . . . Trim the sails . . . so as to sail closer to the wind; . . . change course (lit & fig). . . . 2. Pull or draw with force. . . . b. Worry torment, pester."(1197)

Referring to sailing, changing courses, and pestering (Cher's specialty), the old spelling of *haul* matches that of Mr. Hall's name. In "From the History of an Infantile Neurosis" (1918 [1914]) Freud writes about the Wolf-man's refusal to relinquish his allegiance to a fantasy of anal sex and anal resurrection despite his having already learned about castration and legitimate reproduction: "[H]is mental life impressed one in much the same way as the religion of Ancient Egypt, which is so unintelligible to us because it preserves the earlier stage of its development side by side with the end-products, retains the most ancient gods and their attributes along with the most modern ones, and thus, as it were spreads itself upon a two-dimensional surface what other instances of evolution show us in the solid."[36] In light of such a statement, Gilmore's casting of Cher's mother as a depressed and/or battered Cleopatra makes a certain sense because *Clueless* returns to ancient meanings and old fantasies, resurrecting them to new purposes, confusing starts and stops, beginnings and ends. Yet unlike Gilmore, Heckerling refrains from scripting the Disco Mom and the fantasies of generations, sex, scenes, and movement she represents as stuck in a depressive crypt with the 1990s daughter who revives and identifies with her

Cher wears pink and white in noticeable superfluity only after she meets Christian; in fact, excepting for a second in an opening flash, the first time she wears these colors in the film is when she meets Christian—a fashion decision about as incidental as the film's use of a black-and-white color scheme. After this meeting, she appears wearing these colors with an astonishing frequency, helping Heckerling, it would seem, to carry both Cher and her Disco Mom to the finale in—if the pun can be borne—the pink of health. The colors her mother wears in the one portrait we see of her and the colors associated with "girliness" in culture—pink and white—are also the two colors Cher wears when she and Tai make up and when on the couch after realizing she loves Josh, the colors at the wedding, and the respective colors of the two girls' skirted butts in the cafeteria. Last but not least, Cher wears a bright pink sweater when she decides to "make over" her "soul" in Miss Geist's class. That her "soul" specifically needs a "make-over" highlights the transformational religion set in play by *Clueless*: that she wears a hot pink sweater when announcing her rebirth makes it a resurrection narrative as well for Cher's Disco Mom. She may be a hanging portrait in the vestibule, but the Disco Mom does not sit still or quietly, appearing again not only through specific characters but as the very fabric and hue of the scene itself. Indeed, in many ways her portrait comes to life in Cher's rosy photo-op of her generation of friends and in Heckerling's choice to set Gaston's photo-still reverie in motion at the fountain.

In *Clueless*, the patriarchal law is sick and not the mother, the daughter, or the scenes of desire, identification, and generation either represent. Indeed, Cher's first encounter with her father involves a discussion of inoculating him, and the kiss scene between Josh and Cher turns the question of their "butts" into a fantasy of a sick lawyer. When Josh "rescues" Cher from the harsh critique of the big, bad lawyer who calls her a "dumb kid," he raises the question of their butts. In defense of their flirting, Josh says, "We've been working our butts off on this case." The lawyer retorts, "I don't care what you do with your butts, I'm calling in sick." Contextualized amidst other similar instances, this rescue scene both makes Cher seem unconvincingly timid and sets the film's fantasies of anal sex and anal generation against one of its most rigid and misogynistic incarnations of the law, allowing Cher to continue sailing along—even past the wedding scene.

If the media interprets this revolution at the site of the legitimate laws of genital reproduction as an occasion to celebrate the birth of the girl and the death of grunge, this interpretation while exceeding the film is nonetheless made available by it. Indeed, in conjunction with its resurrectionary aspirations, it represents one of the text's secret fantasies: when Josh accuses Cher of selfishness while with her in the Jeep, he says to her, "I would die of shock if you did something that was not 99 percent selfish for a change." She quips back, "Oh, that would be reason enough for me." Andrew Ross writes of grunge "as a scourge upon the impossibly sanitized, aerobicized world of 90210, the politics of dirt reasserted itself within music culture itself."[37] *Clueless* takes the dirt from the hands of the boys and from the black and blues of misogynistic violence—domestic or otherwise—and gives it to the girls; thus, participating as one text among many in a larger cultural turn that, while having as many hegemonic as subversive effects, certainly works to help us begin thinking about the politics of the rise of the girl in the 1990s from a psychoanalytic perspective and understanding why this particular remake of Austen had such enormous psychological appeal for the girls who viewed it repeatedly. A generous and generative spirit of a generation carries us from jeepin' to sailing and back, right through the ending of the text and beyond—the song after the final image is also about turning: bringing us full circle through the media to the fantasy with which the film begins.[38] The word *Geist* means specifically "the spirit of a group," and it is this spirit, this fantasy of a generation, that helps turn a story that in other hands might result in the bruising of the "Cleopatra Mom" into a tale about the stealing back of Egyptian gold, into a tale that allows the girl of the 1990s not only to play with dirt but to do so in a way that reimagines a new queendom to come.

206 *Denise Fulbrook*

Notes

1. See Carolyn Dever, *Death and the Mother from Dickens to Freud* (Cambridge: Cambridge University Press, 1998).

2. Francis L. Restuccia, "A Black Morning: Kristevan Melancholia in Jane Austen's 'Emma,'" *American Imago* 51, no. 4 (1994): 451.

3. See John Wiltshire, *Jane Austen and the Body* (Cambridge: Cambridge University Press, 1992), 110–155.

4. Peter Stack, "A Romp among the *Clueless*," *San Francisco Chronicle*, 22 December 1995, p. C19.

5. Brian Hoffman, "'*Clueless*' is Plotless, But So What? It's a Lot of Fun," *Sun-Sentinel* (Ft. Lauderdale), 11 August 1995, p. 46.

6. Nick Madden, review of *Clueless, Boston Herald*, 31 July 1995, p. 32.

7. Amruta Slee, "Absolutely Clueless," *Sunday Times* (London), 30 July 1995, p. 3.

8. I do not believe this description of said generation is all encompassing; it is patently not. As *Clueless* makes clear, neither it nor any other text could be representative of a "real" generation. For differing approaches to the phenomenon of Gen X and Y, see Rob Owen, *Gen X TV: The Brady Bunch to Melrose Place* (Syracuse, NY: Syracuse University Press, 1997); Douglas Coupland, *Generation X : Tales for an Accelerated Culture* (New York: St. Martin's Press, 1991); Geoffrey T. Holtz, *Welcome to the Jungle: The Why Behind "Generation X"* (New York: St. Martin's Press, 1995).

9. *Orange County Register* online, 20 July 1995, 30 March 2002 (http://www.oc register.com).

10. While contemporary feminist criticism is not my topic per se, *Clueless* speaks directly to a steady spate of publications about third-wave or third-generation feminism. See, for example, Barbara Finlan, ed., *Listen Up: Voices from the Next Feminist Generation* (Seattle: Seal Press, 1995); Leslie Heywood and Jennifer Drake, *Third Wave Agenda: Being Feminist, Doing Feminism* (Minneapolis: University of Minnesota Press, 1997); Rebecca Walker, *To Be Real: Telling the Truth and Changing the Face of Feminism* (New York: Doubleday, 1995); Devoney Looser and E. Ann Kaplan, ed., *Generations: Academic Feminists in Dialogue* (Minneapolis: University of Minnesota Press, 1997). See particularly, Judith Roof, "Generational Difficulties: or, The Fear of a Barren History," in *Generations: Academic Feminists in Dialogue* (Minneapolis: University of Minnesota Press, 1997) 68–87, who warns against the use of generational metaphors at all. Although Roof aptly critiques the use of mother/daughter language in feminist criticism, her definition of feminist criticism also limits itself unnecessarily to thinking about a "generational metaphor" in those terms.

11. There are many ways to approach the question of the identificatory structures *Clueless* establishes for Cher and itself. I have not, for example, considered the role of the lesbian gym teacher or the complicated racial politics of the film in as much

detail as I would have liked or is required. Despite the critical hesitancy to take *Clueless* "seriously," it is as complex as any Austen text. See Suzanne Ferris, "Emma Becomes *Clueless*" and Devoney Looser, "Feminist Implications of the Silver Screen," *Jane Austen in Hollywood*, ed. Linda Troost and Sayre Greenfield (Lexington: University of Kentucky Press, 1998), 122–129; 159–171 (esp. 167).

12. H.B. Gilmore, *Clueless* (New York: Pocket Books, 1995), 1–2.

13. Walter Hughes, "In the Empire of the Beat: Discipline and Disco," in *Microphone Fiends: Youth Music, Youth Culture*, ed. Andrew Ross and Tricia Rose (New York: Routledge, 1994), 147–157. See also Richard Dyer, "In Defense of Disco," *Out in Culture: Gay, Lesbian, and Queer Essays on Popular Culture*, ed. Corey K. Creekmur and Alexander Doty (Durham, NC: Duke University Press, 1995), 407–415.

14. The video for Madonna's 1999 "Ray of Light" takes place on a roadway. She is dancing amidst the moving lights.

15. Ethan Smith, *Entertainment Weekly Online* (August 18, 1995): Teen Beats (http://www.ew.com/en/archive) 30 March 2002.

16. Jean Laplanche and Jean-Bertrand, "Fantasy and the Origins of Sexuality," in *Formations of Fantasy*, ed. Victor Burgin, James Donald, and Cora Kaplan (New York: Routledge, 1989), 5–28, 26.

17. John Fletcher, "Poetry, Gender, and Primal Fantasy," in *Formations of Fantasy*, ed. Victor Burgin, James Donald, and Cora Kaplan (New York: Routledge, 1989), 109–141, 114.

18. That the series of primal fantasies Freud initially explored lost its multiplicity in the naming of one primal fantasy as the primal scene relates to the way in which a range of sexual possibilities becomes reduced to genital intercourse between a man and a woman. This definition of sex upholds and doubles for the definition of sex as that which identifies a body as female or male in much the same way as the primal scene in Freudian psychoanalysis upholds a theory of subjectivity that most routinely considers this pairing of mother and father as constitutive of the fantasies it allows for the acquisition of a sexual identity. See Eve K. Sedgwick's critique of Kaja Silverman's analysis of primal fantasy in Sedgewick's *Tendencies* (Durham, NC: Duke University Press, 1993).

19. Hughes, "In the Empire of the Beat," 149.

20. Gilmore writes this space into one typically threatening to disco: a frat house. See Andrew Ross on the "DISCO SUCKS" movement. For Ross, disco persists in various genres of music in the 1990s; however, he leaves unanticipated the ways in which disco in the late 1990s would forefront women in that scene and place the girl at the center of youth culture. [See "Introduction," *Microphone Fiends: Youth Music, Youth Culture*, ed. Andrew Ross and Tricia Rose (New York: Routledge, 1994) 1–17 (esp. 11)]. In Heckerling's *Fast Times at Ridgemont High,* the Jennifer Jason-Leigh character's first sex with a "pig" happens under graffiti that reads, "Disco Sucks."

21. This chapter does not subscribe to the developmental claims that would imagine "adult" sexuality as post-Oedipal sexuality. The difference between the Oedipal and

pre-Oedipal is understood here as itself an effect of heterosexist assumptions about what counts as desirable: adult sexuality.

22. Horns play when Cher reaches her epiphany of desire; a close-up of a trombone hole begins the dance scene.

23. Jane Austen, *The Complete Novels*, ed. R.W. Chapman (New York: Oxford University Press, 1994), 1072.

24. Freud writes, "From the very first, children are at one in thinking that babies must be born through the bowel; they must make their appearance like a lump of fæces. This theory is not abandoned until all anal interests have been deprived of their value" "The Sexual Life of Human Beings," *The Standard Edition of the Complete Psychological Works of Sigmund Freud*, ed. and trans. James Strachey [London: Hogarth, 1963], 16: 319).

25. Cf. Henry Tilney's description of "journalizing" in *Northanger Abbey* with the style of Austen's letters and with Oscar Wilde's *The Importance of Being Earnest*—a text in which the rainbowesque Miss Prism mistakes her book for a baby. (See Oscar Wilde, *Plays*, ed. Peter Raby (New York: Oxford University Press, 1995). See also Deirdre Le Faye, ed., *Jane Austen's Letters* (New York: Oxford University Press, 1995.

26. Mary Shelley, *Frankenstein, or The Modern Prometheus*, ed. James Rieger (Chicago: University of Chicago Press, 1982), 229.

27. Jeffrey Masson, ed. *The Complete Letters of Sigmund Freud to Wilhelm Fliess, 1887–1904* (Cambridge: Harvard University Press, 1985), 288.

28. Deirdre Le Faye, ed., *Jane Austen's Letters* (New York: Oxford University Press, 1995), 16–17.

29. Sandor Ferenczi's writings on female fantasies of cloacal reproduction lead to a story about chickens, eggs, and dirt. See his "Two Typical Faecal and Anal Symptoms," in *Further Contribution to the Theory and Technique of Psychoanalysis*, ed. Ernest Jones (London: Hogarth Press, 1950): 327–328. Cf. Josh's "Easter" visit.

30. For an article about the plots of domestication and colonization in *Clueless* see Gayle Wald, "Clueless in the Neocolonial World Order," *Camera Obscura: A Journal of Feminism, Culture and Media Studies* 42 (1999) 51–69.

31. The cover of Richard Keller Simon's *Trash Culture: Popular Culture and the Great Traditon* pictures a dark-haired empire-waisted heroine who might easily be mistaken for Austen (Berkeley and Los Angeles: University of California Press, 1999).

32. John Milton, *Paradise Lost*, ed. Scott Elledge (New York: Norton, 1975), 6.

33. Fittingly, Rolling Stone.com writes of the Ska-core "Plaid Boys of Boston"—note the plethora of plaid in the film: "The Bosstones . . . gratitude toward . . . fans was welcomed in an era of humorless, standoffish grunge icons." See http://www.rollingstone.com and http://imusic.com/showcase/modern/mightyb.html. A review of their CD, "Let's Face It," reads: "As always, the major theme is tolerance: racial, sexual and otherwise. As plainly stated in the album's title track, it's a message aimed at anyone who partakes in racism, homophobia or bigotry of any kind."

34. Hughes, "In the Empire of the Beat," 153.

35. Lyrics for "Shoop" can be found at http://www.ohhla.com/index.htm. While many of its words do not play in this song's brief celluloid cameo, from the start, Pepa's narrative brings us to a scene of sex and motion to which *Clueless* incessantly returns. Indeed, in its stress on "hot rod[s]," getting "digits," "slip slid[ing]," "yum-yum" boys, "kick[in]'" it, "chillin'," boys being "stacked 'specially in the back," coup[in]', and shooping this song is as much a script for *Clueless* as for *Emma*.

36. Sigmund Freud, "From the History of an Infantile Neurosis," in *The Standard Edition of the Complete Psychological Works of Sigmund Freud*, ed. and trans. James Strachey (London: Hogarth, [1955]), 17: 119 [1–123].

37. Ross, "Introduction" *Microphone Fiends: Youth Music, Youth Culture*, ed. Andrew Ross and Tricia Rose (New York: Routledge, 1994), 5.

38. The script is recorded by pacey578@rocketmail.com. The final song is "Need You Around" by the Smoking Popes.

Part IV
In the Bedroom

10

Sleeping with Mr. Collins

❧❖❧

Ruth Perry

Jane Austen's beloved and well-known characters are oddly nondescript, their vague physical descriptions vividly animated by moral qualities. A light, graceful step or an upright posture lives in the mind of the reader as a moral trait as much as a physical one. Perhaps that is why contemporary filmmakers enjoy bringing these novels to the screen—because Austen's texts allow them great interpretative license in translating moral characteristics into physical appearance. Yet something is lost in the translation. Our own reliance on the visual, on physical "chemistry" as we like to call it, falsifies the representation of the body, sexuality, and even marriage in Austen's own day.

Take the match between Charlotte Lucas and Mr. Collins in *Pride and Prejudice* as a case in point. When Charlotte Lucas accepts Mr. Collins' proposal of marriage, Elizabeth Bennet reflects in a moment of free indirect discourse that her friend has "sacrificed every better feeling to worldly advantage."[1] Blurring the line between the narrator and Elizabeth's inner voice gives authorial weight to this sentiment and makes it seem irrefutable. Yet in the subsequent treatment of this subject, Austen makes it clear that Charlotte, who is neither insensible nor crude, has accepted Mr. Collins with her eyes wide open. "Without thinking highly either of men or of matrimony" (122), marriage had always been Charlotte's object, we are told; it was the "pleasantest preservative from want" (122–123) for a woman in her position. "I am not a romantic," she tells Elizabeth. "I ask only a comfortable home" (125). These are sentiments that Austen still espouses years later, when she writes to her niece Fanny Knight in 1817: "Single women have a dreadful propensity for being poor—which is one very strong argument in favour of Matrimony."[2] If Charlotte Lucas is willing to marry Mr. Collins

213

just because he is a man in a respectable position, her successful suitor is hardly more fastidious. For Mr. Collins, women are interchangeable too: one is as good as another. He only wants encouragement to make his selection.

Still, when Elizabeth Bennet visits Hunsford several months later, after Charlotte is settled into married life, she is pleased to see her old friend taking satisfaction in her pleasant establishment while wisely encouraging Mr. Collins to work in his garden and leave her to the enjoyment of their comfortable home. Although the reader is told that Charlotte deliberately chooses not to hear Mr. Collins' long-winded and embarrassingly self-congratulatory speeches, Elizabeth's appraisal of their marital situation is that her friend is tolerably happy. She remarks to Darcy that Charlotte is "one of the very few sensible women" that could have carried off a marriage to Mr. Collins with success:

> My friend has an excellent understanding—though I am not certain that I consider her marrying Mr. Collins as the wisest thing she ever did. She seems perfectly happy, however, and in a prudential light, it is certainly a very good match for her. (178)

Thus, Elizabeth Bennet attests to the success of the match, despite the absence of romantic love on either side. We are not allowed to imagine that Charlotte Lucas has let her "excellent understanding" lapse, nor that Mr. Collins' person or company has any attractions for her. Nevertheless, he has a respectable position in the world and will come into the property of Longbourn when Mr. Bennet dies. The text corroborates the realism of such material considerations in marriage when Elizabeth Bennet confesses teasingly that her own regard for Darcy began when she saw "his beautiful grounds at Pemberley" (373). Both Jane Austen and her character, Elizabeth Bennet, are sympathetic to Charlotte's cheerful adjustment and genuinely glad to see her make the best of "her home and her housekeeping, her parish and her poultry" (216).

One is surprised by Austen's acquittal of Charlotte in this closer look, because to a modern sensibility the inviolabilty of bodily experience is a supreme moral consideration. In our day, the intimacies of marriage with a repellant man would be an insupportable form of prostitution. Yet Charlotte Lucas willingly undertakes all the offices of her new station, from visiting Lady Catherine de Bourgh several times a week to sleeping with Mr. Collins. That they share the conjugal embrace is proved by their "expectation of a young olive-branch" (364). There is not the slightest whiff of sexual disgust about the matter: not from Charlotte, nor from Elizabeth, nor the narrator. However one feels about the marriage—and it can be argued that Charlotte is in fact an appropriate mate for Mr. Collins—the physical repugnance that we in the present century feel at the idea of sleeping with Mr. Collins is entirely absent in Jane Austen's treatment of the matter. The "better feelings" that Charlotte

Lucas is said to have sacrificed do not, apparently, include squeamishness about sex with a pompous and sycophantic man. In this, as in so much else, Austen reveals her eighteenth-century sensibility because Charlotte Lucas Collins is a vestigial character, left over from an era of pragmatic rather than romantic matches, before the discourse of the later eighteenth century created unbridgeable moral conflict over arranged or prudential marriages.

Nonetheless, when adapting Austen's novel to the screen, modern filmmakers cannot resist depicting Mr. Collins as physically repugnant and representing Elizabeth Bennet's shock at Charlotte Lucas's marriage as caused as much by her own physical as well as moral distaste for the man. In bringing *Pride and Prejudice* to a modern audience, they are less interested in historicizing Austen's attitude toward sexuality—representing Charlotte Lucas's sense of her luck without physical distaste for the man—than in playing up Elizabeth Bennet's relief at avoiding a disgusting suitor. The 1940 Greer Garson and Laurence Olivier version, with its prissy Mr. Collins bowing and scraping and pursing his lips, probably comes closest to representing the spirit of the novel with regard to this match because it minimizes the physicality of all of the courtships. Charlotte is hardly plain in this old film, and Mr. Collins is unappealing largely by contrast to Olivier. Nonetheless, the visit to Hunsford is begun by Elizabeth's immediately changing her dress, displaying her old-fashioned, frilly undergarments as well as her intimate ease with her old friend Charlotte. It is the only time in the film that she disrobes, however, and because it is done immediately upon entering Mr. Collins' house, the viewer is reminded that Elizabeth will not be undressing in front of him, that a sexual connection with Mr. Collins is happily not her fate, although it is what Charlotte has contracted for. The scene thus restores the suggestion of unwanted sexuality that the earlier sequence plays down.

The 1979 BBC production, reissued in 1986, for which the dramatization was done by Fay Weldon, casts Mr. Collins as a large, ungainly, awkward buffoon in black clerical garb. He talks too much, in a loud eager voice, and when he dances with Elizabeth he pulls her to and fro with too much energy. He is like an overgrown puppy, and the music accentuates his awkward energy. When he asks Elizabeth for a private conversation, she begs her mother not to leave them alone. The camera moves in and Collins' large, heavy face fills the screen. His appalling physical presence seems unavoidable.

Rejected by Elizabeth, he proposes to Charlotte in the garden. The screen shows several luscious flowers, open to the sun, with a large black bee fluttering and tumbling in. When she declares she will marry him, he smiles broadly and nods and his blubbery lower lip trembles. Charlotte drops her eyes, unsmiling. Nonetheless, when Elizabeth visits Hunsford, Charlotte looks well and happy, and not at all discontent with her new husband. Despite the image of the bee penetrating the sexy blossoms, and the obtrusiveness of Mr. Collins' large and overbearing presence, he is not made physically disgusting in this treatment, but only ridiculous.

The most recent film treatment of *Pride and Prejudice*, the 1995 Andrew
Davies A&E version, exaggerates the physical dimension of everything in the
novel, beginning with Bingley and Darcy galloping toward Netherfield rather
than opening with the teasing dialogue between Mr. and Mrs. Bennet. Elizabeth not only tramps across the fields to visit her sister but romps on the lawn
with a large dog when she gets there. The film is famous for its beefcake:
Darcy without clothes climbing into Bingley's bath or plunging into the pond
to cool off with a swim. All the characters are too beautiful, even Charlotte,
and almost all elements of wit are removed from most of the conversations
which are everywhere stripped down to serve the marriage plot. In its hyper-
physicality, this film, more than any other, emphasizes Mr. Collins' physical
repulsiveness. Although there is not enough focus on anyone's intellectual
qualities in the film to fully demonstrate Collins' pomposity, we watch him
evade a half-naked, giggling Lydia on the stairs with a prudish gesture, when
staying at Longbourn. He is particularly repulsive when he asks his cousin
Elizabeth to dance, his face shining with the exertion at charm and his smile
bared over too many teeth. The way he leans over her much too close, forc-
ing her assent, feels claustrophobic and encourages our vicarious sexual disgust at the thought of necessary physical contact with him. Any historical
difference between Austen's sensibility and our own with regard to sleeping
with Mr. Collins is entirely obviated by this shot.

These cinematic versions of *Pride and Prejudice* add the dimension of
physical disgust for Mr. Collins to Austen's story. But when you go back to
the text, it is simply not there—if you can clear your mind's eye of images
from the movies and other adaptations. Written in an era before love was
universally expected to accompany marriage, the original sequence in the
novel is an interesting window into an earlier sensibility. Charlotte Lucas
gets her establishment and makes the best of the marriage and the author
does not, in the end, judge her harshly. Nor is Austen's novel unique for her
period in portraying marriages that are happy enough despite the absence of
attraction, romance, or even compatibility between the principals. In discussing loveless marriages in late-eighteenth-century fiction, J.M.S. Tompkins compares Mrs. Strictland in Clara Reeve's *School for Widows* (1791) to
Charlotte Lucas Collins and observes that neither is condemned for her
practical choice. Reeve's Mrs. Strictland, says Tompkins, "painfully learns
enough patience and tact to live not uncomfortably beside her boorish
spouse. . . . She holds to her bargain, takes comfort in her children, and,
after the first revolts, finds even in her confined circumstance opportunities
for charity and mental growth. The picture is done in sober tones, without
satire and almost without humour, but there is a quality of unassuming realism about it, a simple attention to important things, that commands respect."[3] In the terms Tompkins uses to describe married life, sex was not
necessarily considered one of the "important things" in late-eighteenth-
century fiction.

The reason that Austen is able to imagine Charlotte's sleeping with Mr. Collins with equanimity is because sex had less psychological significance in eighteenth-century England than in our own post-Freudian era; it was less tied to individual identity, and more understood as an uncomplicated, straightforward physical appetite. Sexual disgust—the feeling that sex with the "wrong" person could be viscerally disturbing—was an invention of the eighteenth century; it was one dimension of an evolving sexual identity for women, a dimension that could control their sexual reactions without the interference—whether policing or protective—of a network of kin relations. A somatized reaction compelling enough to regulate women's sexual preferences and habits, sexual disgust can hardly be found in the repertoire of earlier English written experience. Even rape is recorded more as pain at physical force than psychological horror at unwanted intercourse registered as an invasion of the self.[4] The ribald escapades of such Restoration texts as *The Wandring Whore*, with their gross physical acts, hardly left any place for sexual disgust or sexual delicacy. It is hard to imagine an early-eighteenth-century heroine such as Moll Flanders, or a character from one of Delarivier Manley's fictions, as capable of feeling sexual disgust. Only when the experience of sexual intercourse began to be invested with meaning greater than other bodily experience could its mishandling horrify and shock.

Frances Sheridan's *The Memoirs of Miss Sidney Bidulph* (1761), Elizabeth Griffith's *The History of Lady Barton* (1771), Georgiana Spencer's *Emma: or, The Unfortunate Attachment* (1773), and Henry MacKenzie's *Julia de Robigne* (1777)—novels depicting the tragedy of marrying without love—were part of an emerging discourse about marriage in the later eighteenth century. They built a new attitude toward sexual experience that, when introjected, would construct women as the right kind of sexual property: neither prude nor coquette but trustworthy and warm-blooded. Women had to learn to make distinctions between the right kind of sex and the wrong kind of sex. They had to learn a new kind of physical revulsion for sexual experience when not accompanied by the new sentimental version of romantic love that was supposed to infuse ordinary sexual and domestic relations. They had to feel viscerally how wrong it would be to have sexual relations with the wrong man. This refinement was necessary to develop an inner consciousness of the double standard. If women were to stay put as the sexual property of one man and one man only, they had to be trained to feel repugnance for physical relations with anyone else. The new popular wisdom set up expectations of disgust for sexual acts without love, and even for lustful feelings that had no admixture of moral admiration or mutual social respect. The emphasis on a woman's sexual allegiance to a mate, rather than her obedience to a father, also signaled the realignment of kinship along a conjugal axis rather than a consanguineal axis.

Were there no literary representations of sexual disgust before the eighteenth century? Cannot one find expressions of sexual disgust in Renaissance drama, for example? Certainly Hamlet's charge to Gertrude that she lives "[i]n the rank sweat of an enseamed bed,/Stewed in corruption, honeying and making love/Over the nasty sty"[5] is an expression of sexual disgust. Yet these lines express a more generalized disgust at the fact of human sexuality, and in particular women's sexuality, at the whole wide rank world, rather than disgust with a particular sexual object. Hamlet is sick about sex, and his revulsion extends to Ophelia; he is not distinguishing between a proper sexual object—she to whom he is attracted—and an improper object—she by whom he is physically repelled. In his disturbed state of mind, all women are appalling in their sexuality—potentially deceptive and seductive.

Nor do other early literary examples of sexual aversion, when examined closely, hold up as instances of that peculiar revulsion to sex with the wrong person that signals a violation of one's psychological self and not just one's bodily self. In *Comedy of Errors*, there is a male servant—Dromio of Syracuse—who is pursued by the fat, greasy, kitchen wench—Nell—whose lust he does not reciprocate. He dodges her advances and mocks her size and aspect to his master. But his distaste is played as farce, as slapstick, rather than as the effect of a revulsion that reaches to the very core of his being. The fact that Dromio has no interiority in this dramatic characterization obviates that intensity of feeling and keeps his resistance to Nell's advances comic.

In Thomas Middleton and William Rowley's *The Changeling* (1622), there is a character—Beatrice—who feels repugnance for the man she is bound to have sex with. She is deflowered by him offstage in an unholy quid pro quo. Although she finds De Flores repulsive, she submits to him because he has obeyed her wishes and killed her unwanted fiancé. Hardly an innocent woman, her complicity in the murder complicates the audience's feeling about the sexual payment he demands. Moreover, in the course of the play she warms up to him because they are really soul mates in evil. In the end, there are hints that she has continued their sexual liaison voluntarily because she has come to trust and admire him. Whatever sexual disgust she may have felt for him originally is dissipated by this development in their relationship.[6]

The invention of sexual disgust is part of what Norbert Elias has written about as the progressive regulation of instinctual life. The "civilization-curve" as he calls it, from the middle ages to the nineteenth century, entails the suppression of instinctual and bodily experience from the shared public life of a society and the progressive containment of this bodily experience in private, domestic life. Elias gives examples from table manners, bathroom behaviors, and sexual mores. "The tendency of the civilizing process," he writes, is to make all bodily functions private, to put them "behind closed doors".[7] Moreover, "the greater the transformation, control, restraint and concealment of drives and impulses that is demanded of the individual by society," the more elaborate and complicated the conditioning of the young (189). Elias refers to the discomfort and embarrassment that people feel when that conditioning is violated, and the association of "delicacy" about bodily matters with a higher degree of civilization. I would add that disgust is an important somatic sign marking the complicated conditioning of bodily response, and that sexual disgust, in particular, evolved to condition women's sexual choices. That is, no one expects a heterosexual man to be so put off by the vulgar mind or loose morals of an attractive woman as to be unwilling to have sex with her. As with Dromio of Syracuse in *Comedy of Errors*, sexual disgust in a man is played for comedy and the object of that disgust derided. For a woman, sexual disgust is more serious. It is supposed to operate as a restraint on her desire for inappropriate men, to confine her sexual activity to intercourse with a single partner from the right social class in a legitimate marriage. Sexual disgust is a visceral response that helps to define the social and moral limits of acceptable sexual behavior. It must be understood as one of the bodily forms of discipline that Michel Foucault has famously explained as providing the invisible regulatory mechanisms for policing the most important rules of social reproduction.

Perhaps examples from two novels of the later eighteenth century will further clarify the emotional response that I am calling sexual disgust. There is no reason to believe that Jane Austen knew either one of these books, although they certainly were in circulation in her lifetime. The first is from *Millenium Hall* (1762) by Sarah Scott, the mid-century bluestocking. The early history of Mrs. Morgan, one of the original founders of the community of women, provides an instance of sexual disgust of the sort I am trying to define: revulsion from sex with a particular person because of his unattractive character. Forced into a loveless marriage by her vicious conniving stepmother and her weak father, Mrs. Morgan experienced the worst kind of servitude of body and spirit in fulfilling her marital obligations to a man who neither loved nor respected her. Of the sexual dimension of the union, the narrator has this to say:

> Sensible that his wife married him without affection, he seemed to think it impossible ever to gain her love, and therefore spared himself all fruitless endeavours. He was indeed fond of her person; he admired her beauty, but despised her understanding. . . . Those who know Mrs. Morgan best, are convinced that she suffered less uneasiness from his ill-humour, brutal as it was, than from his nauseous fondness.[8]

Not given to "fruitless" romanticism, Mr. Morgan did not bother to court his wife, but took cold advantage of his marital rights to indulge his fondness for "her person." Despising her mind but glad of her personal beauty, his "nauseous fondness," his sexual appetite for her, devoid even of friendship, was the most insupportable aspect of the marriage for her. For Mrs. Morgan, historically precocious as a literary heroine, sexual pleasure was impossible without caring, mutual respect, or at least common interests;

and sexual congress without any sort of mutuality was repulsive.[9] The quick roll in the hay that would have been possible in a novel by Henry Fielding or Eliza Haywood, or the clear-sighted calculation that was part of the sexual adventures of Daniel Defoe's female protagonists, was out of the question for this new kind of sentimental heroine.

Mary Wollstonecraft's *Maria; or the Wrongs of Women* (1797)[10] also depicts a sensitive woman called upon to endure the embraces of a morally and physically repulsive husband. She describes Mr. Venables in the morning, dirty and unkempt, "lolling in an arm-chair, in a dirty powdering gown, soiled linen, ungartered stockings, and tangled hair, yawning and stretching himself," exhibiting the signs of a squeamish stomach "produced by the last night's intemperance" (I: 140), which he took no pains to conceal. Although she had married him with the illusion of love, Maria was soon disabused of her fantasy and learned the true character of the man to whom she had yoked herself. Echoing Sarah Scott's description of marital relations that disgust, Maria describes her feelings frankly:

> My husband's renewed caresses then became hateful to me; his brutality was tolerable, compared to his distasteful fondness. Still, compassion, and the fear of insulting his supposed feelings, by a want of sympathy, made me dissemble and do violence to my delicacy. (I: 140)

As in the situation described in *Millenium Hall*, it was worse for a woman of "delicacy" to have to endure a sexual connection without love than to put up with mere brutality of language and behavior. To have to fake sexual willingness did violence to a woman's feelings, to her sense of herself; it was an affront to her consciousness, a psychological violence worse than physical violence. That the performance of a bodily function could be so unsettling, and invested with such significance, shows that sexual practice had entered a realm beyond the merely physical. It is as if being forced to eat or drink something distasteful could shake one's identity, violate one's sense of self, make one feel dirty and dishonest.

A woman's relation to sex was coming to stand for her integrity as a woman, to be identified as the expression of her deepest self. Wollstonecraft, for all her radical belief in free love, helped to consolidate this sentimental meaning of sex for women by writing about it as if it were the center of their emotional experience. By taking women's sexual feelings seriously, she sometimes made it seem as if sentimentalized sexual relations were more essential to their self-definition than any other aspect of their lives. "How does the woman deserve to be characterized," she asked in *Maria*, "who marries one man, with a heart and imagination devoted to another? Is she not an object of pity or contempt, when thus sacriligiously violating the purity of her own feelings?" (I: 144–145). Sexual activity could only be a positive experience when the heart and imagination of a woman accompanied it. When they did not, it violated the purity of her feelings and welled up as sexual disgust. This was a far cry from the Renaissance belief in women's insatiable sexual appetite or the Restoration and early-eighteenth-century expectation that lust was wholesome, natural, and inevitable in men *and* in women.

Although the beginnings of this discourse of sexual disgust can be seen in many places—*The Athenian Mercury, The Tatler, The Spectator*, sentimental comedies, conduct books, and finally in novels after about 1740—the classical statement of this repugnance for pure physicality, with or without marriage, was probably Defoe's *Conjugal Lewdness or, Matrimonial Whoredom: A Treatise Concerning the Use and Abuse of the Marriage Bed* (1727). Begun in the 1690s, although not published until 1727, Defoe's treatise evenhandedly warns men and women alike that sexual enjoyment, without mutual affection and regard, is morally reprehensible and bad for your health.[11] He speaks of the degeneracy of the modern age in which marriage, that "divine Institution is made a Stalking-horse to the brutal Appetite" (33).

Defoe's attention to the psychological dimension of sexuality is fairly novel in this period. The seventeenth-century sex manuals and works of anatomy and advice, such as *Culpepper's Midwife* or *Aristotle's Masterpiece: or, the Secrets of Generation Displayed*, did not moralize about attitudes, practices, or legalities. They simply gave the facts of physiological excitation and reproduction as they were understood. Defoe's treatise, subtitled "The Use and Abuse of the Marriage Bed," argues first and foremost, that one must take seriously the business of marriage which is "all that can be called happy in the Life of Man," and "the Center to which all lesser Delights of Life tend, as a Point in the Circle" (96). Defoe grants that moderate sexual pleasure is appropriate in a marriage in which there is mutual affection and especially in which there is the desire for children. But the point that he repeats again and again—and the point for which he apparently wrote the book—is that married couples must keep a lid on excessive sexual desire, even for each other, and they must temper their lust with politesse in the bedroom. "Married persons must keep such modesty and decency of treating each other, that they never force themselves into high and violent lusts, with arts and devices: always remembering that those Mixtures are most innocent which are *most simple* and *most natural, most orderly* and *most safe*" (55). Married persons must not make use of each other as sexual objects; they must try to retain their sense of their whole relation to one another at all times. Defoe wrote, "It is a duty of matrimonial Chastity to be restrained and temperate in the use of their lawful Pleasures" (55). He condemned the expedients that human invention might dream up to fan the flames of desire—some of which have been updated and recycled in our own day in magazines sold in supermarkets offering advice on "how to keep passion in your marriage." His concern historicizes the place of sexuality in marriage—indeed, in human life—and reminds us how much attitudes have changed in 276 years.

Defoe warned that criminally immoderate sexual appetite, whether inside or outside of marriage, would enfeeble the body and take its toll on the health of one's offspring. "Palsies and Epilepsies, Falling-Sickness, trembling of the Joints, pale dejected Aspects, Leanness, and at last Rottenness and other filthy and loathsome Distempers" could be expected in later years of those who overdid sexual activity in youth. Defoe's metaphors are mechanical and hydraulic: sex uses up the body's vitality; ill health will result "if the Fountain is drawn dry, if the Vitals are exhausted, the Engines of Nature worked with unreasonable Violence" (91). As for the progeny of unions too self-indulgent about wanton sex: "Nature speaks plainer in her Reproofs of that Crime than I dare do," Defoe claimed, and the revolting effects were visible for several generations: "The Product of those impure and unlawful, however matrimonial Liberties, carry the indelible Marks of their Parents unhappy Excesses and Intemperances in their Faces," where "scrophulous Humours break out, in Scabs and Blisters" and in the "blotch'd and bladdred Skin of their Posterity" (61–63).

Such titillating detail combined with physical revulsion was a new combination in 1727 and both reflected and contributed to changing popular attitudes toward sex. Defoe fulminated against contemporary licentiousness masquerading as marriage. Too many modern couples were willing "to gratify their vitious Part in the formality of a legal Appointment," he wrote, without "one Ounce of Affection, not a Grain of original, chast, and rivetted Love, the Glory of a Christian Matrimony, and the essential Happiness of Life" (105–106). He describes the delicious freedoms of marriage: how "she freely strips off her Cloths in the Room with him; and whereas she would not have shew'd him her Foot before, without her Shoe and Stockings on, she now, without the least Breach of Modesty, goes into what we call the naked Bed to him, and with him; lies in his Arms, and in his Bosom, and sleeps safely, *and with security in her Virtue* with him, all the Night" (58). Initially describing this openness as peaceful and innocent—a wife sleeping in her husband's arms was like a child on its mother's bosom—he soon warms to his message that, however sanctified, these freedoms are fraught with dangers and one must beware "wanton excesses" and "criminal indulgence"—excesses and indulgences he suggests with pornographic effect. Thus he enlists the aroused energy of his readers in the service of disapproval, mingling descriptions of physical desire with moral disapprobation and physical disgust until a whirlpool of feeling is set up around the marriage bed.

Human sexuality—especially female sexuality—was no longer to be unselfconsciously accepted as part of physical life, but needed to be scrutinized, judged, and regulated. Samuel Richardson's *Clarissa* (1747–1748) was probably one of the earliest texts to naturalize a certain female delicacy regarding these matters. When Clarissa writes about Solmes drawing his chair so close to hers that "squatting in it with his ugly weight . . . he pressed upon my hoop," one feels the threat of sexual violation. Solmes is vile: the word "squat" conjures up the toad shape of John Milton's Satan "close at the ear of Eve" in his first attempt to "reach/The organs of her fancy" (4: 800–802). Solmes' weight trespassing on Clarissa's hoop also suggests his bodily impatience to force himself on a more private circumference. His physical proximity makes Clarissa move involuntarily to another chair, her panic betraying her reason and giving her brother and sister too much advantage. "I could not help it—I knew not what I did," she tells Anna Howe, illustrating the power of even a sexually insinuating gesture to shake her composure and frighten away her self-possession.[12]

In another episode, Clarissa's brother—James Harlowe Jr.—deliberately insults the finely tuned heroine by insinuating that she has sexual feeling like the rest of animal creation—in this case, for Lovelace. He sneers a line at her from Virgil's *Georgics* which, in its original context, refers to the use of animal mating cycles for agricultural advantage: *amor omnibus idem* (All feel the same love).[13] If it were not for his cruelty and greed, one could argue that he was simply teasing Clarissa as Anna Howe has already teased her: about her "throbs" and "glows" for the virile villain. But styling such attraction not as sentiment and feeling but as brute animal instinct appalls her and makes her squeamish, and the reader shares her shock and enters into her way of thinking. Clarissa then reinscribes her squeamishness about being placed in nature's animal continuum when she writes to Anna about her brother's "vile hint." Coming as it does from her crude brother, accompanied by the threat of being carried off to Uncle Antony's moated castle and forced to endure visits from the repulsive Mr. Solmes, the notion that all "love" stems from the same primal instinct of species' survival—that gradations of feeling are ultimately traceable to this one great reproductive imperative—places the sex drive in a context that naturalizes Clarissa's squeamishness and makes it seem the only civilized response to a brutal and threatening situation.

Defoe's *Conjugal Lewdness* helped create the climate for Clarissa's response by arguing that without the right kind of consciousness, sexual intercourse was bestial. Twenty years before Richardson dramatized the matter in *Clarissa*, Defoe argued for the all-distinguishing importance of separating lust from love and argued that sex had to be accompanied by love or else it brutalized the sensibility. Although he castigated spouses who used the marriage bed for wanton pleasure, he reserved his worst opprobrium for those who married with only "slight and superficial Affection." Such persons "are to me little more than legal Prostitutes" (102), he wrote, insofar as they provide sexual services without engaging the affections. He considered parents who forced their children to marry without love as guilty of rape, and gives as an example a dialogue between a knight and his lady in which she testifies " 'twas no Marriage, 'twas all *Forced*, a *Rape* upon Innocence and Virtue. . . . I was dragged to Church, I did not go; I tell you, 'twas no Matrimony, tho' 'twas a Marriage; I was ravished and nothing else" (175). When a woman suffers sexual violence from a man who is not her husband, he wrote,

> she has her recourse to the Law, and she will be redress'd as far as redress can be obtained. Where the Fact is irretrievable, the Man should be punished, and the Woman is protected by the Law from any farther Force upon her for the future.
>
> But here the Woman is put to Bed to the Man by a kind of forced Authority of Friends; 'tis a Rape upon her Mind; her Soul, her brightest Faculties, her Will, her Affections are ravished, and she is left without redress, she is left in the Possession of the Ravisher, or of him, who, by their Order, she was delivered up to, and she is bound in the Chains of the same Violence for her whole life.
>
> HORRID abuse! (198)

Defoe's language both sensationalizes and heightens the horror of sex without love. What appears to have been felt as an irritant or annoyance (for sex was never a pleasure when unwanted) a bare forty years earlier at the end of the Restoration, here is constructed as a violation of a woman's deepest self. What was probably regarded as an unpleasant duty among other unpleasant duties is here written of as a primal affront to her fundamental being. Defoe regards sex as both more important to an individual's identity than it had ever been thought of before, and less a socially significant act that constituted marriage within a community. Thus, marrying when there was no affection and mutual regard—however obediently it might reproduce society—was not properly marriage in Defoe's treatise but matrimonial whoredom. And conversely, marrying to satisfy lust without the matrimonial urge to create a family and live a domestic life was not marriage but conjugal lewdness.

These were the earliest English literary antecedents of what now seems to us to be a natural response of sexual disgust to the idea of sleeping with, say, Mr. Collins. That Jane Austen could construct Charlotte Lucas as rational and unsentimental about marriage, cheerfully undeterred by the idea of sex with that insufferably obsequious man, shows that by 1797 or even by 1811 it was still possible to hold an older, less psychologized, conception of sexual relations. As we study ideological change, we have come to see that earlier cultural formations often linger in a later historical period, coexisting with those attitudes that have come to replace them. Thus, temporally successive ideological positions can be held simultaneously in the same society. Raymond Williams called these lingering elements the cultural "residual," constructed on the basis of "some previous social and cultural institution or formation" but "still active in the cultural process, not only and often not at all as an element of the past, but as an effective element of the present." He emphasized that this cultural residual often had "an alternative or even oppositional relation to the dominant culture," but that it survived alongside of it, often for a long time, before dwindling into the archaic.[14] I am arguing that Austen's treatment of the Lucas–Collins marriage is part of the cultural residual, coexisting with the emerging ideological formation of sentimental love-in-marriage.

Pride and Prejudice occupies an intermediate position in this history of perspectives on sex and marriage. Austen's novel contains both the older and the newer way of thinking about these matters in the diverging views of Charlotte and Elizabeth. If Charlotte Lucas, with her pragmatic sense that marriage to a small-minded and hypocritical man was preferable to an impoverished and dependent old age, expresses the common wisdom of the seventeenth and early eighteenth centuries, Elizabeth Bennet, with her independent manner and her handsome suitor, is an example of the newer sort of nineteenth-century heroine. That Austen herself understood both impulses for marrying—the older, unromantic, practical reasons as well as the newer demand for sexual attraction and sentimental love—can be seen by her double response to Harris Bigg-Wither, who proposed to her in 1802.

He was the brother of her friends Elizabeth, Catherine, and Althea Bigg, and he was heir to Manydown Park. At first she accepted the tall, stammering young man, but thought better of it overnight and recanted in the morning. Caroline (Mary Craven) Austen, daughter of Austen's brother James and his second wife Mary Lloyd, set down her own meditations on the facts of the case as she had heard them spoken of in the family.

> Mr. Wither was very plain in person—awkward, & even uncouth in manner—nothing but his size to recommend him—he was a fine big man—but one need not look about for [a] secret reason to account for a young lady's *not* loving him—a great many would have taken him *without* love—& I believe the wife he did get was very fond of him, & that they were a happy couple—He had sense in plenty & went through life very respectably, as a country gentleman—I *conjecture* that the advantages he could offer, & her gratitude for his love, & her long friendship with his family, induced my Aunt to decide that she would marry him *when* he should ask her—but that having accepted him she found she was miserable & that the place & fortune which would certainly be *his*, could not alter the *man*—She was staying in his Father's house—old Mr. Wither was then alive—To be sure she should not have said yes—over night—but I have always respected her for the courage in cancelling that yes—the next morning—All worldly advantages would have been to her—& she was of an age to know *this* quite well—My

> Aunts had very small fortunes & on their Father's death they &
> their Mother would be, they were aware, but poorly off—I be-
> lieve most young women so circumstanced would have taken Mr.
> W. & trusted to love after marriage.[15]

I have always thought, somewhat facetiously, that Jane Austen rejected
this man because she could not endure the name Bigg-Wither. But Harris
Bigg-Wither was, even more than Mr. Collins, a good match "in a prudential light": more sensible than Mr. Collins, the brother of her close friends,
and heir to a fine old estate, it was an unexceptionable connection. As Caroline Austen says, most young women would have accepted him "& trusted
to love after marriage." That Jane Austen, who must have liked him well
enough humanly, was miserable when she envisioned being married to him,
shows her elevated expectations of marriage. She was not attracted to Harris Bigg-Wither and could not, in the words of Wollstonecraft, violate "the
purity of her own feelings."

The same dialogue is there in Austen's fragment of a novel, *The Watsons*,
written a few years after the Bigg-Wither proposal, in a conversation between Emma Watson and her older sister. "I would rather be a Teacher at a
school (and I can think of nothing worse) than marry a Man I did not like,
declares Emma Watson. 'I would rather do any thing than be a Teacher at a
school'—said her sister. '*I* have been at school, Emma, & know what a Life
they lead; I should not like marrying a disagreable Man any more than yourself,—but I do that think there *are* many very disagreable Men;—I think I
could like any good humoured Man with a comfortable Income.'"[16] Emma
Watson wants to "like" the man she might marry, whereas her older sister
simply wants to avoid a disagreeable husband, which her tolerant imagination tells her is rare anyway. Emma Watson, her sister thinks, has more refined expectations than she because having been raised by a rich aunt, the
promise of a handsome dowry allowed her to be more choosey about the
matter. As for herself, it was not necessary that her "heart and imagination"
be captivated; good humor and a comfortable income would make her
happy enough.

Sexual disgust, of course, is the other side of attraction: both emphasize
the "person" of the other. If Austen does not imagine Charlotte Lucas's sexual disgust for Mr. Collins, neither does she imagine powerful physical attraction between her couples destined for marriage—not until *Persuasion* in
any case. Although some of her heroes are handsome, Austen was also perfectly capable of creating heroes whose attractive qualities are spiritual and
intellectual rather than physical: Edward Ferrars and Colonel Brandon, for
example, or even Edmund Bertram or Mr. Knightley, whose stature is mentioned only once, but whose rationality, education, and moral judgment are
paraded throughout. So although in *Pride and Prejudice* the scenes with
Darcy and Elizabeth have enough erotic energy to satisfy modern readers,

there is the irreducible fact in the same novel of the evident happiness of Charlotte Lucas, which neither the author nor her spritely heroine try to diminish. Alone in her chamber at Hunsford, Elizabeth meditates "upon Charlotte's degree of contentment" (157), "her address in guiding and composure in bearing with her husband" (157), and is forced to acknowledge that "it was all done very well" (157). This working out of the Charlotte Collins subplot reminds us that the expectation of love-in-marriage is of comparatively recent date because Charlotte Lucas was created when marriage was still a matter of practicality rather than romance, a means to perpetuate society rather than the occasion for isolating from society two people who hope to find in each other their entire happiness.

Notes

1. Jane Austen's *Pride and Prejudice* (ed. R.W. Chapman, 5 vols., 3rd edition (London: Oxford University Press, 1933) II: 125. Reference to this text throughout this chapter will be to this edition.

2. Deirdre Le Faye, ed., *Jane Austen's Letters* (Oxford: Oxford University Press, 1997), letter 153, p. 332.

3. J.M.S. Tompkins, *The Popular Novel in England* (London: Constable and Company, 1932), 164.

4. Susan Staves quotes the testimony of a woman who has been raped in her article about scenes of attempted rape in the fiction of Henry Fielding. The statement she reproduces from the trial testimony of 1768 is powerful in its flat, unemotional description of force ("Fielding and the Comedy of Attempted Rape," in *History, Gender and Eighteenth-Century Literature*, ed. Beth Fowkes Tobin [Athens: University of Georgia Press, 1994], 86–112).

5. William Shakespeare, *Hamlet*, ed. G.R. Hibbard (Oxford: Clarendon Press, 1987), act 3, scene 4, pp. 281–282.

6. I am grateful to Curtis Perry for these Renaissance examples of "sexual disgust" and for his clarifying discussions of this issue.

7. Norbert Elias, *The History of Manners* (1939; reprint, trans. Johan Goudsblom, New York: Urizen Books, 1978), 189 (page citations are from the reprint edtion).

8. Page numbers are taken from the excellent edition of *Millenium Hall* edited by Gary Kelly for Broadview Press. (Peterborough, Ontario: Broadview Press, 1995), 135.

9. Sarah Scott's Mrs. Morgan was modeled on Mrs. Delany, whose journal circulated privately in the later eighteenth century. That manuscript included anecdotes of her first marriage to Alexander Pendarves, a man nearly forty years her senior who was fat, dirty, and physically disgusting to her and made no attempt to be agreeable to his young wife.

10. Janet Todd and Marilyn Butler, ed. *The Works of Mary Wollstonecraft*, 7 vols. (London: William Pickering, 1989), 1: 140, 144.

11. Daniel Defoe, *Conjugal Lewdness or, Matrimonial Whoredom: A Treatise Concerning the Use and Abuse of the Marriage Bed*, ed. and intro. Maximillian Novak (1727; reprint, Gainesville, FL: Scholars' Facsimiles and Reprints, 1967) (page citations are from the reprint edition).

12. Samuel Richardson, *Clarissa*, ed. Angus Ross (London: Penguin Books, 1985), letter 16, p. 87.

13. Richardson, *Clarissa*, letters 50.1 and 50.2, pp. 218–219. The original quotation is from the *Georgics*, bk. 3, ln. 244.

14. Raymond Williams, *Marxism and Literature* (Oxford: Oxford University Press, 1977), 122.

15. Quoted in William Austen-Leigh and Richard Arthur Austen-Leigh, *Jane Austen: A Family Record,* rev. and enl. Deirdre Le Faye (Boston: G.K. Hall, 1989), 121–122.

16. Jane Austen, *The Watsons*, ed. R.W. Chapman, in *Minor Works*, vol. 6 (London: Oxford University Press, 1954), 318.

11

Books to Movies

Gender and Desire in Jane Austen's Adaptations

Martine Voiret

"Austenmania" is alive and well. Just as the mid-1990s offered the public a cornucopia of Jane Austen adaptations, the 1990s ended with a version of *Mansfield Park* made by the director Patricia Rozema. The latest avatar of this Austen revival comes in the form of the film *Bridget Jones's Diary*. Austen's most fantasized about male screen hero, Darcy, is back in the guise of his modern brethren Mark Darcy played by Colin Firth, of *Pride and Prejudice* fame. While it is too early to tell if this latest incarnation represents the end or the continuing chapter of the 1990s trend, so much I would like to show in this chapter can be demonstrated: Austen adaptations have been popular among filmmakers and moviegoers, in great part, because Austen's novels provide scenarios addressing contemporary postfeminist concerns. With their complex tales of romance, their diverse cast of male and female characters, they offer scripts that can be used to capture the anxieties, fantasies, and contradictions many men and women experience in the domain of gender and gender relations.

The making of movies based on Austen's novels is part of a larger trend. The 1990s produced an abundance of costume dramas. Many critics and academics have judged the popularity of such movies as the sign of a regressive turning towards the past, a postmodern nostalgic longing for simpler times. The analysis developed by the film critic Pamela Cook is more to the point. According to her, costume drama appeals to the public for a complex set of reasons. Because of its emphasis on masquerade, it allows the spectator to step out of the constraints of his time to try out different selves or identities. To use Cook's term, it facilitates "metaphorical cross-dressing between characters and spectators."[1] With its play on costume and disguise, the historical drama encourages multiple identifications. The genre invites the spectator to try out the different roles presented by the various characters. This process is never a simple movement of going back to outdated modes of being. Part of the attraction of costume drama, of course, is that it gives the spectator license to identify with roles or characteristics now devalued. More important, costume drama is invested with the needs and fantasies of the present. In Cook's words the past is "a place where contemporary dilemmas are worked through, identities are tested and not necessarily resolved in a traditional manner" (73).

In Austen movie adaptations from the mid-1990s, the identities being tested are not so much social or national identities, such as in the Gainsborough Studio movies studied by Cook, but gendered identities. The rich social fabric of the novel is often reduced to a mere background. The plot is streamlined so that the film presents to the viewer sets of characters exemplifying different ways of being male or female. In Emma Thompson's *Sense and Sensibility*, for example, Lucy Steele's sister disappears from the plot.[2] So do Lady Middleton and her children. A moviemaker cannot reproduce all the rich details and detours of a novel. The elision of those characters, however, facilitates the process of focusing on gender issues. So does the bigger importance given in the film to minor characters such as the younger sister Margaret and the mismatched Palmers. Such changes allow the film to focus on a limited and sharply drawn cast of men and women embodying different conceptions of gender and different ways of relating to one another.

It is far from incidental that the spectacle provided by the interaction of those men and women takes place at the beginning of the nineteenth century. Ironically, this movement backward represents for the mostly female audience of those movies a movement forward. With their male characters suggestively dressed in the more flamboyant fashion of the times, these adaptations, unlike the current staple of Hollywood productions, cater to female desires and to the female gaze. They first do so because, in opposition to the prevalent esthetic and visual norms of our times, they bring us back to an era when men could still be the locus of the beautiful. Those movies take place in the beginning decades of the nineteenth century just before the final chapter of what has been called "the Great Masculine Renunciation" or "the Great Divide."[3]

For many centuries, and in contrast to our present esthetic codes, men and women followed similar standards of beauty. Aristocrats, especially, presented to the eye a harmoniously rich and balanced tableau. The clothes of both sexes were made of the same luxurious, colorful, and ornate material. Men and women moved in a similar fashion. This glorious display was a mark of rank and privilege. Men and women's elegant and ornate appearance represented visually their elevated status. The playful shimmer of the rich texture of their garments was the image of their superior refinement, exquisite wit and delicate manners.

Those standards started to change very slowly in the course of the seventeenth century. By the 1780s, portraits show increasing differences in male and female modes of presentations. Men display greater simplicity, women more ornamentation. The previous symmetry is now broken. The size of the woman's apparel is now much bigger than her companion's. This process of differentiation is completed by the 1830s. The requirements of beauty and appearance now become the sole province of womanhood. The period in which Jane Austen novels take place represents an interesting moment in this evolution. Both men's and women's presentations are then pared down to obey the neoclassical ideal of simplicity. The male costume comes to be designed following the principles of the heroic male nude of classical antiquity (interestingly one of those sculptures can be seen in the entrance hall of the Elliots at the beginning of *Persuasion*[4]). The coat is now made of natural wool. It subtly follows the curves of the body and the bone structure. The waistcoat is shortened to form a high line across the waist. The legs are covered by skin-fitted pantaloons made of silk or doeskin. The pants are generally of a light color, thus making the legs look longer. Their matte texture suggests the smoothness of the skin. The framing of the genital area that had disappeared since the Renaissance is now part again of the male attire. This costume, in its time, was meant to present an image of man in his natural physical and moral state. The whole effect is rather striking. The previous fashion with its knee-length breeches gave most men a short-legged pear shape. Now, as Ann Hollander describes, a tailor could give a man: "a lean, well-muscled and very sexy body with long legs."[5] This costume, with its suggestive emphasis on the genital area, appears even more erotic to the modern viewer. As Susan Bordo states in her recent study: "[T]he more a piece of clothing outlines and reveals what is underneath, the sexier it is in our cultural eyes."[6] More important, it allows the female viewer the pleasures of agency and looking usually reserved to the male viewer.

Curiously, as Bordo emphasizes, the sexual revolution of the 1960s brought a plethora of movies exhibiting the female body. The male body as sexual object, however, almost disappeared from the screen. Hollywood became less and less interested in catering to female subjectivities. While the screen was still filled with handsome actors, they were rarely presented to the female viewer as sight. In Jane Austen movie adaptations, the hero by contrast is there to be looked at. He presents an arresting spectacle not only because of his attire but also because the camera capitalizes on the sight he offers. The adaptations favor still frames of the standing protagonist. In the second ball of *Pride and Prejudice,* for example, the camera keeps returning to images of the standing Darcy, each time taken at a different angle, a technique usually used by fashion photographers for their female models.[7] As has been noticed by critics, this framing of the male body is particularly prevalent in *Pride and Prejudice*. *Persuasion, Sense and Sensibility*, and *Emma* similarly focus on the spectacle of their male stars in their physicality and beauty. [8]

Dressed in their skin-fitted attire, the male heroes are often presented in suggestive poses. Two scenes from *Emma* come to mind. Emma and Knightley are having tea. She is sitting rather straight; he is leaning back in his chair as if offering himself to the spectator. Similarly in another scene, the camera playfully lingers on a relaxed and reclining Knightley while Mrs. Weston and Emma look on sitting very straight. Darcy, likewise, is often shown in lounging poses. So is, of course, Colonel Brandon. While in the book *Sense and Sensibility* he is first introduced as part of a small party, in the movie, we first catch a glimpse of him languidly leaning against a door frame mesmerized by Marianne singing. Those representations of the male heroes are appealing not only because they recognize the sexual subjectivity of their female viewers but also because they present an image of masculinity that transcends the restricting conceptions of manhood presently available.

Once again, Bordo's analysis is quite useful here. According to her, our culture presently limits men to two options: a hard or soft type of masculinity. As the present craze for bodybuilding shows, men are supposed to present a hard surface to the world. A real man, like those overbuilt action heroes still filling our screens, stands aggressively, sure of himself, ready to take on the world. Conversely, there is nothing worse than to be considered soft. As a result, men are often represented "facing off" the onlooker in aggressive poses.

Only recently, in part with the influence of gay esthetics, have those representations started to change. Advertisements now show men in what is traditionally considered feminine postures: leaning back, in languid poses. Those representations, however, are reserved for young men. More mature men, by contrast, are supposed to be in control. They cannot exhibit attitudes considered feminine, passive. Austen movie adaptations present many moments embodying a third option: a manhood capable of experiencing what is usually considered the more "receptive" pleasures and attitudes.

Once again, one of the elements of the neoclassic costume comes in handy to emblematize this third option: the pristine linen white shirt. In its original use, the shirt and its long white cravat tied carefully around the neck and the jaw were used to "produce a commanding set of the head on the heroic shoulders." [9] To our modern sensibilities, however, the connotations are quite different. It represents a playful reversal of the modesty and prudishness usually associated with women. It begs to be untied; and it is. In that regard, one of the most famous scenes characteristic of Austenmania is Darcy's famous swim in the pond. It triggered in England a frenzy of Darcy parties. Female viewers would repeatedly play the scene of Darcy diving and emerging in his wet clothes, his opened white shirt sexily sticking to his dripping body. Similarly, one of the turning points in the representation of Colonel Brandon comes during Marianne's illness. He leans against the door frame, disheveled, his white shirt opened after a sleepless night consumed by anguish and passionate worry for the young woman. This scene, like the preceding involving Darcy, does not exist in the novels.

In a similar fashion, *Sense and Sensibility* capitalizes on Hugh Grant's coyness and shyness. Whereas, as has often been noticed by critics, Edward Ferrars, in the novel, is far from being an attractive fellow, the choice of Hugh Grant endows the character with a mixture of handsome vulnerability and virginal attractiveness. In the movie, interestingly, he often seems like the embodiment of a gentler masculinity. His body is often slightly bent forward. As important, in at least three scenes, he is presented sitting awkwardly on the edge of a lower chair like a shy maiden. In all of the aforementioned scenes, the old cultural assumptions concerning sexuality and gender relations are undermined. Women are recognized as agents, the desirable men are shown to be the ones capable of experiencing the "feminine" pleasures of giving and receiving.

Just as Jane Austen's novels provide powerful images translating our desire to go beyond our present stereotyped dichotomies, they also offer a complex sample of male and female characters presenting more or less traditional masculine and feminine traits. The staging of those diverse characters and relationships allow filmmakers to explore unabashedly our conflicting and at times regressive understanding of gender and gender relations.

With their emphasis on romance and courtship the films address the renewed but somewhat ambivalent "postfeminist" interest for marriage. In the 1970s, many women had espoused the feminist rejection of marriage. Many believed that marriage by its very nature was a repressive institution. For a few years Hollywood gave expression to its female audience's desire to find its own voice. Many scenarios told the story of a married woman leaving home and finding herself. The 1980s, as Susan Faludi has aptly described, witnessed a backlash against women.[10] On our TV screens strong single women, with the notable exception of Murphy Brown, disappeared and gave way to thirty-something happy nesters. Most women's lives, however, did not correspond to any of those stereotyped alternatives. They were often torn by difficult compromises between a desire for independence and success, and a desire for companionship or marriage. As Susan Douglas stresses, the 1990s exhibit the "same split personalities about the roles and place of women."[11] Similarly, many women are torn by competing desires: they want "to have love and support, power and autonomy" (273).

Because they focus on the inevitability of marriage in a woman's life and subtly explore the relationship between marriage and happiness, Austen's novels allow filmmakers to explore what has again become a central concern and anxiety of our times and certainly of many women's lives: finding the appropriate mate. Of course, most of the adaptations play on the concomitant fear of never finding such "fulfillment." The image of the nineteenth-century "spinster" is here most useful. *Emma*'s Miss Bates is in that regard exemplary. In the film, the character is more a caricature than she was in the novel. Unappealing, short sighted, incessantly talking, Miss Bates emblematizes the unattractiveness of the single status. While her presentation is rather extreme, in all the movies, the older single women present a rather unappealing picture. In *Persuasion*, for example, the older daughter Elizabeth is first presented lazily leaning back, speaking with chocolate in her mouth. She is shrill and self-indulgent. Such behavior is historically inaccurate. Women were trained to follow rules of decorum but as Rebecca Dickson emphasizes: "[T]he Elizabeth of the novel who could run a house admirably but still be self-absorbed and vain is too subtle for today's filmgoer to vilify."[12] Elizabeth has been cut down to fit our stereotype of unattached women.

The play on old fears and cliches is hardly more subtle in *Sense and Sensibility*. Emma Thompson has added a dramatic scene that does not exist in the book. On what she believes is Marianne's deathbed, Elinor cries: "[P]lease do not leave me alone." Likewise, toward the end of the movie, Elinor is shown doing laundry and wearing the well-known emblem of unappealing spinsterhood: the dreaded apron and its connotations of lifetime drudgery. In *Pride and Prejudice*, it is Mary the younger daughter who represents the unappealing spinsterlike woman. Underlying that she was the only "plain" one among the daughters, the book drew a short but sharp portrayal of the plight of women in the nineteenth century who neither had the means nor the looks to assure their status through the only available means: marriage. In the movie, her bookishness and boorishness are greatly increased to suggest the still-common stereotype that intellectual women are unappealing and will never find happiness.

Through the play on the spinster figure, the movies provide to the viewer a negative pole of identification as well as an outlet for contemporary fears that a woman's life cannot be lived happily on her own. As Patricia Mellencamp asks eloquently, however: "Why do women . . . imagine independence being lonely instead of gratifying, thrilling? Why does female independence coincide with sacrifice? Why is it a loss, not a gain? Why don't women view freedom as positive."[13] She stresses that in the past the answer was often economics, but it is not the case in the mid-1990s. As the recent and unexpected success of *Bridget Jones's Diary* and *Ally McBeal* suggest, the traditional view that a woman is not complete without a man has not lost its potency.

Such ambivalence toward female independence, however, does not signal a return to the age-old narrative that only soft-spoken, selfless, beautiful girls are rewarded by love.[14] Part of the attraction of Austen's novels is that they provide plots fulfilling the contemporary female desire that it is not the traditionally gentle and self-effacing woman who finds fulfilling love but the outspoken, self-assured woman. The recent remake of *Mansfield Park* is in that regard quite telling.[15] *Mansfield Park* was the only story written by Jane Austen that had not been remade into a film. Its central heroine Fanny was endowed with few characteristics a modern female audience could identify with. Gentle, self-effacing, always concerned with other people's feelings, Fanny possessed all the traditional womanly qualities. Considered "insipid" even by Austen's own mother, Fanny's frailty and passivity irked many readers.[16] It is not surprising then that Patricia Rozema would submit Fanny's character to a drastic makeover. In the novel, for example, a few pages are devoted to her poor health and her squeamishly picking up horse riding to get a daily regimen of exercise. In the film, she is vibrant and active. Like her lively consort from *Pride and Prejudice*—Elizabeth Bennett—she saunters around playfully. We now see her energetically riding about the countryside with her cousin Edmund. As important, Rozema has incorporated into the character some of the elements of Austen's life. Fanny is now a writer. As a *New York Times* reviewer points out, if her story still follows the Cinderella script, she has become in Rozema's hands a "feminist Cinderella."[17] Gone also from the film, are all the judgments that because of "the sweetness of her temper, the purity of her mind and the excellence of her principles,"[18] Fanny would have been the perfect complement and ideal wife for Henri Crawford. This nineteenth-century ideal of complementarity has lost a lot of its appeal for a modern audience. Many men and women, in particular, now reject the idea, exemplified by Fanny, that women are the guardians of morality and virtue, that a woman's softening and elevating influence is the necessary complement to a man's more aggressive and passionate constitution.

Accordingly, when Austen movie adaptations offer gentle and soft-spoken heroines, their gentleness and lack of expressivity are often at the very root of their unhappiness. Jane Bennet and Anne Elliot are very good examples. It is because the beautiful Jane Bennet behaves according to all the decorum and appropriateness expected from a young lady that her suitor can be convinced by his friend Darcy that Jane has no feeling for him. Her character is not simple, though. Her loving nature and evenness of temper are not without their attraction. As her sister Elizabeth experiences, she has all the qualities one might expect of a perfect friend: warmth, constancy, generosity, attentiveness to others. Her story demonstrates, however, that those perfect "feminine" qualities, if untempered by more assertive qualities, easily degenerate into mere passivity.

In the same way, it is because of her gentleness and deference to other people's beliefs that the soft-spoken Anne Elliot remains unhappy for many years. Listening to Lady Russell's prudent motherly advice, she follows the timid course of action expected from young ladies. She rejects Frederick Wentworth's marriage proposal because he does not have the means to support a wife comfortably. While many critics find Amanda Root unappealing as Anne Elliot, the actress portrays effectively the evolution of the character from a suppressed, self-sacrificing young woman to a gently but firmly assertive individual. At the beginning of her story, both in the novel and the movie, Anne Elliot consistently lets others determine her fate. As requested, she stays behind to prepare her father's estate for its new inhabitants. She takes care of her hypochondriac sister Mary and her household. Everybody at Uppercross confides in her and uses her as a bridge of communication to other people. When there is dancing, she is requested to play the piano and forgo the fun enjoyed by the rest of the company. When Mary's boy gets injured, she is the one who takes on the function of the soothing and caring mother, while Mary and her husband leave for an evening of entertainment. Through all of those scenes, Anne exhibits the "perfect feminine" qualities of caring, nurturing. Amanda Root's rendition of the character, however, demonstrates that those traditional feminine characteristics do not lead to happiness but, on the contrary, to a shriveling of the body and the soul. In many scenes, a pale Anne looks at the world with big, frightened eyes. Walks tire her very easily. Her constant giving to others, in other words, has not brought satisfaction but a depletion of physical and mental energy. Frederick Wentworth, after an absence of eight years, is shocked by how much the young and intelligent woman he knew has changed.

It has often been noticed that with the exception of Gwyneth Paltrow the young ladies chosen for Austen's movie adaptation lead roles are not "especially" beautiful. This is particularly true for Amanda Root. While some critics have complained about the actress' unattractiveness, it is this very lack of conventional beauty that allows the filmmaker to offer to his audience a more pleasing definition of what constitutes feminine "attractiveness." While women are still to a large extent constrained by traditional expectations of femininity and beauty, Anne Elliot's story demonstrates that a woman's beauty is determined in great part by her character. Wentworth's attitude toward Anne changes substantially when during Louisa's accident she demonstrates not only that she is a caring individual but that she is capable of the more "manly" qualities of initiative and leadership. During the rest of the movie, Anne becomes more and more assured and expressive. She asserts her needs against her father and sister. She takes initiatives to let Wentworth know she cares about him. At the concert, for example, rejecting the requirement of feminine decorum, she throws herself in his way and pursues interaction actively. This mental metamorphosis is accompanied by physical change. Her body is now more alive and energetic. Her face projects a glow of intelligence and happiness. She has become quite beautiful, but it is a beauty that comes from within. Her complexion and features have become more animated. She projects an aura of tranquil assurance, goodness of heart, and sense of purpose. She has, in other words, moved beyond the traditional definitions of femininity. By the end of the movie, she combines the "feminine" qualities of empathy, and nurture as well as those qualities traditionally associated with the "masculine": assertiveness, enthusiasm, aggressive seizing of opportunities.

In a recent article of the *New York Times*, a critic rejoiced that the recent crop of movies finally offered strong, intelligent heroines. According to the author, the common Hollywood equation vulnerability, sex appeal was finally broken. *The Thomas Crown Affair* was given as a fine example of such an evolution.[19] If such a movie can be considered a sign of progress, one understands better the appeal of heroines based on Jane Austen's novels. In Rene Russo's exhibitionist performance, every sign of intelligence or initiative has to be compensated by sexy behavior. Movies based on Austen's novels, by comparison, address in a complex way women's desires to go beyond those stereotypes.

Many critics have commented that in Austen's 1990s movie adaptations, the women who occupy center stage, even more than in the books, are "intelligent, female leads, grappling with conventions."[20] Those modifications reflect the contemporary audience's own struggles because, while it is often assumed that the promises of the 1970s have been fulfilled and that we have entered an era of postfeminism, many women can identify with the dilemmas of their nineteenth-century counterparts. Like the movie heroines, they are strong-willed, intelligent, eager to make the right choice; they still feel, however, greatly constrained by role expectations. As Vicky Pockok emphasizes, women are still, for example, assumed to be more naturally nurturing, caring, and loving.[21] When married, they are expected to fufill competently the duty of a full-time job, while at the same time fulfilling at home the traditional duties of wife and mother.

Whereas much ink has been devoted to herald the advent of "the New Man," gender arrangements and, in particular, conceptions of masculinity have hardly shifted. "New Men" are indeed a rare breed. Even more, the 1980s and the 1990s were times of backlash and confusion regarding male roles. Many men and women were more than ever torn between conflicting expectations. As Anthony E. Rotundo stresses, the cultural types that "have been accumulating sanction for a century"—"the tough man and the tender, the real man and the sissy"—still occupy a large place in our cultural landscape.[22] At the same time, as Richard A. Shwedder states, our screens exhibit few positive images of manhood. Films rarely stage sympathetic representations of men in the context of their family, work, or love life. Men seem "devoid of civility, honor, fidelity, courage and a sense of duty and justice."[23] With their focus on courtship and what qualities are required from a man to make an acceptable companion, Jane Austen movie adaptations address that gap. Ironically they do so, because Austen's male characters embody masculine traits very similar to our own conflicting contemporary ideals of manhood.

As recent studies have shown, we witnessed in the 1990s a "remasculinization of America"; the renewed popularity of the "alpha male" is, in that regard, exemplary. Surprisingly, softness in men is still viewed as a problem. Men are, to a large extent, taught to behave according to nineteenth-century codes of manhood. They must be stoic, independent, self-possessed. "A real man" must embody what is often referred to as the ideal of "the sturdy oak." At the same time, however, as William Pollack points out: "It is no longer acceptable for boys to have to follow the old boy code rules, stuff away feelings and behaviors once labeled feminine."[24] In the wake of the feminist revolution, we now want men to be egalitarian, sensitive, nurturing, and expressive. We, in other words, expect men to possess two sets of somewhat irreconcilable qualities. In Pollack's words we want them to be "tough and gentle, vulnerable, courageous, dependent and independent" (396). Jane Austen's movie adaptations reflect this ambivalence. They translate contemporary desires for a type of masculinity that happily embodies those conflicting features.

Austen's male characters, most critics agree, have been modified to embody the characteristics of the new man. In *Sense and Sensibility*, the bland and rather boring Edward Ferrars is endowed with the sweetness of Hugh Grant. Scenes with the younger sister Margaret have been added in order to show that he is a sensitive, caring individual. Colonel Brandon similarly is shown to be an attentive individual in his dealings with Margaret and in his constant care and concern for his adoptive daughter Eliza. The films, when possible, make the most of this modern sign of sensitivity: liking and enjoying children. Colonel Croft, this paragon of the egalitarian and devoted husband, likes to toss children on his lap. Knightley in *Emma* is shown enjoying and being sensitive to his brother's baby.

More generally, the films invent or focus on moments showing that the principal male characters are sensitive and responsive to other people's needs. At the beginning of *Sense and Sensibility*, for example, Emma Thompson invented little incidents showing that Edward is considerate and attuned to other people's feelings. He, for instance, subtly refuses to take Margaret's bedroom. One can only assume that he does not want to hurt the little girl's feelings and more generally make the Dashwood ladies unwanted in their own homes now that the young Mr. John Dashwood is the rightful owner of the estate. Similarly, the movie stresses Colonel Brandon's discreteness and sensitivity to Marianne's and her family's needs.

The plot of Miramax's *Emma* has been streamlined in a similar way. Many moments of the film highlight Knightley's attentiveness to his friends' and neighbors' predicaments. He makes every effort to ease Jane Fairfax's difficult social situation. He is always considerate toward Miss Bates. Of course, one of the best examples of his sensitivity occurs when witnessing Mr. Elton's refusal to dance with Harriet Smith: He asks the young lady to dance with him, thus saving her from a public affront.

In many of the movies, the male characters have also been modified to emphasize the desirability of an egalitarian relationship. Disparity of age and attitude between the principal male protagonist and his eventual female partner have been greatly reduced. Miramax's Knightley, played by the well-known British actor Jeremy Northam, is a far more sexy and lively companion than the sterner and more fatherly character of the novel. Physically and mentally, there does not seem to be a seventeen-year difference between the two friends. This equality is visually stressed by the staging of scenes, like the archery scene, the tea scene, or the dance, when Emma and Knightley are framed by the camera occupying parallel spaces.

Colonel Brandon's character, every reader of the novel knows, has been submitted to a similar drastic makeover. Brandon is played by Alan Rickman, noted for often portraying dangerous characters. He is more mysterious and does not, as in the novel, wear an insipid rheumatism belt. When the disparity in maturity is highlighted, such as between Louisa and Frederick in *Persuasion*, it is to stress the ill-fated consequences of such a relation. In the movie, Frederick recognizes more unambiguously Louisa's carelessness and his responsibility in encouraging her provocative ways. Her accident would not have happened if Frederick, now a well-situated man, had not been flattered by the attention offered to him by the younger and exuberant young lady.

If *Pride and Prejudice* can be described as the most popular of the Austen productions, it is because it most clearly expresses this longing for a caring, attentive, respectful, and equal partner. It also expresses the hope that such a change is possible. Following the formula of what Janice Radway calls the "good romance," the film provides the viewer with a fantasy of successful male transformation.[25] Aloof, independent, imbued with a sense of superiority, Darcy represents at the beginning of the story the epitome of the self-sufficient, uncommunicative male. His love for Elizabeth, however, leads him to become more emotionally expressive. When they meet at Pemberley, Darcy is a changed man. He reveals he can be loving, tender, and attentive to Elizabeth's needs. In the second part of the movie, Elizabeth remains, to a great extent, ignorant of Darcy's feelings; the viewer, however, is not. By focusing on Darcy's discrete efforts to resolve the crisis triggered by Elizabeth's younger sister's elopement, the movie provides the viewer with the realization of a wish rarely granted in real life: the metamorphosis of a self-centered male into a loving, caring companion.

Persuasion fulfills a similar desire. In the film, Frederick appears at first as a much more "masculine" character than in the book. Gone, for example, is the scene in which alone with Anne for the first time, he loses his composure; and the scene in which he sensitively rescues Anne from the rough play of her young nephew. The tall Ciaran Hinds gives to Frederick a manly, self-assured presence. The effect is reinforced by the fact that the film focuses on the hero's typically masculine activities such as hunting. Indeed, many shots show him wearing boots and a beige overcoat reminiscent by its shape and color of the cowboy overcoat of spaghetti western fame. Conversations highlight his adventuresome life at sea and the prejudices concerning women such a life might have fostered. This more sharply drawn masculine persona makes Frederick's transformation more pleasing. His realization that his self-centeredness is one of the causes of Louisa's accident, his growing appreciation of Anne's subtle qualities such as empathy, and his final avowal of his feelings fulfill the hopeful wish that men can change, that our standards of masculinity can be transformed.

The movies usually provide scenarios that repress the difficulties involved in such a change as well as the contradictions involved in the double bind to which men are usually submitted. A scene from the Miramax production, between Emma and Knightley, is in that regard quite telling. At the end of the picnic during which Emma has openly flirted with Frank Churchill and made a disparaging comment to Miss Bates, an angry Knightley scolds her vividly and grabs her arm in a surprising moment of repressed violence. The gesture is rather startling since Knightley, up to this point, has always conducted himself as a perfect gentleman. With Emma, he has often been a rather playful companion. Knightley's outburst, of course, is not so much, as he would like to believe, triggered by moral outrage as by pent-up jealousy and unrecognized feelings toward Emma. This little incident opens a quickly shut window on masculine potentiality for violence and aggression. The film, subsequently, progresses toward a moment of recognition in which Knightley fairly easily comes to terms with his real feelings and communicates them to Emma.

What is alluded to here, quickly repressed and happily resolved, are some of the emotional consequences linked to our expectations concerning masculinity. The ideal of autonomy, stoicism, strength, and assertiveness to which men are still, to a great extent, expected to conform leads to a repression of feelings, a denial of emotional needs, a lack of emotional expressiveness and literacy that foster frustration, and often only find an outlet through the expression of anger or violence. While in real life this emotional learning cannot easily be undone, the Jane Austen movie adaptations, in the image of our own ambivalent desires concerning masculinity, suggest that it can: a man can possess the traditional "manly" qualities as well as develop the more "caring" attributes usually associated with the feminine.

In agreement with our conflicted expectations concerning manhood, the movie adaptations draw sharper distinctions between the different male characters than were found in the novels. The films establish more clearly marked differences between, in broad terms, on one side the dependable, successful, strong male and on the other side the lively, pleasant, sociable but ultimately unreliable male, the Darcy versus the Wickham, the Frederick Wentworth versus the Mr. Elliot, the Knightley versus the Frank Churchill, the Colonel Brandon versus the Willoughby, and, to a lesser extent, the Edmund Bertram versus the Henry Crawford. As often noted by critics, Willoughby and Brandon are probably the best example of such a polarization. By the end of the novel, Willoughby appears as a more complex character. He comes back and expresses his regrets to Elinor. Kristin Flieger

Samuelian has well described how in the film Brandon has been granted some of the attributes that in the novel solely belonged to Willoughby.[26] He thus becomes, in the eyes of a modern audience, a more exciting and thus a more acceptable companion. The Mr. Elliot of *Persuasion*, similarly, is a more conniving and rakish individual. The narrative always develops along the same line: the strong, and in the films, handsome, well-situated man reveals himself to be the caring, reliable companion who can make the heroine happy; whereas the lively, expressive one reveals himself to be an unreliable, self-centered and ultimately undesirable partner.

Such a narrative remains hugely attractive because it gives voice to what Alison Light nicely terms "the tory in us."[27] This type of narrative expresses values and identities that in our postfeminist world are now devalued and thus are not usually expressed but that nevertheless still exert a strong pull on our imagination and desires, the more so maybe because they are now considered transgressive or regressive. While, on the ideological level, most viewers would probably endorse the ideal of "the new man," expectations and fantasies regarding men have remained unavowedly traditional or ambivalent. A man is still, to a large extent, judged according to the traditional criteria of success, independence, autonomy. The viewer's situation here is very similar to the one exemplified by Elizabeth Bennett in *Pride and Prejudice*. A major turning point in her perception of Darcy occurs after she sees the young man's sumptuous estate of Pemberley. When later on, Elizabeth's sister Jane asks her when her change of mind took place, she jokingly tells her that it happened when she saw the beautiful Pemberley. This criterion of judgment is made light of and quickly repressed in favor of other factors such as his reliability, newly revealed gentleness, and consideration toward others. Darcy, and for that matter the other male leads of the adaptations, have captured so thoroughly the imagination of modern audiences because they happily embody our own conflicted desires and standards concerning men, they fulfill our double expectations of male success and nurture, of "tradition" and "new masculinity."

The films, however, cater to the viewers' fantasies and ambivalence by glossing over the difficulties and contradictions involved in such a conception of masculinity. The persona of the rake is here most useful. The roguish characters have usually been darkened to disqualify the qualities they possess or minimize the problems their characters point to. The likes of Willoughby, Wikham, Mr. Elliot appear at first rather attractive because unlike the main hero, they are lively, outgoing, enjoy conversation and company, and live for the moment. Their expressiveness, their exuberance, is what makes them so pleasant to be around. Moreover, it is often because of the influence of their passionate nature, that the heroine's life powers become fully awakened. Patricia Rozema's Henry Crawford is a good example. The Henry Crawford of the film displays a playful and erotic presence that did not exist in the book. The ball scene is, in that regard, exemplary. It has been drastically modified. The camera follows Henry Crawford's gaze. His eyes rest on Fanny's neck with the passionate gentleness of a caress. The young woman, moved, dances away in a swirl of vividness and sexual awareness. Similarly, in the film *Persuasion*, Mr. Elliot's affirming look at Anne's on the stairs of Lyme marks a turning point in her self-image and in asserting her desires. One of the most attractive of all rogues, Willoughby, not only triggers Marianne's powers of happiness but also seduces all the Dashwood ladies to enjoy the pleasures of life. Those very qualities, however, are what bring the downfall of the roguish characters. Compelled to live for the present, unable to restrain their desires, they prove themselves unable to demonstrate the qualities of which "a man" (and a good husband) is supposed to be made: strength, steadiness, reliability, a will to achieve or maintain a good position in the world. What the movies, however, gloss over is that those two sets of qualities are somewhat at odds. The requirements that men demonstrate strength, independence, stoicism in the face of adversity often lead to a hardening of character, a muting of those very qualities we would like them also to possess: expressiveness, sensitivity, sociability, desire for connection. Commenting on this double and often unconscious standard, William Pollack offers to his readers a cautious but hopeful note: "It is not," he writes, "impossible to be both manly and empathic, cool and open, strong and vulnerable, but it is certainly a difficult and complex task."[28] Movies based on Jane Austen novels remain attractive because while addressing our repressed desires, contradictions, and anxieties concerning masculinity and gender, they also suggest happy resolutions to those difficulties in the form of what Elisabeth Badinter playfully calls the ideal of the "gentle man" and the "true ideal of androgyny."[29]

In agreement with those ideals, men and women should be able to give voice to the feminine and masculine aspects of their being: "True androgyny" should not be construed as a neutral ground beyond the masculine and the feminine but as the possibility for both men and women to develop and express at different times and according to their different personalities those qualities that have traditionally been labeled "masculine" and "feminine." Accordingly, the adaptations present couples who, at their most successful moments, embody such a vision. The main male protagonist demonstrates that he is in love with the heroine because she is intelligent, spirited, strong-willed. Colonel Brandon, for example, loves Marianne because she refuses to submit to the passivity expected from her sex. She follows her desires and does not shun from taking actions to reach her goals. In the film, as in the novel, Brandon insists that Marianne never change, remaining the unconventional young woman he loves. The final pages of the novel are somewhat ironic. They leave us with the vision of a subdued married Marianne. The film, by contrast, ends on a vision of happiness and mutuality, on a suggestion that in Brandon Marianne has found a companion who will not request her to suppress whole aspects of her being.

Similarly the film version of *Pride and Prejudice* stresses that Darcy loves those qualities that make Elizabeth Bennet unlike the other young ladies around her: he loves her will, her determination, her liveliness. In the film, one of the Pemberley visits has been modified to show Darcy enjoying Elizabeth's taking the lead role in protecting his sister against the verbal attacks of the Bingley sisters. The camera focuses on the unusual image of Darcy sitting suddenly blissfully relaxed and happy at the sight of Elizabeth intervening on behalf of his family. The two would-be lovers look at each other with a gaze of happy recognition. This suspended instant points to the satisfaction awarded by a relation in which each partner alternately takes on the leading role according to the requirements of the situation.

The narratives, then, provide to the viewer the pleasure of a story in which a man helps his female companion to express those qualities that for too long have been associated with the masculine—mastery, assertiveness, will, enthusiasm—and which, to an often unacknowledged degree, many of our contemporaries still find distasteful in a woman. Conversely, the scripts also provide the pleasurable narrative of a male who, under the influence of love, learns to give voice to his feminine qualities. Indeed, most of the films only proceed to a happy conclusion after the male protagonist goes through a revelatory moment in which he must display those feelings often associated with the feminine: self-sacrifice, empathy. For example, in the film *Persuasion*, unlike the final version of the novel, Frederick Wentworth has to overlook his personal feelings and inquire of Anne if she is getting married and thus needs to get back the ancestral home that has been rented to his sister. His self-restraint, his solicitude suggest that he has accepted this painful meeting in a spirit of true concern for the woman he loves. Likewise in *Emma*, Knightley has to go through a process of identification with Emma. Despite his feelings of jealousy, he comes back to console the young woman who, he believes, has been greatly affected by Frank Churchill's betrothal to Jane Fairfax. His sole concern is to alleviate the pain Emma might be experiencing. In the film *Mansfield Park*, this requirement of male self-denial and empathy is dramatically translated by the image of the handsome Henry visiting Fanny in her squalid surroundings and eating the indescribable food her mother has prepared. The relationship with Henry Crawford fails, however, because he is incapable of sustaining this mode of relating. Here is a man who, according to Fanny's assessment, wants to be loved but cannot truly love. By marrying Edmund, by contrast, Fanny seems to find a mate capable of true love and empathy. The film concludes on the hopeful image of an Edmund solely preoccupied with Fanny's success as a writer. The conclusion of *Mansfield Park*, however, remains somewhat unsatisfactory. Edmund appears too much like a passive participant, a brotherly reflection of Fanny. He lacks the energy (sexual and otherwise), the life enthusiasm that in his best moments Henry Crawford exemplifies so well. The movie, in other words, fails to embody the "true ideal of androgyny" that gives to the other films their utopian and hopeful dimension.

If Jane Austen's novels have remained a constant source of inspiration for filmmakers and spectators, it is because they provide scripts reflecting the confusion and conflicting aspirations of our "backlash" mentality. In their images and aspects of their narratives they point to a time when men and women will be recognized as having similar needs: "to love and be loved," "be active and passive."[30] They also reflect, to use Susan Douglas's words, that present feminism occupies a middle ground "filled with ambivalence, compromise, tradition and rebellion."[31] As important perhaps, by returning us to the past, they make us look forward to a better future.

Notes

1. Pamela Cook, *Fashioning the Nation* (London: British Film Institute, 1996), 6.

2. *Sense and Sensibility*, Columbia Pictures, 1995.

3. Ann Hollander, *Sex and Suits* (New York: Alfred A. Knopf, 1994), 63.

4. *Persuasion*, BBC, 1995.

5. Hollander, *Sex and Suits*, 88.

6. Susan Bordo, *The Male Body* (New York: Farrar, Strauss, and Giroux, 1999), 30.

7. *Pride and Prejudice*, A&E, 1995.

8. *Emma*, Miramax, 1996.

9. Hollander, *Sex and Suits*, 91

10. Susan Faludi, *Backlash* (New York: Crown, 1991).

11. Susan Douglas, *Where the Girls Are* (New York: Random House, 1994), 269.

12. Rebecca Dickson, "Misrepresenting Jane Austen's Ladies," in *Jane Austen in Hollywood*, ed. Linda Troost and Sayre Greenfield (Lexington: University of Kentucky Press, 1998), 44–57.

13. Patricia Mellencamp, *A Fine Romance* (Philadelphia: Temple University Press, 1995), 49.

14. Douglas, *Where the Girls Are*, 297.

15. *Mansfield Park*, Miramax, 1999.

16. Cited by Barbara Kantrowitz, "Making an Austen Heroine More Like Austen," *The New York Times*, 31 October 1999, p. 17.

17. Ibid. Section 2, 17.

18. Jane Austen, *Mansfield Park*, vol. III of *The Novels of Jane Austen*, ed. R.W. Chapman (Oxford: Oxford University Press, 1988), 468.

19. Marcelle Clement, "Forget Ravages of Age: Over 40 and Sexy Is Fine," *The New York Times*, 12 December 1999, section 2, p. 15.

20. Devoney Looser, "Feminist Implications," in *Jane Austen in Hollywood*, ed. Linda Troost and Sayre Greenfield (Lexington: University of Kentucky Press, 1998) 153–176.

21. Vicky Pockok, *The Illusions of Post-feminism* (London: Taylor and Francis, 1995).

22. Anthony E. Rotundo, *American Manhood* (New York: Basic Books, 1993), 291.

23. Richard A. Shwedder, "A Few Good Men? Don't Look in the Movies," *The New York Times*, 25 January 1999, section 2, p. 1.

24. William Pollack, *Real Boys* (New York: Random House, 1998), 397.

25. Janice Radway, *Reading the Romance* (Chapel Hill: University of North Carolina Press, 1984).

26. Kristin Flieger Samuelian, "Piracy Is Our Only Option," in *Jane Austen in Hollywood*, 148–158.

27. Cited in Cook, *Fashioning the Nation*, 33.

28. Pollack, *Real Boys*, 46.

29. Elisabeth Badinter, *XY de l'identité masculine* (Paris: Odile Jacob, 1992), 231, 249.

30. Ibid., 208.

31. Douglas, *Where the Girls Are*, 244.

12

Gender and the Heritage Genre

Popular Feminism Turns to History

Madeleine Dobie

Over the past decade or so the costume drama or "heritage" film has routinely been subjected to a specific form of political analysis. The argument goes that as the conservative British government, led by Margaret Thatcher, launched economic and social policies that intensified class division and racial tensions, heritage productions functioned as a palliative, promoting a sense of unbroken tradition and reaffirming national identity. And, as the government relaxed restrictions on industrial development and encouraged the spread of enterprise to rural areas, they disseminated bucolic images of an England still rich in verdant meadows and rolling hills.[1] The success of the heritage genre in the United States, achieved largely under the auspices of the PBS Masterpiece Theatre series, has similarly been attributed to viewers' desire to take refuge from the conflicts of the present in a past comfortably imagined as a greener, more harmonious time.

These analyses certainly capture the mood of social conflict that dominated the 1980s. But to apply them to today's heritage dramas is, I believe, to overlook the fact that over the past few years the tenor of these productions has changed considerably. A different spirit of historical representation has emerged, no doubt in tandem with the new political climate that developed following the election, in both Britain and the United States, of more liberal administrations. Films of the 1990s, such as *Jefferson in Paris*, *Carrington*, *Wilde*, and *Orlando*, placed contentious questions of race, gender, and sexuality center stage, making it appropriate, as Claire Monk suggests, for us now to speak of a "post-heritage" genre: historical drama that approaches the past as a terrain on which to explore controversial issues in contemporary cultural politics.[2]

Prior to 1995 relatively few film adaptations of Jane Austen's novels made it to either the big or the small screen. Only seven Austen films/miniseries were produced between 1970 and 1995, and these were all made for television. Merchant/Ivory, the most celebrated makers of heritage cinema in this period, turned to E. M. Forster and Henry James for material, not to Austen. By contrast, since 1995, five of Austen's six finished novels have been made into motion pictures, television miniseries, or both. Although some critics, both in the mainstream media and in academic journals, have received these adaptations as the usual heritage fare, I would situate them rather in the emergent category of post-heritage productions. This is not to say that they distance themselves completely from the representational modes of previous costume drama, but rather to note that they take on political issues and social perspectives that pull in a new direction.

Consider, for example, Roger Michell's recent rendition of *Persuasion* (BBC/WGBH, 1995), a film whose guiding ambition seems to be to present the viewer with a tableau of material life in early-nineteenth-century England. The camera hovers over property and possessions, indulgences and deprivations, dwelling on lavish candle-lit dining rooms, and the confined, dimly-lit interiors of country cottages, highlighting the manifestations and foundations of social class, but also suggesting the fragility of the social order, its dependence on economic structures that, due to the expansion of mercantile capitalism, were undergoing profound change. Other recent adaptations touch on different social issues: *Mansfield Park* (BBC/Miramax, 1999) takes on slavery in the British Caribbean, while *Emma* (Meridian [ITV]/A&E, 1996) alludes to poaching as a reaction to laws favoring the enclosure of private property. However, the key factor in the recent resurgence of Austen has undoubtedly been gender. There has been a rise in interest in filming from a feminist perspective. And, though written in an age before women's liberation, when middle-class women did not work outside the home and barely traveled, Austen's novels have been recognized as a fertile terrain for socially-conscious representations of women's lives—a perception undoubtedly nurtured by the proliferation of politicized readings of Austen in the academy.[3]

There is incontrovertibly a dearth of complex representations of women in mainstream cinema. Given this scarcity, Austen's novels lend themselves to feminist filmmaking for the reason that they are solidly feminocentric. The central characters are all women, and the reader enjoys an access to their thoughts and feelings that is simply lacking in the case of the men. Translated into the medium of film, these characters assume the function of central-organizing consciousness, the implied perspective from which images and events are presented and interpreted. As Laura Mulvey and many other film theorists have argued, this is a structural position that women rarely occupy in commercial cinema.[4] Unsurprisingly, therefore, the feminocentrism of the novels is cited by several of those involved in the recent productions as the primary reason for their attraction to Austen. Thus, for example, Lindsay Doran, the producer of *Sense and Sensibility* (Mirage/Columbia, 1995), says that she was interested in adapting this novel in particular because it offers not one but two female leads.

The complexity, however, begins here. The Austen adaptations are unquestionably more women-centered than most mainstream contemporary films, but does this mean that they are feminist films? Several feminist critics have in fact said no, criticizing the recent adaptations not for promoting heritage-style nostalgia for an age before the women's movement, but rather for a specific set of departures from Austen's narratives. For example, Deborah Kaplan has argued that although early in the film version of *Sense and Sensibility* Elinor Dashwood, played by Emma Thompson, articulates the fact that in nineteenth-century England middle-class women could not earn a living, and were therefore dependent on male relatives, the need for further investigation of women's social condition is obviated by the film's enhancement of Austen's courtship plot.[5] Whereas Austen's novel depicts the marriages of Elinor and her sister Marianne as solid alliances grounded in mutual affection and respect, the film introduces a much higher level of romance, rendering these relationships nothing short of idyllic. To some extent this transformation is accomplished by a redrawing of the principal male characters—Edward Ferrars and Colonel Brandon—who are made more complex, more passionate, and even better looking than their prototypes in the novel. The notoriously lackluster Edward Ferrars, for example, is played by modern matinee idol Hugh Grant, a casting choice that reflects a broader tendency of the new Austen films to portray the novels' heroes as "hunks." For Kaplan, the filmed version of *Sense and Sensibility* ultimately conveys something akin to the postfeminist sensibility that has gained ground in recent years. That is, it acknowledges feminist concerns, but swiftly abandons this mode of reflection, as though the social problems confronting women had fortuitously been resolved.

I am perhaps less inclined to regard these shifts in emphasis as clear-cut signs of a retreat from feminist concerns. There are, after all, debates within the spectrum of feminist thought over the status of romance, and whether a strictly feminocentric plot is always preferable to one that accords a role to heroes who are "new men."[6] I do, however, think that they reflect the fact that the Austen films are the products of an encounter among a number of different cultural forces, including commercial calculations on the part of film and television executives. The commercial factor should not be understated: The five recent Austen films and miniseries have for the most part been box-office or television hits, and have also done well on video. Profits have also been realized through a range of product tie-ins, including new editions of Austen's novels and glossy photo books that recount "the making of" *Sense and Sensibility* and *Pride and Prejudice*.[7]

Film is a significant barometer of culture because its profitability depends on the anticipation and nurturing of aesthetic and social preferences. Over time the major studios have developed a number of strategies to manage risk and maximize revenue, two of the most effective of which have been the repetition of successful formulas, and the identification of target audiences, demographic groups such as teenagers and women. The recent cluster of Austen productions—four films and two televised miniseries in the past four years—must be interpreted in light of these strategies. If Austen became big business almost overnight it is because participants in the industry recognized that these productions were reaching an audience that could be identified, and to which further offerings of the same nature could be pitched. To take an example, the unexpected popularity of the BBC/A&E miniseries, *Pride and Prejudice*, first aired in September 1995, made possible the release of *Persuasion* (BBC/WGBH, 1995), originally made for television, as a feature film, as well as the production of a second miniseries based on *Emma* (Meridian [ITV]/A&E, 1996). Similarly, the box-office success of the film versions of *Sense and Sensibility* (Mirage/Columbia, 1995) and *Emma* (Miramax, 1996),[8] undoubtedly opened doors for Patricia Rozema's *Mansfield Park* (BBC/Miramax, 1999).

The Austen revival has been facilitated by a number of factors prevailing in what is often described as the "new Hollywood." These include the expansion of television, notably through the proliferation of cable networks; the growth of American independent film production; and the rise to prominence of the companies that Justin Wyatt calls the "major independents": production companies such as New Line Cinema and Miramax that were originally independent, but subsequently affiliated with major studios.[9] In combination, these factors have introduced greater flexibility into the processes of production and distribution, facilitating collaboration between film and television companies, the circulation of product between the two media, and the production of more low-budget films that target a specific demographic niche, but have the potential to attract a wider audience.

I would like to make two points about this new landscape and the Austen revival. The first concerns the shift toward "niche-marketing" that in recent years has reshaped the film industry as it has the wider economy. (Niche-marketing is a flexible production system geared to the generation of highly specialized goods aimed at a small but well-defined market. Because targeting is the key element in this mode of production, marketing campaigns play an integral role in ensuring commercial success.) I want to propose that this economic shift is key to understanding the transition from heritage to post-heritage genre that I described earlier. Whereas the heritage films of yore targeted relatively broad demographic groups, offering legitimation of values potentially shared by a great many people—a sense of national identity, or an outlook that is broadly conservative or traditionalist—post-heritage films seem to be pitched to narrower, more clearly defined groups. For example, a film such as *Carrington*, which explores the experience of homosexual and bisexual artists in the Bloomsbury era, reaches out to gay viewers, while the Austen films appeal primarily to women, and in particular to well-educated women versed in classic literature but also attracted to feminist ideas.

My second (though related) point is that although niche-marketing depends on the targeting of specific groups, there is often an underlying aspiration to extend the niche to draw in a wider audience, in other words, to achieve what is known as a "crossover success." For the past decade or so, crossover productions have been particularly associated with Miramax, the company responsible for films such as *Like Water for Chocolate*, *The Crying Game*, and *The Piano* that have won both critical acclaim and box-office success. These films negotiate the fine line that separates independent from commercial cinema. They explore unusual or controversial subjects and experiment with innovative cinematic styles, but they also retain firm links to the cultural mainstream.[10] This strategy is of special interest in the context of the Austen revival because Miramax produced or coproduced two of the six recent films based on Austen's novels: *Emma* (1996) and *Mansfield Park* (1999). I would suggest that these films, like almost all of the recent Austen adaptations, manifest the kind of ideological splitting characteristic of crossover movies. That is, they gesture toward the social and political concerns of feminism, but also venture into the well-charted territory of another genre of film: the date movie or romantic comedy.

We have briefly observed the convergence of costume drama, contemporary feminism, and commercial calculation in the filmed version of *Sense and Sensibility*. To further illustrate this merger I want to focus for a moment on the production that launched "Austenmania," the BBC's miniseries, *Pride and Prejudice*. In her account of the making of this series, Sue Birtwistle, its producer, says that she wanted to give Austen a fresh, glamorous look by using film rather than video.[11] She also reports that she initially tried to sell the project to Britain's ITV, which commands a larger market share than the BBC, and that to do so she represented the novel to network executives as "simply the sexiest book ever written," while concealing its title (vi). When ITV put the project on hold, Birtwistle did turn to the BBC, a more traditional outlet for costume drama. However, she did not abandon the emphasis on sex. Working with screenwriter Andrew Davies, Birtwistle shaped a fuller role for Darcy, and underscored the sexual chemistry between the protagonists. Unsurprisingly, long before the series aired, it had garnered considerable media buzz, with rumors that there would be explicit sex scenes and male nudity (vi). The production is in fact not particularly risqué: The audience is treated to a scene of implied sex, a kiss, and some shots of Darcy swimming, semi-clad, in a country stream.

Nonetheless, these scenes elicited the response that—we may suppose—the producers were hoping for. The series was a smash and Darcy, played by Colin Firth, became an overnight sensation (so much so that *The Guardian* reported that women were holding "Darcy parties" at which the scene in which the hero goes for an impromptu swim was played and replayed).

Pride and Prejudice (the novel) shares a certain number of narrative elements with works of another genre: romantic comedies such as, for example, *Pretty Woman*. In both cases a female character is saved from a life of poverty and insignificance by an encounter with a man whose personal attractions are magnified by his fortune and social standing. In both stories the central couple struggles through a conflict that is rooted in questions of status as well as in personality. Finally, in both instances, this conflict is resolved and the couple is happily united. There are, however, also important differences between these two modes of narration. Whereas the romantic comedy typically underplays the social realities from which conflict springs, a work such as *Pride and Prejudice* dissects them. Commensurately, the romantic comedy places greater emphasis on romance and sexual attraction, building its hero into the object of an all-consuming fantasy. *Pride and Prejudice* (the miniseries) falls between these two modes. It combines a serious investigation of social difference, including gender difference, with the fantasy-driven formula of romantic comedy.

This kind of merger is far from unusual. It reflects the fact that cultural productions are, generally speaking, born of an array of forces and conditions, and convey a mix of messages. But in this instance it is facilitated by an underlying structure: the shared practice of address that connects certain feminist works to other types of films or books made "for women." It is to the process of address, and to the questions that it generates, that I want to turn in the remaining pages of this chapter.

In her memoir of the women's film movement, entitled *Chick Flicks*, Ruby Rich raises a question of terminology. She observes, "There is . . . uncertainty over what name might characterize the intersection of cinema and the women's movement . . . variously called 'films by women,' 'feminist films,' 'images of women in film,' and 'women's films.' All are vague and problematic."[12] For me this passage is important because it articulates not just the problem of naming, but a much wider indeterminacy surrounding the relationship between feminist cinema and the broader category of films that address women. As Rich's reaching for words suggests, a common politics—or strategy—of address to women underlies this indeterminacy.

Popular film embodies and distills the process that Louis Althusser calls "interpellation," the mechanism by which individuals come to absorb social representations as their own self-representations. The mainspring of this mechanism in film, as to a lesser extent in novels, is the invitation to spectators to identify with the characters that are portrayed. In commercial cinema, men are encouraged to identify with male characters, women with female characters, such that, as Teresa de Lauretis has argued, film functions as what Michel Foucault calls a "technology of sex," a social instrument that plays a significant role in the social construction and reaffirmation of gender identities.[13] The politics of identification are not homogeneous—it would be misleading, for example, to claim that the male position is always defined by activity or aggression—but the circuit of solicitation and recognition does necessarily involve the reproduction of predefined models of sexual identity.

The issue of address is one that came into focus for the first time in the eighteenth century, with the emergence of the novel as mass literary genre. The growth of a popular readership inevitably gave rise to questions, both aesthetic and commercial, about address and reception. This reflex in fact connects the novel to cinema, whose mass cultural appeal is similarly interwoven with a self-conscious reflection on the viewing public. Jane Austen herself probed the mechanics of address in her posthumously published novel, *Northanger Abbey*. One of the least admired of Austen's novels, *Northanger Abbey* has often been dismissed as a flawed narrative that fails to reconcile two competing dimensions: the social satire or comedy of manners that occupies the first half of the text, and the spoof of the gothic novel that dominates the second half. The unwieldy structure of the narrative can, however, equally be attributed to the fact that *Northanger Abbey* attempts to synthesize the novel with a metafictional reflection on the novel that involves, among other things, an examination of the interrelationships, structural and sociological, between writers and their readers.

The heroine of *Northanger Abbey* is Catherine Morland, a naive and inexperienced girl who has spent her adolescence voraciously consuming novels written primarily for female readers. Guided by her enthusiasm for gothic tales, she constructs in her mind an elaborate narrative whereby General Tilney, the intimidating father of her suitor, Henry, is a cold-blooded villain who has neglected and perhaps even murdered his late wife. Propelled by her overactive imagination, she furtively explores the hidden rooms and locked chests of Northanger Abbey, where she has been invited to stay as a guest of the Tilney family. The general lends weight to Catherine's dark suspicions when he abruptly expels her from the abbey, sending her home with neither a servant nor sufficient money to pay her way. We subsequently learn that his invitation to Catherine arose from misinformation about her material worth, and that when he learned the true circumstances of her family, he no longer regarded her as a suitable match for his son. In this dénouement we can read the reflection that, although neither Catherine nor Mrs. Tilney has in fact fallen victim to a dastardly plot, both have been subject to the ordinary calculation and everyday violence of their male-dominated society. As several recent feminist critics have suggested, Austen uses this bifurcated conclusion to advance her own "realist" mode of representing women's lives as a gentle corrective to the Gothic genre. Equally important, however, is the fact that, early in the era of mass culture, Austen's novel represents its reading public, imagines the division of this readership into gendered subcategories, and examines how novels reinforce, and perhaps even produce, gendered identities.

Interestingly, the manner in which determinism inhabits the act of address is also raised in two recent independent films that have appeared in tandem with the Austen adaptations, companion pieces that explicitly draw on the legacy of Jane Austen as a storyteller and social commentator, but whose setting is contemporary North America. I want to mention these films, not because they are commentaries on the recent revival of Austen (chronology alone would preclude this interpretation), but because they articulate thoughtful perspectives on the contemporary application of narrative models inherited from another age. An important part of this reflection, as I will show, concerns how historical distance complicates the role of gender in the process of reception.

Westerley Films' *Metropolitan* (1990), produced and directed by Whit Stillman, is a comedy of manners set among preppies in New York City. Shortly after the film's opening credits, a subtitle tells us that the scene is set in "Manhattan, Christmas vacation, not so long ago." The scene in fact seems to be set in the 1980s, though as the subtitle implies, the mores of the preppies that it portrays are so anchored in tradition that it could just as well be the 1950s. The protagonists are Audrey, a shy, sincere debutante who is an avid reader of Austen, and Tom, a self-proclaimed Fourierist who looks down on the preppy lifestyle and also disdains novels, preferring history and literary criticism. Much of the couple's conversation turns on their view of Austen, and in particular of *Mansfield Park*, which Audrey loves, but which Tom (who has actually never read the novel) dismisses on the authority of Lionel Trilling's characterization of it as a rearguard defense of conservative values. From the beginning of the film Jane Austen is thus placed at the center of several interwoven cultural debates: the conflict between progressive and conservative values, the opposition between lovers of fiction and those who prefer the sobriety of nonfiction, and the distance between the sexes. These interwoven debates are actually ones that Austen herself enters into in *Northanger Abbey*, in which Catherine Morland's passion for novels is contrasted with Henry Tilney's enjoyment of history, a difference in taste that stands for the wider cultural and intellectual preferences of the sexes, or at least for dominant prescriptions of these tastes in nineteenth-century England.

The Tom–Audrey relationship in *Metropolitan* is also loosely modeled on the relationship between Fanny Price and her cousin Edmund Bertram in another Austen novel, *Mansfield Park*. Audrey is attracted to Tom, who is dazzled by the attractions of a more captivating, sophisticated woman, in much the same way that Fanny loves Edmund, who is mesmerized by the charms of the engaging Mary Crawford. As the relationships evolve, Edmund/Tom gains a greater appreciation for the sincerity and emotional solidity of Fanny/Audrey, finally coming to the realization that she is his true soul mate. The end of the film, however, gestures again to *Northanger Abbey*, or at least to the Gothic second half of Austen's novel. Tom and his friend Charlie learn that, upset by Tom's apparent indifference, Audrey has gone to a house party at the Long Island home of the rich but disreputable Rick Von Slonocker. They set off in hot pursuit (taking a taxi from Manhattan to Southampton since neither can drive), their minds filled with dreadful images of Audrey being "ruined" by Rick. They make a melodramatic entrance and "save" Audrey, who, needless to say, was in little real danger. Later, when Tom and Audrey are alone together on the beach, he chastises her, saying that Jane Austen would not have gone to Rick's. Audrey, with some amusement, concurs that she probably would not have.

This closing exchange builds on an earlier conversation in which Tom asserts that the values and preoccupations of the age of Austen seem ridiculous to the modern perspective, and Audrey retorts that today's fashions and concerns would probably seem equally ridiculous to Austen. Although in this exchange Audrey seems to be asserting the superiority of Austen, and of the more genteel age in which she wrote, her subsequent "transgression" of decorum suggests that she is actually observing that times change. Her position is, in essence, that there is a place for Austen, but that this place is circumscribed by historical change—for example, by changing social attitudes toward female sexuality. Tom, by contrast, makes the successive mistakes of first overemphasizing historical difference, and then, at the end of the novel, effacing it altogether. The dénouement of this story thus captures, fleetingly, a sense of the dialectic of history, an awareness of the dynamic relationship between past and present, and correspondingly, of the provisional, unstable character of historical models of continuity and discontinuity. A central feature of this historical consciousness is the reversal of expected gender roles. It is not the novel-reading Audrey but the more serious Tom who succumbs to melodramatic anxieties about the dire goings-on at Von Slonocker's. In and of itself this upset registers historical change because it dramatizes the disintegration of the expected correlation between gender and genre. To be more exact, *Metropolitan* stages the collapse of the perceived congruence between the mode of address, the gender of the subject who is addressed, and the fashion in which cultural messages are absorbed by this subject.

The second film that I want to discuss is Republic Pictures' *Ruby in Paradise* (1993), written and directed by Victor Nunez. This quietly powerful film follows the life of Ruby Gissing as she leaves behind the world of her upbringing in rural Tennessee, and seeks her independence in a resort town on the Florida coast. Despite obvious differences, Ruby's story is in many ways like that of an Austen heroine. As in Austen, the seaside resort promises escape from the daily routine of a life that offers few economic or romantic prospects. And, like Austen heroines, Ruby is soon presented with an array of "suitors," men whose merits and flaws become evident as the story unfolds. In Ruby's case these admirers include Ricky, the flashy, reckless son of her employer, and Mike, the sensitive, socially alienated intellectual who works at a local greenhouse. In one scene Mike, who is a voracious reader, lends Ruby a copy of *Northanger Abbey*. She reads aloud the opening passage, and finds herself identifying with Catherine Morland, described as a girl too ordinary ever to become the heroine of a novel. The quotation of this passage acknowledges the film's debt to Austen, making the point that, like *Northanger Abbey*, *Ruby in Paradise* undertakes to dismantle the romantic fantasies sold to women, and to offer in their stead a less sugarcoated narrative. Mike, a devotee of Austen, opines that no one has ever exposed the value systems of society with such lucidity. Ruby, however, hesitates to go this far, and says that for her *Northanger Abbey* is simply "a neat story." Her identification with Catherine Morland thus proves to be short-lived. Unlike Mike, who embraces Austen as a timeless cultural commentator, Ruby focuses on the differences between her daily existence and the story of this nineteenth-century character. The contrasting perspectives of the two protagonists in regard to *Northanger Abbey* mark a fulcrum at which the film breaks away from the Austen paradigm and asserts its modernity.

Whereas in Austen a trip to Lyme or Brighton generally does effect a change in the heroine's circumstances, in *Ruby in Paradise* the glamour and romance of the resort town quickly wear off. Coastal Florida is sketched as a hard-edged, run-down area where women work in unhealthy conditions for low wages. Ruby arrives in the off-season and has to struggle to find and keep a series of low-paying jobs in retail and laundering. But the modern obligation for women to work is one that Ruby ultimately affirms as her choice, and one that she comes to cherish as the guarantee of a small degree of personal freedom. When she loses her job at the Beach Emporium where she works because she refuses to sleep with Ricky, Mike invites her to live with him and, implicitly, to enter into the traditional contract whereby the man establishes himself as provider and protector. But Ruby rejects his invitation and along with it the belief that marriage is a woman's ultimate goal, the happy ending that will forever abolish material hardship and personal fear. In an interior monologue she reviews with skepticism this enduring dream, which she names as "everybody's fantasy, tender unions, precious ties," wondering how many people get anywhere near it, and surmising that in most cases "it's the woman [who] pays the most for the dream, security, belonging." Whereas in the world of Austen marriage represents the only respectable way for a woman to improve her material circumstances and assert her independence, Nunez's film affirms that in the very different social context of the 1990s, labor, for all of its vicissitudes, constitutes a more solid foundation for women's autonomy.

In differing ways, both *Ruby in Paradise* and *Metropolitan* portray the reception of cultural productions as historically determined, and as a result problematize the notion of address across the unbroken continuum of women's history. These films challenge gender-determinism by showing that gender is subject to historical change, and also by highlighting the circuits of address and reception through which deterministic models of sexual identity are channeled. In this regard they do something more sophisticated than the Austen adaptations, not because the latter are period pieces, but because, as we have seen, the aspiration to make films about and for women has supported a drift toward a more commercial mode of address. The object of this form of targeting is, needless to say, to pitch products to predefined groups, not to examine these categories or to challenge their formation.

The limitations of the recent Austen adaptations in this regard may perhaps be seen as a reflection of the continuing problem of women writers' place in the literary canon. Austen has long been accepted as a key figure in the history of English literature, yet like many other women writers, she occupies within this circle of prestige a circumscribed, distinctly feminine position, which at worst amounts to qualified acceptance, or to recognition as a woman writer. This positioning is, to be sure, mostly the product of sexism, but it is also in some measure a reflection of tensions within feminist criticism as an academic movement. Though feminists rightly denounce this kind of qualified recognition as an instance of the cultural drive to position the feminine as distinctive/particular while affirming the masculine as neutral/universal, feminist critical practice not infrequently reproduces this dominant feminization/particularization of women's cultural production—for example, through an exclusive focus on women authors or attempts to isolate the distinctively feminine elements in women's literary production. The recent rash of film adaptations extends these tensions into the broader arena of popular culture because, while they clearly magnify Austen's status as a cultural icon, they also reproduce the predicament of the feminine sub-canon.

In defense of these films, which really have much to recommend them, it should be observed that this is a real dilemma. The continuing marginalization of women in contemporary film, as in the writing of literary history, certainly cries out for correction. The difficulty is to respond without having recourse to a gender determinism that feeds back into the prevailing marginalization of women in the entertainment industry.

Notes

1. The label *heritage film* has been used to articulate the perceived convergence between the soothing images of the past disseminated in costume drama and the National Heritage Act, a piece of legislation brought before the British parliament in the early 1980s. The stated objective of the act, drafted by the moderate conservative MP

Norman St. John Stevas, was to "defend" or "conserve" the natural environment against the encroachment of industry and big business. But, as several critics have asserted, the environmentalist arguments of the act were interwoven with conservative reflexes. To conserve the national heritage meant, in part, to defend the inherited property rights of the rural aristocracy against the anticipated encroachments of the urban working class. On this point see Michael Bammes and Patrick Wright, "Charms of Residence: The Public and the Past," in *Making Histories: Studies on History Writing and Politics*, ed. Richard Johnson, Gregor Mclennan, Bill Schwartz, and David Sutton (Minneapolis: University of Minnesota Press, 1982), 264–299.

2. Claire Monk, "Sexuality and the Heritage," *Sight and Sound 5*, no. 10 (October 1995): 32–34.

3. When we consider actress Emma Thompson's feminist-inspired screenplay for *Sense and Sensibility* (1995), it is worth recalling that Thompson read English at Cambridge in the early 1980s, a time when academic critics were beginning to develop more political views of Austen. Similarly, the repeated allusions made in Patricia Rozema's recent production of *Mansfield Park* to the West Indian plantations that support the luxurious lifestyle of the Bertram family reflect the influence of Edward Said and other academic critics who have placed Austen in a global context. See Edward Said, *Culture and Imperialism* (New York: Vintage, 1994).

4. See Laura Mulvey's seminal essay, "Visual pleasure and Narrative Cinema," *Screen* 16, no. 3 (Autumn 1975): pp. 6–18.

5. Deborah Kaplan, "Mass Marketing Jane Austen: Men, Women, and Courtship in Two Film Adaptations," in *Jane Austen in Hollywood*, ed. Linda Troost and Sayre Greenfield (Lexington: University of Kentucky Press, 2000), 177–187.

6. Devoney Looser has argued that the ways in which the recent films modify Austen's narratives are indicative of a "mainstreaming" of feminism. See her essay, "Feminist Implications of the Silver Screen Austen," in *Jane Austen in Hollywood*, ed. Linda Troost and Sayre Greenfield (Lexington: University of Kentucky Press, 2000), 159–176.

7. Emma Thompson, *Jane Austen's Sense and Sensibility: The Screenplay and Diaries* (London: Bloomsbury, 1995); Sue Birtwistle and Susie Conklin, *The Making of Pride and Prejudice* (Hong Kong: Penguin Books/BBC Books, 1995).

8. According to Amy Stevens, by March 1996, *Emma, Sense and Sensibility*, and *Clueless* (Paramount, 1995; a film based on Austen's *Emma* but set in contemporary California), had grossed $97 million in domestic ticket sales alone (*Wall Street Journal*, 25 March 1996, pp. 74–90).

9. Justin Wyatt, "The Formation of the 'Major Independent': Miramax, New Line, and the New Hollywood," in *Contemporary Hollywood Cinema*, ed. Steve Neale and Murray Smith (London: Routledge, 1998). In 1993 New Line was acquired by Turner Broadcasting and Miramax was bought by Disney. Although Miramax receives financial support from its parent company, it has been allowed to retain a high level of autonomy and to preserve its name-brand identity.

10. On the hybrid politics of crossover films, see ibid., 81.

11. See Birtwistle and Conklin, *The Making of Pride and Prejudice*. One reason for using film is that it made possible the inclusion of more outdoor scenes with the result that the principal characters could be portrayed as physically active beings rather than as drawing-room wraiths.

12. Ruby Rich, *Chick Flicks: Theories and Memories of the Feminist Film Movement* (Durham, NC: Duke University Press, 1998), 62.

13. Teresa de Lauretis, *Technologies of Gender: Essays on Theory, Film, and Fiction* (Bloomington: Indiana University Press, 1987), ix, 12–13.

Appendix

Television, Film, and Radio Productions of Austen

Compiled by Patrick Cooper

Jane Austen's Television and Film Versions

The following was culled from: <http://www.pemberley.com/lane info/*abbcvid.html>; <http://www.geocities.com/Hollywood/Set/2484/>; <http://www.imdb.com>.
Information on a *Pride and Prejudice Musical* can be found at <http://www.musicals.demon.co.uk/ppindex.html>.

Emma

Emma (1948) BBC TV
Dramatized by Judy Campbell
Produced by Michael Barry
Starring Judy Campbell, Ralph Michael

Emma (1960) BBC TV (6 parts)
Dramatized by Vincent Tilsley
Produced by Campbell Logan
Starring Diana Fairfax, Paul Daneman

Emma (1972)
Directed by John Glenister
Starring Doran Godwin, John Carson

Emma (1993) BBCV4997—
Double video, 257 mins.

Dramatized by Denis Constanduros
Produced by Martin Lisemore
Directed by John Glenister
Starring Doran Godwin, John Carson, Donald Eccles, Constance Chapman

Clueless (1995)
Directed by Amy Heckerling
Starring Alicia Silverstone

Emma (initial release August 1996)
Directed by Douglas McGrath
Starring Gwyneth Paltrow

Emma (1996) ITV—2hrs.
Adapted by Andrew Davies
Produced by Sue Birtwhistle
Starring Kate Beckinsale

Mansfield Park

Mansfield Park (1983)
BBCV4333—Double video,
261 mins.
Dramatized by Ken Taylor
Produced by Betty Willingale
Directed by David Giles
Starring Anna Massey, Bernard
Hepton, Nicholas Farrel,
Sylvestra Le Touzel

Mansfield Park (1999)
Directed by Patricia Rozema
Starring Frances O'Connor

Northanger Abbey

Northanger Abbey (1971)
Dramatized by Julian Mitchell
Produced and directed by
Howard Baker
Starring Ann Firbank, Bryan
Marshall

Northanger Abbey (1986)
Directed by Giles Foster
Starring Katherine Schlesinger,
Peter Firth

Northanger Abbey (1990)
BBCV4378—90 mins.
Dramatized by Maggie Wadey
Produced by Louis Marks
Directed by Giles Foster
Starring Peter Firth, Googie
Withers, Robert Hardy,
Katherine Schlessinger

Persuasion

Persuasion (1960) BBC TV (4
parts)
Dramatized by Michael Voysey
Produced by Campbell Logan
Starring Daphne Slater, Paul
Daneman

Persuasion (1971)
Directed by Howard Baker
Starring Anne Firbank, Bryan
Marshall

Persuasion (1993) BBCV4996—
Double video, 225 mins.
(Originally produced by Granada
Television in 1971)
Adapted by Julian Mitchell,
produced and directed by
Howard Baker
Starring Ann Firbank, Bryan
Marshall

Persuasion (1995) BBCV5616—
102 mins.
Screenplay by Nick Dear
Produced by Fiona Finlay
Directed by Roger Mitchell
Starring Amanda Root, Ciaran
Hinds

Pride and Prejudice

Pride and Prejudice Warner Home
Video/MGM/Loew's
Incorporated (1940; video
1989)—B&W
Screenplay by Aldous Huxley and
Jane Murfin
Produced by Hunt Stromberg
Directed by Robert Z. Leonard
Starring Greer Garson and
Laurence Olivier

Pride and Prejudice (1952) BBC
TV (6 parts)
Dramatized by Cedric Wallis
Produced by Campbell Logan
Starring Daphne Slater, Peter
Cushing

Pride and Prejudice (1958) BBC
TV (6 parts) (B&W)
Dramatized by Cedric Wallis
Produced by Barbara Burnham

Starring Jane Downs, Alan
Badel

Pride and Prejudice (1967) BBC
TV (6 parts)
Dramatized by Nemone
Lethbridge
Directed by Joan Craft
Produced by Campbell Logan
Starring Celia Bannerman, Lewis
Fiander

Pride and Prejudice (1979)
Directed by Cyril Coke
Starring Elizabeth Garvie, David
Rintoul

Pride and Prejudice (1993)
BBCV4960—Double video,
259 mins.
(Previously, shorter version
BBCV4331)
Dramatized by Fay Weldon
Produced by Jonathan Powell
Directed by Cyril Coke
Starring Elizabeth Garvie, David
Rintoul

Pride and Prejudice (1995) BBCV
5702—Double video, 301
mins.
Adapted by Andrew Davies
Produced by Sue Birtwistle
Directed by Simon Langton
Starring Jennifer Ehle, Colin Firth,
David Bamber, Crispin
Bonham-Carter and Susannah
Harker

Sense and Sensibility

Sense and Sensibility (1971). BBC
TV (4 parts)
Dramatized by Denis Constanduros

Directed by David Giles
Produced by Martin Lisemore
Starring Joanna David, Robin
Ellis

Sense and Sensibility (1985)
Directed by Rodney Bennett
Starring Irene Richard, Bosco
Hogan

Sense and Sensibility (1990)
BBCV4332—174 mins.
Dramatized by Alexander
Baron
Produced by Barry Letts
Directed by Rodney Bennett

Sense and Sensibility (1995)
(Recently released on video)
Dramatized by Emma Thompson
Directed by Ang Lee
Starring Emma Thompson,
Alan Rickman, Kate Winslet,
Hugh Grant

Kandukondein Kandukondein
(in Tamil) (2000), also
known as *Priyuraalu
Pilichindi* (2000) (India:
Telugu title: dubbed version)
Directed by Rajiv Menon
Starring Tabu, Aishwarya Rai

Other

Jane Austen in Manhattan
(1980)
Directed by James Ivory
Starring Anne Baxter, Robert
Powell

Metropolitan, (1990) Directed by
Whit Stillman
Starring Carolyn Farina, Edward
Clements

Jane Austen's Radio Versions

The following was culled from <http://www.geocities.com/Hollywood/ Set/2484/>.

Emma

Emma (1948) BBC Home Service (12 parts: April 4, 1948–June 20, 1948)
Dramatized by H. Oldfield Box
Produced by Wilfred Grantham
Starring Rachel Gurney, Cecil Winter

Emma (1951) BBC Light Program (15 parts: April 9, 1951–April 27, 1951)
Abridged by Ursula Wood
Read by Julia Lang

Emma (1970) BBC Radio 4 (13 parts: January 4, 1970–March 29, 1970)
Dramatized by John Tydeman
Produced by John Tydeman
Starring Rachel Gurney, Suzanne Neve

Emma (1989) BBC—5 hrs. 15 mins.
Dramatized by John Tydeman
Directed by Brian Miller
Starring Jean Trend, Angharad Rees, Alan Moore

Mansfield Park

Mansfield Park (1952) BBC Home Service (9 parts: September 7, 1952–November 2, 1952)
Dramatized by Thea Holme
Produced by Alary Hope Allen
Starring Thea Holme, Peggy Bryan, John Humphrey

Mansfield Park (1961) BBC Home Service (9 parts: February 12, 1961–April 9, 1961)
Dramatized by Thea Holme
Produced by Norman Wright
Starring Anne Cullen, Beryl Calder, Robin Lloyd

Mansfield Park (1972) BBC Radio 4 (9 parts: September 24, 1972–October 15, 1972)
Dramatized by Thea Holme
Produced by Jane Graham
Starring Jill Balcon, Madeleine Cannon, John Rowe

Mansfield Park (1997) BBC— 2 hrs. 50 mins.
Dramatized by Elizabeth Proud
Directed by Sue Wilson
Starring Hannah Gordon, Michael Williams, Amanda Root

Northanger Abbey

Northanger Abbey (1937) BBC National Service (Serial Reading) (11 parts: October 9, 1937–December 18, 1937)
Read by Sheila Borrett

Northanger Abbey (1949) BBC Home Service (January 31, 1949)
Dramatized by Thea Holme
Produced by Raymond Raikes
Starring Louise Hutton, Moira Lister

Northanger Abbey (1951) BBC Home Service (3 parts: June 19, 1951–July 3, 1951)
Dramatized by Sam Langdon
Starring Jane Barrett, Alan Cuthbertson, Diana Maddox

Northanger Abbey (1953) BBC Home Service (3 parts: August 16, 1953–August 30, 1953)
Dramatized by Thea Holme
Produced by Raymond Raikes
Starring Sarah Leigh, Peter Coke, Brenda Bruce

Northanger Abbey (1962) BBC Home Service (5 parts: August 12, 1962–September 9, 1962)
Dramatized by Denis Constanduros
Produced by Brandon ActonBond
Starring Susan Maudslay, John Bouney, Sheila Steafel

Northanger Abbey (1970) BBC Radio 4 (A Book at Bedtime) (22 parts: April 6, 1970–May 6, 1970)
Abridged by Eileen Capel
Read by Dorothy Tutin

Northanger Abbey (1972) BBC Radio 4 (Saturday Night Theatre) (December 23, 1972)
Dramatized by Constance Cox and Sean MacLoughlin
Produced by Norman Wright
Starring Rosalind Shanks, John Rye, Frances Jeater

Persuasion

Persuasion (1951) BBC Home Service (3 parts: March 4, 1951–March 18, 1951)
Dramatized by H. Oldfield Box
Produced by Mary Hope Allen
Starring Dulcie Gray, Michael Denison

Persuasion (1954) BBC Light Program (15 parts: January 16, 1954–February 15, 1954)
Abridged by Nan MacDonald
Read by Richard Hurndall

Persuasion (1965) BBC Light Program (14 parts: March 12, 1965–March 31, 1965)
Abridged by Eileen Capel
Read by Peggy Ashcroft

Persuasion (1970) BBC Radio 4 (January 31, 1970)
Dramatized by Denis Constanduros
Produced by Brian Miller
Starring Rosalind Shanks, Charles Simon, Betty Hardy

Pride and Prejudice

Pride and Prejudice (1945) BBC Home Service (May 26, 1945)
Dramatized by Helen Jerome
Produced by Barbara Burnham
Starring Angela Baddeley, Reginald Tate

Pride and Prejudice (1950) BBC Home Service (12 parts: May 28, 1950–August 13, 1950)
Dramatized by H. Oldfield Box
Produced by Mary Hope Allen
Starring Hermione Hannen, Hugh Burden

Miss Elizabeth Bennet: A Play (1959) BBC Home Service (November 23, 1959)

Dramatized by A. A. Milne
Adapted for radio by Cynthia
  Pughe
Produced by Audrey Cameron
Starring Dorothy Tutin, John
  Westbrook

Miss Elizabeth Bennet: A Play
  (1967) BBC Radio 4 (December
  25, 1967)
Dramatized by A. A. Milne
Adapted for radio by Peggy Wells
Produced by David Davis
Starring Kika Markham, Derek
  Jacobi

Pride and Prejudice (1971) (A
  Book at Bedtime) BBC Radio 4
  (28 parts: September 22,
  1971–October 29, 1971)
Abridged by Honour Wyatt
Read by Eileen Atkins

Sense and Sensibility

Sense and Sensibility (1949)
  (Women's Hour) BBC Light
  Program (17 parts: March 15,
  1949–April 6, 1949)
Abridged by Janet Dunbar
Read by Ronald Simpson

Sense and Sensibility (1959) BBC
  Home Service (6 parts:
  December 20, 1959–January
  24, 1960)
Dramatized by Jonquil Antony
Produced by Mollie Austin
Starring Ysanne Churchman,
  Angela Brooking

Juvenalia

Lady Susan (1948) BBC Home
  Service (July 25, 1948)
Dramatized by Joanne Holbrook
Produced by Mary Hope Allen
Starring Lydia Sherwood, Edith
  Sharpe

Lady Susan (1972) BBC Radio 4
  (4 parts: December 26,
  1972–December 29, 1972)
Dramatized by Margaret Etall
Produced by Margaret Etall
Starring Caroline John, Jane
  Knowles

Love and Friendship (1936) BBC
  Regional Service (August 17,
  1936)
Dramatized by M. H. Allen
Produced by M. H. Allen
Starring Lydia Sherwood, Patrick
  Waddington, Cherry Cottrell

Love and Friendship (1953) BBC
  Third Program (November 4,
  1953)
Dramatized by Terence Tiller
Produced by Terence Tiller
Starring Prunella Scales, Brenda
  Dunrich, Sarah Caisley, Thea
  Wells, Frank Duncan

Sanditon (1948) BBC Third
  Program (6 parts: August 15,
  1948–August 21, 1948)
Read by Leslie Stokes

Contributors

Virginia L. Blum is an associate professor of English at the University of Kentucky and writes on psychoanalytic theory, nineteenth-century American literature, and popular culture. She is the author of *Hide and Seek: The Child between Psychoanalysis and Fiction* (University of Illinois Press, 1995) and the forthcoming *Flesh Wounds: The Culture of Cosmetic Surgery* (University of California Press).

Mike Crang is a lecturer in geography at the University of Durham. He has principally worked on the geography of the U.K. heritage industry and has published papers on nostalgic and tourist photography, living history, narrative, and open-air museums. He is the coeditor of *Tourism: Between Place and Performance* (Berghahn, 2001), and *Thinking Space* (Routledge, 2000), and *Virtual Geographics* (Routledge, 1999). He is an editor of the journals *Tourist Studies* and *Time and Society*.

Madeleine Dobie is associate professor of French at Columbia University. She is the author of *Foreign Bodies: Gender, Language, and Culture in French Orientalism* (Stanford University Press, 2001) and of articles on eighteenth- and nineteenth-century French literature and culture.

Denise Fulbrook is an assistant professor of English at the University of Kentucky and is working on a manuscript on female anal eroticism and authorship in nineteenth-century British literature and psychoanalytic theory. She has published an introduction on sexuality and sexual orientation with Eve K. Sedgwick for McGraw-Hill and has coedited a collection entitled *Rock over the Edge: Transformations in Popular Music Culture* (Duke University Press, 2002).

Deidre Lynch, associate professor of English at Indiana University, is the author of *The Economy of Character: Novels, Market Culture, and the Business of Inner Meaning* (University of Chicago Press, 1998) and the editor, most recently, of *Janeites: Austen's Disciples and Devotees* (Princeton University Press, 2000). She is currently working on a book entitled *At Home in English: "Loving" Literature, in the Eighteenth Century and After*.

Sarah Maza, a specialist in eighteenth- and nineteenth-century French cultural history is Jane Long Professor and chair of the History Department at Northwestern University. Her most recent book, *The Myth of the Bourgeoisie: An Essay on the French Social Imaginary 1750–1850,* is forthcoming in 2003.

Ruth Perry, professor of literature at MIT and past president of the American Society of Eighteenth-Century Studies, has published widely on eighteenth-century subjects. Happiest when reading or writing about Jane Austen, her favorite current project is a volume of essays on Austen, interpreted in the context of eighteenth-century English culture.

Suzanne R. Pucci is an associate professor of French at the University of Kentucky. Her most recent book is *Sites of the Spectator: Emerging Literary and Cultural Practice in Eighteenth-Century France* (Voltaire Foundation, 2001). She has published essays on Pierre Marivaux, Dennis Diderot, Pierre-Augustin Beaumarchais, Baron Montesquieu, and Antoine Watteau in edited collections and journals and is currently working on a book-length study: *Snapshots of the Family: Domestic Intimacy in Early Modern and Contemporary Culture.*

Kristina Straub is a professor of literary and cultural studies at Carnegie-Mellon University where she serves as associate head of English and associate dean of humanities and social sciences. She has written about the eighteenth-century novelist Frances Burney, actors in eighteenth-century England, and about violence and sexuality in master–servant relations of that period. She is at work on a book on this last topic. She is still an unrepentant and exuberant fan of *Buffy the Vampire Slayer.*

James Thompson is professor and chair of the Department of English at the University of North Carolina at Chapel Hill. He has written on eighteenth-century literature, pedagogy, and politics. His most recent book is *Models of Value: Eighteenth-Century Political Economy and the Novel* (Duke University Press, 1996).

Maureen Turim is professor of English and film studies at the University of Florida. She is the author of *Abstraction in Avant-Garde Films* (UMI Research Press, 1985), *Flashbacks in Film: Memory and History* (Routledge, 1989), and *The Films of Oshima Nagisa: Images of a Japanese Iconoclast* (University of California Press, 1998). She has also published over sixty essays in anthologies and journals on a wide range of theoretical, historical, and aesthetic issues in cinema and video, art, cultural studies, feminist and psychoanalytic theory, and comparative literature. She has also written catalog essays for museum exhibitions. Her new book project entitled *Desire* *and Its Ends: The Driving Forces of Recent Cinema, Literature, and Art* will look at the different ways desire structures narratives and images in various cultural traditions and the way our very notion of desire may be shaped by these representations.

Martine Voiret is an independent scholar based in Acton, Massachusetts. Her area of expertise is eighteenth-century French literature. She has published articles on Voltaire and Restif de la Bretonne. She has also finished a book-length study on incest in eighteenth-century French fiction.

INDEX